D1544050

# REVOLUTIONARY
# ROADS

# REVOLUTIONARY ROADS

*Searching for the War That Made America
Independent... and All the Places It
Could Have Gone Terribly Wrong*

## Bob Thompson

TWELVE

*New York Boston*

Twelve
Hachette Book Group
1290 Avenue of the Americas, New York, NY 10104
twelvebooks.com
twitter.com/twelvebooks

First Edition: February 2023

Twelve is an imprint of Grand Central Publishing. The Twelve name and logo are trademarks of Hachette Book Group, Inc.

The publisher is not responsible for websites (or their content) that are not owned by the publisher.

Library of Congress Cataloging-in-Publication Data
Names: Thompson, Bob, 1950 August 28- author.
Title: Revolutionary roads : searching for the war that made America independent…and all the places it could have gone terribly wrong / Bob Thompson.
Description: First edition. | New York : Twelve, 2023. | Includes bibliographical references and index.
Identifiers: LCCN 2022042073 | ISBN 9781455565153 (hardcover) | ISBN 9781455565160 (ebook)
Subjects: LCSH: United States—History—Revolution, 1775–1783—Battlefieds | United States—History—Revolution, 1775–1783—Monuments | United States—Description and travel | Thompson, Bob, 1950 August 28—Travel—United States
Classification: LCC E209 .T478 2023 | DDC 973.3—dc23/eng/20221014
LC record available at https://lccn.loc.gov/2022042073

ISBNs: 9781455565153 (hardcover), 9781455565160 (ebook)

Printed in the United States of America

LSC-C

Printing 1, 2022

*For Mona, Lizzie, and Deborah*

# Contents

# REVOLUTIONARY
# ROADS

# "Something Different Is Going to Happen"

The particular stretch of tree-dotted meadow I've come to contemplate—where a small battle would be lost or won, and with it, perhaps, the American Revolutionary War—lies just a quarter mile ahead, but I can't see it yet. It's hidden behind a gentle rise in ground. Never mind that for now, however. Army historian Steve Rauch wants the group he's leading to concentrate on what British soldiers *would* have seen as they formed up to attack a rebel army on the South Carolina frontier, on the morning of January 17, 1781, nearly six years after the war began.

"Observing from the British position," Rauch asks, "what do you see out in front of you?"

"Skirmishers," one of his students replies.

"Skirmishers, right—they're spread out across the battlefield." He's talking about the 115 or so expert riflemen in the Americans' first defensive line.

Rauch, fifty-six, retired as an army logistics officer in 2002; since then he's taught for the army as a civilian. His charges today are a couple dozen lieutenants and captains enrolled in a Signal Officer Captain's Career Course at Georgia's Fort Gordon. They range in age from around twenty-five to thirty-five; wear civilian clothes (one woman's T-shirt proclaims her allegiance to the New England Patriots); and have been bused up to Cowpens National Battlefield to refight what is, without question, the most important military confrontation ever to take place in a western South Carolina cow pasture. I'd met Rauch at a gathering of supremely knowledgeable Revolutionary War obsessives near Savannah, where he said smart things faster than I could write them down. Later, he invited me to Cowpens on condition that I keep my nonmilitary mouth shut while he and his students did their thing.

"Where are the Morgans—Morgan One, Morgan Two? Good, you've teamed up already," he says. "So Morgans, your skirmishers are supposed to do what?"

Rauch's students have researched specific topics—in most cases, two have been assigned to each topic—and have prepared to be grilled as they walk the field. The topic here is Brig. Gen. Daniel Morgan, the American commander, whose leadership and battle plan at Cowpens have been widely praised by historians.

"Pick off the officers," Morgan One says.

"Pick off the officers," Rauch echoes.

Walking a historic battlefield to look for still-relevant military lessons is a training exercise the army calls a "staff ride" (in the nineteenth century, horses were involved). Rauch has led nearly a hundred staff rides at Cowpens. It's a beautifully preserved outdoor classroom where you can conjure visions of history unfolding and think about how things might have turned out...differently.

This kind of thought experiment is exactly what I've come here to do. I'm in the home stretch of what I sometimes describe as a ridiculously ambitious, one-person staff ride of the Revolutionary War. The idea is to travel to places where history-shaping events occurred (I've put twelve thousand miles on the car so far) and, in most places, to seek out people like Rauch who can help me understand what happened there. Today, I'll be trying to wrap my mind around a single battlefield moment—lasting just a few seconds—in which things went suddenly, horribly wrong.

Some Cowpens context:

Stalled up north, the British have moved the war south, a strategy that's been a nightmare for the rebels. One Continental Army commander has been forced to surrender around six thousand men; his replacement has been ignominiously routed. A third commander, given a last chance to turn the southern tide, has divided his inadequate force and sent the two halves off in different directions. In hindsight, this looks brilliant, but it's also a desperate move: The troops lack food, so splitting up gives them a better chance to live off the land. Now it's up to Morgan—who leads the western contingent—to avoid getting wiped out.

This is no easy task when you've got the most feared and hated man in the British Army, Lt. Col. Banastre Tarleton, on your trail.

"Tarletons!" Rauch calls out.

By now he has marched us two hundred yards up the dirt-and-gravel track that runs through the middle of the battlefield, just as it did in 1781. We've halted not far from a sign reading "Let 'em Get Within Killin' Distance" that marks the site of the rebels' second defensive line, where Morgan placed the thousand or so local militiamen who comprised more than half his force.

"A thousand militia in a line—Tarletons, is this a problem? Is there anything your men should be doing differently facing militia? Have they done it before?"

"They've done it before," Tarleton One confirms.

Yes they have. As the British Regulars well know, rebel militia often run from them in conventional battle situations, especially when bayonets are involved. But Morgan hasn't asked his men to do what they're not capable of doing. His plan calls for the militia to get off a couple of damaging volleys, retire in good order, and leave the heavy lifting to the Continental Army veterans who form his third line of defense.

"What's the Continentals' mission?" Rauch has asked a young officer earlier.

"Hold the third line," he's been told.

"Hold the line. Stand fast and don't let the British get by. That's the plan. Now we don't know how it would have turned out, do we? Because we know something different is going to happen."

\* \* \*

The Revolutionary War is one of the greatest stories in all history, an eight-year epic replete with self-sacrificing heroes, self-interested villains, and, more interesting, all the shades of complex humanity in between. It boasts large-scale gambles that sometimes paid off but usually didn't (whose idea *was* it to invade Canada through the Maine wilderness?) as well as countless moments like the "something different" that will disrupt Morgan's plan at Cowpens—tiny, fraught tipping points which, had events played out in other ways, could have altered the course of the war. The drama is magnified when you consider what was at stake: not just the future of thirteen colonies complaining of long-distance tyranny, but the fate of a social and political experiment that would transform the world.

Yet we don't know this story as well as we should—or how easily the ending could have changed.

We remember the midnight ride of Paul Revere, but we don't know who fired the first shot in Lexington, or why the famous fight at Concord's Old North Bridge almost didn't occur. We recall that George Washington crossed the Delaware to win an essential victory at Trenton, but not how close he came to having his army wiped out eight days later. We know there was a cruel winter at Valley Forge and a climactic British surrender at Yorktown, but we're weak on context and details. (See "the Capes, Battle of," one of many prerequisites for that surrender.) We admire the idealism of the Marquis de Lafayette, but we would be hard pressed—at least I was, before I started reading up on him—to say what the teenage French volunteer actually did during the war.

Hint: On-the-job training can be scary at times.

We don't know nearly enough about the months-long catastrophe that was George Washington's attempt to defend New York City in 1776. Fought on what would become some of America's most expensive real estate—Brooklyn Heights! Midtown! The Upper West Side!—the New York campaign added up to a series of humiliating defeats or miraculous escapes, depending on who's telling the tale. On the night of August 29, to take just one example, Washington and his badly beaten army were ferried across the East River from Brooklyn to Manhattan by a bunch of sailors and fishermen from Massachusetts. Great skill and fortitude were involved. But if the wind had changed a day earlier, nine thousand men would have been captured and the war could have been over.

We know little about what Benedict Arnold did before turning his name into a synonym for Traitorous Scumbag—but we should. Among other things, his fingerprints are all over the Saratoga campaign, widely viewed as *the* turning point of the Revolution because its triumphant conclusion helped bring the French into the war. How much credit does the ferociously combative Arnold, not known for playing well with others, deserve for Saratoga? Historians are still duking this one out; it's fun to watch.

African Americans, free and enslaved, worked and fought for both sides during the Revolution (though more sided with the British, who started liberating those enslaved to rebels early on). Americans today are at least beginning to be aware of this story. Yet few understand how slavery's end might have been accelerated if we had recruited enslaved men to fight in return for their freedom—as Rhode Island did, briefly—or how such a plan came to be fiercely debated in South Carolina. That plan's idealistic young author, John Laurens, would remain obscure, at least until he made his Broadway debut as a sidekick in *Hamilton*.

I should confess right now that I had never heard of Laurens before I started reading for this book. Just about everything else I've mentioned was news to me as well, despite my having grown up ten miles from the Old North Bridge. And when it comes to another vitally important aspect of the war that most of us don't grasp—how much of the endgame played out far below the Mason-Dixon Line—I plead guilty as well.

We underplay the significance of the fighting in the South, not only because some of us are Yankees, but because we were taught that after Saratoga, winning was just a matter of time. The real story was more uncertain and grim. One theme was Americans killing Americans: Rebels and loyalists fought each other throughout the Revolution, but most bitterly in Georgia and the Carolinas, where, in the words of Maj. Gen. Nathanael Greene, they pursued one another "with as much relentless fury as beasts of prey" and people were "frequently murdered as they rode along the road." Another theme was the debilitating string of British victories noted above. A third was the heroic tenacity and brilliant leadership it took to end that string.

All of which brings me to a final, crucial point: We almost never think about what would have happened if *neither* the rebels nor the British had won the war.

One of the most persistent misconceptions about the American Revolution is that it had to end with one side victorious. But by 1781, a more likely scenario—fueled in part by French reluctance to throw more scarce resources at a cause that might be lost—was peace negotiations in which the European powers would hold all the cards, and which would, at best, preserve much of the territorial status quo. Picture a fragile new nation lacking Georgia, the Carolinas, New York City, Long Island, and parts of northern New England, with Great Britain still holding vast swaths of territory west of the Appalachians, and you'll have a better idea why the battles fought late in the war were critical to the future of the Republic.

So yes, Saratoga was a turning point, and a hugely important one. But if you go looking, you'll find turning points all over the revolutionary landscape. By the time I got to Cowpens, I'd seen dozens of them. I was about to see one more.

\* \* \*

As Rauch leads his students up the battlefield toward a marker titled "The Continental Army at Cowpens," Tarleton Two shares a premonition with Tarleton One.

"Brace yourself. Get ready," she tells him. "Because we're going to *lose* this."

But they haven't lost it yet.

Sharpshooters and militia have thinned the British ranks and fallen back, as instructed. Tarleton's cavalry has charged. Morgan's has driven them off.

Still the Regulars come on.

Their job is to break the line of Continental veterans that waits behind that gentle rise of ground—and they have reason to believe they can.

Both sides start to blast away at short range. The Continentals hold the line. Tarleton calls up his infantry reserves, some 250 Scotsmen from the Seventy-First Highland Regiment, and sends them to attack the rebels' right flank. Col. John Eager Howard commands Morgan's third line. Howard sees the Highlanders coming. Amid "the roar of musketry, the shouting men, the cries of the wounded and the dying, and the thick smoke that always engulfed eighteenth-century battlefields," as one historian describes the scene, he has a decision to make. Fast.

"Howards?" Rauch says.

Two tall young men step forward, join hands, and raise them over their heads. "We are Howard!" they chant. There's a burst of laughter before the rapid-fire questioning begins.

"What's happening here? You've got the Seventy-First coming around your flank—is that an issue?"

"Yeah," says one of the Howards laconically. He might just as well have said: *Are you kidding me? Elite enemy troops are about to smash into us from the side!*

"What are you going to do about that?"

What Howard does, in the midst of that smoke and deafening chaos, is issue an order—but his order is misunderstood. Instead of wheeling ninety degrees to face the oncoming Highlanders, as Howard intended, the two companies on the far right of his line do an about-face and start to retreat. The rest of the Continentals, seeing this, assume that they, too, must have been ordered to retreat—and soon every single one of Howard's men has his back to the enemy.

"Wait a minute, stop! Retreating—was that part of the plan? Morgan! Is this part of the plan?"

"No, no, it wasn't part of the plan," says one Morgan. The general has been behind the Continentals, psyching up the militia to return to the fight, but now he rides up to ask Howard, "What's going on?"

"So what do you guys talk about?"

Howard: "I'm like: 'Dude—open your eyes, look at the battlefield. We're allowing our men to break contact and move to a position of advantage.'"

Morgan: "And I'm like: 'Yeah, that sounds like a good plan. Go ahead and do that.'"

High five! This time, the laughter goes on awhile.

What we're cracking up about, besides that wonderfully anachronistic "dude," is the word "plan," because there's no way the garbling of Howard's order could have been anticipated.

Yet after it happens, everything changes.

Tarleton's men see their enemies retreating and think they've won. They break ranks and surge forward like a mob. Howard and Morgan give a few quick orders that are correctly understood. The Continentals turn around, deliver a point-blank volley, and charge with bayonets. Rebel cavalry and the revitalized militia join in, putting both British flanks under attack at once. Close to 80 percent of Tarleton's stunned force ends up killed, wounded, or captured—mostly captured, because they surrender—with Tarleton himself barely escaping to bring his boss, Lord Cornwallis, the bad news. Cornwallis needs those prisoners back. He tears off after the rebels, but can't catch them. Pretty soon, he fights a battle in North Carolina and loses a quarter of his army. In April, he abandons the Deep South and marches toward Virginia. In August, he digs in at a small port on the York River near the Chesapeake Bay.

Good luck with that.

The war won't officially end until two years later, when the Treaty of Paris is signed. But its last major fight will end on October 19, 1781, when Cornwallis's army marches out of Yorktown to lay down its arms.

Where would that army have been that day if Morgan, Howard, and their men had not recovered—calmly and bravely—from that near miss at Cowpens? Short answer: We'll never know. What-if questions are as unanswerable as they are irresistible. Yet it's essential to keep asking them, because one of our basic impulses, when we think about the past, is to assume that things happened because they *had* to happen.

\* \* \*

Army staff rides end with group discussions designed to reinforce what's been learned. The wrap-up Rauch leads is fact-based, not speculative, and the fact he most wants to reinforce is that the simultaneous two-flank attack that finished off the British was completely unplanned. "There's no grand double envelopment thought of by anybody when they show up here," he says, using the technical term. In the wake of the misunderstood order, Morgan and his subordinates simply realize: *Hey, here's an opportunity to take advantage of the situation.* And they do.

"Isn't that what it's supposed to be about in terms of adaptive leadership and agility?"

It's time for everyone but me to get on the bus. I walk the battlefield again with a last, nagging what-if stuck in my brain. This one came courtesy of historian Jim Piecuch, then at Kennesaw State University, who has spent his professional life studying the war in the South.

*What would have happened if Howard's order had not been garbled, but instead understood and obeyed?*

Well—something different.

"If the order is understood properly," Piecuch told me, answering a question I hadn't thought to ask, those two companies on Howard's right flank will turn to face the oncoming Highlanders instead of retreating—and be overwhelmed. "The Continental line is going to be rolled up and the militia is going to disappear," he said. "And that's the end of it. The battle is a disaster." In other words, Morgan, Howard, et al. wouldn't have had the *chance* to be so adaptive and agile and do the right thing—for which, let me be clear, they deserve every word of praise they've received—unless someone on their own team had done the wrong thing first.

To this day, we're not sure who it was.

One candidate is Capt. Andrew Wallace, to whom the order was first given. He was killed in battle two months after Cowpens, but decades later Howard was still trashing him for screwing things up. Another candidate is Capt. Conway Oldham, to whom Wallace would have repeated the order. There may be more. I'm not going to solve that puzzle here. If we care that the Revolutionary War came out the way it did, however, we might want to dedicate a statue to the Unknown Dude Who Screwed Up at Cowpens. Or at least raise a glass to him now and then.

# CHAPTER 1

# "You'll Have Noise Enough Before Long"

There are dozens of places you could begin a time-traveling journey through the Revolutionary War. I chose a three-hundred-year-old stone tower in Somerville, Massachusetts, that looks like a giant bullet. Why? Because what happened there on September 1, 1774, could have sparked the war seven months early and kept the names "Lexington" and "Concord" out of the history books.

The Powder House rose thirty feet above a small hilltop in Nathan Tufts Park, which is across a nasty traffic circle from the Tufts University campus. "Dogs Must Be Leashed at All Times," a park sign warned, but true to their revolutionary heritage, most dog walkers ignored it. A street-level marker told passersby that the tower was built as a windmill around 1703, repurposed as a storage space for gunpowder, and "rifled by General Gage of the colony's powder on 1 September 1774"—which was fine as far as it went, assuming people knew that Thomas Gage was then the military governor of Massachusetts and that gunpowder was a scarce commodity at the time. But it said nothing about the story I had come to pursue, which was about what *resulted* from Gage's powder-rifling venture.

Back up the hill I went to look harder.

Only then, gazing at the Stars and Stripes waving from the Powder

House's conical top, did I notice an ancient metal marker—high off the ground and so close in color to the surrounding stone that it blended in—which added some tantalizing detail. Gage had seized 250 half barrels of powder, it said, and "thereby provoked the great assembly of the following day on Cambridge Common, the first occasion on which our patriotic forefathers met in arms to oppose the tyranny of King George III."

Tantalizing but inadequate!

Which patriotic forefathers would we be talking about here? Met in *arms*? What exactly happened in Cambridge on September 2, 1774?

If I wanted to understand the incendiary confrontation soon to be known as the Powder Alarm, I figured, it was time to take a Cambridge walk with a man who lives the Revolution every day.

*  *  *

The first thing one notices about the proprietor of *Boston 1775*—a blog with the tagline: "History, analysis, and unabashed gossip about the start of the American Revolution in Massachusetts"—is the pair of nineteenth-century-style sideburns that threaten to rendezvous under his chin. Otherwise, he looks like a well-groomed graduate student: jeans, blue-and-white-checked shirt, thick dark hair, and a youthful face that made me surprised to hear he was forty-nine when I met him. He writes as "J. L. Bell," the world being overstocked with John Bells, yet it would be hard to mistake the eclectic erudition of *Boston 1775* for the work of anyone else.

How does a longtime book editor evolve into an everyday revolutionary blogger? Over a sandwich a few blocks west of Harvard Square, Bell told me the story of the eleven-year-old cause of it all.

He had started to think about writing a historical novel for kids when he ran across a reference to a boy who had been shot and killed a week and a half before the Boston Massacre. "It's very unusual to find events in history where children are agents and their decisions actually matter," Bell said, but in 1770, "the boys of Boston were doing their own picket lines" as part of a boycott of British goods. One day some boys got into an altercation with a boycott opponent and began chucking rocks through his windows. The man fired into the crowd and the rest was history—more than a thousand people showed up for young Christopher Seider's funeral—except that Bell didn't *know* that history. Growing up in Revolution-proud Massachusetts, he had assumed that all the important stories had been thoroughly explored. He was wrong.

Intrigued, he did some serious digging. After a while, he noticed that the internet was revolutionizing how history could be researched and written. Should he be thinking about a blog? he wondered. "Just do it," a friend urged.

Ten years and 3,624 posts later, *Boston 1775* had credentialed Bell to an extent few would have predicted. Academics consulted him; lecture opportunities found him; the National Park Service hired him to write a book-length report on George Washington's Cambridge headquarters; and random history-minded journalists began pestering him for help. When I got in touch, he was deep into finishing *The Road to Concord*, a book that devotes its first two chapters to the events of September 1 and 2, 1774.

After lunch, we set out on our Powder Alarm walk. First stop: a yellow colonial at 42 Brattle Street, between the Brattle Theatre and an Ann Taylor store.

Today, 42 Brattle houses the Cambridge Center for Adult Education. In 1774, as tensions between Great Britain and New England neared an all-time high, it was home to William Brattle, a sixty-eight-year-old gentleman farmer and Massachusetts militia general, who kicked off the September craziness by writing the governor a letter. Composed in late August, it informed Gage, who was his boss, that gunpowder was starting to disappear from the Powder House. Gage took the hint. Before dawn on September 1, longboats ferried upwards of 250 Boston-based British soldiers three miles up the Mystic River, where they got out and marched another mile to their destination. Removing hobnailed boots lest a spark blow them to kingdom come, they collected the remaining powder in the tower; a few went to Cambridge to confiscate a couple of artillery pieces as well. All were safely back in Boston by noon, and the governor was a happy man.

Not for long, though.

Later that day, Gage's enemies somehow got their hands on Brattle's letter. A crowd of local protesters showed up outside his house, but by then the owner was gone. "He went into Boston," Bell said, "and never saw Cambridge again." Unsatisfied, the crowd reassembled half a mile up the street, at the home of a colonial official named Jonathan Sewall, whose wife said he wasn't home. The protesters didn't believe her and tried to break in. Someone inside fired a pistol—accidentally, it was claimed—which sobered everybody up, and the crowd dispersed.

As Bell and I walked up to Sewall's house (now 149 Brattle), I asked what the tony twenty-first-century neighborhood had been like in 1774. For one thing, he said, it was far less crowded: Just seven elegant residences, widely spaced, sat along a mile-long stretch of what was then called the Watertown Road. They were "estates with farms, not town houses; this was out in the country." Enslaved people did the farming, and many families on Tory Row—"a name that came along later"—had fortunes based on Caribbean sugar plantations. All of which made these folks very different from the several thousand farmers and tradesmen who materialized on Cambridge Common, just a few blocks away, on the morning after the September 1 disturbances.

To understand what those men were doing there, we need to back up a bit.

When I first had the idea for a traveling revolutionary history, tracing the events of the war itself seemed plenty challenging enough, and I decided to skip sites related to *causes* of the Revolution. I knew about taxation without representation, of course, and had a pre-Lexington timeline in my head that included the French and Indian War, the Stamp Act, the Boston Massacre, and the destruction of British tea by angry guys wearing face paint. But now that the Powder Alarm was on my radar screen, I needed a refresher course on the Massachusetts Government Act—which I had entirely forgotten until Bell reminded me it was crucial.

Briefly: When news of the Boston Tea Party reached England, early in 1774, the British government went ballistic. It closed the port of Boston, ordered redcoats into the center of town, and, somewhat less famously, set out to eliminate local self-government in Massachusetts.

Before this, Bell said, there had been "a balance of top-down and bottom-up power" in which the top, in London, "appointed the governor, who appointed the sheriffs and judges," while the bottom, "which was really the middle, the property-owning white males," elected legislators, town officials, and local militia officers. Now, however, members of the legislature's upper house, known as governor's councilors, would be appointed directly by the Crown. Judges and other court officials, formerly under the indirect control of citizens, would serve exclusively at the governor's pleasure. Town meetings would be limited to one per year unless the governor gave special permission.

Resistance began the minute news of the Government Act crossed the Atlantic. Within weeks, royal authority outside Boston had almost disappeared.

"Huge crowds showed up in court sessions in western counties, where there were no British troops. They often showed up in their militia units, not armed, but with a clear implication of, you know, there are thousands of us and fourteen of you." The crowds demanded that courts stop doing business under the Government Act and that all the "newfangled" governor's councilors resign. By the time Brattle wrote his letter, Gage knew he was in trouble. Without reinforcements, he didn't have enough men to put down what historian Ray Raphael calls "the first American Revolution." The best the governor could do was go after the insurgents' military supplies.

So that was what he did.

But the unintended consequences of the Powder House raid kept getting worse.

News of the raid spread through the countryside that night, accompanied by alarming rumors: Gage's troops had shot and killed people! The British Navy was bombarding Boston! The town was burning! The rumors didn't all make sense (why burn a town where your own men are quartered?), but there was no time to confirm them, and by now, the country people were used to acting forcefully on their own. "Each individual community got together and decided: 'Now we march,'" Bell told me. A traveling merchant, in one of the few detailed accounts that survive, described repeated scenes of purposeful chaos: "at every house

Women & Children making Cartridges, running Bullets, making Wallets, baking Biscuit, crying & bemoaning & at the same time animating their Husbands & Sons to fight for their Liberties, tho' not knowing whether they should ever see them again."

By early morning on September 2, thousands of men with muskets filled the roads to Cambridge.

Somewhere, the truth caught up with them: No one had been killed; Boston wasn't burning. They parked their guns outside of town and proceeded to the Common "armed only with sticks," one newspaper reported, but still with business to conduct. As long as they were here, why not demand resignations and apologies from Cambridge men who had taken office under the Government Act? This was what they were doing, peacefully enough, when six anxious resistance leaders from Boston showed up. These gentlemen, Bell said—and they *were* gentlemen, with the best-known being Dr. Joseph Warren—were "worried about the farmers attacking somebody" and discrediting a movement whose chief hope, still, was that London would back down.

The Bostonians tried to take charge. For a while, they appeared to succeed. Then—boom!—someone recognized a customs commissioner named Benjamin Hallowell, who happened to be passing through Cambridge in his chaise. It was as though a grenade had been tossed into the gathering: More than a hundred men mounted up to pursue Hallowell toward Boston. Many of the riders got talked out of it, but some didn't, and the chase continued. Others in the crowd went back to retrieve their muskets. Before long, Thomas Oliver, the lieutenant governor of Massachusetts, heard a knock on his Tory Row door.

Set back from the street, surrounded by outbuildings and lush green space, Oliver's mansion—now occupied by the president of Harvard—helped me imagine the 1774 neighborhood better than any other stop on Bell's tour. Less easy to picture, however, was the angry crowd that materialized outside it for the final act of The Day the War Could Have Begun.

Lieutenant Governor Oliver, like those six nervous gentlemen from Boston, had spent much of September 2 trying to keep the peace. That morning, a delegation from the militiamen had asked him to travel to

Boston and urge Gage not to attack them; Oliver had complied, returning to report that Gage had no plans to send troops. After declining a
relatively polite request that he resign—besides being lieutenant governor, Oliver served on the governor's council—he seized the opportunity
of the Hallowell furor to head home. But the mood on the Common
had changed, Bell said, and "the crowd decided that they weren't going
to let *anybody* in Cambridge remain on the council." This meant walking a mile west to confront Oliver en masse.

Inside his house, Oliver—presented with a resignation document to
sign—once again refused.

Outside, thousands of men—a quarter of them armed—got impatient.

"The leaders of the crowd had lost control," Bell said. Men pressed
up to Oliver's open windows; his wife and children freaked out. Members of the delegation inside "were pleading with him to sign, because
they didn't know what these men were going to do." Finally he gave in,
adding a line of explanation to the prepared text.

"My house at Cambridge being surrounded by about four thousand
people, in compliance with their command," Oliver wrote, "I sign my
name."

The Powder Alarm was over.

Technically, the Revolutionary War had not broken out.

Yet thanks to the actions of thousands of forgotten men—their
names, unlike those of the elite leaders on both sides, do not appear in
the historical record—few illusions remained about how soon the shooting might begin.

One day later, Gage began to strengthen British defenses at the only
place Boston could be attacked by land.

\* \* \*

It was called Boston Neck or just "the Neck," and it was among the most
significant chunks of revolutionary real estate in Massachusetts. To follow the action when the war finally did break out, 229 days after the
Powder Alarm, you need to know how the Neck dictated the starting
point for Paul Revere's famous ride, not to mention the route the British
Regulars would take on the way to Lexington and Concord.

It would also be nice to go *see* what the Neck looked like in April 1775, but you can't. Here's why:

From the time of its founding through the eighteenth century, Boston was a virtual island. If you wanted to enter or leave without getting in a boat, your only option was a 120-foot-wide isthmus that connected the south end of town to the mainland. It was the Neck toward which a terrified Benjamin Hallowell spurred his horse during the Powder Alarm, seeking protection from the British troops there. It was the Neck at which Gage began to beef up British defenses the next day, and it was the Neck that Revere needed to avoid the following spring. In the nineteenth century, however, massive landfill projects more than doubled the size of the city and radically reshaped its shoreline. Back Bay, which used to be a real bay that rose and fell with the tides, became a fashionable urban neighborhood. And the Neck, with huge tracts of filled land on either side, essentially disappeared.

I thought I'd look at what remained anyway.

Walking down Washington Street in modern Boston's South End, as instructed, I came to a nice little ballpark called Luis Tiant Field. Between street and field stood a long, low sculpture, five feet high at its crest, with one side covered in sea-blue tiles and the other in planted earth. *LandWave*, it was called, and the Neck had been its inspiration. I could make out no reference to the Revolution. Later, I would learn, it was condemned as "a dangerous playground for skateboarders and climbing kids" and removed.

Oh well. My next Boston stop would reconnect me with Joseph Warren, a man who understood that on April 18, 1775, geography was destiny.

A thirty-three-year-old widower with a thriving medical practice, Warren was charismatic, ambitious, and fiercely committed to colonial liberty. Had he not died young, his admirers believe, he would have achieved Founding Father status. He was also the highest-ranking resistance leader in Boston on April 18—most others, fearing arrest, had left town—and he knew how dramatically the world had changed in the seven months since he and his colleagues had tried to rein in the Powder Alarm because they weren't ready for war.

During those months, Massachusetts courts continued to be closed, and Massachusetts counties passed resolutions that foreshadowed the Declaration of Independence. The colony also created an illegal shadow government, the Provincial Congress, which started collecting taxes, stockpiling arms, and reshaping its militia into a force that might someday resemble an army. Meanwhile, the Crown's position hardened. Contemptuously underestimating the strength of the opposition, one of Gage's London bosses demanded that the governor do something *right now*—using his own best judgment, of course.

Thanks, pal.

Hand forced, Gage decided to send hundreds of red-coated troops on a supposedly secret mission into the countryside. It's hard to imagine him not knowing that he risked war by doing this. It's equally hard to imagine Warren not knowing that *he* risked war by sending out messengers to warn that the Regulars were coming.

His first move was to send a tanner named William Dawes to try the land route through Boston Neck. Then, needing a Plan B—what if Dawes got turned back by the guard?—Warren sent for Paul Revere.

They met at Warren's rented house on Hanover Street, which doubled as the doctor's medical office. No trace of it remains, unless you include the fact that City Hall Plaza, one of the ugliest urban redevelopment projects ever built, sits on the ashes of a neighborhood that took its name from William Scollay, the brother of Warren's fiancée.

Revere was the son of a French immigrant (original name: Rivoire) who had married a Yankee woman, and he was one of the best-connected men in town. A skilled artisan, primarily a silversmith, he was "a great joiner" who "knew everyone and moved in many different circles," as historian David Hackett Fischer put it, thus helping "link one group to another." He was also "supremely good at getting things done" and was often asked to carry important news to liberty-minded contacts as far away as Philadelphia.

The task Warren assigned to Revere and Dawes on April 18 was the same: Ride to Lexington and warn Samuel Adams and John Hancock that British troops were headed their way. The doctor didn't *know* the Regulars were after the two most important opposition leaders in

Massachusetts, but he didn't want to risk Adams and Hancock being surprised in their beds. Plan A, as we've seen, was Dawes trying to make his way past the guards at the Neck. Plan B, which Warren and Revere activated at Warren's house around 9 or 10 p.m., was even riskier. Two friends would row Revere to Charlestown, across the mouth of the Charles River from his home in the North End, without attracting the notice of a British warship anchored directly in their path. If he made it, colleagues there would have a fast horse waiting for him.

There was a Plan C as well, arranged by Revere and those Charlestown colleagues two days earlier. As everyone knows, it involved signal lanterns and the Old North Church, a fifteen-minute walk from City Hall Plaza, much of it along Boston's famed Freedom Trail.

A few hundred yards into the North End, I found myself at the brown, clapboard-covered house where Revere had lived. Its revamped visitor center was still under construction, so I didn't linger. Then I came to another Revere site that was both wonderful and unexpected.

Being a twenty-first-century American, I had seen the name "Paul Revere Mall" on a map and assumed it had something to do with shopping. But "mall" can also mean "sheltered walk or promenade," and here it was—a long brick walkway with a crowd-pleasing statue of the Midnight Rider on one end and the elegant steeple of the Old North Church rising above the other. Between statue and church, embedded in a high brick wall, was a treasure trove of 1930s-era historical markers designed to exalt the neighborhood and mesmerize history obsessives like me. Dozens of North Enders who helped make Boston "the pride of later generations" are celebrated, among them Ann Pollard, who came ashore with the Puritans in 1630 to find her new home "covered with blueberries."

The mall's namesake is honored with a few lines from the poem that begins "Listen, my children, and you shall hear / Of the midnight ride of Paul Revere." Cobbled together from Henry Wadsworth Longfellow's much longer original, they describe what happened after someone climbed the steep stairs inside the church to send a signal to Charlestown about which way the British were coming—by land, across Boston Neck (in which case one lantern would be lit), or by sea, in boats launched from Boston Common (in which case two lanterns would be displayed):

> *On the opposite shore walked Paul Revere...*
> *A glimmer and then a gleam of light!...*
> *A second lamp in the belfry burns!...*
> *And so through the night went his cry of alarm*
> *To every Middlesex village and farm.*

The first thing to say about this poem is that it isn't true. Well before he got in that boat to be rowed past that warship, more of Revere's friends, at his request, had lit those two lanterns in the church's highest window. They already knew which way the troops were going; the point was to let the folks in Charlestown know, so they could have a horse ready—and, by the way, start spreading the word themselves.

The second thing to say about "Paul Revere's Ride"—which is full of such errors—is that without it, few of us would know Revere's name today.

Until 1861, Revere was a regional hero, not a national one. But when one of the most popular poets in American history took an interest in him, he went permanently viral. Writing on the eve of the Civil War, Longfellow wasn't striving for historical accuracy. He intended his poem, Fischer wrote, as "a call to arms for a new American generation, in another moment of peril," as well as an argument "that one man alone could make a difference, by his services to a great and noble cause." That cause, historian Jill Lepore has noted, was not only preserving the Union but ending slavery.

It's not that he didn't do any Revere research at all. For poetic purposes, he ascended to the steeple window of Old North Church, startling pigeons as he climbed. I would have followed suit, except that tours no longer went all the way to the top. So I stood outside and admired the steeple for a while—it's not original, having been blown down twice in storms—then walked across the Charlestown Bridge to see if I could find the spot where Revere's brave oarsmen dropped him off.

Sure enough, in an isolated corner of waterfront not far from the USS *Constitution*, a marker with a hokey painting of Revere standing up in a boat notes that he landed "near here," walked "a short distance" into town, and got on a horse. Just after midnight, he would gallop up to the Lexington parsonage where John Hancock and Sam Adams were staying and find at least nine militiamen already on guard.

They had been alerted hours before that *something* might be up.

* * *

Hancock had strong family connections in Lexington. The Reverend Jonas Clarke had succeeded his grandfather as the town's Congregationalist minister, and Clarke's wife, Lucy, was his cousin. When Revere showed up, no fewer than fifteen people were sleeping at the parsonage, among them nine Clarke children, Hancock's aunt Lydia, and his fiancée, Dolly Quincy. Aware of this, militia sergeant William Munroe urged the Midnight Rider to keep the noise down.

"Noise!" Revere replied. "You'll have noise enough before long—the Regulars are coming out." Half an hour later, William Dawes turned up bearing the same message.

"We don't think *anybody* went back to bed that night," Jane Morse said as she led a tour of the two-story, timber-frame structure now known as the Hancock-Clarke House.

Morse was for years the head guide for the Lexington Historical Society, where she worked to eliminate "rampant mythology and hearsay" from the guides' repertoire. Since retiring from the management part of the job, she told me, "I just do the fun stuff." She walked us into the downstairs room where Hancock and Adams shared a four-poster bed, pointing out the small round table at which "the two most famous instigators of the patriot cause" took tea the night before the battle. Their presence explains why the town was on high alert hours before Revere and Dawes showed up: A note had arrived warning that mounted British officers had been seen on patrol northwest of Boston and might be headed for Lexington. The note does not survive, but whatever it contained, it didn't stop anyone in the parsonage from going to bed—albeit with militiamen guarding the door.

Next, Morse led us upstairs to talk about what happened after Adams and Hancock left the house.

It had taken them far too long to put themselves out of harm's way. Revere had said goodbye, ridden off toward Concord, and gotten himself captured by a British patrol. He was eventually released and trudged several miles back to Lexington (his captors having taken his horse), only to find his original mission unaccomplished. "Guys, what the *heck* are you still doing here?" is Morse's version of what he might have said to the irreplaceable leaders he had risked his life to warn. But finally, off they had gone, leaving Hancock's fiancée and aunt behind.

From their bedroom window, Dolly Quincy and Lydia Hancock could see Lexington Common, a five-minute walk away. They were still in the house when the shooting started. As an old woman, one of the Clarkes' daughters—who was twelve on April 19, 1775—plainly recalled seeing "the British troops marching off the Common," Lydia "wringing her hands and helping Mother dress the children," and "Dolly going round with Father, to hide Money, watches and anything down in the potatoes and up in the garret."

Later, Betty Clarke watched her father help bury the Lexington dead. But that's getting ahead of the story.

I talked with Morse for a while between tours. She urged me to head for the Munroe Tavern, another house museum managed by the historical society, to meet a colleague who would be on guide duty there for another half hour.

"John is an unbelievable researcher-scholar," she said, shooing me toward the door. "He's wonderful. And he will talk about Lexington for three days straight if you like."

# CHAPTER 2

# The Grassy Knoll of the Revolution

Ask John Denis how he got obsessed with Revolution-era history and he'll tell you about reading a novel because four students had been killed at Kent State University.

"It's 1970, it's spring, I'm at Dartmouth," Denis said, answering questions at the Munroe Tavern after it closed for the day. His roommate kept telling him to read the celebrated historical novelist Kenneth Roberts, and Denis kept not reading him. Then came Kent State, and colleges around the nation canceled classes. Time to read Kenneth Roberts, he thought. "And I'm sitting in my dormitory one day reading this incredibly dramatic passage"—in which, true story, starving soldiers led by special operations pioneer Robert Rogers rafted down the Connecticut River in a desperate search for food—"and I look out the back window of my room at . . . the Connecticut River! I've been living on the banks of the river that Rogers floated down in 1759. And there was the epiphany: Hollywood had lied. All the exciting stuff *didn't* happen west of the Mississippi. Oh my God, what else am I missing?"

Well, the Revolutionary War for one thing, about which Roberts had also written novels. Denis read them. Then he read a narrative history of the war's first days and found himself hooked for life on the nonfiction version.

A broad-faced, white-bearded man who sometimes used a cane but never a computer, Denis was a retired teacher of high school Latin and Greek. We talked for six hours over two days, during which I got a crash course in what is and is not known about April 19, 1775. At our second meeting, he showed up with a black three-ring binder, three inches thick, filled with every primary source he had been able to find, carefully retyped and arranged in chronological order. He used an electric Smith Corona for the typing, he said, and when he needed a new cartridge, he went down to the Cambridge Typewriter Company, where "the guy has told me there's *one* factory in China that produces them and when that factory burns down, that's it."

"So you'll be getting a computer!" I said.

He laughed, then went back to expanding my limited knowledge of how the war began.

Take those Regulars said to be heading Lexington's way. I knew roughly where they climbed into boats from Boston Common (there is a nonobvious marker on Charles Street, within hailing distance of the Swan Boats in the Public Garden; once again, landfill has made history harder to see) and I knew roughly where they waded ashore in East Cambridge (another well-hidden marker, two blocks from the old Lechmere Station, marks the landing spot). But I didn't know how *many* came out that night, having seen numbers ranging from six hundred to nine hundred.

"I did a paper on that," Denis said, producing a copy. Ten typewritten pages filled with carefully weighed evidence persuaded me to go with "more than eight hundred."

The troops got off to a late start. Marching through Cambridge around 2 a.m., they heard church bells in the distance and deduced that they weren't going to surprise anyone. This was partly Revere's doing, but hardly the solo act portrayed by Longfellow. "For the word to have been spread so efficiently and so quickly," Denis explained, "there had to have been a preconceived plan. When Revere hits Medford, the captain in Medford knows who his messenger is and what town he's going to. And when he gets to where *he's* going," the same thing happens. The whole thing reminds Denis of a scene from 1950s TV. "Remember the old Walt Disney show trying to explain nuclear fission? And they have all the mousetraps with the Ping-Pong balls? Just throw one Ping-Pong ball" at the mousetraps "and they *all* go off eventually."

The analogy is hardly perfect. Still, those Ping-Pong balls evoke the rapid, collective nature of the response to the British foray into the countryside. They also—bonus points!—conjure up the chain-reaction chaos sparked when the Regulars reached Lexington Common and someone fired the first shot of the war.

Key word: "someone."

We don't know who fired that shot and almost certainly never will. Think of Lexington Common (also known as the Battle Green) as the Grassy Knoll of the Revolution, locus of a centuries-long argument in which inadequate information, conflicting sources, political bias, wartime propaganda, and conspiracy theories are all part of the mix. That said, Denis has worked this fraught territory with as much rigor and perseverance as anyone, and I was happy to hear what he thought.

"If I'm doing a talk on the Green, I point out that the first shot was from *us*," he said.

To set the scene: It's dawn, but barely. The two hundred or so men of the British vanguard are marching up what's now called Massachusetts Avenue toward the triangle-shaped Common. On the near end is the Lexington meeting house, where Reverend Clarke preaches on Sundays. To its right is Buckman Tavern, which, unlike the meeting house, still stands today. On the far end of the Common—which the Regulars can't yet see—about eighty Lexington militiamen have formed up in two lines, holding loaded muskets. Enter British lieutenant William Sutherland on horseback, accompanied by a few men on foot.

"Sutherland is riding ahead of the vanguard, heading toward the Green," Denis said, citing a Sutherland letter—it's in his binder, as you'd expect—written eight days after the battle. The lieutenant is headed for the gap between the meeting house and the tavern "when somebody standing off to the right, roughly around where the visitor center is today, levels his piece and pulls the trigger. It flashes in the pan, the main charge doesn't go off, but that's enough for Sutherland," who turns around to report to his superior. "He then says that 'as I hope for mercy'—which is a rather strong statement in those days"—three shots then came in his direction from what his letter calls "a corner of the large house to the right of the church," which can only be Buckman Tavern.

"If musket balls go past you, you can hear that *vvvpppp* sound," Denis said. "There's no doubt about what's going on." This is just one of many reasons he thinks Sutherland is telling the truth.

Next question: What, exactly, had Capt. John Parker hoped to accomplish by ordering those militiamen onto the Common as the Regulars approached?

Before trying to answer, it's worth noting a few facts. First, the British troops had almost certainly *not* been sent to arrest Hancock and Adams. Gage's orders were for them to go to Concord, six miles farther down the road, to seize and destroy a cache of weapons and military supplies there. "It would have been a fool's errand to send the infantry after guys who have horses," Denis said. Second, there were excellent reasons for opponents of the Crown to believe, in April 1775, that their leaders faced arrest at any moment. Thus for Parker, "As long as the two politicians are here, that's your primary duty: You've got to protect these guys." But third, the politicians had left town—as Parker had to know—by the time the Regulars arrived.

Once again: Why were those men with muskets lined up on the Common at dawn?

Several hours earlier, summoned by an alarm bell, perhaps 130 members of the 144-man Lexington Militia Company had mustered on the Common. They had discussed the Regulars' reported approach with their commander, as was their democratic habit, and, according to sworn testimony Parker gave six days later, they had "concluded not to be discovered, nor meddle" with the Regulars "unless they should insult or molest us." Not long afterward, having received no confirmation from scouts that the British were near, Parker dismissed his men; they were to be recalled, if necessary, by the beat of a drum.

So: If your plan is "not to be discovered" by advancing troops, how do you end up standing with loaded weapons a few feet from the road down which those troops must go? Was Parker, a forty-five-year-old man said to have fought in the French and Indian War, simply a fool?

"No, no. He made a *really* bad miscalculation, but he's not a dope of any kind," Denis said. "As a military move, it was incredibly stupid, but I don't think it was a military move. I think it was a political gesture."

There is no evidence for this, only speculation. Might Parker have changed his mind on his own, unwilling to see an occupying force march through his hometown without at least a show of resistance? Did others in Lexington that night—the fiery Reverend Clarke, perhaps, or the saber-rattling Hancock—push him in this direction? Might Samuel Adams have urged Parker to stand firm, secretly hoping for a confrontation he could exploit as a rallying point, just as he had done with the Boston Massacre?

It was dawn, in any case, and eighty militiamen—many fewer than had mustered earlier—stood on the Common with the Regulars a few minutes' march away. Other men stood to the side, whether near the tavern and its outbuildings, behind a stone wall, or elsewhere; these men were not under Captain Parker's control. Sutherland reported seeing the flash in the pan. The men of the British vanguard stopped to load their own weapons, then advanced onto the Common. Seeing Parker and his men, they sped up and began to shout.

Think Ping-Pong balls and mousetraps: The situation was about to explode.

Were there more shots from the side? Did a British officer fire his pistol in the air, triggering an undisciplined reaction from his men? Did someone's gun go off by accident? All these and more are reasonable possibilities. One of the few things that seem clear, amid a welter of conflicting testimony, is that none of the militiamen lined up *on the Common* fired at the Regulars before being fired upon themselves. Parker, assessing the hopelessness of their position, ordered his men to disperse. Most turned and hastened away, still carrying their weapons, though a few, not hearing the order or choosing not to obey it, stood their ground. "Lay down your arms, damn you, why don't you lay down your arms?" a mounted officer shouted, according to a witness looking out the window of a house close to the action. In the grotesque, one-sided skirmish that followed, seven militiamen and an unarmed civilian were killed, ten more were wounded, and there was so much smoke from the Regulars' volleys that the few Lexington men who returned fire couldn't see much but the heads of some officers' horses. The British infantrymen—professional, yes, but nervous and mostly without combat experience—had run wild, and it took longer than it should have for their officers to get them under control and back on the road to Concord.

Then came what Denis thinks is the most remarkable part of Lexington's day.

"Sometime in the middle of the morning," he said, "having discovered just how awful things can be when they go horribly wrong," a significant number of the town's militiamen shouldered their arms, marched up the road the British had taken, and put themselves in a position to confront the Regulars again. "*That's* courage, when you know how bad it can be but you go out and try it one more time." He whacked the table emphatically, three times, to echo the rhythm of the last three words.

Concord was up next. But on my way out of town, I paused for a last look at a statue so famous that the word "iconic" is unavoidable.

The Lexington Minute Man is a well-realized idealization of revolutionary fortitude. Ruggedly handsome and sculpted in bronze, he stands astride a pile of rocks with a musket resting on his raised left leg. The idea was that he should represent a generic Lexington hero, though perhaps inevitably, he became identified with Captain Parker. But it's important to note a couple of historical realities here.

First, the real Parker wasn't actually a minute man. That term applies to members of rapid-response units that were created, not long after the Powder Alarm, to mobilize faster than the local militias from which they were drawn. Lexington never formed such a unit. All who mustered there on April 19 were militiamen.

And second, while no reality-based images of Parker exist, he has been described as "a stout, large framed man, of medium height" and in April 1775, he was five months from dying of tuberculosis.

More human and less iconic, in other words—and even easier to admire.

* * *

Concord has a statue, too, of course. It's called simply the Minute Man, having gone up a quarter century before Lexington's, and there are other significant differences. In addition to holding a musket, Concord's bronze guy rests a hand on a plow, suggesting a connection with the noble Roman said to have returned to his farm after leaving it to fight in time of need. And he also boasts—carved into his base—four lines of immortal verse:

> *By the rude bridge that arched the flood,*
> *Their flag to April's breeze unfurled,*
> *Here once the embattled farmers stood,*
> *And fired the shot heard round the world.*

Ralph Waldo Emerson, whose grandfather watched the Concord fight from his home a hundred yards away, wrote those lines in 1837. They still stir hearts, mine included. Dishearteningly, however, by the time Emerson's words ended up on the statue, Lexington and Concord were decades into an unseemly pissing match over which deserved the glory of being the Town Where the Revolutionary War Began. When it came time to plan centennial celebrations in 1875, all attempts to coordinate proved futile: An aide to President Ulysses S. Grant told the feuding towns that if they couldn't get their acts together, Grant might not even come. The towns called his bluff, put on entirely separate events, and made the president go to both.

It was a perfect blue-sky day when I showed up on the east bank of the Concord River, across from where the citizen-soldier stands, to think about the 1775 confrontation. I watched a great blue heron swoop down to land near a couple lying on the grass and admired the graceful curve of the bridge itself, which—though rebuilt many times, once out of concrete—now looks roughly like the plank structure the embattled farmers would have seen. An old marker helped set up the drama. "On the morning of April nineteenth," it began, "while the British held this bridge, the minute-men and militia of Concord and neighboring towns gathered on the hill across the river."

Those minute men and militia (Concord, unlike Lexington, had both) were still gathering at around 9 a.m. But Concord's day had really started seven hours earlier, with a warning delivered by Samuel Prescott, the man who finished Revere's ride for him.

Prescott was a twenty-three-year-old Concord physician who, the story goes, had spent the evening courting a sweetheart in Lexington. Heading home after midnight, he ran into Revere and William Dawes, fresh from delivering their messages, who had decided to go on to Concord. Would the doctor help alert the countryside en route? Yes indeed! Then, out of nowhere, came the aforementioned British patrol, which took Revere prisoner. Dawes escaped, but his horse threw him and ran off. Prescott jumped *his* horse over a stone wall and galloped away.

Soon an alarm bell was ringing in Concord and men were gathering near the town center, a bit less than a mile south of the North Bridge.

As the British of course knew, Concord was a major storage point for provincial arms and military supplies—at least it had been. Warned days earlier that the Regulars *could* be coming, however, the man in charge of those arms and supplies, Col. James Barrett, had already organized the removal of the most important. Still, Prescott's warning was a literal wake-up call for the town to get more of them out of sight. Many citizen-soldiers got to work on that. Around 7 a.m., perhaps as many as two hundred of them, including some men who'd come in from Lincoln, took a position overlooking the road the Regulars must take into town. By then, they knew there had been a confrontation in Lexington, but not the grim details. Pretty soon they saw a ribbon of redcoats winding down what's now called Hardy's Hill, bayonets flashing in the sun—and suddenly, as John Denis put it, "it wasn't a question of imagining David versus Goliath. It was, 'Oh my God, that *is* Goliath.'"

Sensibly, they withdrew to the Concord River, crossed the North Bridge, and regrouped on the hill above it, wondering what they should do next.

Poised to walk up that hill myself, I noticed a modern military procession approaching from the other direction. A couple dozen teenagers in camouflage pants and bright green T-shirts marched straight to the graves of two British soldiers near the bridge, saluted, and held their salutes as a recorded bugler played something that sounded like "Taps." The teens, I learned, were junior ROTC cadets attending a weeklong training camp, and what I'd thought was "Taps" turned out to be the British equivalent. Now Col. John Murray, a retired army aviator and passionate amateur historian, began to tell the cadets what took place here and what lessons they could take from the story.

One was that the Concord fight was *not* inevitable.

"The militia didn't jump out of bed and say, 'Hey, man, I'm going to start the American Revolution today,'" Murray said. The British didn't, either. "What occurred was simply—it was a mistake, okay? It was a set of bad circumstances. The conditions were set because of the anger between the two groups, but it just happened.

"And I'm going to tell you why."

After the British marched into Concord, he said, their commander split them up. The main body began "search and seizure of colonial arms and ammunition" in the town center. Four companies crossed the North Bridge and marched a couple of miles west to Colonel Barrett's farm, where intelligence reports indicated that more arms were stored, "including cannon, which were very important in those days." Three other companies, totaling roughly a hundred men, took positions near the bridge. Their job was to keep it open for the troops returning from Barrett's farm.

That was the plan, anyway.

"Everybody look behind you," Murray said. "On the high ground, that pasture that slopes up, four hundred men from towns in and around this area had gathered. Now, the colonial militia had been ordered by their leadership not to take any offensive action, to assume a defensive posture. So what happened on that day, at this place where the American Revolution begins?"

Well—smoke happened.

In the center of Concord, British troops searching for hidden military supplies turned up "a minimum amount," including wooden carriages for cannon, and "took them out to the street and set them afire, in bonfires. One of those bonfires got away from them and set a meeting hall on fire, which began to burn, which sent up deep, dark smoke." Which meant that those men standing on the hilltop—who could look down into Concord, because in 1775, unlike today, no trees blocked their view—were left to conclude that the British were burning the town.

Being New England citizen-soldiers, they discussed this. Then they marched down the hill.

Seeing them coming, the British troops fell back to the other side of the bridge.

"They're eighteen miles into enemy territory, they're alone, and they're afraid," Murray said—and this time, they definitely shot first. Two minute men recently arrived from Acton fell dead. "Fire, for God's sake fire" ordered Concord's Maj. John Buttrick, and the colonials did, killing two Regulars outright and wounding ten others, one of them mortally. The British panicked and ran, abandoning their fallen comrades and leaving the four companies at Barrett's farm "hanging in the breeze" with no one to secure their return. Luckily for them, their opponents *still* didn't know what to do next, and remained reluctant to take the offensive. Not only didn't they pursue the British toward the town they had marched down that hillside to protect, but they chose not to attack those vulnerable men coming back from their largely fruitless search at Barrett's.

The cadets were on a tight schedule and Murray was running out of time. I was already impressed by the amount of complexity he had crammed into a ten-minute presentation. Then he surprised me with another story. Remember that mortally wounded soldier, he asked, the one who got left behind at the bridge? At some point, "a teenage militiaman wandered by and he happened to have a tomahawk," which he decided to use on the fallen man. Returning from Barrett's, British troops found a comrade with his head split open and assumed the militia had scalped him; later that day, they would commit atrocities themselves. "That barbaric act," Murray said, "may have encouraged them to act the way they did."

This led to one last point about the Concord fight.

"Keep in mind: This was just a skirmish. Lexington was a skirmish. But on the afternoon of the nineteenth—from twelve o'clock in the afternoon to seven o'clock in the evening—the British had to march eighteen miles back to Boston, the entire time under attack."

\* \* \*

The British commander, Lt. Col. Francis Smith, ordered his men out of Concord around noon, having failed to turn up enough military supplies to begin to justify a mission that had already lasted since the previous

33

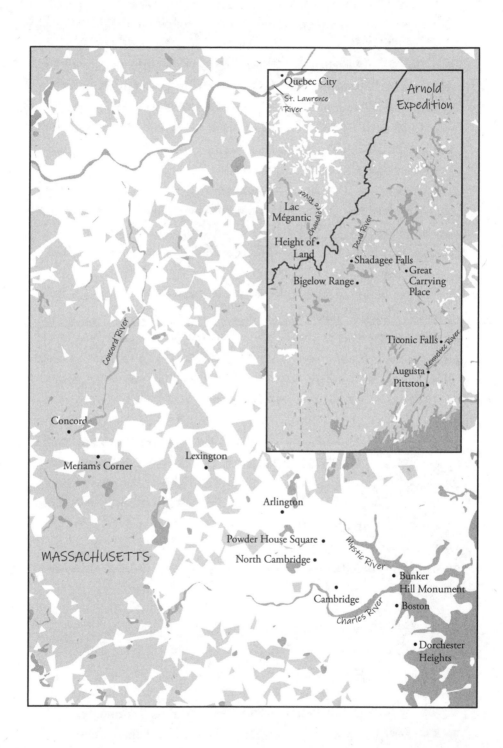

day and cost thirteen lives. The best way to think about what happened next, I figured, was to walk to Boston in the footsteps of the embattled Regulars. Full disclosure: I did this over several days, not seven hours, and ended up driving a couple of the less dramatic miles. Also, no one was shooting at me. Still, I wouldn't trade the experience for months of book learning, despite the distractions I encountered immediately on Lexington Road.

For one thing, it was rush hour.

How hard is it to imagine hundreds of exhausted eighteenth-century soldiers tramping a route now bumper-to-bumper with angry Massachusetts drivers? Very hard—at least until you realize that the troops were moving, at a pace of three miles per hour, about as fast as the cars.

For another thing, you can't swing a dead cat by the tail in Concord without hitting the home of a literary icon.

Look, here was the house where Emerson wrote "Self-Reliance" and that shot-heard-round-the-world thing. Here was the house where Louisa May Alcott wrote *Little Women*. Here was one where Nathaniel Hawthorne lived for a few years, and a trail leading up the hillside behind it, and an old marker saying that Hawthorne "trod daily this path to the hill to formulate as he paced to and fro upon its summit his marvelous romances." I couldn't resist the Marvelous Romance Path, which led, not to a true summit, but to the top of a long ridge from which the traffic noise seemed mercifully far away. Walking back down, I noticed a small marker that's hard to see from the road. A drawing on it showed a young African American man running with a musket in his hands; its text, titled "Casey's Home," explained why it was here:

> In 1775 Casey was Samuel Whitney's slave. When revolution came, he ran away to war, fought for the colonies, and returned to Concord a free man.

I made a note to find out more about Casey, then dragged my mind back to April 19.

Almost a mile into their return march, the Regulars were not yet under attack. Smith had sent out light infantry companies to protect the flanks of his main column, a standard precaution made especially important by that long ridge on which Hawthorne walked. I had first noticed the ridge at the Old Hill Burying Ground in Concord Center, and it had continued to run just north of the road, offering a perfect position from which to surprise troops below—precisely what the flankers had been sent up there to prevent. It worked. Militia and minute men who were shadowing the British kept their distance.

Then the ridge ran out.

Meriam's Corner, half a mile past Hawthorne's house, marks the beginning of the four-mile Battle Road Trail in Minute Man National Historical Park. The corner, where Lexington Road meets Old Bedford Road today, is one of those magical spots where being in a historic landscape makes everything you've learned about the history click into place. You see the end of the ridge those flankers came down, and the flat, boggy area with a brook running through it that greeted them at the bottom. You're reminded by a little park footbridge that in 1775, a larger bridge spanned this brook. You recall that the flankers moved toward the road, rejoining the main column, so they could cross the brook without getting their feet wet (bad move) and that the rebel militia and minute men, echoing this, moved closer to that column themselves. "Musket Shots Rang Out" reads the cautiously worded description on a park marker; it's unclear which side fired first. Not far away stands a memorial to one British soldier who died there.

Sixteen miles to go.

The Battle Road Trail soon took me into a world of treeless fields, stone walls, circling hawks, and a farmer plowing—pretty much what I'd have seen on a peaceful day 250 years ago, except that today's plowman drove a big John Deere. "The field patterns are much the same as when colonial militiamen ran through here to get to new positions ahead of the British column," a marker noted. It also mentioned a disturbing social pattern: Farms had been subdivided so often by 1775 that there wasn't enough land for the next generation, leaving children "with the prospect of having a lower standard of living than their parents."

The farmland turned out to be just a short stretch of the trail, however, and the rest—while gorgeous—was more removed from historical reality. Those marshy songbird habitats protected as wetlands today? Ditched and drained to form hay meadows. Those trees we imagine militiamen hiding behind? Not there, except for occasional woodlots. Most of the area had been cleared. This is why, when men ran to get ahead of the British after Meriam's Corner, one of the first places they went was a sharp bend in the road where there actually *were* some trees. They set up an ambush and did enough damage that the place became known as the Bloody Angle. This was at 1 p.m., according to a park marker, which also estimates that 1,500 colonials were now in the field. Some men who'd been at the North Bridge were still fighting, and they'd been joined by men from Billerica, Chelmsford, Woburn, Framingham, Reading, and several other towns. Lieutenant Colonel Smith, remember, had left Boston with about eight hundred troops. He had sent for reinforcements hours before shots were fired at Lexington. None had appeared.

Fourteen miles to go.

Smith's flankers were back on duty, and they did some damage themselves. Militiamen too focused on the main column to see them coming had short life expectancies. More importantly, the flankers kept most of the militia far enough from the road to be out of effective musket range. Still, "British soldiers fell at every hill or curve where the colonists had position," as another marker put it—including one such position held by men with a grudge. Half an hour's walk from the Bloody Angle, I saw a marker titled "Parker's Revenge," complete with a photo of Lexington's idealized statue. The rocky hillside above looked like a good spot for an ambush, though recent battlefield archeology suggests that the fight took place farther west. Never mind: The Lexington men blazed away, possibly killing a couple of Regulars, then joined the pursuit.

The Battle Road Trail dead-ends about a hundred yards from I-95; a final park marker notes that the day's fiercest fighting was still to come. The whup-whup-whup of a traffic helicopter reminded me that in a modern war, help can reach embattled troops in minutes, not hours. But as far as the Regulars knew, no help was coming. They had marched twenty-three miles with no sleep; were running out of ammunition; and were now subjected, as one officer wrote, to "such an incessant fire as it's impossible to conceive." Small wonder they lost their cool. As they got to what another officer described as "within a mile of Lexington," most likely meaning the Common, they began to run.

Historians have placed this chaos in different places, but I'm persuaded by those who think it began on Concord Hill, just east of the interstate. From the hilltop, in tree-deprived 1775, the frantic Regulars would have had a clear view of Lexington Common—half a mile beyond which, at a site now commemorated by a granite cannon on the lawn of a condo building, acting Brig. Gen. Hugh, Lord Percy and 1,100 fresh troops were just arriving.

Finally.

A few things I'd learned about Lord Percy had struck me. First, he was the most competent British officer, by far, to take the field on April 19. Second, he lived in a castle that appears as the Hogwarts School of Witchcraft and Wizardry in the first two Harry Potter movies. (Coincidence? You be the judge.) Also, it wasn't his fault that he didn't show up until twelve hours after Smith sent for reinforcements. Marching orders were delivered to two officers who weren't around to read them, delaying his departure by nearly five hours. We can't know how the rest of the day might have gone if Percy's men had joined Smith's—as they should have, absent the screwup—before the running fight broke out at Meriam's Corner.

Once in Lexington, Percy took charge. He drove back the pursuing militiamen with the help of two small cannon, burned houses that might have given those pursuers cover, commandeered the Munroe Tavern as a field hospital, gave Smith's exhausted men as long a respite as he judged he could afford, then marched them back toward Boston.

Unfortunately, they had to get through Arlington first.

The Town Formerly Known as Menotomy has no claim to being the place where the first shot of the war was fired. It boasts no minute man statue and no National Historical Park. What it can say is that more men on both sides were killed in Arlington on April 19—a total of sixty-five, by one historian's widely cited count—than everywhere else combined. The number of colonials engaged by this time is uncertain, but it's likely that more than 1,500 additional militia poured into Arlington, joining the men who had hounded Percy since his return march began. This created a nightmare for the Regulars, especially the flankers, and they reacted accordingly.

Following their bloody trail through town, mostly on Massachusetts Avenue, I began to conjure images of a savage firefight moving down the crowded thoroughfare. Militiamen took aim from behind the used Impalas at Mirak Chevrolet; flankers charged through the aisles at Stop & Shop, then looted Mystic Wine next door; noncombatants sought shelter behind the counter at Retro Burger & Ice Cream. My urban warfare fantasies were misleading, though. Menotomy was a farming village in 1775, not a commercial center, and buildings tended to be surrounded by forty acres of land. To get a feel for what really played out here on April 19, I needed to check out the residence of a local man who died that day.

The Jason Russell House dates to 1740, though it's been expanded since. A volunteer from the Arlington Historical Society used a modern painting to set the scene. You can see the main British column coming down the road, he said, pointing to the front of the house, "and you can also see the flanking parties coming in from the rear and ambushing the militia." Some militiamen were killed outside the house, as was the owner, too lame to move fast. Others sprinted inside, where they had a life-or-death decision to make. If they hid on the first or second floors, they died: "The redcoats went and killed them." If they chose the cellar, they lived: Following them downstairs was too dangerous, though "we can see bullet holes in the stairs." A third option was to "jump right through this window, with the window in place. Think how desperate they'd have to be to jump through that. But the redcoats all had bayonets." Two men jumped. The first died—"we don't know if it was bullets or glass"—but the second survived.

The Regulars didn't stop to chase him down. Time was an issue for them in Arlington. They killed men who had surrendered, not wanting to take the time to deal with them. To the frustration of their officers, they wasted time looting houses they entered in search of militia. Occasionally they set those houses on fire, but didn't wait to make sure the flames took hold.

Six miles to go.

That number requires some explanation. Unlike Smith, whose men had been rowed to Cambridge, Percy had taken the land route through Boston Neck, crossing the Charles River on the only bridge available, near what's now the Harvard Business School. Going back that way would have meant marching eight miles from the Russell House, not six. More important, Percy knew that his enemies were likely to have taken up the bridge's planks. (They had.) Backed up against the river, low on ammunition, he'd be finished. Heading for Charlestown was a better idea. As with Boston, the Charlestown Peninsula was connected to the mainland by a pre-landfill isthmus—and once crossed, Charlestown Neck would be easy to defend.

Percy knew where this alternate route began, because an officer with him had scouted it in March. I wasn't sure, but a marker in North Cambridge helped. After flankers surprised and killed four men near the corner of Rindge and Massachusetts, it noted, the British column "barely paused before swinging left onto Beech Street, continuing its retreat down Somerville Avenue." The names may be modern, but the route seemed plausible, so off I went.

Three miles to go.

They were long miles for the Regulars, though this part of the day got less ink than most. I read every marker I saw; none mentioned April 19, though I lingered over one about the alleged discovery of "the first complete Anchisaurus skeleton" nearby. This turned out to be a hoax, the marker explained, created by mixing the bones of a German shepherd and a horse. A cautionary tale, perhaps, about how hard it is to get history right in a world of self-serving falsehoods and missing information? Yup—especially if you know, as I would learn, that the marker *itself* was a hoax, and that the city had debated whether to take it down or leave it up as a piece of performance art.

Two miles to go.

At Prospect Hill, Percy again used his cannon to fend off attackers. I followed him down Washington Street past Liquor Zone, AutoZone, Empire Tattoo, and—Washington having evolved into Cambridge Street—the Tavern at the End of the World. I'd have liked to drop in, as would those exhausted Regulars before me, but on I went, underneath

I-93, past another hellish traffic circle, past a bus honking at an ambulance, until I came to the old Schrafft's candy factory at 529 Main Street, which, I had been told, served as a landmark for where Charlestown Neck used to be. Some time between 7 and 8 p.m., Percy's men crossed the Neck and marched up the steep slope on the other side. I followed their ghostly footsteps to the top of Bunker Hill.

Two hundred seventy-three Regulars were dead, wounded, or missing, along with ninety-five colonials. Boats from Boston arrived with reinforcements and returned carrying wounded men. Before the night was over, the surviving British troops were back where they started.

The next morning, they found themselves besieged by an army that hadn't existed twenty-four hours before.

CHAPTER 3

# "A Middle Finger Raised to the Powers That Be"

Two months later, on June 17, 1775, the British Army returned to the Charlestown Peninsula. Nearly two and a half centuries after that, reenactments not being permitted at the site of the actual fight there, I drove sixty miles north to watch "The Battle of Bunker Hill" play out on a wide green hillside in Epping, New Hampshire. Standing with a couple hundred other spectators on Nottingham Square Road, I looked up to see scruffy militiamen gathered behind the walls of an earthen redoubt—a small fort recently constructed with the help of a backhoe—and watched some move into position to defend a rail fence that ran along the crest of the hill. Behind us, the British attackers were forming up, and I walked back to hear Maj. Gen. William Howe address his troops. Channeled by veteran reenactor Paul O'Shaughnessy, Howe was fired up:

"Gentlemen, we have an opportunity to end this rebellion *today*. Are you with me?"

"Huzzaaaaaaaaaahhhh!"

"A mob of farmers in a shallow ditch on the top of a hill. What could go wrong?"

"Huzzaaaaaaaaahhhh!"

"Our plan is simple. Heavy battalion will attack in a frontal attack— this is a feint. The lights will break through in the back. By the time you reach the top of the hill, they will be in disorder and fleeing…I ask of you today to go no farther than I and your officers lead."

"Huzzaaaaaaaahhhh!"

And off they marched, in their splendid red coats, to reenact an hour or so of ghastly mayhem that would radically alter the course of the war.

Reenactments can't do ghastly mayhem, of course, and there were other elements of the battle that were impossible to replicate on a New Hampshire hillside. No British Navy guns were available to lob cannonballs at the defenders before the infantry attack began (though the reenactors used a few noisy field pieces as stand-ins) or to fire red-hot shot into the wooden houses in Charlestown, south of the redoubt, setting them afire and flushing out rebel snipers who had sheltered there. No Mystic River flowed north of the battlefield, awaiting its critical role in the day's events (though a few pieces of brush had been dragged over to represent the riverbank). No waist-high grass or annoying farm fences slowed the attackers. "What we have here is a golf course compared to what they were facing," General Howe told me before the battle.

Now here were the redcoats moving up that golf course—which was actually a lot steeper than the average fairway—in a neatly formed horizontal line.

The rebels blazed away from the hilltop.

Howe's men stopped to fire back.

They were right in front of me, and I couldn't take my eyes off them—but why wasn't anyone falling down?

Whoops. I'd been fooled by the feint, just as Howe hoped his opponents would be. The serious fighting was well off to my right. It didn't seem to be going well, however. Down came the redcoats in disarray. Up they went once more. The crackle of musket fire came more rapidly now, with gunsmoke drifting across the rail fence, and large clusters of men in red began to fall.

Another retreat. Another regrouping.

"They're going to do it *again*?" a spectator asked.

They were indeed. This time, finally, they drove their enemies off the hill. The victory was illusory, however. Under the conventions of eighteenth-century warfare, the side that controlled a battlefield when the shooting stopped was said to have won. But those losers on Charlestown Heights—part of a wildly uncoordinated army described by one British general as a "rabble in arms"—had stood their ground long enough to kill or wound more than a thousand professional soldiers, nearly half of those Howe had sent against them.

No rebellion would be ended this day.

The landscape of the real battle would help me understand why.

\* \* \*

Two hills, a redoubt, a fence, and a beach shaped the story of the Charlestown Heights fight on June 17, 1775. Only the hills are still there. Before considering the roles they played, however, we must first tip our hats to a piece of high ground four miles away—Dorchester Heights, just south of Boston Neck—because that was where William Howe *thought* he was going to begin the attack that would end the rebellion.

Howe was a rising star with close family connections to George III. In 1759, he had been tapped to lead the army's climb up the cliffs that protected Quebec City, setting up a famous victory on the Plains of Abraham and the conquest of Canada. Sixteen years later, on May 25, 1775, he sailed into Boston accompanied by not one but two other major generals and some less exalted reinforcements. The generals put their heads together with lame-duck commander in chief Thomas Gage and came up with a plan. On June 18, they would first occupy Dorchester Heights and drive a contingent of rebels out of nearby Roxbury. After that, they would send troops waltzing across the Charlestown Peninsula and have them swing around from there to strike the main rebel base in Cambridge.

Would this have worked if they had managed to keep it a secret?

Maybe.

But they didn't—and their opponents, forewarned, did their disorganized best to screw up the plan.

On the evening of June 16, some 1,200 men under Col. William Prescott marched out of Cambridge carrying muskets and entrenching tools. They crossed Charlestown Neck, just as Lord Percy's retreating column had done two months before, and walked up the hill with the famous name, which they had been ordered to fortify. So far, so good. But then, in the middle of the night, Prescott and a couple of other officers started to argue about whether Bunker Hill was really the right place to make a stand. Should they perhaps build their redoubt on a different *part* of Charlestown Heights?

Decision time, guys.

There were maybe five hours before dawn, at which point the British would see them.

Standing in front of Saint Francis de Sales Church, an imposing gray stone edifice at 303 Bunker Hill Street, it was easy for me to grasp the rebels' options. They could get right to work here on the crown of Bunker Hill, the highest point in Charlestown, and fortify a position that feels comfortably far away from Boston, or they could march half a mile downhill, descending thirty-five vertical feet, to Breed's Hill. A redoubt there would be a lot closer to Boston, making it both more provocative and more vulnerable to attack.

It's also easy to see, walking down from the church today, what choice Prescott and the others made. They picked Breed's, despite the inconvenient fact that the 221-foot granite obelisk now rising above the site of the redoubt (and the Battle of Bunker Hill itself) would end up misnamed forever.

Who made that middle-of-the-night decision?

No one knows. The evidence is murky and the arguments are speculative, though Prescott seems to me the most likely to have taken the lead.

The more important question, however, is *why*.

Continuing down Bunker Hill Street, I was reminded of a chunk of its twentieth-century history that seemed weirdly relevant. I'd read about it in J. Anthony Lukas's *Common Ground*, part of which is set in Charlestown. Starting in 1925 and continuing for at least a couple of decades, the town's young men indulged in a pastime called "looping." The rules: You stole a car in Boston and roared past the Charlestown police station in City Square to provoke a chase. You led the pursuing cop "up the long slope of Bunker Hill Street to St. Francis de Sales' Church at the crest, then down again, picking up speed, often to 70 or

80 miles per hour," then circled back to City Square. A successful loop ended when you ditched the car before you could be arrested. "Looping was an initiation rite, proof that a Townie had come of age," Lukas wrote. "But it was something else as well: a challenge flung at authority, a middle finger raised to the powers that be."

Exactly. Building a redoubt on Breed's Hill was like flipping the bird at the British Army. Whoever made that decision wanted to be sure an attack would come.

For what was left of the night, Prescott's men dug, and they were still digging when dawn revealed how shockingly exposed they were. "The Danger we were in made us think there was Treachery, & that we were brot there to be all slain," young Peter Brown wrote his mother a few days later. A cannonball fired from a British warship promptly killed a man, further demoralizing Brown's comrades. Prescott has been described, irresistibly but unreliably, as trying to calm everyone down by climbing onto the parapet, strutting back and forth, waving his hat and shouting, "Hit me if you can." Later in the morning, still digging, the men were ordered to add a breastwork extending a bit north from the redoubt. Even so, as anyone could see, the left flank of the rebel position remained distressingly vulnerable.

Fortunately, someone did see—most likely it was Capt. Thomas Knowlton of Connecticut—and by early afternoon, with a British attack imminent, work had begun on yet another makeshift fortification. No trace of it remains, unless you count an old marker that says something cryptic about "the rail fence and grass line of protection." Running across the peninsula almost to the Mystic River, its ingredients were an existing ditch with a stone and rail fence in front of it; a new fence right in front of the old one, made with rails pulled from farm fences nearby; and anything the defenders could find, including a bunch of new-mown grass, to pack into the gap between those fences.

In his excellent *Bunker Hill*, Nathaniel Philbrick calls the result "a kind of wood-and-grass sandwich." He and every other historian I've read agree that the rail fence, as it's commonly known, was a key to the battle. But it was far from the only key. For one thing, as you may have noticed, that fence didn't go *all* the way to the Mystic River.

Enter Col. John Stark.

A laconic farmer and lumberman from what's now Manchester, New Hampshire, Stark was a French and Indian War veteran (as were Knowlton and Prescott) who had led a large contingent of New Hampshire troops down to join the siege of Boston. Stark's men were among the last to arrive before the battle began, and they pitched in to help with the rail fence. Meanwhile, their commander noticed that where the fence ended, at its farthest point north, was a sharp drop-off to an undefended beach that ran along the river. If the British sent troops down that beach, he knew, they'd be able to attack the American position from behind.

Stark needed a little time to fix this.

Mercifully, he had just enough.

*  *  *

If you had to pick one reason to explain why Bunker Hill turned into a war-altering disaster for the British, it would be this: They gave the defenders too much time.

Or, to put it another way, they didn't listen to Henry Clinton.

Clinton was the youngest and brightest of the three major generals who sailed into Boston on May 25 (the others being Howe and John Burgoyne, of whom more later). He was also the most socially awkward, which created problems that would haunt him throughout his service in America. Philbrick summed up Clinton's persona nicely at a Revolutionary War conference I attended: "We all know people like this, who are actually really smart," he said, "but they are so annoying that if they propose something, it's guaranteed you're going to do the opposite."

Doing the opposite, early on June 17, meant telling Henry to calm down and go back to bed, neither of which he did.

Sometime during the night before the battle, Clinton, who couldn't sleep, had decided to take a walk. Wandering north from his quarters in John Hancock's Beacon Hill mansion, near where the Massachusetts State House is today, he heard digging noises floating across the water from Charlestown Heights. Time to wake up the commander in chief. Meeting with Gage and Howe, he urged an attack on the rebel position at daybreak, which would mean getting ready right now.

But Gage decided to wait and see what things looked like when the sun came up.

Clinton was of the same mind when sunrise made the Breed's Hill work visible to all. He wanted to attack as soon as possible, preferably in two places at once, and he volunteered to lead five hundred men who would be ferried around to Charlestown Neck to take the rebels from behind. There were reasonable arguments against landing at the Neck, among them the chance that rebel reinforcements could close a trap there. There was no good argument against the ASAP part of Clinton's advice.

But Howe—who, as the senior major general, would lead the attack—decided to wait for high tide. He didn't want his troops to have to wade too far to get ashore.

So it wasn't until 1:30 p.m., at least twelve hours after Clinton heard noises in the night, that the first navy barges filled with close-packed, standing men, their bayonets gleaming, pulled away from Boston's Long Wharf and moved around the North End to where, in the words of historian Richard Ketchum, "the worn, dirty, shirt-sleeved farmers, staring over the walls of their earthen fort," could see them coming.

Howe's plan, contrary to the assertions of various early historians, had never been simply to "assault the redoubt in the good old British fashion of marching up to its face." To be sure, he would send troops in that direction, but he intended to win by exploiting the obvious vulnerability of the rebel left—a vulnerability that Knowlton and the builders of the rail fence, along with Stark down by the Mystic, had now made disappear.

It was too late to land Clinton at Charlestown Neck. So Howe landed on the far northeast corner of the peninsula, sent for reinforcements, and . . . waited.

Finally, *finally*, the assault began, with a column of redcoats marching four abreast up the Mystic River beach. Unluckily for them, they couldn't see around corners, and so didn't know Stark was already there.

Reliable details on the barricade Stark's men had improvised are scarce, though it's said to have been built from stones rolled down to the shore. The colonel prepared his men for the coming confrontation—as did officers up and down the rebel line—by ordering them to hold their fire until it could do serious damage. Did anyone say, "Don't fire until you see the whites of their eyes"? If so, we have no proof. Stark reportedly told some men to wait "until they could see the enemy's half gaiters" (a type of lower legwear); he is also said, by the same problematic source, to have set up some kind of *fire-when-they-get-here* marker a short distance from the barricade to serve as a visual aid. What's not in dispute is the result of the New Hampshire men's disciplined, devastating fire. British soldiers died in droves, bodies piling on bodies. Minutes later, horrified survivors were fleeing back down the beach, leaving the defenders free to rejoin their comrades at the rail fence.

There, the slaughter was bloodier still.

Howe, who led this part of the attack from the front, saw his neatly formed lines disrupted by farm fences and other obstacles in the tall grass. He saw his troops disobey orders by pausing to fire instead of pushing on with bayonets to sweep the rebels away. All around him, men were shot down, among them every single member of his staff. At one point, a British officer wrote, he saw the general standing, briefly, "quite alone."

The Battle of Bunker Hill wasn't just high drama, it was high drama played out on a public stage. Desperately interested in the outcome, men and women in Boston climbed up hills and church steeples and onto rooftops to watch. The opening act on the beach was out of their sight, but the watchers saw Howe brutally repulsed at the rail fence, and, as British focus shifted to the redoubt, they saw the redcoats driven back there as well. Prescott's men, like Stark's, did a superb job of holding their fire. One time their guns fell so silent that some watchers believed they had fled. But Prescott had simply told them not to shoot until their targets were thirty yards away, when, as he wrote, "we gave them such a hot fire, that they were obliged to retire nearly 150 yards before they could Rally and come again to the Attack." For the people on those Boston rooftops, hills, and steeples, all this would have unfolded against a terrifying backdrop of Charlestown in flames, its own steeples "great pyramids of fire above the rest." For the defenders, the battle unfolded against a different kind of backdrop, equally terrifying:

They were about to run out of powder and shot.

Gunpowder, in particular, was scarce in the colonies. Ingredients weren't readily available and decent grades of powder were difficult to make, so most had to be imported—hence the prewar scrambles for stores at places like the Powder House. But on June 17, there was at least *some* powder in Cambridge that could have been sent. It wasn't. Worse, as the men on the front lines couldn't help but notice, hundreds of their comrades spent the battle milling around uselessly back on Bunker Hill. Poor leadership by Gen. Israel Putnam, combined with indiscipline and cowardice, had kept them safely out of range.

*Those* men had powder and shot, if only they would put themselves in a position to use it. They didn't.

And here came the British one more time.

\* \* \*

"So one more time, we're going to try to take this hill!" Teri Jobe was saying. "Oh boy."

A National Park Service ranger with a superenthusiastic delivery ("As you've probably noticed, it does not take much to get me excited"), Jobe was doing the closest thing you can do to a reenactment in Charlestown itself: She was shepherding a group of tourists on a route similar to that of the final British attack. As we wound up streets lined with Victorian brownstones, she rehashed the day's fighting and explained what she wanted us—enlisted as redcoats for the duration of the tour—to do now. No more trying to sneak around to the back: We would just go straight at the redoubt. No more stopping to shoot: We would charge with bayonets only. "Everybody know what bayonets are? Yeah, they're about eighteen-inch blades that go on the end of the musket. Yikes."

Straight at 'em, then, with bayonets.

*"Are you ready to take this hill?"*

"No," said one of Jobe's younger soldiers. "I'd rather go back and get a root beer float."

He was no fool, that kid. Given the havoc the rebels had wreaked so far, why would anyone want to go at them again? But up those soldiers went, and they finally broke through at the breastwork next to the redoubt. This made the redoubt itself untenable to defenders *with* ammunition, let alone to those without it. Participants' memories of intense battlefield moments are notoriously, and understandably, unreliable. That said, a British officer who helped lead that last charge described the interior of the redoubt—with dead and dying men strewn about and maddened redcoats stabbing those yet living—as "a sight too dreadful for me to dwell any longer on."

Walking the few yards toward the monument itself, I passed a statue of an elegantly dressed Colonel Prescott pointing his sword—or so it seemed—at a man in a black T-shirt reading "Never Again Will I Let You Fuck with My Head." Many years after the battle, Prescott's son would write that when it came time to retreat, his father had walked, not run, out of the redoubt and fended off British bayonets with that sword.

To climb the Bunker Hill Monument, I had to walk through an adjacent building known as the Lodge. It housed another heroic statue, this one honoring the battle's most famous casualty.

The story of Joseph Warren on June 17 is both puzzling and tragic. Despite his lack of military experience, the Provincial Congress had recently named Dr. Warren a major general. No one knows where he was on the morning of the battle, though one theory has him visiting a young woman who would soon bear his child. Later in the day, after learning what was happening on Charlestown Heights, Warren walked from Cambridge to Bunker Hill and on down to Breed's, sensibly declining offers to take command. Like Prescott, he was one of the last men out of the redoubt; unlike Prescott, he did not survive. In April 1776, after the British left Boston, Warren's body was dug up and identified by means of a couple of false teeth.

On the back wall of the Lodge, I noticed a portrait of an old man with thin shoulder-length hair, fierce eyes, and lips pulled together in the beginning of a frown. John Stark, thirty-five years after the battle, still looked like a man unlikely to allow a flanking attack down his personal stretch of beach.

Where is that beach today? Under a bunch of landfill, of course. But you can see where it once was from the top of the monument, if you know where to look and are willing to climb 294 steps filled with sweating humans saying things like "I hate heights" and "My legs are like Jell-O right now." Looking out the north-facing window, I found the roofs of the Bunker Hill Housing Project: dozens of three-story brick buildings, seventy-five years old at the time and scheduled for replacement. Just beyond them was Medford Street, which roughly traces the original Mystic shoreline. Up Medford a few blocks, I located Charlestown High School, which knowledgeable people had told me was where Stark's men built their barricade. The school is less than half a mile from the monument, but feels as if it's in another world. Standing in front of it later, looking down a short drop-off toward a landfill-enabled playing field, I watched nontourists fly kites, toss footballs, and swing small children around in circles on or near an unmarked killing ground where a few minutes of quick thinking and courage changed the course of American history.

Is that an overstatement? I don't think so.

Bunker Hill was the first set-piece battle of the war, and for the British, it turned out to be the bloodiest day of the eight-year struggle. They lost more than twice as many killed and wounded as the defenders, including a shocking number of officers, and a traumatized Howe stated the obvious when he wrote that the victory had been "too dearly bought." But had the day gone badly for the rebels from the start—as it surely would have done, had that column of troops gotten down that beach and charged them from behind—the most likely scenario is that they'd have been driven out of their makeshift defenses and killed, captured, or chased off the peninsula with their confidence in shreds. Maybe they'd have been chased all the way to Cambridge, as Howe and his colleagues had intended. Maybe there wouldn't have been any army *left* for George Washington to take charge of when he rode into town fifteen days after the battle.

And as long as we're doing counterfactuals, here's one more question to consider:

If June 17 had been a disaster for the American army, would its new commander in chief have agreed, just two months later, to send a sizable chunk of it paddling through Maine with Benedict Arnold?

# CHAPTER 4

# "The Difference Between Life and a Frozen Death"

I n 1775, Arnold was a prosperous New Haven merchant with a painful family history. Three of his four siblings had died before he was thirteen, and his father had become a drunk. Thirty-four years old that year, he headed a Connecticut militia company—and when the news from Lexington and Concord arrived, he got a move on. Did he need powder before he could march off to join the fight? No problem: He forced the guardians of the local powder house to supply it. Did his men need shelter in Cambridge? No problem: Soon he had them sleeping in Thomas Oliver's Tory Row mansion. Was the rebel army desperate for artillery? No problem: Arnold talked Joseph Warren into sending him to Lake Champlain to lead an attack on Fort Ticonderoga, which had plenty.

What about when he discovered that Ethan Allen and his Vermont irregulars, the Green Mountain Boys, had the same idea?

Okay, that was a problem. Still, Arnold managed to team up with Allen long enough to help take Fort Ti, barely three weeks into the war. The next thing anyone knew, he had taken over a loyalist's schooner, mounted a few guns on it, sailed it north, and captured a seventy-ton British sloop of war at Saint-Jean-sur-Richelieu, Quebec, giving the rebels control of the lake. And the next thing after that—leaving out the part where his wife died and he returned to New Haven to arrange for the care of his kids—he was back in Cambridge talking to Washington about invading Canada.

Whoa! If you were George, wouldn't you have said, "I wish I had twenty more guys like this" and ignored the complaints, already starting to come in, from people Arnold had rubbed the wrong way?

Their meeting took place early in August. But way back on June 13—before the Continental Congress had even chosen its new commander in chief—Arnold was lobbying for a Canadian campaign. He wrote the delegates to propose an attack via Lake Champlain and Montreal that would end with the rebels taking Quebec City. Congress went for the idea, but put someone else in charge.

No problem.

Why settle for just one Canadian invasion when you can have two?

* * *

The plan Washington and Arnold agreed on was simple enough, though plenty daunting. Washington would detach 1,100 men, mostly volunteers, from the army besieging Boston. They would sail up the Kennebec River to what's now Pittston, Maine, where they would transfer their supplies into two hundred smaller boats. They would then row, paddle, pole, and tow those boats beyond all trace of civilization; carry them thirteen miles west to the Dead River; lug them over the Height of Land at the Canadian border; and proceed down the Chaudière River to Quebec City. With luck, the French inhabitants would reject their British conquerors and join the rebellion. In any case, by seizing and holding Canada's strongest city, the rebels would reshape the strategic landscape of the Revolution— preventing the British from retaking Fort Ti, proceeding down the Hudson, and cutting New England off from the rest of the colonies.

It was a bold plan, but it came with a few problems.

Take those "bateaux," as everyone calls the Arnold expedition's principal mode of transportation. Heavy, flat-bottomed river craft with high, pointed bows and sterns, they were designed to carry four men and perhaps half a ton of cargo. Reuben Colburn, whose boatyard was commissioned to build them, performed a small miracle by having all two hundred bateaux ready before Arnold and his army arrived. Alas, that miracle was achieved using green pine (seasoned wood being unavailable) and fewer than the usual number of nails (which were in short supply).

Arnold promptly asked Colburn to build twenty more.

The Major Reuben Colburn House still stands on the banks of the Kennebec where the bateaux were built. It's rarely open to the public, but if you do get in, you can check out the bedroom where Arnold slept and the Maine River Bateaux Museum in the barn. My own visit came courtesy of one of the greatest organizations I ran into on my travels. The Arnold Expedition Historical Society has spent six decades keeping Maine's overlooked Revolutionary War history alive. Among other things, it organized a bicentennial reenactment of the invasion—check the AEHS website to learn what happens when you tell your insurance company you'll be driving to Quebec with a stash of black powder in your truck—and worked tirelessly to preserve and mark Arnold's wilderness route. Longtime AEHS mainstay Stephen Clark also wrote a book about the expedition that's a historical tourist's dream: Without Following Their Footsteps—and a lot of help from Clark himself—I wouldn't have found half of what I wanted to see.

My first stop after the Colburn House was obvious enough. Fort Western, ten miles upriver in Augusta, is where the expedition really got going. There, Arnold split his army into a number of parts and staggered their departures by a day or more, the idea being to avoid traffic jams on portage trails. Touring New England's oldest surviving wooden fort, I learned that Arnold did *not* sleep here—he bedded down in a house nearby—but Aaron Burr and Daniel Morgan did.

Burr was nineteen at the time. The future vice president, duelist, and alleged treasonous conspirator against the United States (he was tried and acquitted in 1807, but that verdict is still debated) had chosen to accompany the expedition as a gentleman volunteer. He was in no way central to the effort, though he acquitted himself well. Decades after his death, a fantastic tale arose of how a lovely Native American princess fell in love with Burr, followed him to Canada, and bore his child. Regrettably, it seems not to be true.

Daniel Morgan was a whole different story.

\* \* \*

Morgan didn't talk much about his childhood, which most likely took place in northern New Jersey. He left home in his teens after a fight with his father, turning up in Winchester, Virginia, according to his best-known biographer, with "scarcely any personal belongings." Winchester in 1753 was a frontier village, Don Higginbotham wrote, comprising "sixty crudely built dwellings, stores, and taverns. What it lacked in size, it made up for in noise. Cursing, drunkenness, quarreling, and fighting were so prevalent that Moravian missionaries and other pious souls skirted it during their travels through the back country." Morgan thrived there. Employed as a wagon driver, he soon saved enough money to buy a team of horses and start working for himself.

The French and Indian War interrupted his rise and almost killed him.

Pressed into service by a British general who needed wagoners, he lost his temper—always short—and knocked a redcoat officer down. A brutal whipping resulted. For the rest of his life, it's said, Morgan enjoyed recounting how his tormentor lost count and gave him one fewer lash than the hundreds he was due. Later in the war, as a member of a Virginia ranger company, he and a companion rode into an Indian ambush. The companion died but Morgan survived, albeit with fewer teeth and a hole in his cheek.

Six feet tall, phenomenally strong, and fond of rum, Morgan was a ferocious brawler; his name turned up so often in court records that you'd never have pegged him as a future pillar of the community. By 1775, however, that was exactly what he was. He had married, fathered two daughters, turned to farming, and started buying up land, as well as a few enslaved people to work it. When Congress voted to raise ten companies of "expert riflemen" for the Continental Army, Morgan was chosen to recruit a company and lead it north. He marched his men six hundred miles to Cambridge in three weeks, arriving on August 6. A month later, having whiled away some time using British sentries on Boston Neck for target practice, the Virginia riflemen joined the invasion force. On September 25, they headed out from Fort Western as part of Arnold's first division, with Morgan in command.

No men were better prepared to endure what followed—but that didn't mean they knew it was coming.

I set out to trace their route on one of those perfect mid-September days that Maine teases you with before the weather gets serious. Eighteen miles north was Ticonic Falls, the first major obstacle around which Arnold's men had to haul their four-hundred-pound bateaux. (The green wood made them even heavier than expected.) Roughly sixty-five road miles farther on, I pulled over and parked on a hillside near the start of the "Great Carrying Place," a narrow trail created by Native Americans to portage birchbark canoes—which did *not* weigh four hundred pounds—between the Kennebec and Dead Rivers. Getting here from Fort Western had taken the army two weeks. The bateaux were falling apart already: One man described them in his journal as "nothing but wrecks, some stove to pieces." Meanwhile, the weather had turned cold enough to freeze wet clothes solid, and Morgan reported that much food had been spoiled by water leaking into wooden barrels. The day before arriving at the Great Carrying Place, Arnold, who also kept a journal, wrote that he'd seen "mountains begin to appear on each side of the river, high, & snow on the tops."

I found a sign for the "Arnold Expedition Portage Trail" and got ready to walk.

The trail had been reopened not long before by the AEHS. Thick with dead leaves and blazed, apparently, by a crew with a thrifty respect for the cost of orange paint, it wasn't always easy to follow. But the day was warm and the woods were lovely, and whenever I found myself thinking, "I'm all alone out here—do I really know where I'm going?" I would spot a blaze on a tree ahead. A satisfying but hardly strenuous three-mile hike brought me to the shore of East Carry Pond, the first of the three ponds the portage trail crosses, where I sat for a while, eating lunch and mulling the wildly different circumstances under which Arnold's men had walked this way.

They had carried the damn bateaux over thirteen miles of canoe-size trail with only axes to help them widen it. They had carried them up 1,200 vertical feet in the process, having no topographic map to warn them about the elevation gain. They had hauled all their supplies and ammunition as well, which meant they'd had to put down the bateaux and go back for more loads, repeating the whole thing five to seven times. Cold rain and illness, including dysentery, increased their misery; Arnold ordered a log "hospital" built, not far from my lunch spot, and left the sickest behind. Near the end of the portage came a mile-wide bog in which men sank to their hips in black mud and some had boots sucked off their feet.

Right after that…

Actually, I couldn't go where they went right after that, because the first part of the Dead River has disappeared under the enormous, man-made Flagstaff Lake. But if the weather held, maybe I could climb up to the long, high ridge that forms Maine's stunning Bigelow Range—named after one of Arnold's officers, said to have climbed it to see if Quebec was visible from there—and have a look? I chose the easiest route, which still meant ascending a couple thousand feet in less than three miles on what my mountaineer father would have called "an efficient trail." Cranberry Peak (elevation 3,194 feet) rewarded me with a view that helped me grasp the scale and grandeur of the wilderness Arnold and his men traversed. Yes, my knees hurt coming down, and no, I didn't set any speed records, but I was pretty proud of myself nonetheless.

That was before I learned about a man who climbed a higher Bigelow peak eighty-nine times in eighty-eight days, not to mention doing the whole Arnold Trail in a canoe.

\* \* \*

Duluth Wing, whose friends called him "Dude," was born and raised in the village of Flagstaff, which lay on the part of the expedition's route later drowned by the lake. Staring up at the Bigelow Range, he couldn't help wondering about the men who gazed at the same ridge from their leaky bateaux. When he graduated from high school, he heard about a job manning a fire tower on the second highest of the Bigelow summits (elevation 4,088 feet) and asked his father if he could do it. Yes, came the answer, as long as he climbed down every night to milk the cows. One day, because of a fire, he had to climb the mountain twice. Another day, he met a young woman who had asked *her* father if she could climb it, by herself, as an adventure. They were married sixty-five years.

And until the day he died, in 2013, Dude Wing stayed curious about Arnold's mind-boggling trek.

He read everything he could find, including *Arundel*, Kenneth Roberts's fictionalized version. He pored over *March to Quebec*, the collection of journals by expedition members that Roberts put together. He helped found the AEHS in 1968. Somewhere around that time, he and his friend Cecil Pierce decided to retrace Arnold's route, which no one had ever done. Pierce had lost four fingers to a woodworking accident, adding an additional level of difficulty to an already nontrivial excursion.

"My father said Cecil was the worst canoe partner he ever saw," Wing's son told me. "Because he could only paddle right-handed."

Kenny Wing had agreed to meet me at the Dead River Area Historical Society in Stratton, near the west end of the Bigelow Range, to show me a couple of display cases labeled "Duluth 'Dude' Wing's Collection of Arnold's Artifacts." Some years after the canoe trip, Kenny said, Dude acquired a metal detector, and he spent decades putting it to good use. Two of his prize finds told of increasing desperation as the expedition approached Canada. One was a batch of handmade nails laid out in a pattern suggesting they were all that remained of an abandoned bateau. The second was 832 musket balls, all found in one place, from a keg left behind because no one had the strength or the will to haul it any farther.

Kenny also told me—persistent legend and Wikipedia to the contrary—that Mount Bigelow certainly did *not* get its name because anyone from the expedition climbed it in late October 1775. "No. The mountain was snow-white. It was frozen!" The steep slopes I had scrambled up in perfect weather would have been covered with ice.

* * *

Leaving the Bigelows and Flagstaff Lake behind, I drove north on Route 27, following the unsubmerged portion of the Dead River. Eight miles from the historical society, I parked and walked down a fisherman's trail to what's now called Ledge Falls. The line of rocks that stretched across the river here clearly would have made a portage necessary, but otherwise the Dead seemed unthreatening. Fortunately, I had brought along *March to Quebec*, which includes Arnold's journal, to remind me how deceptive modern appearances can be.

Exhausted by the Great Carry, the army was spread out for miles, with some units running out of food. The rearmost division had been entrusted with reserve supplies, so Arnold sent some troops back down the river to collect more and bring it north. The commander himself and a small party pressed forward; portaged around Ledge Falls after paddling through heavy rain for days; made a cold, wet camp; and went to sleep. At 4 a.m., they woke to find a torrent of water washing over them.

The Dead River, Arnold wrote, had risen "8 feet perpendicular in 9 hours."

Happily, they found a hillock on which to huddle. Unhappily, when dawn came, they could no longer find the river. Floodwaters had turned their campsite into a storm-tossed lake. They didn't know what had hit them, but modern weather experts think it was a "wandering West Indian hurricane" that had veered inland from the coast.

At Shadagee Falls, another stretch of white water a few miles upstream, I tried to picture a chaotic scene Clark had described for me. Persevering after the flood, Arnold's men neared the falls with "seven bateaux in a row, one behind the other, that they were pulling up the fast water with ropes." The first bateau "broadsided"—turned sideways in the current—"and hit the next in line." In minutes, all seven were wrecked and all the supplies in them lost. Among the losses was a keg filled with coins that were to have been used to buy supplies. A great story comes with this, and Clark told it with relish. Two young Maine men named Getchell, he said, were serving as expedition guides. Both made it home safely. The next summer, the Getchells disappeared for a while. Then "very quietly and very slowly," always paying with hard currency, they started buying up land.

Back in 1775, though, the men of the expedition faced bigger problems than a lost keg of coins. They had maybe ninety hard miles to go before they reached the southernmost French settlements—and if they didn't get more to eat by then, they would die.

On the evening of October 23, Arnold held a council of war. Several decisions emerged. Fifty men would go north in a screaming hurry to find food. Arnold, too, would head for the settlements to see what he could do. Sick men would be sent back to Fort Western. Finally, orders would be sent to Roger Enos, commander of the army's rearmost division—the one assumed to have extra supplies—to hasten forward with as many men as he could furnish with "fifteen days' provisions."

Enos and his officers decided to bail instead.

They took roughly a third of Arnold's healthy troops with them and had to be cajoled into leaving even two barrels of flour behind.

* * *

The Canadian border is sixteen miles from Shadagee Falls; you can drive it in twenty-five minutes if you're not slowed by log trucks or the occasional moose lolloping down the road. Gawking at the scenery can add time, too. I stopped at a viewpoint overlooking the Chain of Ponds—a gloriously unspoiled five-mile stretch of interconnected lakes, bordered by cliffs and mountains—and again at Natanis Point Campground, where I stood on a strip of gravelly beach and admired the distant Bigelows, still visible thirty miles to the southeast. Then I drove a few more miles up to the Height of Land, beyond which water starts flowing north toward the Saint Lawrence River, and crossed the border without incident.

Arnold's men had a harder time, of course.

Weak from hunger, many discarded their ponderous bateaux, including the one that left the boat-shaped pattern of nails Duluth Wing found. Others, notably Morgan's riflemen, sucked it up and shouldered a few to the Height of Land through snow and ice. Most men eventually straggled down to a place they called the Beautiful Meadow. (A Fontaine Lumber mill now occupies this site, with the Motel Arnold serving as another landmark.) From there, if they'd had boats, they could have floated down what's now the Arnold River to Lake Mégantic, from which they could have continued on the Chaudière River to Quebec City as planned—but most no longer *had* boats. Only about twenty of the original 220 made it as far as the Beautiful Meadow. And now Arnold, having raced ahead to the lake, sent back an order that can be shorthanded as *Whatever you do, don't walk into the horrible swamp that's right ahead of you.*

Part of the army left the meadow before the order arrived. Those men fared poorly.

They tried to follow the river, but sundown found them lost in the swamp. Some died. Others managed to build a fire on a soggy hummock "so small that the men lay like spokes of a wheel, with their feet to the fire and their heads almost touching the surrounding swamp." That proved "the difference between life and a frozen death."

Hundreds of men *did* follow Arnold's advice. They fared worse.

Uncharted rivers and (yes) swamps slowed their progress as they staggered along the shore of Spider Lake. They spent a starving, freezing night worried they'd been walking in the wrong direction (they had), then got up and kept going, with every man aware that if he fell behind, he would die. Finally, miraculously, they reached Lake Mégantic and the Chaudière, though their trials were far from over.

Somewhere on the banks of this river, Jemima Warner, one of at least two women known to have come north with the expedition, left the straggling column to stay with her weakening husband. When he died, she covered his body with leaves, took his gun, and caught up. Somewhere, too, an officer allowed starving men to kill his beloved dog. "They ate every part of him, not excepting his entrails," Henry Dearborn recalled, then pounded up his bones for broth. Given that the men were also eating powder bags, hair grease, and moose-hide breeches, it's amazing the poor beast had lived as long as he had.

The army was now scattered over twenty miles of the Chaudière, with no dogs left to eat and dozens of miles to go. Then, to their joy, men saw "a vision of horned cattle" being herded toward them. Arnold had reached the first of the French settlements and sent back lifesaving nourishment on the hoof.

* * *

I spent a delightful couple of days in Quebec City, looking for traces of the invasion and trying to figure out how Arnold and the maybe six hundred ragged troops who had made it this far planned to take the place. But I can sum up my first impression in four words:

You *must* be kidding.

Crossing the Saint Lawrence on the ferry from Levis, I craned my neck to gaze up at the Château Frontenac. The famous castle-like hotel, which wasn't around in 1775, nonetheless serves as a reminder that Quebec was a fortress city, built high on a rocky promontory surrounded on three sides by water. Turning to look up a river now populated by container ships and tankers, I tried to picture Arnold's army crossing it at night in canoes and under the guns of British warships that could have blown them away. Remarkably, hundreds of men made it across. Up the cliff they climbed and onto the Plains of Abraham, just as William Howe and James Wolfe's army had done in 1759.

Okay, now what?

When Arnold planned his invasion, he seems to have believed that he would be able to sneak up on the largest and most important city in Canada and take it by surprise. Why? Your guess is as good as mine, but it didn't happen. Quebec's defenders had known he was coming for quite a while, and had recently received a small but important contingent of reinforcements. When Arnold and his men arrived, they found the gates closed against them. All they could do was parade loudly around for a few days, bluffing, then withdraw to a less vulnerable position and wait for Richard Montgomery to show up.

Richard who?

The leader of the other invasion of Canada, that's who.

General Montgomery outranked Colonel Arnold and had far more military experience, having served in the British Army during the French and Indian War. He'd had a less arduous trek north and taken Montreal in mid-November, on the same day Arnold began crossing the Saint Lawrence. Eighteen days later, the two joined forces outside Quebec. A month after that, on December 31—not coincidentally, one day before the enlistments of Arnold's men were to expire—they launched a desperate attack in a raging snowstorm.

I walked the city walls, Clark's book in hand, to see where their plans went wrong.

Near St. John's Gate, on the west end of Quebec's Upper Town, picnickers ignored signs reading "Attention! Danger de chute" and sat on the edge of the wall facing the Place d'Youville. This was where the battle began, with an officer named James Livingston—an underappreciated gentleman we'll meet again—trying to create a diversion. The idea was to make enough noise to lure defenders here while Montgomery and Arnold led attacks on the weaker defenses of the Lower Town, the part of Quebec below the cliffs and outside the walls. With luck, they would then break through to the Upper Town.

Livingston's diversion didn't work. Given what came next, it probably didn't matter.

Montgomery attacked along the Saint Lawrence, below Cape Diamond on what's now the Boulevard Champlain. At the first fortified barrier he and his four hundred men encountered, the outnumbered defenders surprised them with musket and cannon fire. The general died instantly. His second-in-command—too shocked to continue, though a determined push likely would have cleared the way to the Lower Town—ordered a retreat.

It's a safe bet Daniel Morgan wouldn't have done that. But he was busy elsewhere.

Arnold attacked from the northwest. He, too, came to a fortified barrier blocking the way into the Lower Town, and he, too, soon lay in the deepening snow—not dead, but with a musket ball in his leg. A couple of men carried him to the rear. The rest fought on, with Morgan taking the lead. Surmounting the first barrier with reckless courage, they pressed forward to the next. Years later, Morgan would maintain that Quebec was theirs for the taking, had his fellow officers not insisted on waiting for Montgomery to show up. But "to these arguments I sacrificed my own opinion," he wrote, "and lost the town."

We can't know if he was right. What we do know is that he was a man who really, really hated to lose.

From the Rue des Remparts, on the north side of the Upper Town, I looked over the cliff and spotted the site of Arnold's wounding. (There was a marker on a wall below, though I'd have needed binoculars to read it.) A few hundred yards farther east I looked down again, toward where the second barrier had stood. The cliff here had mesh on it to keep rocks from falling on pedestrians below. Nothing prevented Quebec's defenders, however, from shooting down on their enemies in 1775. Others charged through a gate in the wall that no longer exists, taking the Americans from behind. Some escaped. Most did not. Two-thirds of the men who had made it all the way north with Arnold ended up killed, wounded, or captured; Clark gives the numbers as 35, 33, and 372, respectively.

Was it all for nothing, then? All that effort, all that suffering, all that heroism?

It sure looked that way. Even if the Americans had managed to take the city, Clark told me, no good would have come of it. In London, plans were already afoot that would send ten thousand troops to Canada in the spring. They could easily have retaken Quebec, capturing "the entire American army in the North, lock, stock and barrel" in the process.

Clark is thoughtful about the hazards of what-ifs. Speculation about "scenarios and outcomes beyond this point," he cautions in *Following Their Footsteps*, "has too many variables to seriously consider."

That said: Arnold was still alive, if not yet kicking.

So was Morgan.

They would show plenty of fight between December 31, 1775, and October 7, 1777, when the man tapped to lead those British troops to Canada would find himself in deep trouble in upstate New York.

Stay tuned.

# CHAPTER 5

# "Are You Here for the Knox Marker?"

Smack in the middle of Cambridge's Tory Row stands a yellow Georgian mansion built by one of the loyalists who skipped town after the Powder Alarm. In the front hall is a terra-cotta bust of 105 Brattle Street's most famous occupant, George Washington. Placed there by the house's second-most-famous occupant, Longfellow, the bust is vintage Father of Our Country stuff: George looks formidable, but also old and tired.

Like most images of Washington stuck in our twenty-first-century brains, however, it is profoundly misleading.

The man who took command of the rebel army on July 3, 1775, and soon established his headquarters in this house was a vigorous forty-three years old. Passionate, reserved, thin-skinned, ambitious, fearless, obsessed with control, and brimming with leadership potential, Washington was also too inexperienced for the overwhelming task he had taken on, and he knew it. The more I learned about him, militarily and personally, the more fascinating he seemed. Yet his deeply rooted reputation for boring virtue sometimes made this fascination hard to explain.

"*Why* do you think he's interesting?" a friend asked over dinner one night, her skepticism readily apparent.

It seemed simplest, under the circumstances, to talk about just one surprising thing: a letter Washington wrote to the wife of a close friend, four months before he married the wealthy widow Martha Custis. Washington scholar Peter Henriques describes the letter as "a deadly serious—if somewhat awkward and veiled—assertion of love, which he wanted to be kept secret." It was. The only reason we know about it is that Sally Fairfax kept it for more than fifty years, until the day she died.

Here are a few other things I might have mentioned:

George's father died when George was eleven. His half brother, Lawrence, filled the surrogate dad role admirably, if you don't count one nearly catastrophic misjudgment. Worried about the boy's prospects (as a younger son in a middling gentry family, George's chances of inheriting were small), Lawrence proposed that his little brother start a career in the British Navy at age fourteen. History has been unkind to George's mother, who is accused, basically, of being impossible to please. But history may want to think a little harder about what could have happened to the American Revolution if Mary Ball Washington hadn't quashed Lawrence's plan.

Like Daniel Morgan, Washington did a lot of his growing up on the wild Virginia frontier. Unlike Morgan, he got his start there through a family connection. In 1748, William Fairfax—who was Lawrence's father-in-law—gave the sixteen-year-old his first significant job, as a surveyor. Why? Well, Fairfax oversaw millions of acres of Old Dominion land controlled by one of his cousins. There was plenty of surveying to be done, and hey, the Washington boy needed work.

Then the Washington boy started the French and Indian War, and things got *really* interesting.

* * *

The story wasn't quite that simple, of course. Clashing imperial ambitions in North America would have sparked conflict at some point. But it remains true that as an over-his-head Virginia militia officer in 1754, Washington led a party of men into western Pennsylvania; teamed up with Indian allies to ambush a smaller party of Frenchmen he thought were planning to attack him; and learned only after ten or twelve men were dead that the French had been on a peaceful mission.

Unsurprisingly, France made a lot of noise about this. The war was on, though it would not formally be declared for a while.

Britain's first move was to dispatch Gen. Edward Braddock with two regiments of British Regulars. Recruiting some colonial help, Braddock marched into that same contested wilderness with the intent of taking a French post at the Forks of the Ohio (now Pittsburgh). Washington went along as a volunteer aide, which gave him the chance to experience a perfect storm of a military defeat—one so shocking that if he hadn't been there himself, he wrote, he would scarcely have believed reports of what happened.

On the morning of July 9, 1755, some 1,400 of Braddock's troops crossed the Monongahela River, twelve miles from their destination, and walked into a trap. A couple hundred French troops attacked from the front. Six or seven hundred of *their* Indian allies waited in the forest awhile, then opened up on both flanks. In four hours, two-thirds of the men who crossed the river that morning were killed or wounded—but not George. Those who saw him fight that day testified to his fearless, selfless heroism. With two of his horses killed and his clothing shot full of holes, he helped carry the mortally wounded Braddock back across the river, then rode all night to seek aid.

"If Washington had been killed in action in this battle," as I once heard the author of *Braddock's Defeat* point out, "history would have remembered him as an utter failure." Instead, he was a hero, and his life and career were transformed.

He was twenty-three years old.

Twenty years later, he headed north to take his seat at the Second Continental Congress. A few bullet points from the intervening decades: He commanded Virginia's militia, learning how much work it took to build a disciplined army. He wrote Sally and married Martha. He inherited his brother's Potomac River estate and farmed it with enslaved labor, a practice he took entirely for granted. He pushed to increase his holdings in western land, which he saw as the surest route to real wealth; got himself elected to the colonial legislature; and came to believe—sooner than many of his peers, for a mix of personal, economic, and political reasons—that it was time to reject second-class citizenship in the British

Empire, by force if necessary. Arriving in Philadelphia just weeks after Lexington and Concord, he knew exactly what job he was in line for.

Did he want it?

Of course he did. It was no accident that he showed up for meetings resplendent in a militia uniform. Yet the full story of his rise to power is both more complex and more interesting.

Congress voted unanimously to name him commander in chief on June 16, 1775. His military experience looked good, at least compared with that of potential competitors, as did his character and his martial bearing. But what clinched the deal was that he came from Virginia. All but the most foolish of the New Englanders who had taken the lead in the rebellion so far (we're looking at you, John Hancock) saw that if it was to succeed, it could not be just a New England thing. Washington accepted the job the day it was offered. Two days later, he wrote Martha that *"far from seeking this appointment I have used every endeavour in my power to avoid it."* The italics are mine, because, well, sheesh. Only a handful of the couple's letters have survived Martha's (and presumably George's) desire to keep their private life private, but we have no reason to believe they were in the habit of telling each other blatant lies.

So why was Washington lying now?

My vote for best educated guess goes to Washington biographer Joseph Ellis, who thinks it was because his subject had "trouble acknowledging his own ambitions." The false claim, Ellis writes, was part of "an essential fabrication that shielded him from the recognition that, with a Continental Congress filled with ambitious delegates, he was the most ambitious—not just the tallest—man in the room. He needed to convince himself that the summons came from outside rather than inside his own soul."

In other words, he was trying to hide the truth, not from his wife, but from himself.

What Washington did not try to hide, from Martha or anyone else, was his concern that he was taking on "a trust too great for my Capacity." He underlined his limitations in his acceptance speech to Congress, calling on everyone in the room to remember "that I this day declare with the utmost sincerity, I do not think myself equal to the command

I [am] honoured with." Many have assumed this to be false modesty. It was not. He understood the odds against success and the learning curve he faced, and knew that his to-do list, when he got to Cambridge, would be daunting.

To mention just one item:

Driving the British out of Boston would require him to scrape together some artillery. It took him months to get going on that. But in mid-November, he finally ordered a twenty-five-year-old former bookseller named Henry Knox to ride off to Fort Ticonderoga and bring back some really big guns.

\* \* \*

I first saw Fort Ti when I was five years old, when my family stopped there on the way to Niagara Falls. All I remember is the cannon. Maybe that's because my father snapped a photo of me (worst haircut ever) posing next to one, or maybe it's because I've been using a souvenir Ticonderoga cannon as a paperweight ever since. Naturally, the first thing I wanted to do when I got back, many decades later, was admire the lethal row of bronze metal tubes, green with age, positioned to smash any enemy foolish enough to come up Lake Champlain from the south. But when I joined a dozen other visitors for the 10:15 tour, our guide immediately hit us with a non-cannon question.

"Anybody know who started the French and Indian War?" Gordy Hamilton asked.

"George Washington!" I said proudly, having been possessed of that knowledge for maybe two weeks.

"I'll slip you the five dollars later," Hamilton joked. Then he told the story of the deadliest British defeat in that war—the deadliest battle in North America, in fact, before Antietam in 1862—about which I knew nothing at all.

The Battle of Carillon, it's called, after the French name for the fort. On July 8, 1758, some 3,700 French defenders under the Marquis de Montcalm routed sixteen thousand British and colonial attackers, killing or wounding more than two thousand of their brave but hopelessly outgeneraled opponents. It's an astonishing story that I can't do justice to here. But I bring it up because it hinged on one of those minuscule events, like a butterfly's wing flap in chaos theory, that carried within it the potential to alter everything that came next.

Two days before the battle, units of the armies skirmished briefly. Bang, just like that, a musket shot killed George Augustus Howe, the general who was to have planned and led the attack. Would Howe have done better than the tactics-challenged logistician who ended up leading it instead? Absolutely—but the horrific defeat may not have been the biggest consequence of his death. At thirty-three, Howe was the best British general in North America. A pioneer in adapting army practices to conditions troops would encounter here, he was as charismatic as he was intelligent, a born leader beloved of British and colonial troops alike. But he died, and as it happened, his less-talented younger brother, William, would be Washington's opposite number for three years of the Revolution.

What if George Howe had lived to get that job instead?

I know, I know—we'll never know. Still, the question seems a useful counterpoint to frequent, rarely disputed assertions by historians that if the *other* George had been killed at Braddock's Defeat, the course of the Revolution would have been different.

By now, Hamilton had led us from the fort's outer wall into its parade ground, an interior courtyard with two cannon on display in the center of it. Another British general, he told us, showed up in 1759 and took the fort, renaming it Ticonderoga. ("Mohawk word, means 'Place Between the Waters.'") The French lost the war and signed a peace treaty, in 1763, which left King George III ruling over everything from Quebec to Georgia. Suddenly Fort Ti was "in the middle of nowhere" without a mission. Roofs started to leak. Walls started to collapse. When Benedict Arnold, Ethan Allen, and the Green Mountain Boys came knocking in May 1775, Fort Ti barely had a garrison.

Seven months later, in December, Henry Knox showed up to borrow fifty-nine cannon.

Knox just took the tubes, Hamilton said, not the rotting wooden carriages. Total weight: sixty tons. Now all he had to do was float them down Lake George before it froze; drag them along the banks of the

Hudson *after* it froze; cross the river multiple times; maneuver the guns up and down the slopes of the Berkshire Mountains; and haul them east to the Continental Army, completing a dead-of-winter trek of roughly three hundred miles. "By the way, those are two of the original fifty-nine," Hamilton added, gesturing toward the pieces behind him on the parade ground and causing me to swivel my head in their direction.

I had come to Fort Ti to retrace the route that Knox and his "borrowed" cannon took to Boston. The two Hamilton was showing us—the only ones ever to make it back here—would be my starting point.

\* \* \*

The man Washington chose to schlep those desperately needed guns would go on to become one of his most trusted generals, serving as his chief of artillery for the rest of the war. But when the commander in chief dispatched Knox to Fort Ti, Henry was a volunteer artilleryman just seven months removed from peddling a "large and very elegant assortment of the most modern Books in all branches of Literature, Arts and Sciences" out of a Boston bookstore he had opened a few years earlier.

He grew up near the wharves, the son of a merchant and shipmaster. His parents were well enough off to enroll him at Boston Latin Grammar School, whose students tended to end up at Harvard. Then came an economic downturn in which Knox's father lost everything, abandoned the family, and decamped to the West Indies. Henry was nine. His mother got him a job with some friendly booksellers, and in the years that followed, he went into self-education mode. He read science, math, and the Greek classics, and taught himself French, which would be handy when he got interested in military engineering, because many of the best military texts came from France.

He also learned to fight. As a grown-up, Knox would weigh more than three hundred pounds. As a teen, he was already heavy, strong, and over six feet tall, which made him an asset to the boys' gang in Boston's South End. "All the neighborhoods had gangs," said Matthew Hansbury, who, as collections manager of the Knox Museum in Thomaston, Maine, when I dropped by, might have been the world's only full-time professional Knoxologist. "They would basically meet at various spots and beat each other up, and whoever was standing at the end of the day was the champion."

Henry was a champion many times. "He was probably angry that his father took off," Hansbury said, and that anger could have channeled itself in many ways. "But being with the booksellers—I think that changed his course in life. He really latched on to books."

At twenty-one, he opened that bookstore.

At twenty-four, he married Lucy Flucker, the daughter of prominent loyalists—a young woman spirited and stubborn enough to overcome her father's objections to Knox's insufficient wealth and prerevolutionary politics. After Lexington and Concord, the couple fled Boston; legend has Lucy smuggling her husband's sword out of town in her quilted cloak or, more poetically, in "the silken lining of her dainty petticoat." In any case, she never saw her parents again. Henry, who found his book learning more helpful than any sword, soon began using it to help the rebel army build fortifications.

Three weeks before his twenty-fifth birthday, he ran into George Washington—who had been in command of the army for all of two days—and made an excellent impression. Five months later, he was on his way to Fort Ti.

He knew success would be good for his career. What he couldn't have imagined was that 150 years later, New York and Massachusetts would team up to strew dozens of granite-and-bronze monuments along his path—or that ninety years after that, historical tourists like me would still be setting out on Henry Knox Scavenger Hunts in the hope of finding them all.

\* \* \*

I made up a few rules before I started. First, I wouldn't skip any monuments. Second, I would confirm that they all carried the same text. ("Through this place passed Gen. Henry Knox in the winter of 1775–1776," it read, "to deliver to Gen. George Washington at Cambridge the train of artillery from Fort Ticonderoga used to force the British Army to evacuate Boston.") Finally, I wouldn't allow the looming presence of the Saratoga battlefield, just west of Knox's route, to distract me. There were endless what-ifs to be navigated before a major turning point could take place there in 1777. And a big one, as I'd read over and over again, was: What if those cannon hadn't gotten to Washington in time?

Knox thought he could get them east in a month or less.

Have I mentioned that he was an optimist by nature?

The first couple of Knox Trail monuments are on the grounds of Fort Ti. I located the third in the town of Ticonderoga, in a small park on the route to thirty-two-mile-long Lake George, the best eighteenth-century option for travel between the fort and the Hudson River to the south. Yes, as expected, it had the standard "used to force the British Army to evacuate Boston" text as well as the equally standard bas-relief showing a big guy in uniform supervising gun-toting oxen. But no, I hadn't anticipated finding another metal plaque, a few yards away, displaying eight lines of time-traveling verse:

> *There is a joy in footing*
> *Slow across a silent plain,*
> *Where Patriot battle has been fought,*
> *When glory was the gain.*
> *There is a joy in every spot*
> *Made known by times of old—*
> *New to the feet, though each*
> *Tale a hundred times be told.*

John Keats, poet of historical tourism! Who knew?

Keats wrote this poem while footing around Scotland in 1818. Actually, he wrote a much longer poem, but some clever editor had abridged it.

More surprises were to come. The next awaited me just a mile away. It took the form of a full-scale replica of John Hancock's Boston mansion—the one where Henry Clinton had insomnia the night before Bunker Hill—built on a whim by a Ticonderoga-born paper tycoon in 1926, the same year New York and Massachusetts were creating the Knox Trail. "People in Boston are still angry that Hancock's house was torn down," I told the woman from the Ticonderoga Historical Society who took my $5.

"If they want to see it, they can come here," she said.

Up the stairs I went. On the second floor I found a wall full of ads for Ticonderoga pencils ("A Fine American Pencil with a Fine American Name"), at least one featuring the aircraft carrier *Ticonderoga*. Nearby hung a photo of nineteen-year-old heiress Stephanie Pell, who had been chosen to smash a bottle of champagne across the *Ticonderoga*'s bow at the carrier's 1944 launch. It took her two tries. As Pell recalled, an admiral handed her a rope with the bottle attached, advising her to swing it like a baseball bat. She had never swung a baseball bat in her life. "I christen thee *Ticonderoga*," she cried, then swung and missed. Spectators gasped, as well they might: Superstition had it that a failed christening would doom the ship and its crew. "Stephanie Pell, what have you done?" was all she could think. So she grabbed the champagne on the rebound, ran to the carrier—which was already slipping toward the water—and smashed the bottle by hand.

No champagne bottles were harmed during the launch of Knox's boats on Lake George. Near the Mossy Point Boat Launch, I checked off my fourth Henry—already, I was on a first-name basis with the man's monuments—then drove down the lake to look for the fifth. This Henry turned out to be at Sabbath Day Point, hiding behind a suburban-style house that didn't seem to have anyone in it. "You can walk right back, they don't mind," a neighbor told me, and sure enough, there he was in front of a magnificent lake view. Knox kept a diary on this part of the expedition; coming ashore here after a hard day, he wrote, he and his crew warmed themselves at "an exceedingly good fire in an hut made by some civil Indians who were with their Ladies abed."

He didn't mention missing Lucy, but we know he did.

Thirteen miles farther on, I found Henry gazing toward a rehabbed version of what another marker called "the age of splendid Lake George Hotels." The Sagamore, on Green Island, used to be the kind of place where visitors "lounged by the lake, sketching or reading, or paddled about in boats," often for whole summers at a time. At the south end of the lake, I tracked down a Henry near the twentieth-century replica of

Fort William Henry (no relation), a French and Indian War site familiar to fans of *The Last of the Mohicans*. By the time he got there, he was praying for snow.

He'd gotten the guns down the lake, as hoped, before it froze. Now his plan was to acquire "40 good strong sleds" and the oxen or horses to pull them (he would end up using mostly horses), but the weather was not cooperating. Nor, for that matter, was the price-gouging gentleman with whom he contracted for the sleds and draft animals. All this would be sorted out eventually, but in the meantime, Knox set off toward Albany to check in with his New York boss, Gen. Philip Schuyler, leaving what he called his "noble train of artillery" to wait for the necessary snowfall.

My next Henry was hidden in a stretch of unspoiled woods between Route 9 tourist traps. At one, I counted seventy-five carved wooden bears and moose lined up outside and considered purchasing a bear holding a sign that read "Thank God for Beer!!!" (Sanity prevailed.) At Glens Falls, Hudson Falls, and Fort Edward, I bagged Henrys at a park, a library, and a school; another stood guard close to the Turning Point Wesleyan Church. Crossing the Hudson from east to west, I pulled off on Stark's Knob Road and spotted a Henry framed by lush green hillside. Then I glanced to my right and saw Knox's ghost. It was a steel-gray sculpture, actually, made of what appeared to be scrap metal, showing a pair of oxen pulling a sled full of cannon with Henry, on horseback, looming over them. The oxen looked like longhorns bred with *Star Wars* creatures. The horse looked like a Tyrannosaurus. But seen as a whole, the piece seemed to me indescribably marvelous.

Between Stark's Knob and Albany, I checked off eight more Henrys, not counting two that had gone missing. The second missing monument had been in Albany itself, near where the cannon crossed the Hudson one last time. There I tried to picture the river as Knox saw it—quiet, bridge free, and covered with ice that wasn't quite thick enough.

He wrote Washington that "a cruel thaw" had delayed him. He wrote Lucy that he "trembl'd for the Consequences" to his mission. He ordered holes cut in the ice, hoping to strengthen it, as one biographer wrote, "by flooding it and letting more ice freeze over to support the artillery train." This didn't work. When the river finally froze hard enough for him to try a crossing, one of the bigger guns fell through. Fortunately, it had ropes attached, and "the good people of the City of Albany" helped Knox's drovers haul it out.

Onward.

I searched out five Henrys east of the river before dusk: in Rensselaer, East Greenbush, Schodack, Kinderhook, and West Ghent. Getting to a sixth required driving four miles of gorgeous but confusing country roads, and only some excellent directions from a gentleman walking a well-groomed dog kept me on track. Standard Poodle Man didn't know about the Knox Trail, though, and talking with him made me realize that since leaving Fort Ti, I hadn't run into a soul who seemed to grasp what Knox had accomplished. So it came as a happy surprise when a woman in a minivan hailed me as I got out of my car on Harlemville Road, near the Taconic Parkway. "Are you here for the Knox marker?" she asked, explaining that her children couldn't fathom why she kept pointing the darn thing out to them.

By now it was almost dark. Time to find a motel.

"Just one more Henry," I thought, and fifteen minutes later there he was, with a plastic goldfish, a wind-up turtle, and no fewer than eight rubber ducks perched on his granite shoulders. Meaning no disrespect, I burst out laughing. I'm pretty sure the ghost of Henry Knox would have done the same.

\* \* \*

On January 14, 1776, almost two weeks later than he had promised delivery, Henry the Optimist was still trying to wrangle sixty tons of cannon through the rugged hills of western Massachusetts. At the same time, back in Cambridge, Washington was tearing his hair.

"We are now without any Money in our treasury—Powder in our Magazines—Arms in Our Stores," he wrote a confidant, yet this wasn't the worst part of his army's predicament. It also lacked *men*. Many troops had decamped after their short-term enlistments ran out in December, and so far replacements were scarce. Washington knew who'd be held responsible should disaster result, and this knowledge might have inspired the plunge into self-pity that followed. "I have often thought, how much happier I should have been," he wrote, "if, instead of accepting of a command under such Circumstances I had taken my Musket upon my Shoulder & enterd the Ranks, or, if I could have justified the Measure to Posterity, & my own Conscience, had retir'd to the back Country, and livd in a Wig-wam."

If you can picture Washington in a wigwam, your historical imagination is better than mine. What I have even more trouble imagining, however, is how the commander of the desperately flawed army he had just described could even *think* about flinging it against a fortified city defended by veteran troops.

Aggressive by nature, not yet the beneficiary of hard-earned lessons about the need for patience when facing a stronger opponent, Washington was wild to attack Boston. He wanted to put his men in boats, send them down the Charles River, then have them row straight into cannon fire from British batteries. Failing that, he wanted to send them slip-sliding across the frozen Back Bay, right into that same cannon fire, as soon as the ice got thick enough to hold their weight. (Sometimes he went down to test it himself.) He wanted to attack with or without the artillery Knox's beasts of burden were so laboriously hauling in his direction. The only thing that stopped him was a commendable belief in civilian control. The civilians in Congress had instructed their rookie commander in chief to consult his subordinate generals before making major decisions—so he did.

Again and again, he consulted them.

Again and again, they voted him down.

They used words like "improper" and "impracticable" and "too great a Risque" before adding that maybe it would be okay to attack *sometime.* Just not right now.

Would some big guns help?

Maybe. But Knox had yet to bring them home.

I picked up the Knox Trail at the New York state line and followed it east. The Massachusetts Henrys carried the same text about the cannon being on the way "to force the British Army to evacuate Boston," though the one in Egremont had a sobering modern plaque on its base: "This monument is dedicated to the thousands of innocent and brave men, women and children killed by terrorist attacks in New York City, Washington D.C. and Pennsylvania on September 11, 2001. They died for our country and our freedom. We shall not forget."

Near Otis, with Route 23 getting steeper, I tried to meld today's hilly but peaceful landscape with the "ominous confusion of mountains, precipices, chasms and deep valleys" described by Knox's biographer. At Blandford, I recalled the drovers balking at a daunting downhill grade before Knox "arranged for two span of oxen to supplement their horses." Once through the Berkshires, however, the level of difficulty dropped, and at some point after reaching Springfield, Knox left others in charge while he dashed ahead to report.

A couple of Henrys later, I broke my rule about not skipping monuments and dashed ahead myself, eager to see where the end of the Boston siege played out.

By late January, the cannon were stashed in barns in Framingham, twenty miles west of Cambridge. The idea was to keep them safely out of sight until Washington and his generals decided how to use them. On February 16, at yet another council of war in his Tory Row headquarters, the commander in chief once again pushed for an all-out infantry assault. There were enough men now, he argued, more militia having come in; the ice was finally thick enough; and attacking across Back Bay would allow them to avoid the strongest British defenses, on Boston Neck. But the ice wouldn't last!

Then, one more time, he asked what people thought.

"A novelist would fill the next few moments with nervous coughs and shuffling feet," writes Edward Lengel in *General George Washington: A Military Life.* "The officers had considered the problem from every possible angle, and their conclusion was that Washington did not know what he was talking about"—though no one put it quite that bluntly. He had "overestimated the capabilities of his troops," Lengel writes, "an odd miscalculation given his repeated difficulties in training them." Few had bayonets "or had ever fired a shot in anger." Sending them against "fixed positions held by well-armed regulars...would have meant the destruction of the American army." But his men *could* fight behind fixed positions themselves, as they had proved at Bunker Hill.

Maybe they should try it again, on Dorchester Heights this time—and with some serious artillery support.

* * *

Why the high ground near the Neck remained unoccupied in February 1776 is a mystery. Dorchester Heights, which overlooked the town and harbor from what's now South Boston, was a crucial strategic position. The British, as you may recall, had been poised to occupy the heights before the rebels flipped them the metaphorical bird from the Charlestown Peninsula, and Artemas Ward, the Massachusetts general who had commanded the army before Washington showed up, had long argued in favor of putting troops there. For months, Washington didn't listen. (He didn't much like Ward, and the feeling was mutual.) But after his attack plan was rejected yet again, and with the Fort Ti guns now available, he did what wise leaders across the centuries have done: took a subordinate's idea and made it his own.

Nearly three weeks of planning preceded the move onto Dorchester Heights, a luxury unavailable to the men who had so hastily improvised the Charlestown defenses in June 1775. Remarkably, Washington still hadn't given up on attacking Boston across Back Bay, which was no longer frozen. The four thousand troops he set aside for this mission, however, were to be ordered into boats only *after* the new hilltop fortifications had lured the British into a full-scale engagement across town.

Now it was the night of March 4, and here came oxcarts dropping huge bundles of hay to obscure the enemy's view of the army's movements. Here came eight hundred troops to guard the operation from unexpected attacks and 1,200 more to ascend the Heights, along with the artillery. The general chosen to lead the men up the hill said that by 10 p.m. they had put up fortifications "sufficient to defend them from small arms and grape shot." On and on they worked, replaced eventually by fresh men. Shortly after dawn, the British got their first shocked look at what the rebels had wrought, and William Howe—seeing Knox's cannon positioned to reach both Boston itself and the fleet in the harbor, albeit at long range—had a difficult choice to make.

Within hours, the British Army was observed making preparations to attack.

Its officers and men, and Howe himself, surely knew the odds. What was to come would likely be a second Bunker Hill, but worse. Their opponents' position was stronger, with its defenders better trained and its artillery—which had been scarce and ineffective in the Charlestown fight—poised to mow the redcoats down as they climbed.

Why even *try* this?

Howe is reported to have said he thought "the honor of the troops" required it. But it's hard to believe those troops were unhappy when a sudden, violent storm blew up on the afternoon of March 5, preventing them from fighting that day, or when Howe came to his senses, using the weather as an excuse, and called the whole thing off.

A delegation of loyalists emerged from Boston with a message for the commander in chief: The British would refrain from burning the town if he let them leave in peace. On March 17, Howe and his army sailed away, bringing with them every loyalist who wanted to leave—thus making Knox the first American husband to drive away his in-laws with artillery. Washington was suddenly all the rage, the man who had authored what would be called "the first great strategic success of the Americans in their war for independence." Harvard gave him an honorary degree; Congress gave him a gold medal.

None of this satisfied him, however.

He had wanted so badly to fight that battle. The move onto Dorchester Heights, he wrote, had "seemed to be succeeding to my utmost wish." A smashing victory might even have ended the war. But then along came that damn storm—in fairness, I should note that Washington described it as a "remarkable Interposition of Providence" undoubtedly "designed to answer some wise purpose"—and screwed things up.

Howe, by contrast, could only have been pleased.

That's because—as I did not know when I first got hooked on the story of the cannon—the British had long planned to evacuate Boston *anyway*.

Why base the army in the kind of implacably hostile territory where Bunker Hills could happen, Howe and Gage decided, when they could move it to where it would get more support? The only reason British forces were still in town, as J. L. Bell has explained, was because their commanders couldn't make such a move without London's blessing, and that blessing "arrived too late for Howe to assemble a fleet before winter."

With this complication to the famous story in mind, I headed off to commune with Henry one more time.

\* \* \*

I found him on a green hilltop, in the shadow of one of the loveliest Revolutionary War monuments you'll ever see. It's a white marble Georgian Revival tower, dating from 1902, at the Dorchester Heights National Historic Site. I'd have loved to take in the panoramic view of modern Boston from the top, but the tower was closed for safety reasons. So I settled down next to my forty-third and final Henry to consider what that enterprising young man had really done for his country in the winter of 1775–1776.

Yes, technically, his guns were "used to force the British Army to evacuate Boston"—but the truth is that they only moved Howe's timetable up a bit. What the rebel army did on the Heights, however, turned out to matter a lot. Through a combination of skill, effort, and good fortune, it made people *think* it had driven the mighty British out of town. This did wonders for morale, civilian and military. Worth remembering, too, is that when Howe first saw that artillery, he very nearly made a massive, war-changing blunder.

But the most important thing Henry Knox and his cannon did—or so I ended up believing—was to save his *own* commander in chief from a massive blunder. How much longer, do you think, could Washington's generals have resisted his ill-conceived attack plans, which could have destroyed both his army and his military reputation? Wasn't it Knox's guns that allowed them to persuade their boss that fortifying Dorchester Heights was a far, far better idea?

CHAPTER 6

# Toward the Gap in That Brooklyn Ridge

Trains shrieked and rumbled on overhead tracks held up by rusting steel supports. Trucks honked, sirens wailed. And as he peered down a street lined with police cars and New York City Transit Authority vehicles, not to mention piles of trash, Barnet Schecter—a man who knows as much as anyone about where the Battle of Brooklyn was fought—had momentarily lost his bearings.

"I'm just trying to locate Jamaica," he said. "So maybe we want to backtrack a bit."

Schecter and I had taken the A train from Manhattan to Broadway Junction, a major transit hub halfway between the Brooklyn Bridge and John F. Kennedy Airport. Now the author of *The Battle for New York: The City at the Heart of the American Revolution* was leading me toward the site of the Howard House, a long-gone tavern where—at around 2 a.m. on August 27, 1776—sixteen-year-old William Howard woke up to find a British soldier standing beside his bed. Soon young Howard was watching a British general demand that his tavern-keeping father guide a patrol toward a crucial gap in the low ridge that ran lengthwise across Long Island, including the part that makes up today's borough of Brooklyn.

"We belong to the other side," his father said, according to a nineteenth-century history, "and can't serve you against our duty."

"If you refuse," came the reply, "I shall have you shot through the head."

Nineteenth-century historians were not fastidious about quotations. "They're making up all this dialogue," Schecter said. Still, off the Howards went, father and son. If the patrol confirmed that the gap in the ridge was undefended, ten thousand troops would pour through it, march several miles west, and hit the unsuspecting rebel army from behind.

Dark haired, fifty-something, wearing a baggy coat that emphasized his slimness, my own guide had come armed with a canvas tote full of documents and maps, but in this case, he pulled out his phone to find what he was looking for. Standing at a chaotic intersection where Jamaica Avenue and four other streets converge, he pointed to a nondescript brick building that likely occupied the spot where the Howard House drama unfolded in 1776.

I took his word for it.

For one thing, I was distracted by city buses careening in our direction, intent (or so it seemed) on mowing us down. For another, I was eager to climb the hill behind us, where Schecter had promised a view of about half the borough. Seeing it would help me understand how five months after sailing away from Boston—and just hours after the Howards led them toward that gap in that Brooklyn ridge—the British came oh-so-close to stopping the American Revolution in its tracks.

\* \* \*

Long before the British Army abandoned Boston, George Washington had a pretty good idea where it would show up next. In January 1776, he sent one of his most experienced generals to New York to see what could be done to defend the place. A talented, eccentric, and, it would prove, highly problematic subordinate, Charles Lee accepted the assignment with enthusiasm—indeed, he volunteered for it. After looking around for a couple of weeks, however, he sent back a clear-sighted answer to Washington's question:

*Fuggedaboutit.*

I'm paraphrasing, of course. But firsthand observation had reminded

Lee that New York was surrounded by water, and that the British—unlike the rebels—had a navy.

Washington couldn't afford just to throw up his hands, though. New York City's population of twenty-five thousand or so, clustered on the southern tip of Manhattan, was the second largest in the colonies, behind only Philadelphia's. Much more important was its strategic location. "The British saw New York as the key to subduing the rebellion," Schecter writes early in his book. The city "secured one end of the Hudson River, and they expected their northern army, descending from Canada, to hold the other." And if they controlled the Hudson, they could isolate New England—home of the incorrigibles who had started the war in the first place—from colonies more likely to return to the fold.

Strategic considerations aside, Washington and Lee both knew that conceding New York without a fight would *look* bad. It would cause problems with Congress and lower morale. Also the French, whose help was desperately needed, would not be impressed.

The alternative? Build fortifications all over the place and hope. At worst, the two generals believed, they could make the British pay a Bunker Hill–like price for the city.

Washington rode into New York in April, by which time Lee—whose military stock was soaring—had been sent south to worry about defending Charleston. This left others to supervise the fort-building over the next few months, and they made a number of changes—some for the better, some maybe not; it wouldn't turn out to matter much once the enemy showed up.

That started to happen in late June.

General Howe, since leaving Boston, had been holed up in Nova Scotia, preparing for his next move. On June 25, he sailed into New York's Lower Bay with a dozen ships. Within a few days, the rest of Howe's fleet followed—part of a stunning display of British military might, "the largest expeditionary force in their history prior to the great embarkations and landings of World Wars I and II." Before they stopped coming that summer, more than four hundred ships would carry some thirty-two thousand soldiers and sailors to New York, among them thousands of hired troops from such German principalities as Hesse-Kassel.

Soon, many of those troops set up camp on Staten Island. No fortifications hindered them as they landed.

Good news briefly interrupted the bad: In Philadelphia on July 2, the same day those hordes of redcoats disembarked, Congress voted to dissolve all connections with the nation employing them. On July 4, the delegates formally adopted the Declaration of Independence, pledging "our Lives, our Fortunes, and our sacred Honor" to the cause. When copies reached New York, Washington ordered the Declaration read to his men. Some then joined celebrating civilians and marched down Broadway to Bowling Green, a small park near where the bronze Wall Street Bull enthralls tourists today. There, they toppled a statue of George III, cut off the king's nose, and chopped off his head, leaving the lead from the statue to be molded into bullets. The next day, their commander in chief reprimanded them for the "appearance of riot" and urged his army, in the future, to let projects like statue-toppling "be executed by the proper authority."

He didn't press the point, though, because he had more important things to worry about.

Should he, for example, attack the British on Staten Island? It would be unbelievably risky, but Washington knew the buildup wasn't finished; a preemptive strike might be just the thing. He asked a council of war whether a complex plan to attack the island from six directions at once would be "advisable."

The unanimous answer: Nope.

Okay, then: Was there anything he could do about the inferiority of his army to Howe's? Not only did he have many fewer troops in total, but as a classic history of the revolutionary military points out, he "lacked even a small hard core of well-trained and seasoned veterans." Fixing this would require him to talk Congress out of its (reasonable) fear that a standing army could lead to tyranny, allowing him to enlist soldiers for long enough that serious training and seasoning could take place.

This wouldn't happen until things got much worse.

On July 12, two British warships sailed blithely past fortifications at Red Hook, on Governors Island, in Lower Manhattan, and along the Hudson, finally anchoring thirty miles upriver near where the Tappan Zee Bridge is today. Many rebel cannon were fired. At least one blew up, killing some artillerymen. The ships shelled New York in return, terrifying its inhabitants. At the end of a long day filled with noise and smoke, Washington was strongly reminded that the British could land troops pretty much anywhere they wanted: in the city itself, or somewhere on Long Island, or—most frighteningly—near the northern tip of Manhattan, where they could cut off the Continental Army's line of retreat.

So many options.

How could he defend against them all?

Guessing would be involved. Stakes would be high.

* * *

"All right, let's go for our vista," Schecter said. He led me past Knights Collision Experts, Bushwick Monuments, and Popeyes to the Cemetery of the Evergreens, an oasis of green straddling the border of Brooklyn and Queens, where we climbed a winding path to William Howard's grave. The sleep-deprived sixteen-year-old who helped guide the British patrol, it seems, lived seventy-eight more years to tell the tale.

We had come for the view, however, not to commune with the dead. Below us stretched mile after square mile of dense, mostly red-brown, mostly low-rise urban landscape unlike anything a soldier standing here in 1776 could have imagined. The future borough of Brooklyn in those days (population: low four digits) was a breadbasket farmed by mostly Dutch landowners who used enslaved labor and tended to support the Crown. I had seen maps showing the arc of the British Army's bold flanking march across this territory, but as I gazed down at it now, I couldn't begin to tell where any part of that march might have taken place.

Oh wait—yes I could.

"There's the bridge!" I said excitedly, noticing the tops of two barely visible towers nine miles to the southwest. "The Narrows Bridge!"

"Yeah, that's the Verrazano," Schecter agreed.

On August 22, 1776, not far below where the eastern end of the span that now links Staten Island to Brooklyn would be built, transports began off-loading troops. Howe had spent the summer waiting for supplies and reinforcements he had been promised—including some brought by his surviving brother, Adm. Richard Howe, chosen to head the navy's American war effort—but now, finally, it was time to get a move on.

Twenty thousand men eventually got off the transports.

"They fanned out across southern Brooklyn," Schecter said, with some getting as far east as Flatlands—"about here, where I'm pointing." Half the twenty thousand stayed farther west, their positions out of sight from the Evergreens cemetery. But on the night of August 26–27, the other half began to march, as quietly as possible, toward the gap in the ridge we'd been talking about.

That gap, Jamaica Pass, was just west of the high point where we stood; its precise location is unclear, because so much of the ridge (known as the Heights of Gowan) was leveled during Brooklyn's explosive nineteenth-century growth. Guarding the pass's mouth were five rebels on horseback, whose job—at which they failed, because they were promptly captured—had been to gallop back to Washington's army if any redcoats showed up. Still the British worried: What if there were defenders at the *top* of the pass? They checked this out by forcing the Howards to guide the patrol up a narrow alternate route.

"It was a really risky thing," Schecter said of their night march through terrain they didn't know. "They could have been ambushed." But the flank attack worked, thanks to Howe, who chose to take the risk, and to his second-in-command, who came up with the idea in the first place.

And hey—it wasn't even Henry Clinton's best idea.

We last saw Clinton in Boston, unsuccessfully pushing a plan to put men in boats and land them behind the rebels on the Charlestown Peninsula. He pushed a similar idea in New York, Schecter said, except on a larger scale. Instead of landing in Brooklyn, "Clinton was saying: 'Go up the Hudson—push the ships up and cut the Americans off at Spuyten

Duyvil,'" where the river meets the creek that separates the northern
tip of Manhattan from the mainland. If the British had done that, "the
whole game would have changed, because the Americans would have
been basically trapped on Long Island and Manhattan."

So why didn't Howe try it?

Well, Clinton hadn't gotten any less annoying since he left Boston.
The surprising thing was that Howe said yes to Clinton's next idea, the
attack through Jamaica Pass.

Make it so, he said on August 26, a day after receiving the
suggestion—and let's do it right away.

* * *

Barnet Schecter got interested in the Revolution through a kind of intellectual flank attack. I'm pretty sure he's the only battlefield expert I've
met who began his working life as a sculptor, and he's definitely the only
one with whom I've talked about how cities are really giant sculptures
themselves, shaped and reshaped by historical forces.

His father was a *Time* correspondent, so Schecter got early exposure
to history and politics growing up in places like Tokyo and Moscow—
"but also a big dose of art," because his parents filled their houses with
it. Equipped with a BA in history and a master's in fine arts, he began
sculpting in New York. Branching out, he wrote a novel about historical
forces shaping the city in the 1990s—"big developers versus open-space
advocates," he says, laughing, "when community gardening was a big
thing, and squatting." He couldn't sell it. Then he met a publisher who
wanted a short book on an amusing incident related to the British invasion. Schecter researched it, then told the publisher: "There's a bigger
story here! The five boroughs and Westchester were this raging battlefield, and educated Americans have never heard about it." *The Battle for
New York* was the result. More books followed, and to support his writing habit, he sometimes guided people like me to battle sites sculpted
into oblivion by modernity.

Take our next stop, for example:

Left to my own devices at the corner of Bedford Avenue and Fulton Street, three miles west of Jamaica Pass in the Bedford-Stuyvesant

neighborhood, the only trace of history I'd likely have noticed would have been a lamppost banner that celebrated a twentieth-century revolutionary. "Brooklyn Icon Jackie Robinson," it read. "Bed-Stuy and proud of it."

Schecter saw ten thousand redcoats on the march.

Picture them advancing down Fulton in column formation, he said, "right where this car's coming." Now picture them stopping to fire two cannon shots. "Right at 9 a.m. Boom! Boom!" The shots were a prearranged signal to Howe's *other* men in Brooklyn, and they meant that the jaws of the British trap were about to close.

Schecter and I would soon move toward those jaws. "Down there," he said, gesturing across Fulton toward the Zam Zam Stop & Shop store to indicate the direction we'd be heading. By this time, however, we'd talked a good deal about what was happening on other parts of the battlefield, so let me pause to sum up what I'd learned.

For starters, Washington had guessed wrong.

Yes, he knew an attack could come in Brooklyn, but something made him sure the British would go at New York City more directly. Even after the landing on the twenty-second, he persuaded himself that the landing was a feint and the real attack would come in Lower Manhattan. It would be three days before he fully abandoned this misguided notion.

He had also taken some bad advice.

Fortifications were already in place in Brooklyn: A line of redoubts and trenches ran close to its western edge, from Red Hook to what's now the Navy Yard. But at the last minute, one of Washington's generals had an idea. Why not move 3,300 men out of the fortifications—more than a third of the total rebel force in Brooklyn—and ask them to defend that long, low, unfortified ridge with the multiple gaps? Go for it, said the commander in chief, who knew very little about the terrain and had no experience in managing battles on this scale.

Might this have worked?

Sure—assuming the defenders weren't stretched too thin, which they were, and that they had sent more than five guys to guard the easternmost gap in the ridge, which they hadn't, and that they wouldn't proceed to fall—hook, line, and sinker—for the diversion designed to keep them from noticing the ten thousand men tiptoeing around their left flank.

Here it came, that diversion, starting before the sun rose. A different column of redcoats marched toward a different gap in the ridge, this one on the rebels' *right* flank—about as far from Jamaica Pass as you can get. A different nineteenth-century burial ground, confusingly enough, preserves part of this landscape today. If you take the tour of Green-Wood Cemetery that Schecter occasionally helps lead, you can see the sharp rise in ground up which the British attacked the rebel defensive line, just vigorously enough to be convincing. You can climb Battle Hill, where three hundred of those stretched-too-thin defenders fought to plug a gap in that line. And you can hear Green-Wood's historian recount what happened next. After beating back two British counterassaults, those three hundred defenders realized "that things had gotten kind of quiet up here." They'd been too busy to notice that no defensive line existed anymore. Their comrades had heard the sound of gunfire in their rear and were trying to make it to the forts before the trap snapped shut.

Boom! Boom!

Whether they would succeed was still unclear.

* * *

From Bed-Stuy, where the British fired the signal guns, Schecter and I took the subway south to Prospect Park. The plan was to be on foot the rest of the day. Walking past the carousel and behind the zoo, we came to yet another gap in the former Heights of Gowan. Bicyclists huffed up East Drive, following a route through which Howe's hired German troops—known throughout the war as "Hessians," no matter which principality they came from—stood ready to attack on cue. Near the top of the gap, we followed a side path to a hillock from which rebel field pieces could have wreaked havoc on attackers below.

Could have—but didn't.

By the time the Hessian advance really got going, most of the defenders on the American left and center—who were closer to the shocking flank attack than were the defenders near Battle Hill—had begun what Schecter calls a "terrifying sprint" for their lives. They ran through the park's Long Meadow (I'll use modern terms here), which had more trees on it in 1776; across Prospect Park West, with its beautiful old apartment buildings (Schecter called it "the Fifth Avenue of Brooklyn"); and down through Park Slope, seeking the safety of fortifications beyond what today is the Gowanus Canal.

Many would make it. Some would not.

Yet their plight was nothing compared to that of the men on the American right, who got a later start.

These men, too, would end up in Park Slope (arriving from the south instead of the east), but would find their way blocked at an old stone farmhouse that British guns had turned into a fortress. They, too, would need to cross the water to reach safety, but would find that the necessary bridge had been burned. Their commanding general, with no good options, had to choose the least bad one immediately. He ordered the bulk of his men to flee across the swift-flowing Gowanus Creek however they could, then led about 250 of his best troops "on what appeared to be a suicide mission"—repeated, insanely courageous attacks on and near the old farmhouse—to buy time for the others' retreat.

The general, who would somehow live to fight another day, was one of the war's more unlikely heroes. William Alexander believed himself heir to a Scottish earldom, though his claim had been denied, and insisted that even fellow revolutionaries call him Lord Stirling. Living beyond his means, he blew his inheritance and lost the contents of his New Jersey mansion to creditors. "Neither he nor anyone else," in the words of a Stirling biographer, "could have predicted that this overweight, rheumatic, vain, pompous, gluttonous inebriate would be so ardent in battle."

The men who followed him were mostly from the First Maryland Regiment. Confusion remains about their numbers (early mistakes resulted in their being memorialized as "the Maryland 400") and about how many would be captured as opposed to killed outright (more were captured, though being sent to a British prison ship was often a death sentence). What's not in doubt is that their sacrifice kept a disastrous day from getting much worse.

"So there's your Old Stone House," Schecter said, as we walked down Third Street.

The most important man-made Battle of Brooklyn site still in existence is flanked by a playground and a practice field. "Still in existence" needs an asterisk: As I had learned from the Stone House's director of education, Maggie Weber, the original, thick-walled 1699 farmhouse was in ruins by 1898. Rebuilt as part of a Depression-era parks project—"supposedly they used 70 percent of the original stones on the outside"—its main function for years was to house park toilets. Finally, in the 1990s, history-minded locals won a fight to make it a community center and museum.

Schecter and I kept walking. Like those terrified sprinters, we needed to cross the Gowanus and head toward Brooklyn Heights, and we were running late.

But at least we didn't have to swim.

Not long ago, according to the EPA, the Gowanus Canal was "one of the nation's most seriously contaminated water bodies," filled with "polycyclic aromatic hydrocarbons, polychlorinated biphenyls and heavy metals, including mercury, lead and copper." In 1776, by contrast, the creek was a cornucopia of foot-long oysters, though without a bridge it would have been a lot harder to cross. It was really more a tidal marsh than a creek, Schecter told me, and when the tide was high—as was the case when those soldiers were trying to wade and swim it—"the Gowanus was eighty yards wide."

Washington had crossed over to Brooklyn from Manhattan around midmorning, Schecter said, and he most likely watched the end of the rout from "a donut-shaped earthwork" at what's now the corner of Court Street and Atlantic Avenue. Nothing remains of the fort or of the hillock on which it stood, unless you count the plaque on the side of an old bank building that's now a Trader Joe's. Yet the legend of what Washington said there, as he watched the Marylanders' heroic attacks, echoes through two centuries' worth of battle narratives:

"Good God! What brave fellows I must this day lose!"

Is this quotation for real?

Good question: It first showed up in a letter from an unnamed soldier who had been in the thick of the fighting, and thus couldn't have heard his commander in chief emoting a mile away. Which makes it hearsay, though not necessarily untrue.

Better questions: Just how close did Washington and his ill-trained, poorly led, outnumbered army come that day to losing, not just the Battle of Brooklyn but the whole war? And how close would they *keep* coming to losing it in the days and months ahead?

Trader Joe's was the last stop on Schecter's tour, but before he and I went our separate ways, we traded thoughts on these questions and more. He also volunteered advice on a number of sites, in Brooklyn and other parts of the city, that I would need to explore on my own, and I was grateful.

Still, the first site I decided to visit without him was one he had warned was dubious.

It was a vacant lot between Eighth and Ninth Streets, ten minutes from the Old Stone House by foot. "Here lie buried 256 Maryland soldiers," read an old marker on the American Legion post next door, though a more recent marker said the precise location of the burial site was "unknown." A funky mural on the post's side wall, facing the vacant lot, showed giant figures in red and blue brandishing bayonets and leveling muskets. Graffiti covered the lower half of their uniformed bodies. Still, it felt good to stand there and consider what might have happened if those Maryland men—wherever they came to rest—hadn't followed a "vain, pompous, gluttonous inebriate" toward death's door.

One more nagging quibble, though:

Wouldn't the Marylanders' sacrifice have been for naught—or perhaps not happened at all—if William Howe, that day, had let his army push ahead and finish the job?

\* \* \*

It's a much-argued point, though hardly a new one. By the time I started second-guessing Howe, he had been in history's dock for 240 years, on trial for pissing away the earliest and best chance to crush the American rebellion.

The case for the prosecution:

*For starters, what in God's name was Howe doing in Brooklyn in the first place? Why didn't he sail around and attack Manhattan from the north, as that clever Henry Clinton suggested?*

Sit down, Henry—you're out of order.

*Okay, so why did he stop to fire those damn cannon at 9 a.m.? If he'd just kept going, he "probably would have surrounded the American outer lines and cut off every escape route back to Brooklyn Heights."*

The Court thanks Barnet Schecter for the amicus brief raising this excellent point.

*Cannon or no, shouldn't Howe have attacked the rebel fortifications as soon as he'd finished chasing those terrified sprinters, while the defenders were still in disarray? Didn't he admit that his men were wild to do this, and that "it required repeated orders to prevail on them to desist"? Didn't Henry Clinton write that HE, unlike his boss, had "little inclination to check the ardor of our troops when I saw the enemy flying in such a panic before them"?*

Sit down, Henry. The Court won't warn you again.

*Your Honor, it's hard to tell whether the defendant's behavior resulted from an excess of caution or from simple laziness in the performance of his duty. But it's an indisputable fact that the man is SLOW. And a third possible reason for his sluggishness has been whispered, which is that he and his brother the admiral didn't really WANT to smash Washington's army. Both Howes had opposed the war. Both had been appointed peace commissioners, at the admiral's insistence, and would have preferred to end the conflict through negotiation. Might this sympathy for the rebels have had to do with their late brother George—killed, as Your Honor will recall, during the French and Indian War—who was so popular with colonial troops that Massachusetts ponied up for a George Howe memorial in Westminster Abbey?*

Interesting notion—but let's get on with it.

*In sum, may it please the Court, if the general hadn't called off his oh-so-willing men, he'd have captured Washington and half his army. End of story! But William Howe is just about the last man on Earth you'd want to entrust with vigorously pursuing a victory. The prosecution rests.*

The case for the defense:

*Your Honor, ladies and gentlemen of the jury: Does anyone here remember Bunker Hill? Do you recall what happened there after a flank attack failed—unlike, thank God, the one that the clever but insufferable Henry Clinton came up with in New York—and my client's brave troops had to go straight at the fortified rebels? If not, let me remind you: More than half of them were killed or wounded. At one point, my client found himself alone near the top of the hill, because every man in his vicinity had been shot down. Now let me ask this: Do you really think William Howe was some kind of SISSY because he didn't want to go through something like that again?*

Objection, Your Honor! The defendant is on trial for poor generalship, not cowardice.

Sustained.

*Well, okay. Perhaps it's worth noting that those eager troops in Brooklyn, the ones who wanted so badly to hurl themselves at the rebel fortifications, had marched all night before the battle even began. Yes, their adrenaline was flowing. But my client knew exhaustion would catch up with them, especially if musket and artillery fire started mowing them down.*

Objection! As Henry Clinton said—

Overruled. Henry also said that "in Howe's position, he, too, would have 'judged it prudent' to hold back." The Court thanks historian David McCullough for his amicus brief on Clinton trying to have it both ways.

*Thank you, Your Honor. And let's not forget that my client was making a hardheaded choice here. If he could have replaced dead soldiers, he would have been less worried about getting them killed. Trained troops, however, were a scarce commodity on this side of the Atlantic, and William Howe's bosses couldn't be counted on to send more. Why "risk the loss that might have been sustained" by charging fortified positions when a siege could produce the same result "at a very cheap rate"?*

Excellent point—but let's get on with it.

*Finally, may it please the Court, how could anyone in my client's position have been expected to foresee the series of unfortunate events—the very UNLIKELY series of unfortunate events—that would allow his seemingly trapped quarry to escape? The defense rests.*

* * *

Resting wasn't an option for the rebels on the afternoon of August 27. Not knowing Howe's intentions, they waited in trenches for what they assumed would be a full-scale assault. "Guys with the equivalent of hand grenades," Schecter had told me, "walked along the line with slow fuses burning, scanning the horizon for the British." Then they noticed "white tents being pitched on the ground between the ridge and the line of defense."

No more fighting today! That was the good news.

The bad news, for those men in the trenches, was a violent storm that brought two days of drenching rain. "They can't stay in their tents, because they've got to be looking at the British, so they're not able to cook...Imagine standing in a trench up to your chest in water and maybe you're chewing on some raw salt pork, if you're eating at all." True, the same northeaster creating this misery was keeping British warships out of the East River, where their guns would end all hope for the defenders. But the wind was bound to change, and in the meantime, Howe's men were pushing siege lines toward what's now Fort Greene Park.

No trace remains of those siege lines. The river is still around, however, so I walked down to the Brooklyn Heights Promenade to take a look.

Despite its name, the East River is actually a tidal arm of Long Island Sound. It was wider in 1776 (before land-fillers did their thing) and someone looking across toward Manhattan would have seen "shipyards and ropewalks, where ropes were fabricated" instead of the jaw-dropping panorama of skyscrapers that draws wedding photographers and tour guides today—none of whom, as far as I could tell, gave even a passing glance to the iffy text on the Revolutionary War marker at one entrance to the Promenade.

On this spot, it said, stood the house "in which the council of war was held August 29th 1776, when it was decided to withdraw the American army from Long Island."

"It's inaccurate," Brooklyn historian Bob Furman told me, citing contemporary evidence that put the council in a house several blocks away. I think he's right. The more important inaccuracy, however, is that by the time that council of war was held, its job wasn't to *decide* whether to evacuate. It was to ratify a decision Washington had already made.

Even so, he was almost too late.

The day before, acting on his orders, more than a thousand rein-forcements had crossed over to Brooklyn from Manhattan. This cheered up the beleaguered defenders and suggests he was still planning to fight. It also shows that, should he change his mind, he already had a large number of boats at his disposal.

On the morning of the twenty-ninth, finally coming to grips with reality—the wind will change! the British have a navy!—he put out an urgent call for more.

At 4 p.m., he convened that council of war.

At 8 p.m., his men were to start getting into boats. They were to embark at the ferry landing in Brooklyn, near where the River Café is today, just below the Brooklyn Bridge. More than nine thousand guys and all their stuff, cannon included, on short notice, with the British Army on their asses and the British Navy just a few miles away—what could possibly go wrong?

Nearly everything. But somehow, it didn't.

Additional boats were gathered, with the secrecy of the operation maintained.

Men marched quietly to the landing when their turn came, ordered "not to speak, or even cough."

As the evacuation began, according to one eighteenth-century his-torian, a general at the landing tried to abort it, sending Washington a message about an adverse combination of wind and tide that made the retreat impracticable. But the messenger never found the commander in chief.

The wind changed, making it possible for warships to cut off the retreat. They didn't.

Washington, meanwhile, had deployed his secret weapon: a contin-gent of Massachusetts sailors and fishermen—most famously from Col. John Glover's regiment of Marbleheaders, though other mariners were involved as well—who rowed tirelessly back and forth through the tidal waters. Among many notable attributes, Glover's men were a naturally integrated unit, including both African Americans and Native Americans drawn from the (comparatively) egalitarian world of New England seamen.

Sometime in the early morning hours, a Washington aide made a near-fatal mistake. The general had chosen some Pennsylvania troops to bring up the rear of the evacuation, intending them to be the last to withdraw from opposite the enemy's lines. The aide garbled an order and insisted they decamp immediately. This left the British free to waltz down to the landing; even if they didn't, early arrival there by the Pennsylvanians would create mass confusion. "I am afraid you have ruined us," Washington told their commander, and angrily ordered them to turn around.

Back they went to the trenches—where, as we now know, the British *had* noticed their absence, but for some unfathomable reason had done nothing about it.

What else could have led to disaster? It's a long list, so I'll just mention the approaching dawn, which would reveal that far too many men were still waiting at the ferry landing. Just then, however—as a grateful young lieutenant named Benjamin Tallmadge would recall in his memoirs—"a very dense fog began to rise, and it seemed to settle in a peculiar manner over both encampments," allowing the rest of the army to escape.

"I think I saw Gen. Washington on the ferry stairs when I stepped into one of the last boats," Tallmadge wrote.

* * *

That moment on the ferry stairs gives us a glimpse of the commander in chief at his best: brave, calm, apparently indefatigable (he hadn't slept in two days), and acting decisively to save his army from destruction. Yet as I set out to examine the remaining months of the New York campaign, two competing images came to mind. One was of Washington weeping like a child as that campaign came to its disastrous end in mid-November. The other was of him going berserk with rage and frustration on

September 15, just two weeks after the Brooklyn evacuation, as Howe's army stormed ashore in what's now Midtown Manhattan.

Once again, he had guessed wrong about where an attack would come.

Eighty cannon announced this one, which came at Kips Bay, a few blocks south of today's United Nations building. Earsplitting broadsides from warships in the East River sent rebel militiamen diving for cover. British and Hessian troops in flatboats moved toward the shore. Packed tight and fearful they would come under fire while still afloat, the Hessians sang hymns. At his headquarters, six miles to the north, Washington heard the guns and leaped onto his horse, joining up with some reinforcements he encountered as he rode. Reining up on a hill above the bay, he saw a cornfield and a road with stone walls on either side.

Up the road marched a column of British grenadiers.

Through the field ran panicked American militiamen.

"Take the walls!" Washington shouted to the reinforcements. "Take the cornfield!" They tried, but confusion prevailed. Still more men, and some of their officers, joined the retreat. What came next shows how quickly fact can morph into legend.

"So many stories have been told about Washington's reaction," Edward Lengel writes, "that it is difficult to know exactly what happened during the next half hour. Certainly he lost his temper." One likely eyewitness wrote that Washington "laid his Cane over many of the Officers who shewed their men the Example of running." Other, unverifiable tales, "modified after circulating for days, said the commander-in-chief drew his sword and 'snapped his pistols,' 'caned and whipped' his men," threw his hat to the ground three times, and yelled something like " 'Good God have I got such Troops as Those[?]' "

Speaking of legends:

Washington had his meltdown in or near the quietly elite neighborhood of Murray Hill. In 1776, it was even more elite: The area was the country estate of a wealthy merchant and loyalist named Robert Murray. And it was Murray's wife, Mary Lindley Murray, who starred—on the same day Washington went berserk—in the amusing incident that first got Schecter interested in revolutionary New York.

As it happened, I had run into the Mary Murray story around the same time he did, thanks to an illustrated treasury of American folklore my wife and I read to our girls. In it, clever Mistress M and her beautiful daughters find themselves "heart and soul" on the side of the rebels, never mind what Dad thinks. Now along come Dad's pal William Howe and his staff officers, mid-invasion, dropping by the family mansion to pay their respects. Why not invite them in, ply them with cakes and wine, and buy Washington's army some crucial time? "Nothing will give me greater pleasure," Howe says, accepting. In the final illustration we see a gaggle of happy, red-coated men waving goodbye, hours later, having blown another chance to crush the rebellion.

Irresistible! At least it was to me, which was how I found myself inside a fenced-off median strip on Park Avenue, scrabbling around in search of a 1903 tribute to Mistress M. No police took notice, mercifully, and after whacking back ground cover and scraping away mud, I was able to confirm that the Daughters of the American Revolution had honored her for "entertaining at her home, on this site, Gen. Howe and his officers, until the American troops under Gen. Putnam escaped."

Sadly, modern historians don't buy this, dismissing it with phrases like "a romantic story" or "an amusing but probably spurious legend."

Yes, Howe might have paid a call on the Murrays, but that doesn't mean that Mistress M's actions delayed the British "even in the unlikely case they were intended to," Schecter writes. For one thing, neither she nor Howe would have known that 3,500 men under Israel Putnam were retreating up the west side of the island (guided by Aaron Burr, safely back from Quebec, who knew the Manhattan roads). For another, Howe's decision to call a halt was hardly spur-of-the-moment. The idea that an initial wave of troops under Henry Clinton would hold up until the rest of the army had landed was "written into Clinton's orders before the invasion"—and never mind that Henry would complain that those orders kept him from cutting off and bagging "great numbers of the enemy."

But why not give our heroine the last word?

"He who fights and retreats a way, lives to fight another day," says the folklore version of Mary Lindley Murray—a truth Washington and his overmatched army would embody again and again during the New York endgame.

* * *

The day after the panicked Kips Bay flight that so infuriated their general, Washington's men gave him his first battlefield victory. It began when a scouting party led by Thomas Knowlton, who fought behind that brilliantly improvised rail fence at Bunker Hill, ran into enemy scouts near today's Broadway and 106th Street; continued as British units attacked to the accompaniment of derisive horn calls used in fox hunting; climaxed in a buckwheat field where the Barnard campus is now; and ended with the overconfident redcoats pushed back to where they started. Knowlton was killed and Washington lamented his loss. But he knew that a day filled with what he called "smart skirmishes"— now known as the Battle of Harlem Heights—had produced a desperately needed boost in his army's morale as well as his own.

Did he, perhaps, drift off that night thinking, "Heck, maybe we *don't* have to haul our asses out of Manhattan right away"?

One could ponder this impossible question, I learned, outside the very bedroom where he slept. To get there, I drove fifty blocks north on Broadway, slaloming around delivery trucks and construction sites, and jogged east into an alternative universe. A serene white Palladian house stood on the heights above the Harlem River, surrounded by gardens, lawns, and trees. "Esteemed guests: We are proud to offer electricity and many other modern conveniences at Morris-Jumel Mansion. Please use the doorbell," read a notice taped next to the door knocker.

"You're walking on the same floors as Washington, Jefferson, Hamilton, Adams, Knox, and Burr," said Chris Davalos, the enthusiastic director of visitor services who let me in. Built as a summer place in 1765, when "there was nothing up here but rolling hills, farmland, and the old post road," the house is now Manhattan's oldest. On September 14, 1776, its loyalist owner having fled, Washington moved his headquarters here. Up I went to check out his room. There's still a bit of uncertainty about which it was, but gosh, those floors! And the relevant marker text taught me something else. "Washington's personal slave,

William Lee, accompanied the general to the mansion," it read. I knew about Lee, who served Washington throughout the war, but it hadn't occurred to me that he "most likely slept in the hall outside the door of Washington's bedchamber." Close to where I was standing now, I thought, looking down at my dirty shoes.

Postwar history was on display, too. Washington, as president, hosted a cabinet dinner at the mansion; Burr, in his old age, married a rich widow who owned it; and Lin-Manuel Miranda wrote part of *Hamilton: An American Musical* in the Burr Bedroom. Still, I stayed preoccupied with the question that brought me here in the first place:

What was George Washington *thinking*?

Why on earth did he keep sleeping here for five weeks after Kips Bay and Harlem Heights? Was he so enamored of his south-facing defensive position that he forgot the British had a navy? I don't think so. But if anyone knows the real reason he and the Continental Army sat around waiting for Howe to sail north and bottle them up, I'd love to hear it. Because eventually, belatedly—close your eyes and you can hear Henry Clinton gnashing his teeth—the British commander in chief bestirred himself and ordered a landing at Throgs Neck, in what's now the southeast part of the Bronx. The landing place hadn't been scouted properly, however. It was a tidal island, and when the tide was high, twenty-five riflemen behind a woodpile could—and did, on October 12—check the British long enough for more defenders to come up.

Howe & Co. found a better landing place farther north, but it took them six days to get there.

On the fourth day, Washington finally decided to get the hell out of Dodge. The idea was to retreat north to White Plains and take a defensive position on high ground, but it took him two more days to get started. Most of the army began straggling toward Westchester on October 18, but when Howe's troops landed that morning at Pell's Point, in what's now Pelham Bay Park, Washington's men were strung out and vulnerable. Fortunately, John Glover had been sent to see what he could do. Unfortunately, the man who helped ferry the army across the East River had little experience fighting on land. Now here came the British and Hessians marching up Split Rock Road.

Overcoming his inexperience and anxiety, Glover improvised a force-multiplying plan with the four depleted regiments under his command. Outnumbered five to one, he kept his own regiment (the Marbleheaders) in reserve and placed the other three at "staggered intervals" behind stone walls that lined the road. As their enemies advanced, a regiment rose, fired several volleys, then retired to a position behind the others. The Brits and Hessians charged forward, thinking they had won, only to have the next regiment rise up, blast them, and retire in its turn. "No professional soldier could have done better," historian George Billias writes.

In Pelham Bay Park I found an old marker, inset in a massive boulder, that sums up what the colonel and his men accomplished. "Near this site," visitors learn, they held out long enough "to save Washington's troops from destruction, enabling them to withdraw to Westchester and ultimate victory." Historians agree that Glover's Rock is in the wrong place. But the phrase "near this site" covers a multitude of sins, including mine, because I wasn't brave enough to trespass on the Split Rock Golf Course or to dash across an I-95 on-ramp, which would have gotten me closer to where the real fighting happened.

Also, I had run out of time. I needed to get to the last stop of the New York campaign—the place where George Washington ran out of luck.

\* \* \*

It was called Fort Washington, not coincidentally, and you can visit the site today at a small park on Fort Washington Avenue in Washington Heights, maybe five hundred yards from an on-ramp to the George Washington Bridge. When I got there, I saw a small boy perched on the barrel of a replica fieldpiece, blasting away at invisible enemies.

"Ammo, ammo, ammo! Fire, fire, fire!" he yelled.

The kid was going to need all the ammo he could get, I thought, to defend one of the dumbest military fortifications ever built. "The place looked like a half-ruined sand castle," as one acerbic historian put it. "Amateurishly constructed as a five-sided earthwork in July 1776, it included no barracks to shelter the garrison, no internal water supply, and feeble outworks... No one could have imagined it capable of enduring a siege."

No one except Washington and some of his most trusted advisers, that is.

After Glover's vital delaying action, Howe had pursued Washington's army (once again, too slowly) and defeated it at White Plains (once again, not decisively). Then he had marched back to Manhattan to deal with the one remaining problem there. The rebels had left a substantial garrison at Fort Washington, the main purpose of which (together with Fort Lee, on the Jersey side of the Hudson) was to keep the British from sailing upriver. This proved a vain hope. Nonetheless, Washington, who by now had led part of his own army into New Jersey, had been assured that his namesake fort could be held—and he chose not to follow his own strong instinct to the contrary.

On November 16, the British and Hessians showed him what a huge mistake he'd made.

According to a marker not far from where the "ammo! ammo!" boy was playing, Fort Washington fell only after "a heroic defense." This is true, but it could scarcely have consoled the commander in chief. He had crossed the Hudson that morning to observe the fighting; missed being captured himself by fifteen minutes; and been rowed back to New Jersey by the time 2,800 of his men—packed into their inadequate sand castle and facing a bloodbath if they didn't surrender—marched out to lay down their arms. And as he watched the battle's end through a telescope from across the river, he broke down.

At least that's what the author of "Rip Van Winkle" and "The Legend of Sleepy Hollow" would have us believe.

Washington Irving was born in 1783, the year the war officially came to an end, and he was named for the Father of His Country. Seven decades later, he published a five-volume *Life of George Washington* in which he described the general's reaction to the defeat as follows: "It is said so completely to have overcome him, that he wept 'with the tenderness of a child.'"

The phrase "it is said" should always raise eyebrows. Still, Irving's tale seems irresistible to historians and biographers advancing a thesis with which I agree: that Washington was far more passionate than his modern image suggests. Buffeted by strong emotions, he worked hard to rein them in, yet didn't always succeed.

Here's what's beyond dispute, however:

Given what he'd been through in the past three months—and what he would face in the weeks to come—the man had every reason to weep.

# CHAPTER 7

# Where the Hell Was Charles Lee?

I f Washington had wanted to blame someone else for the war's worst catastrophe so far, there was an obvious candidate. Nathanael Greene was a thirty-four-year-old Rhode Islander who had entered the army without significant military experience and quickly risen to the rank of major general. In August 1776, while commanding rebel forces on Long Island, he became deathly ill, leaving historians to wonder how the Battle of Brooklyn might have turned out if someone who'd had time to study the landscape had been in charge. In November, he was responsible for both Fort Washington and Fort Lee, just across the Hudson to the west, and when his commander in chief expressed strong doubts about the wisdom of trying to defend the Manhattan fort, he brushed them aside.

No one knows whether Greene shed tears over what happened next. But we do know he took it hard.

"Never did I need the consoling voice of a friend more than now," he wrote to Henry Knox the day after Fort Washington fell. "This is a most terrible Event. Its consequences are justly to be dreaded."

And here they came, those consequences: Two nights after Greene put down his pen, thousands of British and Hessians crossed the river; landed north of Fort Lee; and improbably, in the rainy darkness, climbed a steep path up the Palisades. Fifty rebels at the cliff top could have stopped the attack "if they had only hurled stones down on us," a Hessian officer wrote, but none were on hand to do so. Washington was miles away. By the time the men at Fort Lee got the news, retreat was the only option, unless you count breaking into the rum supply and hiding in the woods. Greene rounded up hundreds of shirkers, but some were still missing as the rest of the garrison—abandoning tents, entrenching tools, more than two thousand cattle, and the artillery batteries along the Hudson—fled toward the Hackensack River, frantic to cross it before the enemy could cut them off.

They lucked out.

Lord Cornwallis, the normally aggressive British commander, had orders to take the fort, not to chase bedraggled rebels around the countryside.

But Cornwallis's orders would change, and soon there would be more rivers to cross.

\* \* \*

I got lost on my way to the next of those rivers, the Passaic, though perhaps "defeated in a valiant attempt to escape a North Jersey traffic jam" would be a less embarrassing way to put it. Eventually, however, I pulled into the parking lot of a Lebanese restaurant (hookah lounge, belly dancing on weekends) near the east end of the Kazimierz H. Slomiany Memorial Bridge (named for a man killed in Vietnam). A faded marker confirmed that Washington's men had crossed the Passaic River here on November 21, "destroying the wooden bridge behind them." Safe from pursuit for the moment, they spent the night in the town of Passaic, then called Acquackanonk Landing.

Off I went across the bridge to look around. Maybe 150 yards north, at Saints Peter and Paul Church, I found a hunk of granite that offered a hymn of praise to Washington. "Unique in Character," it read. "Blameless in private Life and Public Office—Champion of Liberty—Friend of Man—Alone in Greatness—Honored by the World."

There are plenty of things one could say about this tribute. "Well earned" and "over the top" are two. What really struck me, though, as I stood in front of Passaic's Washington monument, was how very hard it is for us to imagine a fraught historical moment such as November 21, 1776—because we know how the story comes out.

How did it feel to order that bridge destroyed, with little time to spare, and to understand that at dawn you'd be retreating again, with no end in sight?

George didn't say. And in all likelihood, a myriad of pressing issues drove any thoughts of future glory out of his brain that day:

*His army wasn't big enough.* The problem wasn't just that he'd lost those men at Fort Washington. It was also that even before heading to New Jersey, he'd split the rest of the Continental Army into three parts and left two of them behind—at Peekskill and North Castle, in New York State—in case the British decided to move up the Hudson or toward New England. Call it the Cover All Your Bases Strategy and don't bet on it working.

*His army would get a lot smaller very soon.* The enlistments of two thousand men were set to expire November 30. Most of the rest would be free to go home a month after that.

*The British were loading troopships in New York and he didn't know where they were going.* If they sailed south to Perth Amboy, they would trap him between two armies, which happened to be exactly what clever Henry Clinton wanted to do.

*A missing persons report had been put out for the New Jersey militia.* Photos on milk cartons would not have helped, though if the technology had been available, Washington surely would have used it.

Instead, he marched his dispirited men south from Passaic to Newark, where another Champion of Liberty and Friend of Man—then serving as a volunteer aide to Greene—got to work on his own version of a missing persons report.

Thomas Paine had emigrated from London in the fall of 1774, when he was thirty-seven. Before that, he'd been a teenage runaway, a privateer, a corset maker, an English teacher, and a tax collector. Once he skipped town to avoid debtor's prison; years later, he saw all his worldly goods put up for auction. Who could blame him for seeking a do-over across the Atlantic? Or for begging a letter of introduction from a

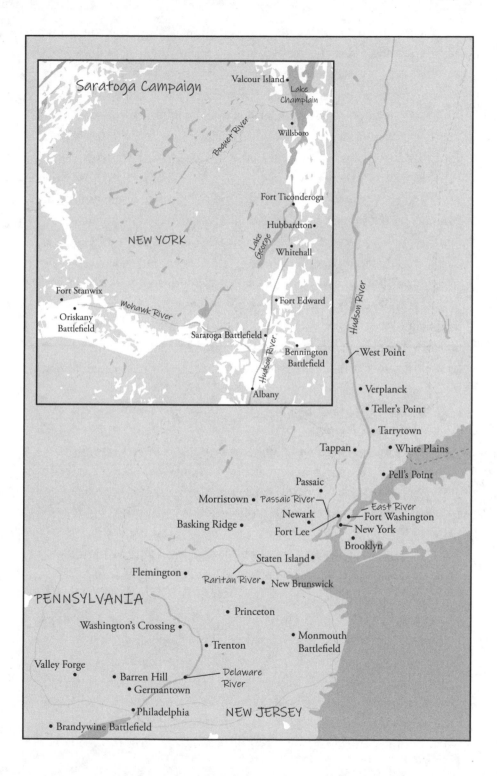

Saratoga Campaign

Valcour Island

Lake
Champlain

Boquet River

Willsboro

Fort Ticonderoga

Hubbardton

NEW YORK

Lake George

Whitehall

Fort Stanwix

Mohawk River

Oriskany
Battlefield

Fort Edward

Saratoga Battlefield

Hudson River

Bennington
Battlefield

Albany

Hudson River

West Point

Verplanck

Teller's Point

Tarrytown

Tappan

White Plains

Pell's Point

Passaic

Morristown

Passaic River

East River
Fort Washington
New York

Newark

Basking Ridge

Fort Lee

Brooklyn

Staten Island

Flemington

Raritan River

New Brunswick

PENNSYLVANIA

Princeton

Washington's Crossing

Monmouth
Battlefield

Trenton

Valley Forge

Barren Hill

Delaware
River

Germantown

Philadelphia

NEW JERSEY

Brandywine Battlefield

prominent Philadelphian he met through a friend? And who could possibly have predicted that fifteen months after Benjamin Franklin recommended Paine as "an ingenious worthy young man" who might make a good "clerk, or assistant tutor in a school," he would produce one of the most influential political polemics in history?

At a time when most colonists still hoped to reconcile with their king, Paine's explosive pamphlet, which was almost fifty pages long, relentlessly attacked both George III ("the Royal Brute of Great Britain") and the institution of monarchy itself. Published anonymously in January 1776, *Common Sense* sold roughly one hundred thousand copies in three months. Passed from hand to hand throughout the colonies, it reached an extraordinary percentage of the population and catalyzed the shift toward full republican principles that culminated with the Declaration of Independence. Soon Paine put his body where his mouth was and volunteered. In late November, with a front-row seat at the military horror show playing out in New Jersey, it occurred to him that another pamphlet might help. Here's how it began:

> These are the times that try men's souls: The summer soldier and the sunshine patriot will, in this crisis, shrink from the service of his country; but he that stands it NOW, deserves the love and thanks of man and woman. Tyranny, like hell, is not easily conquered; yet we have this consolation with us, that the harder the conflict, the more glorious the triumph.

In a few weeks, with Greene's blessing, Paine would head to Philadelphia to finish *The American Crisis* and get it published.

Would it help? No one knew.

But it was hard to see how the army could survive unless a few more winter soldiers and foul-weather patriots showed up.

* * *

For Washington, the most soul-trying time of the eight-year war came during the three days he spent near the Raritan River in New Brunswick, twenty-three miles southwest of Newark. At least that was what his most assiduous biographer came to believe. Specifically, Douglas Southall Freeman pinpointed November 30, 1776, as the "most miserable of his wretched days."

Sound like a great story? It is. You wouldn't guess this, however, from reading the plaque at the town's most important Washington site. It's on the wall of a restaurant at 78 Albany Street, a stone's throw from the world headquarters of pharmaceutical goliath Johnson & Johnson and a few hundred yards from the Raritan, which the army had just crossed. "Under the rooftree of the inn which occupied this site," the plaque says, "General Washington tarried when in New Brunswick."

"Tarried" may not be the best verb to describe Washington's time here. That said, it does evoke the infuriating behavior of his second-in-command.

Ten days after the fall of the fort that bore his name, Charles Lee was tarrying with a vengeance. He and seven thousand men, the biggest chunk of the Continental Army, had been left east of the Hudson to block any British move toward New England, with the understanding— or so Washington believed—that if the enemy chose to invade New Jersey, Lee would hustle down to help out. To that end, on November 21, the commander in chief sent him a polite note suggesting that right now would be a terrific time to start.

Lee had other ideas.

A former British Army officer who had emigrated a year before Paine, Lee held views on monarchy that were almost as radical as the ones in *Common Sense*, and when he joined the rebels, he brought with him more military experience than his peers. During the French and Indian War, he not only survived Braddock's Defeat but campaigned in Canada and upstate New York, where a musket ball at the Battle of Carillon shattered two of his ribs. Returning to Europe, he distinguished himself fighting in Portugal, then, with England at peace, went to Poland as a soldier of fortune. Lee's politics, résumé, and intellect— he was "that rarity in any age," historian John Shy writes, "the soldier who is also an intellectual"—impressed many in Congress from the start, and so far, his performance had borne out their high opinion. He had supervised the building of fortifications around Boston and at New

York; gone south to help fend off an attack on Charleston; and returned just in time to tell Washington to stop tarrying, for God's sake, and get off Manhattan Island before it was too late.

Yes, he had a few issues. He was "remarkable for his slovenly personal habits and coarse speech"; liked dogs more than people; and "would say almost anything," no matter whom he might antagonize. His sex life would also come under historical scrutiny.

So what? He was a winner!

And by this time, he was far from alone in thinking Washington was not.

Reluctant to give up what he saw as an independent command, Lee noticed that his commander in chief had only urged, not ordered, that he do so. Also, assuming the British and Hessians caught up with Washington soon—and why would they not?—George seemed unlikely to be anyone's commander in chief much longer.

This was the state of play when Washington rode into Brunswick (as the town was called in 1776) at the head of an army described by one shocked observer as "almost naked and hardly able to walk or rather wade through the mud." Lee was its most likely source of help, yet no one knew where he was or when he might arrive. But look! Here came a courier with a letter from the man himself. It was addressed to Washington's close friend and aide Joseph Reed, but Reed wasn't around—he was off asking the governor of New Jersey to look under his bed for the state's militia—so Washington opened the letter, hoping it would contain news about Lee's approach. Instead, it only added to the list of unhappy tasks he needed to accomplish.

Gentlemen don't read each other's private letters.

When you open one, even for good reason, and learn that a trusted friend and a willful subordinate both believe that your "fatal indecision of mind" renders you unfit for your job, you must write a short message of apology, seal it up with the original letter, and send both documents on to the intended recipient.

Then you must go on with the rest of your day.

In Washington's case, on November 30, this included pleading with two thousand men to stick around despite the fact that their enlistments were up, and having them show not the slightest interest in doing so. The following day, they packed up and left. Quite a few others decided it was a good time to desert, forcing Washington to send out patrols to try to stop them. At this point, Greene would write, "we had not 3,000 men—a very pitiful army to trust the liberties of America upon"—and the British and Hessians were hours away.

Time to retreat, again. That afternoon, the two armies exchanged artillery fire across the Raritan, with a young officer named Alexander Hamilton commanding the American guns. By dusk, Washington had his pitiful remnant on the road that led toward Princeton and Trenton.

Before he left, however—thinking ahead—he wrote a letter about boats.

\* \* \*

"We should have neon lights pointing it out," Clay Craighead told me. A veteran interpretive specialist at New Jersey's Washington Crossing State Park—not to be confused with Washington Crossing Historic Park, just across the Delaware River in Pennsylvania—Craighead walked me over to the chief treasure on display at the park's visitor center, which I had failed to notice on my own. Washington's thinking-ahead letter was in a small but centrally located document case. Dated December 1, it instructed a certain Col. Richard Humpton to put the ferries at Trenton "in the best Order" and to scour the Delaware, upriver and down, for every other boat he could find, making all things ready to get the army and its baggage to Pennsylvania in the "most expeditious Manner."

"It's a critical document," Craighead said. "Without the boats, nothing good happens. If the British get the boats, bad things happen."

Everything about those statements is true, I thought afterward, but there's a third possibility to deal with. What if the Brits are so close behind that Washington has no *time* to get his men into those waiting boats? Bad things happen then, too, right?

Yes they do. Being backed up against a river is a notoriously terrible place for an army to come under attack. Yet no such disaster occurs.

This brings us back to the ever-fascinating question of what William Howe thought he was doing.

Howe's original plan, as we know, was just to have Cornwallis take Fort Lee. This mission accomplished, Cornwallis asked permission to pursue the retreating rebels. Sure, said Howe, but not until I send you reinforcements, and by the way, don't go farther than Brunswick. At the same time, the commander in chief waved off Henry Clinton's ideas on how he could help to trap Washington's army, among them the one about landing at Perth Amboy. Instead, Howe told Clinton to sail to Rhode Island, take Newport, and establish a winter base for the navy there.

Why? Well, you could argue that Howe and his brother the admiral had good reasons for this move, though by definition it reduced the chance of ending the war quickly. You could point out, again, that William Howe was congenitally slow and that the brothers preferred to resolve the conflict through negotiation anyway. And you'll want to add that Clinton, in a recent burst of frustration, had confided to Cornwallis that he couldn't *stand* serving under Howe, and that Cornwallis, for reasons best known to himself, had ratted Henry out.

So Clinton fumed off to Rhode Island and Cornwallis marched down to Brunswick, reaching the Raritan the day Washington wrote his letter about boats. Back and forth went messengers to New York. Again, Cornwallis asked Howe to let him continue the chase. Howe said he'd come down and scope out the situation himself.

Five days later, he showed up. He'd been busy! Really!

The Howes had decided it was time to bring New Jersey back in the fold—peacefully. On went their Peace Commissioner hats and out came a proclamation offering amnesty to anyone, no matter how rebellious, who swore to "remain in a peaceable obedience to his Majesty" and "not take up arms, nor encourage others to take up arms, in opposition to his authority." This was a serious effort, not a propaganda stunt, and with the rebel cause looking more and more hopeless, it seemed likely to work. When William Howe finally headed for Brunswick, he passed out amnesty proclamations on his way. Once there, however, he decided he had a military opportunity as well, and ordered the pursuit to resume immediately. History has no record of Cornwallis's face going purple with rage. Perhaps he was too busy getting the troops ready to march, which they did at 4 p.m. on December 6, only a few hours after Howe arrived.

Washington had not wasted the gift of extra time. Retreating from Brunswick, he had left a sizable force at Princeton "to watch the Motions of the Enemy," then continued on to Trenton and the Delaware. Into the waiting boats went the army's wagons and supplies. It took three days to get the stuff across the river and safely stowed. At this point, sick of running, he decided to take "such Troops as are here fit for service" and head back toward Princeton, hoping he could make *something* positive happen—an understandable impulse, but a bad idea. Luckily, he got word of the British advance and turned around. The last of his men were still in the boats, making for the Pennsylvania side of the river, as Howe & Co. hit the outskirts of Trenton on December 8.

Whew. Everyone could relax—briefly. Yet over the next few days, on both sides of the Delaware, you could hear the same urgent question being asked:

Where the hell was Charles Lee?

\* \* \*

By December 8, miraculously, Lee was in North Jersey, but he still wasn't moving fast.

He had crossed the Hudson six days earlier, though with a much smaller army than he'd had in November. (Expired enlistments, illness, and desertion had all played parts.) Yet while finally heading in the right direction, he kept pushing his preference to operate independently. The British weren't really going to attack Philadelphia, so never mind that Congress and the city had their knickers in a twist. Surely the best plan would be for him to hang around the upper part of the state and harass the enemy from their rear.

You'd think that Washington, who was legitimately worried about Philadelphia, would have flat-out ordered Lee to join him by now.

Arthur Lefkowitz, author of the most thorough account of the New Jersey retreat, suggests two main reasons he hadn't. For one thing, the commander in chief "doubted himself after the loss of Fort Washington," not to mention the whole New York campaign. For another, he knew that "open controversy within the officer corps" could prompt Congress to intervene, the last thing he wanted. So he stuck with urging, dispatching a couple of officers to track Lee down and—besides delivering written messages—plead his case in person.

Missions accomplished, sort of.

The officers each caught up with Lee in the vicinity of Morristown. When the general finally put his army in motion, however, he kept his options open. "There is no way to tell for certain what was on his mind," Lefkowitz writes, yet as late as December 12, his line of march would have allowed him to veer off and attack Princeton or Brunswick rather than head straight to a rendezvous with Washington.

December 12, as it happened, was the day the British got serious about finding Lee, too. Having an army in your rear is bad; having to guess its location is worse. So Cornwallis sent thirty-three men from an elite cavalry unit, the Queen's Light Dragoons, to look around.

North they galloped. After an unrestful night (the house where some were lodging burned down) they rose early on December 13 and rode on. A few hours later, their commander got some startling news, presumably from a helpful loyalist. Not only was Lee's army in the vicinity, but Lee himself had spent the night at a tavern in Basking Ridge, just four or five miles away—and he was still there.

Lt. Col. William Harcourt had a choice to make. He went for the daring option.

Lee's decision to stay at the Widow White's Tavern (long gone, though there's a small marker near where it stood) has generated endless second-guessing. He was three miles from his army, after all, with only a token guard. One frequently offered explanation is that he chose the spot to facilitate a sexual adventure, though I've run across no source for this that seems even semireliable. At any rate, Lee was finishing his correspondence on the morning of the thirteenth when he was interrupted by the arrival of Harcourt's dragoons, with an uncommonly aggressive junior officer in the lead. The not-yet-notorious Banastre Tar-leton reported his triumph in an excited letter to his mom, including the part where "An old Woman upon her Knees begg'd for Life and told me General Lee was in the House." Tarleton threatened to burn the place and kill everyone inside unless Lee surrendered. Lee did. The dragoons put him on a captured horse and hightailed it south. The whole encoun-ter had taken something like twenty minutes, and after the dragoons got Lee safely back and into custody, they were so giddy they got the horse the general rode in on drunk.

Or maybe not. The story of the horse getting drunk is as poorly sourced as the one about Lee getting laid.

But surely those thirty-three men got drunk themselves.

They had just improvised a stunning coup. Their prisoner, as one Hessian officer exulted to his diary and many British officers believed, was "the only rebel general whom we had cause to fear." How could they know that the 1776 campaign wasn't over yet—or that one of their number had fewer than twenty-four hours to live?

* * *

To reach Francis Geary's grave, I drove north from Pennington, where Cornwallis had his headquarters at the time of Lee's capture, and where a marker on South Main Street noted that "British troops exercised their horses over this wall" while saying nothing about the drinking habits of men or beasts. Eleven miles on, I turned into a suburban neighborhood, parked between jumbo-sized houses with lush green lawns, and walked a quarter mile up a gravel path to one of the most poignant, thought-provoking sites I had seen so far.

The man memorialized there, like Tarleton, was a junior officer in the Light Dragoons; each held the rank of "cornet," an archaic term for second lieutenant. Tarleton, of course, lived to tell of the scouting mis-sion that bagged Lee, but to my knowledge, only one primary source mentions that Francis Geary played a part. The next day, December 14, Geary led eight dragoons on another scouting foray, this one to Flem-ington, where rebels had stashed a supply of salt pork and beef. Return-ing, he rode into an ambush and a militiaman shot him dead. More than a century later, his body was exhumed and identified, and in 1907, his great-nephew had a rough-hewn stone placed on his grave.

"To the memory of Cornet Francis Geary," the inscription reads, "killed in action here in the service of King George III."

It's hard to spend time at Geary's resting place—in a grove of ivy-covered trees, almost out of sight of the houses, with nothing to break the evening silence but the quiet singing of birds—without being moved.

That's not the reason I'm telling his story, though.

The last two days of Geary's life included both the high-water mark of the British occupation of New Jersey (Lee's capture) and early signs of a turning tide. Which makes his memorial a good place to think about the bigger historical picture on the day he died.

On the morning of December 14, William Howe formally declared the campaign over and ordered his troops to "immediately march into Quarters," by which he meant a chain of garrisons strung through the state between the Hudson and the Delaware.

Later the same day, Howe and Cornwallis set out for New York. Howe would winter there with his mistress; Cornwallis planned to sail to England to join his wife.

The Army Formerly Commanded by Charles Lee spent the day marching to join Washington, though bad route planning would further delay it.

Meanwhile, as Geary's killing showed, not all of New Jersey's militiamen were missing persons anymore.

Already some had been harassing Howe's supply lines in the north. Along with militia from Pennsylvania, they soon began making life uncomfortable for garrisons along the Delaware. On the fourteenth, the same Hessian diarist who had crowed about Lee was in a gloomier mood. "It is now very unsafe for us to travel in Jersey," he wrote. "The rascal peasants . . . have their rifles hidden in the bushes, or ditches, and the like. When they believe they are sure of success and they see one or several men belonging to our army, they shoot them in the head."

One more December 14 fact of note:

Washington had not yet learned that the top British generals were heading home. His letters that day show him still obsessed with the threat to Philadelphia. But he also expressed the hope that when Lee's corps and a few more veteran troops showed up, "we may yet effect an important stroke." Which, as you probably know, they did. To tell *that* story, I needed to bid poor Cornet Geary farewell and go watch General Washington's Rowing Club do its thing.

# CHAPTER 8

# The Battle of the Rusty Pole

We were important because we were the water men," Robert Scordia said. "Washington said, 'Oh, man, if these guys could get me across the East River, maybe they could get me across this frozen Delaware!'"

I ran into Scordia near the old wooden boat barn at Washington Crossing Historic Park (the one in Pennsylvania). From there, as a sergeant with Glover's Marbleheaders, he would help row a small army of his fellow reenactors over to New Jersey. The real crossing began on the night of December 25, and the park reenacts it every Christmas, weather and river conditions permitting, but today's event was a dress rehearsal. Less crowded, more fun, I'd been told—and so far, I hadn't been disappointed.

"Testing one, two, three—Colonel Knox! Colonel Knox!" boomed a voice over a loudspeaker. This Henry had a perfect large-bodied look for his part. Reenactors of lower rank patrolled the park's main drag, carrying muskets and dressed in outfits that looked great to my untrained eye, if you don't count a pair of dubious checked pants. A number of women carried muskets and dressed as soldiers, too, though others stuck with traditional eighteenth-century attire. "You couldn't show your elbows. That was vulgar," one said. "But you could have your décolleté down to *here*." My fellow spectators were a more ordinary-looking bunch, though I found myself doing a double take at a shirt one woman wore. "Elegant

Violence," it proclaimed in huge yellow type, but the reference turned out to be to rugby, not the Revolutionary War.

Scordia had been rowing the Delaware for a decade. His legwear had no checks and looked, quite properly, as though it hadn't been washed in a while.

"Water's a little low today," he said. "When we load the boats up, they may bottom out, but I don't think they will." Durham boats, they're called, and the originals were the workhorses of the Delaware, built to haul iron ore, timber, and other goods. Three replicas would be crossing, each manned by eight rowers plus two men with poles and one at the steering oar. And no, the Marbleheaders wouldn't do *all* the rowing. Even back in the day, there hadn't been enough of them to do that.

Before he went back to work, Scordia made a couple more points about his proud outfit:

"We were an interracial group," he said. "We had African Americans and people of complexion from the Indies, because we sailed around the world." In a few minutes, when today's Marbleheaders lined up for a musket demonstration, I would notice that two of the eight were Black.

As for the significance of what those mariners did, there's a metaphor he likes to use:

"When the fire of the Revolution was down to embers, it was Glover and his Marblehead regiment that kept the fire alive," he said, cupping his hands as if cradling something not hot enough to burn them.

On December 25, 1776, the dying fire was as much political as military. Congress had fled Philadelphia, lacking faith in Washington's ability to defend the city. Pragmatic former supporters of the rebellion continued to accept the Howes' amnesty deal. Thomas Paine published his call to action in a Philadelphia newspaper on December 19 and as a pamphlet on December 23, but its impact, as one historian put it, "remains conjectural." Meanwhile, a week after Christmas, most of the Continental Army would be free to go home. Embracing realism at last, Congress had authorized the enlistment of replacements for three years or the duration of the war, but given the widespread gloom, it was unclear how many men would respond.

All of which put Washington in a terrific bind.

Without "the Speedy Inlistment of a New Army," he wrote, "the game will be pretty well up." Yet he couldn't afford to wait and see whether a new army would materialize. He had to use the old one.

Right now. Before it disappeared.

And however political his motivation, he couldn't afford to screw up the military part.

As the reenactment began, I squeezed into a spot just behind the rope line. The amplified voice now belonged to Daniel Dailey, sergeant major of the U.S. Army, who told us that Washington, desperate for a "bold stroke," had drawn up a complex plan. Three contingents of troops were to cross the river from Pennsylvania to New Jersey at night, at three separate places, then meet up like clockwork to surprise the Hessian garrison at Trenton. "Let your imagination travel back in time," Dailey said, "to that bitter wintry day of 1776. Try to imagine what it was like to be a soldier in that ragtag military. Imagine the fear, the trepidation, the suffering. But most of all, imagine the bravery and the sacrifices made to secure the freedoms you and I enjoy today."

This was no easy task for a twenty-first-century crowd eating hot dogs and chili mac in the kind of unseasonable December weather—it was seventy degrees—that had us shedding layers and sweating through shirts.

The Marbleheaders helped, though.

Here they came up the grassy riverbank, shouldering eighteen-foot oars that weighed upward of thirty pounds, then holding the oars vertically, like flagpoles, as a tall, stern Washington inspected the army. Now they were marching down to a small dock and boarding three Durham boats, and now they were pushing off into the gentle current, and now, one by one, the boats were rounding an orange buoy and pulling for the opposite shore. One boat scraped its flat bottom briefly, then moved on. Painted black and pointed on both ends, the Durhams looked like supersized canoes. I did my best to imagine the real ones making trip after trip, with the troops packed in and standing up, because— as I knew from reading David Hackett Fischer's essential *Washington's Crossing*—Durham boats lacked seats, and anyone sitting in the bottom of one "would have been sitting in ice water."

These days you can walk across the river in minutes. On the Jersey side of the Washington Crossing Bridge, I saw the general graciously posing for photos. His buff-and-blue uniform was completely dry.

* * *

No one took a single photograph on December 25, 1776, of course, and no one made any sketches of the crossing, either: too busy, too wet. By far the most powerful image we have of the day is *Washington Crossing the Delaware*, painted by a German artist in 1851. Accuracy was hardly Emanuel Leutze's goal—he was hoping to inspire revolutionaries in Europe—but critics have made much of historical sins such as the painting's anachronistic flag, its undersized boats, its substitution of day for night, and the "small icebergs" it depicts instead of the broken sheet ice that actually filled the river and hampered the water men.

It also left out the ferries. And for anyone trying to understand one of the war's decisive moments, that may be Leutze's biggest sin of all.

Washington chose his crossing place partly because it was far enough away so the Hessians might not notice what he was up to. Just as importantly, however, he needed the two ferries based there, McConkey's and Johnson's, on opposite sides of the river. Because with due respect to every hero who pulled on an oar that day, it would have been impossible to get eighteen cannon, not to mention enough horses to haul them, across the Delaware in Durham boats. And without those cannon... well, we'll get to that part of the story soon enough.

I learned how the ferries worked at the house where the New Jersey operator had lived, a few hundred feet up from the riverbank. Thick rope cables stretched across the river, interpretive specialist Nancy Ceperley told me. The ferryboats were basically "long moving docks with sides and landing flaps"; ropes connected them to wooden pulleys on the cable. The whole setup was designed so "the current did your work for you," which meant that from the Pennsylvania side, those horses and cannon would have angled downstream and ended up where the east end of the bridge is today.

Ceperley had worked for the park for three decades, much of the time at the Johnson Ferry House. "It's the most significant structure we have," she said, the only one here on the night of the crossing that has survived. And at some point, Washington and his generals most likely "came in here, stood around this hearth to warm up and dry off," and talked about what came next.

Wait, wait—right *here*? Right where she and I were standing, in front of the same huge "winter warming fireplace," under the same white-oak crossbeams, looking at the same old wainscoting and interior doors? Yes, with an important caveat. As Ceperley made clear, she was talking about something park people had come to believe, not something they could prove.

I had no trouble conjuring the scene, though.

Knox likely wouldn't have been part of it. In addition to being responsible for Washington's artillery—not the same as the big guns he'd brought from Fort Ti, by the way, which would have been too heavy for an army on the move—he'd been put in overall command of the crossing, which would have kept him frantically busy until the last ferry load came ashore. Right away, there had been delays in moving the troops down to the riverbank. Changing weather made things worse, with a drizzle that began around sunset morphing into a massive storm. One teenage soldier would recall, years later, that "it rained, hailed, snowed, and froze, and at the same time blew a perfect hurricane," but as Fischer points out, John Greenwood "forgot to mention sleet."

So much for the notion of a predawn attack. In Washington's shoes, wouldn't *you* have wanted to talk things over—preferably somewhere out of the rain, hail, snow, and sleet—before marching your army off to Trenton four hours behind schedule?

It took me twenty-five minutes to drive his route, not counting a couple of educational stops. The first was beside Jacob's Creek, at the bottom of a steep stretch of the Bear Tavern Road. There I read how the exhausted men lost time "securing their cannons to nearby trees, which they used as mooring posts to lower the guns to the bottom of the ravine." They were three miles into a nine-mile trek that by most accounts was worse than the crossing. At least two men froze to death. One time Greenwood sat down "so benumbed with cold that I wanted to go to sleep"; if a sergeant hadn't forced him to keep walking, he, too, would have died.

My next stop was in West Trenton, at an intersection just past I-95 and the Trenton-Mercer Airport. On three of its four corners stood a gas station, a Dunkin' Donuts, and a 7-Eleven, but on the fourth I found a lovely, slightly scruffy little garden and an equally lovely, even scruffier marker in a wooden frame with half its paint peeled off.

"Near this site," it began, "George Washington divided his Continental Army of 2,400 men for a two-pronged, surprise attack on the Hessian garrison at Trenton." Nathanael Greene would head over to the Pennington Road and hit the town from the northwest; another general would move down the Old River Road and attack from the southwest. "This brilliant strategy," the marker concluded, led to "a major military victory" that was "the turning point of the American Revolutionary War."

Reality check: A two-pronged attack wasn't what George had in mind. (Remember the men who were supposed to cross the Delaware downriver and help? They never made it.) Militarily, the victory was minor; its political and psychological effects were what mattered. As for Trenton as the turning point, we could argue that one forever. The war had dozens of turning points. And what we tend to forget, while lauding Washington's unquestioned resolve and enshrining his glorious December 26 achievement, is that the *next* turning point—which came along seven days later—could have turned the revolutionary world upside down.

But I doubt Washington was thinking that far ahead as he joined Greene and his men for the final push.

\* \* \*

The Trenton Battle Monument rises 148 feet from the high ground at the intersection of North Warren and North Broad Streets, called King and Queen Streets in 1776. A formidable granite column topped by a bronze Washington, who seems to be waving at the dome of the New Jersey State House, it was designed by the architect of Grant's Tomb. The best view of the battle site used to be from the observation platform just below the statue, but the ancient elevator inside the column became unsafe. Still, you can get a feel for the battle's opening act from the monument's base. Imagine Washington leading his men into town just north of here "through dense clouds of swirling snow." Imagine a row of Knox's cannon, hauled to Trenton with such infinite pains, lined up right where you are standing.

Now imagine those cannon pointed downhill at enemy troops, most of whom have just woken up.

How do you pull off a surprise attack four hours late? The Hessian commander's arrogant overconfidence was a major factor. Warned several times that the rebels were up to something, he played down the threat. Blind luck helped, in the form of a foolish, unauthorized raid on Trenton by fifty Virginians; this made the Hessians less alert, because they thought *it* was what they'd been warned about. Most important, the fierceness of the snow lowered the garrison's guard. Who would be crazy enough to launch an attack in weather like this?

Oh, right. Benedict Arnold and Richard Montgomery.

But as John Ferling points out, that desperate attack on Quebec had been "the only major offensive action by the Americans" in the whole twenty-month war. So maybe we shouldn't be too hard on Col. Johann Gottlieb Rall for not anticipating a replay.

Standing at the monument, I had an artillerist's-eye view down the former King and Queen Streets, which were pretty much all there was to Trenton in 1776. Four or five blocks below me, three Hessian regiments had hastily formed up; Rall had about 1,500 troops in all. Hot fire forced them to withdraw to an orchard a block or two to the east. Bravely, if unwisely, the commander led his men back for more. That didn't go well, either. Rall fell, mortally wounded, and most of the Hessians soon surrendered, though about a third of the garrison managed to flee before the rebels sealed off the escape routes south of town. Numbers point to the ease of the victory: Twenty-two Hessians died and almost nine hundred were captured, including many wounded. American casualties were minimal, the most notable being an eighteen-year-old from Virginia. If a doctor-volunteer hadn't quickly clamped James Monroe's severed artery, the future president would have bled to death.

Washington had rolled the dice and won, big-time.

Back across the Delaware he went, prisoners and all.

Then he took a deep breath and rolled those dice again.

I had learned enough about that second gamble to be more than a little obsessed by the story, and while in Trenton, I went looking for traces of it. Most of all, I wanted to locate a historical marker titled "The Second Battle of Trenton," a photo of which I had seen online. The marker's text made note of a "great concentration of artillery" on which, I knew, the fate of the army—and maybe the new nation itself—would depend. In theory, it should have been near the bridge where South Broad Street crosses Assunpink Creek, below the center of town. In practice, the only marker I saw there had to do with a triumphal arch Washington rode through on his way to be inaugurated in 1789. I spent half an hour walking both sides of the creek, during which time I ran into a fourteen-foot Italian-marble statue of George in his crossing-the-Delaware pose and passed a much-traveled historic house—it's in the wrong place, having been moved three times—in which he'd held a council of war on the night of January 2, 1777. The house was closed for restoration, however, and nothing I saw told me about the Second Battle of Trenton.

Luckily, I knew the perfect person to call.

Ten minutes later, I'd been guided back to that bridge over the Assunpink and was staring at a rusty pole.

The pole was maybe 140 feet shorter than the monument to the first battle. No trace remained of the marker that once topped it. But thanks to the researcher, writer, photographer, and designer of RevolutionaryWarNewJersey.com—who was still on the line trying to help when I burst out laughing—at least I knew where the thing had been.

\* \* \*

His name is Al Frazza, though I sometimes think of him as the Man Who Loves New Jersey. When I met him, he had been working for nearly seven years to document all the marked revolutionary sites in his home state—county by county, town by town, on his own time, with his own money, while earning his living as a web designer. He still had a ways to go, so I asked the obvious dumb question: Did he know what he was getting into when he started?

"No, no, no—I didn't!" he said, then laughed as hard as I had when I first saw that rusty pole.

Not knowing what we're getting into, however, is the way life works. It's the way life worked for the eighteenth-century people he had been researching, too. "Every moment is like that," Frazza said. And when looking back at something that happened more than two centuries ago, "I always want to be *in* that moment."

Frazza was in his midforties when we met, though the brown curly hair that fell below his shoulders made me think he was younger. He had driven over to Montclair, where a friend's guest room served as my New Jersey headquarters, and we were walking and talking in Edgemont Park on a warm summer evening. At any moment, one of us could have been struck by a batted ball ("Heads up!") or run down by a beginning cyclist on the park's oval path ("Sorry!"), but we were too deep in the past to worry about these hazards. Two hours later, I still wasn't sure why Frazza woke up one day and decided to create *Revolutionary War New Jersey*—most likely because he wasn't sure himself.

He'd started reading American history in his twenties. The more he learned, the more his state's crucial role in the war seemed underappreciated, and there didn't seem to be an adequate guide to where that history had unfolded. "In the beginning, I was thinking about just going out and taking pictures and giving a general idea," he told me. His first day of shooting took him, among other places, to the grave of Francis Geary, which, oddly enough, was the first thing I ran into on his website. I'd used his map to find the place; had his photos in mind as I walked that suburban path; and learned much of what I know about the ambush from an obscure article he included in his footnotes.

Question: Did he always know he was going to do footnotes?

More laughter. "I didn't know I was going to get so carried *away* with them!"

His photos, maps, text, notes, and links helped me with every part of New Jersey I visited. In Passaic, for example, I got excited about a marker lauding one John H. Post, "whose destruction of the Acquackanonk Bridge saved General Washington's army from capture in its retirement from Fort Lee." Then I looked more carefully at Frazza's site, on which he calls the story of Post's involvement "an incorrect bit of local lore that began appearing in print at the end of the 1800s." And speaking of footnotes: I should mention a particularly great one exploring the question of whether Thomas Paine began writing *The American Crisis* in Newark or waited until he got to Philadelphia. Paine himself is the source of both versions. But after seven paragraphs of thoughtful back-and-forth on the topic, Frazza goes with Newark.

He's right, I think. Though it's at least conceivable that Philly's non-Jersey location hurt its case.

The war touched every part of the state. Tracking it took Frazza from Sussex County in the northwest, where an unknown soldier died of an unknown illness (disease killed far more revolutionary troops than combat), to Cape May County in the southeast, where British ships intercepted a blockade runner carrying gunpowder from the Caribbean (one of the army's big logistical problems was its need to import powder). Immersing himself in New Jersey's physical geography, he found, gave him a visceral connection to the men and women who experienced the Revolution in the same landscape. "For instance, right over there is one of the Watchung Mountains," he said, pointing west toward a low green ridge of volcanic origin. Less than a thousand feet at their highest, the Watchungs aren't really big enough to be called mountains—but try telling that to a British general who would have had to cross them to attack one of Washington's encampments.

Right over there. "At this time of day, this time of the year," Frazza said, the sun would be hitting them from the same angle.

He thinks about this all the time as he tries to move beyond the tendency of historical paintings to make us see the war as a kind of pageant. Two guys walking and talking here in 1776, he said, would have been "walking around in real life; they wouldn't have been walking around in a *painting*." Everyone on all sides, including people on their farms who were just hoping no soldiers showed up and took their livestock, was living in the moment: "They didn't know how this was going to turn out."

The generals didn't either. How could they?

"So much hinged on randomness," Frazza said, "like the weather changing."

Decisions made at any given moment, on or off the battlefield, "affected everything that came afterward." If one battle had gone differently, "other battles wouldn't have occurred," because the people who ended up fighting them "wouldn't have been in the same place at the same time."

People like Washington and Cornwallis, I thought, after I'd thanked Frazza and said goodbye.

We don't know where Washington would have been on January 2, 1777, if he'd come up snake eyes at Trenton the week before. He could have been dead, or hiding out somewhere behind the Watchungs. But he would not have been camped on the banks of the Assunpink waiting for Cornwallis, for the simple reason that if he had lost his Christmas gamble, Lord C would have been on a ship in the Atlantic, heading home to his much-loved, not very healthy wife.

Instead, leave canceled, he was slogging down the road from Princeton with eight thousand troops and orders to smash the rebel army once and for all.

* * *

One of the amazing things about the Second Battle of Trenton is that there was a rebel army *left* for a British general to try to smash. Washington knew his men were beyond exhausted. He could count on the fingers of one hand the number of days before most of their enlistments would run out. Yet he expected the British to come after him, and he wasn't sure what to do.

Then along came some randomness to help him make up his mind.

On December 27, Washington got word that 1,800 troops, mostly from an enthusiastic militia unit called the Philadelphia Associators, had crossed the Delaware a day late. Part of the original multicrossing plan, the Associators had been foiled by river ice, but now they were sixteen miles downriver from Trenton and itching for action. Why shouldn't he cross the river again and, taking advantage of their presence, figure out some way to wreak more havoc in Jersey?

His generals didn't like this idea, but he somehow brought them around. The crossing was scheduled for the twenty-ninth. Cold and ice messed this one up, too; it wasn't until New Year's Eve that the Continental Army was back in Trenton, in position for whatever it was its commander planned to do. But Washington couldn't plan *anything* until he knew how many men he could talk out of going home the next day.

What he told those men is subject to debate: It would be fifty-five years before a moving, much-quoted appeal attributed to him appeared in print. A more solid fact is that he promised $10 in hard currency to anyone who would stay an extra month. This was serious money at the time, but it didn't stop a lot of men from leaving anyway—among them the Marbleheaders, who knew their maritime skills could earn them a great deal more as privateers than as soldiers. Enough stuck around, however, including some whose time of service hadn't yet run out, to keep the army viable. Washington lost "about 2,600 of his Continental veterans to illness and the expiration of enlistments," Fischer writes. "But he had preserved a veteran force of about 3,300 men" to stiffen the militia now mustering to help.

Late on New Year's Day, less than twenty-four hours before what I was starting to think of as the Battle of the Rusty Pole, he and his generals were still debating their next move, an obvious possibility being to get out of Trenton ASAP. Around 9 p.m., he made his decision. Off went a message to the commander of the Associators, now seven miles away, ordering him to get his troops on the road and join the main army before dawn. Washington's idea was to concentrate his forces and fight from a strong defensive position south of the Assunpink, but he didn't have much time to prepare.

The British advance had to be slowed somehow.

Once again, randomness would do its part.

\* \* \*

Three miles north of that Trenton pole, following Frazza's directions once again, I pulled off Route 206 and into the parking lot of Notre Dame High School. The football team was practicing in the autumn twilight; a sign announced a production of *It's a Wonderful Life*. A few yards away, I found what I'd come to see: a small marker at Shabakunk Creek honoring a "successful delaying action" that deserves a major monument of its own.

Weather had already slowed Cornwallis's progress on January 2—nothing as dramatic as the Christmas storm, just a couple of unusually warm days and some rain that turned the Princeton-Trenton road into a muddy mess for men, horses, and guns. To further delay the attack, Washington had sent one thousand men under Matthias Alexis Roche de Fermoy, an itinerant French officer from the West Indies, to harass the British and Hessian column on its way south.

Good idea; wrong guy.

Before the serious action began, as historian Mark Boatner understates it, Fermoy "unaccountably left his post." Fortunately, Edward Hand was there to take his place. Hand was an Irish-born doctor and British Army veteran whose regiment of Pennsylvania riflemen had performed well in New York. Now he led them and the other units originally commanded by Fermoy, including a small artillery company, in a running fight that lasted much of the afternoon. They did their greatest damage from the south bank of the Shabakunk, surprising Cornwallis's column and forcing it to waste time forming a line of battle and bringing up its own artillery.

*It's a Wonderful Life* stars a man named George who's in big trouble before a guardian angel bails him out. Washington had this experience many times. But if you want to cast Edward Hand as the angel in this particular production, that would be fine by me.

Hand and the rest kept up the fight all the way to Trenton, where, hard pressed, they fell back toward Washington's position across the Assunpink. Out came a Rhode Island brigade to cover their retreat. "We met them, and opened our ranks to let them pass through," recalled John Howland, one of the Rhode Islanders, who were soon scrambling to get back across the bridge themselves. Little daylight remained, but the fighting continued, and to many who were there, the stakes appeared impossibly high. "On one hour, yes, on forty minutes," Howland believed, "depended the all-important, the all-absorbing question, whether we should be independent States, or conquered rebels!" To be more specific: If Cornwallis's men made it across the creek, and "unless a miracle intervened," there might have been no more American army.

What held them off during those fateful forty minutes?

It wasn't just American courage; there was courage to spare on both sides. Nor was it the kind of randomness that had influenced the timing of the confrontation.

It was Henry Knox's cannon.

Knox had at least twice as many guns available at Second Trenton (the high estimate is forty) as he'd had at the first battle. He and Washington had positioned them, Fischer writes, "with interlocking fields of fire on the critical crossings of Assunpink Creek," including several fords and especially a stone bridge at what's now South Broad Street (where I'd found the rusty pole). Time after time, the Hessians and then the British charged the bridge. Time after time the artillery, supported by Washington's infantry, drove them back. "The enemy came on in solid columns; we let them come on some ways," recalled artilleryman Joseph White. "Then, by a signal given, we all fired together." They "retreated off the bridge and formed again, and we were ready for them." The third time was no charm. "We loaded with canister shot, and let them come nearer. We fired all together again, and such destruction it made, you cannot conceive. The bridge looked red as blood, with their killed and wounded and red coats."

An infantryman would tell the story differently, and there's no question the infantry fought well at Second Trenton—but cannon were the difference makers. Knox's fire at the Assunpink, one military historian believes, "was the heaviest ever delivered on any field anywhere in the Western Hemisphere until that time."

Wisely, Cornwallis called off his attack. At daybreak, he planned to send troops across an upstream ford and smash into the rebels' right flank. Legend has him telling his generals, "We've got the Old Fox safe now. We'll go over and bag him in the morning."

Washington didn't appear to *have* a plan yet. He'd been too busy surviving today to focus on tomorrow.

The house where he and his officers finally convened to discuss this stood 175 yards south of the creek, on ground now occupied by the

Lutheran Church of the Redeemer; an old marker on the church's brick wall notes the place's importance. Standing there, I thought about the options those men considered. Crossing the river again wasn't one of them (too late, too much ice). They could retreat south, but by a difficult route that would invite pursuit and destruction. They could stay and fight, but Knox, for one, was not sanguine about the prospect. "The situation was strong to be sure," as he wrote Lucy a few days later, yet "had our right wing been defeated the defeat of the left would almost have been an inevitable consequence, & the whole thrown into confusion or push'd into the Delaware."

What choice was left?

Well, the army could tiptoe away in the middle of the night, hoping the British would be too sleepy to notice; and circle around the enemy lines on some back roads, hoping the weather would get cold enough to make them passable; and march to Princeton, hoping to arrive in time to attack its garrison before dawn. We can't be certain who first raised this idea, but Washington—who probably had it in mind himself by this time, and who liked the fact that "it would avoid the appearance of a retreat"—quickly agreed. Leaving campfires burning, a few hundred militiamen noisily digging, and a couple of howitzers lobbing occasional shells at the enemy camp, the army packed up and left.

The weather cooperated, freezing muddy roads.

The Brits did, too, overlooking or misinterpreting reports of rebel movements.

So far, so good. But Washington's sleep-deprived men, who had a roundabout route to follow, didn't make it to Princeton by dawn—and the delay allowed one more random event to threaten everything they had gained.

* * *

When I first visited Princeton Battlefield State Park, a couple of miles southwest of the main Princeton University campus, I had some trouble getting oriented. It didn't help that the park's battle map had gone missing from its stubby brick base.

Still, as I stood beside the elderly white farmhouse of Thomas Clarke—built five years before the fight and used as a field hospital afterward—the basics began to take shape in my mind. Somewhere behind me was a Quaker meetinghouse, near which Washington's army crossed Stony Brook on its backroads trek. Somewhere in front of me was the main road from Princeton, down which a British column marched with orders to reinforce Cornwallis. As the two forces met, neither could judge the other's strength, but British lieutenant colonel Charles Mawhood—whose seven hundred or so troops were in fact seriously outnumbered—chose to turn and confront the enemy. The Regulars fought with disciplined ferocity. A bayonet charge threw the rebel front line into disorderly flight. The flight proved contagious, especially after Gen. Hugh Mercer went down with multiple wounds, and soon much of the unit coming up behind Mercer's reeled back in confusion as well.

History-changing defeat seemed all too possible.

Shortly afterward came one of the bravest and most consequential acts of Washington's career. Seeing the chaos from a distance, he spurred his horse toward the line of fire, exhorted the retreating men to follow his lead, and—with the help of those previously panicked men, some steadier veterans, and whichever guardian angel was on duty as his life hung "by a single hair with a thousand deaths flying all around him"—saved the Revolution.

But where had this *happened*?

Nothing I saw that day pointed me toward the site.

Later I would learn that Washington's charge took place not in the park as then constituted, but on land owned by the Institute for Advanced Study, the noted center for "curiosity-driven basic research" whose most famous scholar was Albert Einstein. Intent on building more faculty housing, IAS had turned a deaf ear to preservationists and historians who believed, as Fischer wrote, that its land was "as central to the Battle of Princeton as the field of Pickett's Charge is to Gettysburg and as Omaha Beach is to D-Day." After years of bitter confrontation, IAS agreed to sell most of the disputed land to what's now called the American Battlefield Trust, so the story ended happily, though not before administrators had sent bulldozers to rip up the ground over which the Father of His Country had galloped to victory.

What I learned on that first visit to the park, however, was that there'd been another Revolution-saving drama that January morning—one I'd managed to overlook.

It came after the British bayonets wreaked their havoc but before Washington had time to react. Amid the spreading panic, two rebel artillery pieces went into action from the edge of a wooded area near the Clarke House, directing "intense and accurate fire" toward the advancing enemy. Commanded by a sixty-two-year-old Philadelphia sailmaker named Joseph Moulder, the guns were handled by youthful recruits from the city's docks who had seen their first combat just eight days before. Militia captain Thomas Rodney and a few of his men soon sprinted through enemy fire and crouched behind nearby haystacks to support the artillerymen.

The line between victory and defeat was thin, and one way to characterize its thinness is to say that Moulder and those artillerymen bought Washington "just enough time" to do his thing. But Rodney's diary offers a fascinating variation on this theme. What stopped Mawhood and the British from continuing their charge, he believed, was the fact that they couldn't see how few men were in position to *defend* the guns. "If they had known," he wrote, "they might easily have advanced while the two brigades were in confusion and routed the whole body." And if that had happened, as Rodney did not write, the mad-as-a-hornet Cornwallis, now marching his army back up the road from Trenton, might have showed up in time to complete the rout.

What if, what if, what if.

Mawhood's men fought bravely after the tide turned, but eventually had no choice but to run. The rebels mopped up the few remaining British in the town of Princeton and headed north to spend the winter behind the sheltering Watchungs.

CHAPTER 9

# "It Was One Afternoon in August—But It Made a Difference"

The general who took center stage when the war's next major campaign began was fifty-five years old. Summed up by one historian as a "complex man of modest talent and towering ambition," John Burgoyne came with a reputation for boldness, a side career as a playwright, and a lifelong gambling habit—though not yet, I was surprised to learn, with the nickname "Gentleman Johnny," which wouldn't be attached to him until more than a century after his death.

He was also a man with a plan—a three-pronged plan, no less, partly of his own devising—that would give him his best shot to date at the glory he craved.

It would kick off from Canada on June 13, 1777. Burgoyne himself would lead Prong One, pushing straight south into New York State with an army of British and German Regulars supplemented by Canadians, loyalists, and Native Americans. They were to head down Lake Champlain, some in boats, some on foot; retake Fort Ticonderoga; cut over to Lake George, just as Knox and his cannon had done; then make their way down the Hudson River to Albany. Prong Two, a smaller force more dependent on Native American allies, was to attack from the west via the Mohawk Valley, creating a strategic diversion. Prong Three was the responsibility of William Howe in New York City. Howe was supposed to send part of the main British army *up* the Hudson to Albany, completing the trifecta.

Just like that: Hudson River controlled, New England quarantined at last. War as good as over, right?

Well, perhaps.

Burgoyne's talent might have been modest, but he wasn't an idiot. He knew things could go wrong on campaigns and had foreseen some of the problems that might derail his. But gamblers tend to be optimists, and what's more, this particular gambler had just elbowed aside the competition to obtain his first major independent command.

Whatever his doubts, there was no chance he would fold his hand before playing it.

The months-long drama that followed is known as the Saratoga campaign—not to be confused with the Battles of Saratoga that were its culmination—and I needed a place to start following the action. Which was how I ended up in one of the most striking settings to which my travels would take me, listening to Peter Paine talk about the time Gentleman Johnny's men camped in his front yard.

\* \* \*

When Peter S. Paine Jr. was a boy, spending summers at his grandfather's place on Lake Champlain, British Army relics kept turning up in the plowed fields.

This was in the 1940s. Paine, who turned eighty shortly before we met, could have been "sent off to tennis camp on Long Island," he said, with other New York City sons of privilege. Instead, he headed upstate to the small town of Willsboro, New York, some forty miles north of Fort Ti, where his family owned a pulp mill and several miles of Champlain shoreline—including an active farm—that became his emotional home. He took care of chickens and horses and helped with the haying. The plowing was done with Percherons too big for him to handle, but he was allowed to do the harrowing afterward. And out of that plowed and harrowed ground, overlooking the lake and the blue-green mountains beyond, would come "musket balls, buttons, a buckle, and things of that nature" left behind when Major General Burgoyne stopped by for a few days in June of 1777.

I was there because I had heard you could still find traces of Burgoyne's passage through Willsboro. Paine's old friend Tom Spierto had driven me up to the same salmon-colored brick house Paine had visited when he was young. Town historian Ron Bruno had joined us on a patio overlooking one of the fields where the troops had camped.

"Just past that stone wall?" I asked, trying to picture tents and fire pits but distracted by the stunning view.

"Between there and the mouth of the river," Paine said. "We can drive down and I'll show you."

Off we bounced in his Subaru. Half the field had been mown and half not, to preserve cover for pheasants. The mouth of the Boquet River has moved over the centuries, Paine said, yet what we were seeing, as we got out to walk beside it, was "not terribly different from what Burgoyne saw." There would have been deer tracks in 1777, too, as soldiers scrambled gratefully out of their cramped bateaux, and clean blue water, and the silhouettes of four-thousand-footers like Mount Mansfield and Camel's Hump rising above Champlain's eastern shore.

There was another Willsboro site I wanted to see, and Spierto took me there later. The invading army, as noted, included Native Americans who had signed up to fight on the British side. While here, Burgoyne gave an inflammatory speech to hundreds of warriors; Bruno thought this happened on Paine land now leased to the town (for a dollar a year) and used as soccer fields. Along with his speech, the general issued a bombastic proclamation in which he threatened to "give stretch to the Indian Forces under my direction" if disloyal colonists didn't return to the fold. Speech and proclamation were angrily condemned and mercilessly mocked, but the truth is that in addition to terrifying the frontier, Burgoyne's allies—because of their wilderness fighting and scouting abilities—presented the rebels with real military problems.

Benedict Arnold knew just how to fix them, though.

When we last encountered Arnold, he was lying in a Quebec snow-bank with a musket ball in his leg. He'd had an eventful year and a half since, which I'll recap soon, but in July 1777, a month after Burgoyne's Willsboro speech, he joined the ragged rebel army the British were then chasing south. "We are dayly insulted by the Indians," he informed Washington in a letter late that month; they were wreaking havoc with rebel pickets and had recently killed and scalped a local woman "in the most shocking Manner."

His solution?

Send Daniel Morgan!

If the Virginian and his riflemen could be spared, Arnold wrote—as they would be, eventually—"we should then be in a Condition to see Genl Burgoyne with all his Infernals on any Ground they might choose."

\* \* \*

Catching up with Arnold is going to take us a while. There won't be any dull moments, though.

It took him months to recover after having that ball cut out of his leg. Then, in May 1776, the British began landing ten thousand troops at Quebec. The inevitable American retreat became a hellish ordeal, with the army "broken and disheartened," half of it diseased, "without pay, without discipline, and altogether reduced to live from hand to mouth." By mid-June, with one of the generals sent north to take over from Arnold already having died of smallpox, it had reached a swampy island in the Richelieu River, just north of Lake Champlain, where the infections peaked. A doctor reported seeing a barn full of vermin-covered men who "could not see, speak, or walk." The semihealthy were set to digging mass graves. In July, survivors staggered into bateaux and made their way south, where they eventually would be assigned to the defense of Fort Ticonderoga.

Arnold got a new assignment, too.

You can read about this on a proud historical marker in Whitehall, New York, at the southern tip of the lake, twenty-five miles below the fort. "Birthplace of the United States Navy," the title proclaims, and the text goes on to assert that a naval battle Arnold fought in October 1776, while commanding a tiny rebel fleet built here, caused the British to turn tail and sail back to Canada, thus "delaying their ill-fated march south toward the Hudson and Saratoga" for a crucial year.

It's a mind-blowing story, whether or not you buy the cause-and-effect part.

As a merchant, Arnold had sailed his own ships to Canada and the Caribbean, which gave him more maritime experience than most of his colleagues and informed his strategic vision. That said, he was hardly the only officer who knew it was vital to control Lake Champlain. Over the past year, Philip Schuyler—in charge of the army's Northern Department, but not yet Alexander Hamilton's father-in-law—had worked hard on building bateaux to move men and supplies on the lake. He'd also decided to start building gunboats, and in late July, Arnold was ordered to Whitehall, which was then called Skenesborough, to hasten their construction.

Nobody ever accused Benedict Arnold of wasting time. A month later, he led a half-built mini-armada toward the Canadian border, where the British were assembling a fleet of their own. Word was that he planned an attack, but this was a bluff. All he really wanted was to fire off a few cannon and let his enemies know—hoping it might give them pause—that they couldn't sail south without a fight.

To get an idea what Arnold had to work with, I dropped by the Lake Champlain Maritime Museum in Vergennes, Vermont, where visitors can climb aboard a replica of one of his gunboats—known as a "gondola," but with no resemblance to the Venetian kind. "It's like a pirate ship!" a woman exclaimed, but that comparison, too, misleads; the *Philadelphia* looks like an oversized bateau with a few cannon and a single mast. When I arrived, it was swarming with sixth graders asking questions about the effect of grapeshot on humans.

Afterward, I drove to the New York side of the lake to see where the original *Philadelphia* met its fate.

Naval sites are a problem for us battlefield-walking types. If I could have borrowed a canoe and recruited Duluth Wing to help, maybe I'd have paddled out to this one. Instead, following expert advice, I trespassed on the grounds of an inn and conference center in Peru, New York, maybe thirty miles south of the Canadian border, and was rewarded with a good view across the water to the southern tip of Valcour Island—behind which, on October 11, 1776, Arnold lay in wait to surprise the enemy fleet.

His idea was that the British, cruising along before a favorable wind, would sail right by the east side of the island before noticing he was there. To attack him, as James Nelson writes in *Benedict Arnold's Navy*, they would have to "come around, and work their way to windward in the face of the rebels' fire"—a better scenario for Arnold than fighting in the open lake, where British firepower, maneuverability, and naval training would make defeat inevitable.

Gazing across the strait toward Valcour, I pictured myself as a half-trained landlubber waiting to confront the best navy in the world. I could almost hear Arnold pounding a fist on a table as he told his captains: "The object of this fleet isn't to save itself! We've got just one job—to keep the British from getting through to Ticonderoga and the Hudson on this campaign—to save the lake from them for this year."

I should say right away that this is fiction. The speech comes from *Rabble in Arms*, a Kenneth Roberts novel I'd been told would give me a feel for the drama of the Valcour fight. With a few caveats, I'd still recommend it for that purpose: Roberts brings the battle to life in ways nonfiction rarely has the tools to equal, and when not indulging in passionate pro-Arnold advocacy, he sticks close to the basic military facts:

The fleets battered each other for five or six hours.

A rebel schooner was run aground and burned.

Cannon fire sent the *Philadelphia* to the bottom.

Men threw the dead overboard and kept fighting.

By dark, the British still hadn't managed to get their most powerful vessels into the battle. During the night, the American fleet snuck past its complacent enemies and sailed south. With luck, all the surviving gunboats would have gotten away (a few did anyway), but a wind change aided the pursuers, and when the British caught up, two days after the first shots were fired, more carnage resulted. Vastly outgunned but refusing to surrender, Arnold ran his remaining boats ashore in what's now Arnold Bay and burned them.

Still, hadn't he bought his side another year, giving it the chance to fight at Saratoga?

Fans of the pre-treason Arnold tend to take this lost-the-battle-but-won-the-Revolution narrative as gospel. But the more I learned about the 1776 campaign, the more skeptical I got. Arnold's move was indisputably gutsy, and he and his men had, without question, displayed a great deal of nonfictional heroism. Yet Valcour Island and its aftermath delayed the British for just three days.

How, exactly, could that have been decisive?

The whole campaign had been filled with delays, necessary or otherwise. Guy Carleton, who commanded the Crown forces, was a cautious man, and caution had served him well in Quebec City, where he'd ignored Arnold's attempts to lure him beyond the walls. Reinforcements put Carleton on the offensive in May, but the list of factors slowing a move toward Fort Ti was long—among them the need to drive the rebel army out of Canada first (details, details) and the need to build a bunch of boats because the rebels (annoyingly) had failed to leave any behind. Whether those boats could have been built faster is a complex and, to my mind, unresolved question. It has been argued, for example, that by sailing up to the border in September and firing off those cannon, Arnold made Carleton think "he had no choice but to strengthen his own armada" by building one last, humongous ship. If so, and to Arnold's great credit, this may have caused a longer delay than Valcour Island.

For whatever combination of reasons, Carleton didn't get within striking distance of Ticonderoga until late October. He looked around for a few days and—not keen on besieging ten thousand rebels there so late in the year or spending a frozen northern winter trying to keep his supply lines open—turned around and headed back to Quebec. His decision inspired some vigorous second-guessing, notably by John Burgoyne, who had served as Carleton's second-in-command that year. After sailing to London, Burgoyne put his head together with Lord Germain, the secretary of state for America, who hated Carleton. Then back he came in the spring of 1777, armed with his three-pronged plan and orders that he, not Carleton, would be in charge.

Burgoyne had no rebel army, however ragged, to drive out of Canada; no boats to build; and not much of a rebel fleet left to contend with. Small wonder Prong One was knocking on the door of Fort Ti in early July.

* * *

The best place to think about the shockingly one-sided confrontation that followed is a large hill a mile southwest of the fort. From the 853-foot summit of Mount Defiance, I could track the basic moves of the opposing armies just by rotating my head 180 degrees.

Looking to the north, for starters, I pictured the invading force moving grandly down Lake Champlain, accompanied by regimental bands. Burgoyne's army was roughly eight thousand strong, with Germans from Brunswick (not Hesse-Kassel) comprising half of it. The British Regulars disembarked on Champlain's western (New York) shore, a few miles above Fort Ti, while most of the Germans landed on the eastern (Vermont) side.

To the northeast, closer at hand, I saw the famous old bastion itself, on a peninsula jutting out from New York. The French had built it to defend against waterborne invaders from the south, so it was badly positioned to stop enemies coming from the opposite direction.

To the east, I saw a low bluff stretching toward Fort Ti from Vermont. This was Mount Independence, where the rebels built additional defensive works, hoping to create problems for attackers from Canada. Peering at the quarter-mile stretch of lake between the two positions, I imagined the narrow bridge of boats built for men to cross from one to the other.

Now for the shocking part:

Moving my head twice more—southeast, toward Hubbardton, Vermont, then south, toward Whitehall, New York—I envisioned rebels streaming away in both directions. They abandoned Fort Ti and Mount Independence in the early morning hours of July 6, just days after Burgoyne showed up.

Cakewalk! Few involved had expected this—not Burgoyne, who, anticipating a siege, had hauled some 140 artillery pieces along; not

Washington, Congress, or the citizens of the new republic, who had fancied Ticonderoga impregnable; not even King George III, who, when he heard the fort was back in British hands, "was said to have run into the boudoir of Queen Charlotte exclaiming, 'I have beat them! Beat all the Americans!'"

So what happened?

The story most often told has been that the British, being no fools, noticed that the rebels, who *were* fools, had failed to fortify Mount Defiance. Burgoyne's men promptly built a road up the back side of the hill, and the rebels, discovering this—and having miraculously regained their senses—knew they had to skedaddle before cannonballs started falling on their heads.

The real story wasn't that simple.

As I learned from Gordy Hamilton, my Ticonderoga guide, a crucial fact gets overlooked in the rebels-were-fools narrative: *They didn't have enough men to defend the forts anyway.* Had Carleton attacked in October 1776, as noted, he would have faced ten thousand defenders. Nine months later, Burgoyne faced a quarter that number—and before his troops even started building that steep road, they were poised to surround Mount Independence and Fort Ti. "If the Americans stay in the forts," Hamilton said, "they are going to have to surrender, and the entire army is going to be captured. The choice they make is kind of an obvious choice: We want to save the army."

The appearance of redcoats on Mount Defiance, then, triggered the rebel retreat, but didn't cause it. The defenders already knew that unless Burgoyne obliged them by hurling men at their strongest works, there was no way they could beat him. Arthur St. Clair, the rebel commander, talked the situation over with his officers and then did the right thing, knowing full well he would be vilified.

St. Clair had fought under Washington in New Jersey. He has been plausibly credited with suggesting (after Second Trenton) that the army could escape destruction by taking obscure back roads to Princeton. Six months later, he led most of his own army onto another obscure road—described as "a mere wagon track, cut through the woods"—that went through the village of Hubbardton. Hundreds of other men, including those unfit for duty, piled into boats and made for the Birthplace of the United States Navy at the southern end of the lake.

The British pursuit was fast and furious in both directions—but not quite fast and furious enough.

I spent a lovely sunset hour walking the Hubbardton hilltop where the men of St. Clair's rear guard held off their pursuers for almost three hours. An intense, bloody contest won by the British at high cost (and only because some Germans showed up in the nick of time), the battle arguably "saved the northern Continental army and, perhaps, the American cause." Maybe so, maybe not—but as an avid collector of turning points, I was happy to add this one to my list.

Meanwhile, most of the rebels who'd fled south in boats barely had time to get off them, at Whitehall, before their pursuers arrived. Yet they, too, would live to fight another day.

None of these events were part of Burgoyne's plan. He'd planned on *capturing* the rebel army at Fort Ti, not having to pursue it. I starred St. Clair's decision to retreat on my turning-points list, then set out to explore what else would go wrong with Prong One, Prong Two, and Prong Three.

*  *  *

On July 6, 1777, the same day John Burgoyne took Ticonderoga, Henry Clinton was in New York City going ballistic about the intentions of William Howe.

Clinton, like Burgoyne, had wintered in England, so he knew about the plans for a three-pronged campaign and the ministry's fond hope that it would end the rebellion. Not unreasonably, he assumed Lord Germain had explained to Howe that Prong Three was kind of a big deal. But Germain, whose aggressively incompetent management of the war was amplified by the difficulty of communicating across the Atlantic, had not done so—and Howe had other ideas.

Prong Three be damned. He was going to spend *his* summer vacation taking Philadelphia.

Howe was "Sir William" now, thanks to his Clinton-aided victory in Brooklyn, and Clinton was "Sir Henry" because he hated serving under

Howe so much that he had to be bribed with a knighthood to keep doing so. Deal done but Atlantic passage delayed, he sailed into New York Harbor in July to find that Howe had wasted half the campaign season already. Attacking Philadelphia now would ruin any chance for significant coordination with Burgoyne.

Could anything be stupider?

Sir Henry didn't think so.

And being Henry, he didn't zip his lip about it.

For weeks, he fought his boss "with a tenacity that even by his standards was extreme," as biographer William Willcox writes. Clinton left detailed (if hard to decipher) notes on three of the conversations, which Willcox deconstructs over ten fascinating pages, but the gist of his argument was plain enough: Philadelphia "would swallow the army" and Howe "had no prospect of ending the war there." But moving north "to make contact with the Canadian army and cut the enemy's vital communications with New England" would "impale Washington on the horns of a dilemma," forcing him to choose between "abandoning what he dared not abandon or risking everything on a battle."

Nothing Clinton said mattered. Howe sailed for Philly on July 23. Prong Three was toast.

And Prong One—though Sir Henry and Sir William didn't know this—had slowed to a crawl.

\* \* \*

To be more precise, Burgoyne came to a dead halt for two weeks and only then began crawling. But the math looks as bad either way. From Whitehall, it took him twenty-four days to move his army twenty-four miles south to Fort Edward—where he was to pick up the Hudson River—and he didn't get there until July 30. Twenty-four days! If he had just sent a flying column ahead to take the place immediately, one of his Saratoga campaign opponents believed, "he would have reached *Albany* by the end of July."

But that would have been risky—and for once, Burgoyne wasn't in a gambling mood.

To begin with, he had to rethink his plans. Prong One, as noted, was supposed to leave Fort Ti and go down Lake George. Chasing St. Clair's men south on Lake Champlain, however, had screwed this up, and Burgoyne didn't much want to march his infantry back to Ticonderoga. That would look like a retreat.

Also, he had to wait for supplies, which were on carts, which the army didn't have enough of to begin with, and which were falling apart because, guess what, they had been hastily built with green wood.

Meanwhile, his enemies—reunited, reinforced some, and now led by Schuyler—seized the chance to obstruct the already terrible road to Fort Edward. They dropped tangles of trees across it, destroyed its bridges, and dammed nearby creeks to form bogs, forcing Burgoyne's men to clear or rebuild it, mile after mile.

Finally, a few days before reaching his destination, he got word of a brutal murder that would doom his campaign, or so numerous historians came to believe.

The victim was Jane McCrea—whose killing Arnold mentioned, without naming her, in his plea for riflemen—and her story is the most famous thread now connecting Fort Edward to the war. Driving through town you can see McCrea's current resting place (her body has been dug up multiple times); a supposedly haunted house where Indian warriors might have captured her; a pyramid-shaped rock sculpture near where the Daughters of the American Revolution, in 1901, believed she died; and a modern marker that asserts, without explanation, that her death "helped to defeat General Burgoyne at Saratoga."

When I got to the Old Fort House Museum, I stopped to see if I could learn more.

"Headquarters of Schuyler-Arnold-Burgoyne-Stark," read a marker outside the yellow Dutch Colonial occupied, at different times, by those gentlemen. In one downstairs room hung a framed image of George III's little brother, after whom Fort Edward was named. In another stood an elegant sideboard probably made by Stephen Douglas, he of the debates with Abraham Lincoln in 1858.

Wait—Stephen Douglas made furniture?

"He was a carpenter's apprentice in Middlebury, Vermont," said the smart young woman showing me around. "He hated it."

The biggest surprise in the museum, though, was a small upstairs room containing, among other items, a quilt-covered bed, a violin, and an open Bible with a pair of wire-rimmed glasses sitting on one page. This was where a free Black man named Solomon Northup slept sometime in the late 1820s and early 1830s. Years later, Northup would be kidnapped, sold down the river, and enslaved on a Louisiana plantation. Finally freed, he published a harrowing memoir called *Twelve Years a Slave* that aided the abolition movement and became, 160 years later, the basis for an Oscar-winning film.

It's not clear where Burgoyne slept during his stay here, but that didn't stop me from thinking about the strange bedfellows history creates.

Eventually, the tour moved on to what I'd thought I might see: a room filled with images of the Murdered Beauty Who Saved the Revolution. There was McCrea on one knee in a pale blue dress, looking up in terror as one warrior raised his tomahawk and another yanked at her hair. There she was again, similarly posed but in a wasp-waisted frock, and again, on a white horse, turning apprehensively toward some of the warriors who surround her. At last, near an image from sheet music for "Sweet Jane McCrea"—written for the 150th anniversary of her death—I saw a wall text that explained why her killing had been declared a turning point.

"The countryside was horrified," it read, and McCrea's killing "led people throughout the region to join the American forces at Saratoga. It is said that the reaction to her untimely death was one of the major factors leading to Burgoyne's defeat."

Was this true?

I wouldn't know the answer for a while.

\* \* \*

Storm clouds gathered as I drove to my next turning point. I had abandoned Burgoyne to catch up with Prong Two—the one led by good old what's-his-name.

"You know, that guy who came in from the west," a noted Revolutionary War obsessive once said to me at a gathering of the similarly obsessed. "Begins with *L*," I thought, keeping my mouth shut because I wasn't sure. A minute later, someone nearby put us out of our amnesiac misery: Lt. Col. Barrimore Matthew "Barry" St. Leger was our man. St. Leger's fifteen minutes of fame came at Fort Stanwix, a frontier outpost in what's now downtown Rome, New York, a hundred miles west of Jane McCrea's grave. Had he made it *past* that outpost—well, the Park Service ranger showing me around the reconstructed fort was pretty sure what would have happened next.

"We would absolutely, positively, unquestionably have lost the American Revolution," she said.

St. Leger's mission, as originally envisioned, had both military and political objectives. At Fort Oswego, on the southeastern shore of Lake Ontario, he was to assemble his motley invasion force—two hundred British Regulars, a couple of sizable loyalist units, a few German troops, and as many warriors from the Iroquois Confederacy as could be persuaded to sign on—then lead them east, almost entirely by water, to the Mohawk River and on to the Hudson. In the process, he would rally the loyalists in the Mohawk Valley, the site of a bitter civil war with the rebels as well as a breadbasket for whichever side controlled it. Prong Two would siphon scarce rebel resources away from Prong One; firm up an Iroquois alliance with the British; and, in the planned happy ending, rendezvous with Burgoyne at Albany.

Fort Stanwix stood in the way of those plans.

The old wooden fort guarded a crucial portage on the route between Lake Ontario and the Mohawk. The rebels had busted their guts to repair, garrison, and supply it, and St. Leger, arriving in early August, lacked the firepower to knock down its walls or the ability to persuade its determined young commander to surrender. A siege would be required. Before it really got going, though, one of the expedition's Native American leaders received an urgent warning. His Mohawk name was Thayendanegea—the Mohawks being one of the six nations of the Iroquois Confederacy—but history knows him better as Joseph Brant.

Brant was thirty-four. He'd grown up in the middle of the Mohawk Valley, roughly sixty miles east of the fort he was helping attack.

## BATTLE ROAD – APRIL 19, 1775

Above: The Powder House, in an old drawing, and a more recent painting of the fight along the Battle Road. Right: Howard Pyle's illustration of the Battle of Bunker Hill as viewed from Boston rooftops.

The start of the carry over to Dead River

Clockwise from near left: Benedict
Arnold, in an engraved copy of a
rare image painted from life; Daniel
Morgan by Charles Willson Peale;
and a twentieth-century evocation of
the Great Carrying Place, where the
men of the Arnold expedition hauled
400-pound bateaux uphill from the
Kennebec River. Above: The earliest
known portrait of George Washington,
from 1772, when he was forty. Right:
Martha Washington at forty-one. Both
portraits are by C. W. Peale.

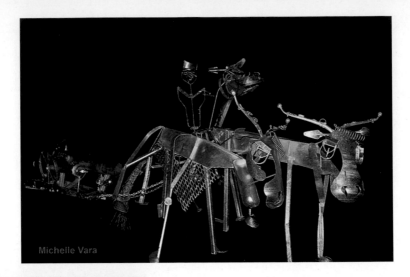

Michelle Vara

Above: Michelle Vara's marvelous, ghostly sculpture of Henry Knox, a team of oxen, and the cannon they're hauling. Left: The former bookseller turned chief of artillery, painted from life by C. W. Peale. Below: Alonzo Chappel's nineteenth-century rendering of the chaos in Brooklyn as the routed Americans tried to escape through what's now the Gowanus Canal.

Above: In a watercolor painted at the time by a British officer, Lord Cornwallis's troops climb cliffs above the Hudson to capture Fort Lee. Right: John Glover, commander of an army-saving regiment of Marblehead mariners, in a drawing by John Trumbull. Below: Durham boats lined up on the Delaware River during a reenactment of Washington's Crossing.

Above: Fort Ticonderoga, whose defenders abandoned it—with good reason—when confronted by John Burgoyne's invasion. Opposite page, clockwise from top: Burgoyne has been described as a "complex man of modest talent and towering ambition"; Horatio Gates became one of two main contenders for the title of Hero of Saratoga; the Boot Monument honors the other, Benedict Arnold. Below: Thayendanegea, also known as Joseph Brant, may have chosen the site of the deadly ambush at Oriskany.

At the Battle of Brandywine, British attackers form up at the foot of Birmingham Hill. One of them came back to make this painting a day later. Brandywine was the first battle for the Marquis de Lafayette, who was barely out of his teens.

Sometime during his childhood, valley tradition has it, his older sister, Molly, leaped onto a horse ridden by an officer at a militia muster "and hung onto him as the horse dashed about the field," attracting the attention of Indian Affairs superintendent Sir William Johnson, over whose household Molly Brant would preside "with intelligence, ability, grace and charm" until his death in 1774. However the Johnson connection began, it would change Joseph's life as well: Sir William sent him to school, where he learned English; employed him as an interpreter and a translator; and endowed him with a powerful network he could not have built on his own.

As a young man, Brant was all too aware of the relentless pressure white settlement put on his people's land. He attended a 1768 gathering, for example, at which Johnson oversaw the cession of mind-boggling swaths of territory in return for the promise of a boundary line beyond which settlers would never go, and he saw how fast that promise—and others—were violated. Late in 1775 he sailed to England as part of a delegation of Indian department officials, hoping his pleas for justice might be heard. Brant was not yet a top Iroquois leader, but the British couldn't tell the difference. He scored an audience with George III and two with Lord Germain, a man who would promise anything if it meant he could turn Indians loose on rebellious colonists, and who was unmoved by what Brant's biographer calls "as near to a lecture on good faith in government as the powerful secretary was likely to hear from anybody." Socially, meanwhile, Brant was the talk of the town: attending balls, sitting for portraits, and getting written up in a London magazine by none other than future biographical hall of famer James Boswell.

Back home, Brant worked hard—with mixed results—to talk the Iroquois nations into abandoning neutrality and fighting for the king. Then on August 5, 1777, outside Fort Stanwix, he got that urgent warning.

It was from Molly. Eight hundred rebel militiamen were on the march, his sister told him. Led by Nicholas Herkimer, an old Mohawk Valley neighbor of the Brants, they would be ten or twelve miles from the fort by nightfall.

St. Leger sent four hundred warriors and one hundred loyalists to intercept them, setting the stage for a battle far more haunting and consequential than its scale implies.

The Oriskany Battlefield State Historic Site is six miles east and a bit south of Rome, but there was little trace of the city nearby. "Green Landscape with Obelisk," a painter might call it. At the visitor center, I asked about a tour. "Okay, but we're going to get wet," Pam Mellor said, grabbing a raincoat and her broad-brimmed Smokey Bear hat. For the next hour, as a light, steady rain fell, we had the battlefield to ourselves.

Mellor had been telling the Oriskany story for two decades, and she knew how to leaven its inescapable grimness with lively narration. On the night of August 5, she said, those eight hundred rebels ("you can't really call 'em troops, you know, they were farmers, they were shopkeepers, they were the militia") camped a couple of miles east of where we stood. From there, Herkimer sent three men to try to sneak past the besiegers into the fort. If they made it, he said, " 'I want to hear three rounds of cannon fire, boom-boom-boom. That way I'll know *they* know we're on our way.'

"Next morning: nothing. No cannon fire."

Herkimer wanted to wait. Others didn't. They were in the middle of a civil war. They knew their general had a loyalist brother serving with St. Leger, "and they figured Herkimer was getting word to his brother" to get out of harm's way. So they egged him on "just like little kids: 'C'mon, I want to go, I want to go, I want to go' " until at last "he said, 'Fine, let's go,' and the way the story is told is that he and his men came down that hillside over there and down into the ravine."

There's virtue in that phrase "the way the story is told." Much remains in doubt on this small battlefield, including which of two possible ravines the military road dropped into. But for scene-setting purposes, the ravine Mellor pointed out would do. It had a stream edged with purplish flowers and a curving path down to a wooden footbridge, though we were left to imagine the old-growth trees that crowded the area before it was cleared for farming—and, of course, the eight hundred undisciplined militiamen, happy to find water, straggling along. "The horses were thirsty, so the guys kind of spread out a little bit—filling up canteens, whatever," Mellor said.

Then the ambush hit.

A marker a few feet away from us noted that "Joseph Brant, familiar with the terrain, probably selected the place," though again, the language is rightfully hedged; some historians think Seneca chiefs made the decision. Whoever it was arranged the attackers in a U shape, with the warriors on both sides of the ravine and the loyalists at the base of the U to block one exit. The idea was to draw Herkimer's whole force into the trap before closing the top of the U and surrounding the rebels entirely—and it almost worked to perfection.

"I don't know if you can have an itchy trigger finger with tomahawks," Mellor said, but before the rear of Herkimer's column was fully inside the U, some warriors "just decided, 'Hey, they're here, let's go.'"

The horrors that followed are difficult to describe. "You think of battle now," Mellor said, "and it's bombs and it's airplanes and everything. This was up close, in your face, hand-to-hand combat—bayonets, muskets, tomahawks, atlatls, you name it, the weapons they could use, they did." Hundreds of militia would be casualties that day, many of them felled in that initial "let's go" assault. Herkimer would go down early, shot in the leg and off his horse. The way the story is told, his men propped him up under a beech tree, where he calmly smoked his pipe and directed the battle. This is the chief image people have of Oriskany, Mellor said, and whether or not it's at least partly folklore—she takes no position on this—it remains indelible.

The desperate, no-quarter agony lasted for hours, during which two utterly unexpected things took place.

One was a heaven-sent intermission.

"While the battle was taking place, it rained," Mellor said. "Not a nice quiet *ahhhhh* rain like we're having today; it was a summer thunderboomer." Muskets don't work if the powder in the pan is wet, and in hand-to-hand fighting, a slip on muddy ground can be fatal. "So when it started really pouring it was as if everybody went back to their corners and waited for that weather to break." Militiamen made their way to higher ground. By the time the storm ended, they had adopted a new defensive tactic, pairing up so that while one man was reloading, the other could cover him.

And the second unexpected thing?

Herkimer's "we're on our way" message finally got through to the fort. Out sallied a couple hundred men to help. They didn't know the battle was happening, though, and they got distracted. Because—look! There were some Iroquois and loyalist camps with almost no one in them! Why not haul off everything useful and trash the rest? St. Leger's Iroquois fighters may have learned about this while the battle was still going on, though just when and how is unclear. "Somebody ran back to camp for something" is the way Mellor told it. In any case, already unhappy with their losses, they called it a day.

This left the militia holding the field. A modern marker says they "suffered 500+ casualties and lost most of their commanders," including Herkimer, who later died from his wound. With further effort out of the question, the survivors carried away the wounded, leaving the dead to the elements and the wolves.

Mellor's voice was quiet now.

"There were whole families in the Mohawk Valley that were wiped out," she said. "It was Dad and the older boys and Great-Uncle John—they all were in the militia, so they came and fought. And in some families, they were all lost." For the Iroquois, too, the battle was a nightmare. Oriskany marked the end of their long confederacy and the onset of a destructive internecine war, because for their own reasons (and despite Brant's urgings), most of the Oneidas chose to support the rebels. Perhaps sixty Oneida warriors fought alongside the militia that day.

"It may not have been a Saratoga, it may not have been a Valley Forge. It was one afternoon in August. But it made a difference," Mellor said.

With rain still falling, she pointed to a marker near a lovely maple that made a grander claim. "Near this spot," it read, "stood the beech tree which during the Battle of Oriskany sheltered the wounded Gen. Herkimer while he gave orders that made Saratoga possible and decided the fate of a nation." Erected in 1912, the marker had migrated around the battlefield—once moving to the far side of the parking lot—because nobody really knows where that mythic beech was.

Nobody knows whether Oriskany actually saved the Revolution, either. But here's what happened next:

Back at Fort Stanwix, Brant and other leaders suggested to St. Leger that he send some loyalists and Iroquois to pursue the devastated militia. They could rally more loyalists en route, allowing them to join Burgoyne with a significant force.

St. Leger said no, they had to finish the siege first.

Did someone warn him that the Iroquois had zero interest in siege warfare? If so, he didn't listen. Then came word that Benedict Arnold was on his way.

Schuyler had sent Arnold west with as many men as he could spare and orders to relieve the siege. Arnold accomplished this with what historian John Luzader calls an "application of psychological warfare that has few parallels in American history and folklore." The rebels had foiled a poorly designed loyalist plot and sentenced the plotters to hang. Among the condemned was a man usually described as not quite right in the head, whose mother and brother showed up to plead for his life. This gave one of Arnold's officers an idea, and Arnold ran with it. I'll spare your life, he told the man, if you'll go tell the Iroquois at the fort that I'm on my way *really soon* with an army that's *way* too big for them to deal with. Off the fellow went, with his brother held hostage for his good faith.

It's unclear what the recipients of this message made of Arnold's ploy. But we do know, Luzader writes, that it gave them "an excellent excuse for doing what they wanted to do," which was to forget Fort Stanwix and go home.

Prong Two was dead.

Prong Three wasn't happening.

It was time to go back to Prong One and see another small, stunning battlefield, 120 miles to the east.

\* \* \*

The Battle of Bennington wasn't fought at its Vermont namesake, though that town boasts a memorial obelisk three times as big as Oriskany's, but in Walloomsac, New York, a few miles across the state line.

The historic site was unstaffed when I showed up, but a short walk past the gate and up a gravel road—I'd been told this was okay—took me to a grassy hilltop where I could explore, in an almost eerie quiet, my last pre-Saratoga turning point.

The battle took place on August 16, six days before the siege of Fort Stanwix would be abandoned. But no one knew that was about to happen, and John Burgoyne had been behaving as if everything were fine.

Burgoyne was still in the vicinity of Fort Edward, getting ready to move down the Hudson. On August 3, he'd gotten a weeks-old message from Howe—which said, in effect: *Off to Philly! Good luck up there!*— but the Man with a Plan had not felt it necessary to share this news with his subordinates. It was no secret, however, that his supply lines were dangerously long, so he detached around seven hundred men and sent them into Vermont with orders to, among other things, rustle up some grub.

Monday morning quarterbacks have had a field day with this decision, and it's hard to disagree with their judgments. Burgoyne sent the wrong troops and not enough of them; put the wrong man in charge; and gave Friedrich Baum far too many objectives: In addition to raiding a rebel supply depot at Bennington, the German colonel was supposed to recruit American loyalists, acquire a thousand horses, and dupe New Englanders into thinking the whole army was veering off in their direction. Blind overconfidence was surely a factor, as it had been throughout Burgoyne's campaign.

But hey, how was he to know that cranky old John Stark would show up at precisely the wrong time?

Just weeks earlier, Stark—a born leader who has also been accurately described as "contentious, suspicious, opinionated . . . and contemptuous of authority to the point of insubordination"—had been sulking in his figurative New Hampshire tent. After his defense of that vital beach at Bunker Hill, he had accepted a commission in the Continental Army and shared its triumph at Trenton, but when a lesser man (in his view) had been promoted over him, he had quit in disgust. Stark's beef was with Congress and the Continentals, though, and he was the kind of bold, experienced commander his state needed in the face of the Burgoyne threat. Asked in July to take charge of the New Hampshire militia, he said sure, as long as I don't have to take orders from *those* guys. By August, he and nearly 1,500 men were poised to join the fight. Before they did, however, a Continental general named Benjamin Lincoln showed up with orders for Stark's men to join the main army on the west side of the Hudson.

No way, said Stark. We're going to stay on the east side and harass Burgoyne whatever way we think best.

Go for it, said Lincoln, whose pragmatic capitulation could be said to make him an accidental hero of the Saratoga campaign.

Because look: Here came Baum & Co., marching blindly and optimistically into Stark's wheelhouse.

The preserved hilltop is only part of the battlefield, but it's an evocative one. Steep-sloped and green, it has granite memorials honoring the militiamen from New Hampshire, Massachusetts, and Vermont who converged there, as well as more recent markers that lay out Stark's battle plan. Baum, belatedly seeing he was in trouble, had fortified the hilltop and sent for help. Stark, who had more than twice as many men, sent hundreds of them tiptoeing around each enemy flank; once they were in position, he would strike from the front as well. We're talking double envelopment, for those of you scoring at home, and Luzader—who calls this maneuver "the most difficult tactic available," even for seasoned veterans—thinks Stark was courting disaster by trying it with militia. But it worked out, as did pretty much everything else John Stark and his impromptu army did on August 16.

Baum's Germans fought bravely but surrendered after their commander received a mortal wound. When the requested reinforcements finally showed up, so did some of Col. Seth Warner's Vermonters, who helped send them packing. "With one hour more of daylight," Stark wrote, "we should have captured the whole detachment"—but even so, the Bennington disaster shrank Burgoyne's invasion force by nearly a thousand men.

Still alone on the hilltop, I walked down an unmarked path into the woods. Might it intersect with the route the militia took as they encircled Baum?

It seemed likely, but I saw nothing to confirm this—just a clearing with a deer in it, about where I guessed Stark's double-envelopers would have been.

# CHAPTER 10

# The Accidental Battle That Won the Revolution

I had no intention of walking around Saratoga National Historical Park without a guide. It was home to the Mother of All Turning Points, after all, and having toured it on my own, a decade earlier, I knew how confusing it could be. For one thing, what many of us think of as the Battle of Saratoga was really two separate battles fought on the same ground eighteen days apart. For another, the story has been complicated further by a fierce historical brawl over which general deserves credit for these critical victories. Was it Horatio Gates, the newly appointed commander of the northern army and, as such, the obvious Hero of Saratoga? Or was it Benedict Arnold, whose backers argue that he was a hero before he turned traitor, and that he did the heavy Saratoga lifting, both tactical and physical, while Gates stayed behind the rebel lines in a defensive crouch?

"I lean toward being a non-Arnold fan," Jim Hughto warned when I called to ask about arranging a tour. This proved a serious understatement, but didn't keep me from being extremely glad I'd hired him.

Hughto was an official Saratoga Battlefield guide, one of two independent contractors then authorized to offer the kind of personalized tours the park itself lacked the staff to provide. A gray-haired, solidly built man in his sixties, he had worked with a lot of psychologists before retiring from what's now New York's Office for People with Developmental Disabilities, and he often began comments on the foibles of Saratoga notables by saying dryly, "I look at it from a behavioral perspective." He'd been studying the battles for nineteen years, beginning as a park volunteer, a process that had left him with well-informed and strongly held opinions. But like all good students of history, Hughto had revised his views as he got deeper into his subject, and he made it clear that the tour I'd be getting would be more than a recitation of incontrovertible facts.

"We have an *interpretation* here," he said. "That's why we're historical *interpreters*."

Starting from the visitor center on a damp September afternoon, we set out to walk as much of the battlefield as we could, covering the two battles sequentially. The main thing we'd be skipping was the line of American defensive works on the bluffs overlooking the Hudson, where no actual fighting happened. River and fortifications are both central to the Saratoga story, however, so a brief recap is in order.

After the Bennington debacle, Burgoyne spent weeks pulling together what supplies he could from the north. On September 13, about ten miles downriver from Fort Edward, he began moving his army across a bridge of boats to the west bank. Then he ordered the bridge disassembled. He needed the boats to float his supplies to Albany, assuming he could fight his way past the rebel army—current size and location unknown—that would be trying to stop him.

Horatio Gates, meanwhile, was building fortifications. Like Charles Lee, he was an ambitious former British Army officer reborn as a revolutionary. Sent north in 1776, he had shored up what was left of the force retreating from Canada and started pushing to replace Schuyler as head of the Northern Department. It took a while, but by late August 1777, Schuyler was gone—done in by political enemies amid a spasm of "Who Lost Ticonderoga?" finger-pointing—and Gates took command.

None too soon, in my guide's view: You didn't want Schuyler deciding where you were going to fight a major battle. Gates took a quick look at his predecessor's chosen position and promptly marched the army fifteen miles farther north, along the west side of the Hudson, to some much better terrain at a place called Bemis Heights.

"That's an aggressive move," Hughto said—because now he was just seven miles from Burgoyne.

Aggressive but defensive, too: As we walked a mostly open, rolling section of the Saratoga Battlefield park toward our first stopping place— a medium-sized hillock on a ridgeline within sight of the visitor center but not the Hudson—Hughto gave me a tutorial on how difficult it would be to get past the new American position.

Could Burgoyne's men push south on the riverbank?

No. Defensive works, including the bluffs on which Gates concentrated cannon, made that a bad idea, as did another terrain feature called the Great Vly—"vly" being a Dutch term Hughto translated as "swamp wannabe"—which would further muck things up.

How about if they went straight at the rebel center?

Not a good idea, either. Deep ravines made that route inhospitable.

So their only choice was to attack the American left?

Yep. Assuming they wanted to attack at all.

Gates knew his left was the least secure part of his line, which was why he put his headquarters and his best troops there. Burgoyne, by contrast, "had no idea where the American left *was*." Most of his Native American allies had abandoned him by now, and the scouts he did manage to send out kept getting intercepted.

Not a lot of good options here.

"Military theorists from 500 BC on have basically advised that when faced with a situation like this, you retreat," Hughto said. "You pull back, lure the enemy..."

Hang on, I asked—what kind of situation, exactly?

"Strongly entrenched enemy across broken ground. You pull back and try to deal with the enemy where the odds are more in your favor. It's what Julius Caesar did at the Battle of Pharsalus." Long story. Caesar wins. "But what does Burgoyne do? He decides to attack."

On the morning of September 19, he splits his army into three parts. He keeps the Germans by the river, where his boats and irreplaceable supplies remain; sends a center column west and then south toward those problematic ravines; and orders a trusted subordinate, Brig. Gen. Simon Fraser, to move even farther west and south, toward the hilltop where Hughto and I now stood. Fraser's mission is to find and attack the left wing of the main rebel defenses. But there's a problem: The two attacking British columns, Fraser's and the center, are out of communication. Why? Because Burgoyne—instead of staying behind those columns, where he could coordinate their movements—has embedded himself with the center. "He wants to be close to the fight," Hughto said.

No good will come of this.

Hughto led me down from what he called Fraser's Hill, across some swales and a lower ridge, then down again to a creek hidden in some woods. Advance elements of the British center were supposed to cross this creek and keep heading south. The walk took us a while: "It illustrates just how far apart those columns were." At some point, each fired a cannon to let the other know it was ready to roll. Across the creek went British scouts, and up the slope on the other side. Ahead of them was a stump-strewn clearing with a house and a few outbuildings in it.

"This is where the scouts emerge—along the tree line," Hughto said, pointing.

Then he led me out of the woods, to where loyalist John Freeman's farmhouse once stood, and began telling a story you might call the Accidental Battle That Won the Revolution.

* * *

"Here we are at Freeman's farm, September 19, 1777," he began. It's near midday. The British scouts emerge from the woods. "American scouts have been posted along here, behind fence posts, behind tree stumps, etc."

Right where we're standing?

"Yeah—and now they're firing away. But they have rifles. The British have muskets. Muskets can be reloaded and fired three to four times a minute; a rifle takes over a minute to reload. The rest of Morgan's command is on that high ground out there—see where the knoll is?—and in the trees beyond that."

Daniel Morgan update: Back from imprisonment in Canada, he and a new brigade of riflemen have been sent north, as Arnold hoped. Dispatched this day to harass the oncoming enemy, most have just now reached the edge of Freeman's cleared fields, perhaps a mile and a half in front of Gates's fortified line.

"They hear firing. The riflemen, not being terribly disciplined, are running across the field to rescue their brethren here. Then you have Dearborn's light infantry, they're more disciplined—they are *marching* down."

Henry Dearborn update: He, too, is back from Canada, albeit without his dog.

More British troops now double-time it across the stream to join the fight. "This is why Jomini would call it an 'accidental battle,'" Hughto explained. "It starts with the scouts, then all of a sudden new forces are being drawn in." Give yourself points if you recognize Antoine-Henri Jomini as the author of *The Art of War*.

"So Morgan's men are rescuing their brethren, and they succeed. They drive the British scouts back." But here come those additional Brits, and now, up on his hill to the west, Simon Fraser hears firing and "sends elements of *his* force in this direction. They come through the woods and hit the Americans in the flank." At which point the riflemen—"What did I say? Not terribly well disciplined?"—run for their lives.

As the pace of Hughto's storytelling sped up, I stopped trying to grasp precisely where different units were moving and when, focusing instead on a stream of action images. The riflemen sprint for shelter in some trees...somewhere. Dearborn's more-disciplined guys retreat toward...where they came from. The First New Hampshire shows up to help...on some part of the field. Dearborn sees this and "orders his men to double-time across in support." The Brits load a couple of six-pound cannon with grapeshot and...uh-oh. "The First New Hampshire gets blasted with grapeshot and breaks immediately." Dearborn's guys "do a U-turn and end up...over there in the trees."

By moving there, Hughto said, Dearborn "basically puts himself between Fraser and the center column." Hold that thought.

More Americans pour into the battle. Some of the newcomers see the First New Hampshire running away and say, essentially, "Where the heck are *you* guys going?" So they all head over to join Dearborn's line. Pretty soon, "the American line is like an S curve. It's a very weird line." Morgan and the riflemen are on the opposite end of the S from Dearborn. "The British think they're completely out of the picture, but you know, they're being quiet, climbing trees—they're setting *up* over there!"

Meanwhile, "the British have decided, 'Ah! We're going to turn the American left!'"

"Left" here means Dearborn's end of the S curve, not the elusive left of the overall rebel defenses. Out march three regiments from the British center, and two of them angle out to hit the American flank. It's a classic maneuver, Hughto said, and in the textbook version, you'd send troops from one of your *own* flanks to attack the enemy in *addition* to sending those men from the center. Which means, in this case, that you'd order Fraser to hustle down from his hill and help.

"Makes sense, doesn't it?"

Simon Fraser is a forty-eight-year-old Scotsman who served under James Wolfe at Quebec and befriended Burgoyne during the 1776 campaign. This July, after the rebels fled Ticonderoga, Fraser pursued them with great energy, though he had to be bailed out by the Germans at Hubbardton. In today's battle, as we've seen, he has already sent a few of his troops—on his own initiative—to help out near the Freeman farm. Now those two regiments from the center are angling out, and Dearborn's men are at the end of that S curve, ripe for the picking, and what does Fraser do?

He does nothing.

And where is Burgoyne?

In the center, busy not telling Fraser to attack.

And what happens next?

Terrible things, from the British point of view.

The Sixty-Second Regiment of Foot, in particular, gets hung out to dry. They're blasted by musket fire from the front and the riflemen "are picking them off from behind." Eventually the Sixty-Second collapses: "They've lost about two-thirds of their men, killed and wounded." And with them, the attempt to turn the rebel flank collapses, too.

The accidental battle rages on for the rest of the afternoon. Back on the attack, the rebels try to turn a *British* flank. William Phillips, a general Hughto has come to admire, rallies the Brits. Some Germans show up, once more, at a crucial moment. And look, here comes Simon Fraser! Too late! Still more rebel units have joined the fight, and he's driven back. Now the sun's going down, "the Americans can't *see* the British, and they're out of ammunition," so they fall back to their defensive line.

Technically, this makes September 19 a British victory: They held the field. Yet Burgoyne suffered some six hundred casualties, twice as many as his foes. He can't replace them. He's no closer to Albany. And the army that fought him to a standstill continues to block his path.

So who should get the credit, I asked, for putting this devastating hurt on the invasion—besides, of course, the ordinary soldiers who mastered their fears and fought with such furious determination?

I expected Hughto to say simply "Horatio Gates." But his real answer was both more measured and more provocative.

"It's Arnold's division fighting," he said, almost half the army. "He orders the men onto the field," though he does so from behind the scenes. At one point, with yet another unit about to head into the fray, Gates "makes a weak protest" but doesn't order that unit back. Bottom line: "I say the decision to move forward is both Gates's and Arnold's."

Except here comes the provocative part:

Hughto thinks that decision was *wrong*, because it put the army at too much risk. "It was a formula for disaster," he said. "Because if Fraser had coordinated his move..."

We were back in the moment when those British regiments advanced against Dearborn while Fraser—did not. "If it had been a coordinated attack," Hughto said, Dearborn's light infantry would have been swept away "and the American left would have caved." Goodbye First New Hampshire, and goodbye Morgan, too: "The riflemen would have seen that they were in a difficult situation and booked out of there."

So: a whole different battle. And what would have come next is impossible to know.

* * *

The British spent the night of September 19 camped on the ground they paid such a price to win, but they didn't sleep. "Burgoyne suspects the Americans are going to do a sneak attack," Hughto said, "so he has his men stand on their arms—stay awake all night, with loaded weapons— and wait for that attack." No attack comes. But the dead and wounded "are still out there on the field" and the men standing on their arms spend the night listening to the wounded "crying out in pain, asking for water, calling for their mothers." On the morning of the twentieth, Burgoyne "orders the army out to attack the American left. Still doesn't know where it is."

It's not a popular idea.

"His generals—they stomp their feet, basically. They say, 'Time out! You just had the men stay up all night. We've got all these dead and wounded out there.'" So Burgoyne postpones the attack for a day, until the twenty-first.

Then he gets a letter from Henry Clinton and starts thinking differently.

Sir Henry has been fuming the summer away in New York, left with barely enough men to defend the city after Howe sailed off toward Philadelphia. But now he tells Burgoyne that he might (assuming he gets some timely reinforcements) be able (ten days after that) to create a diversion by heading up the Hudson to take some enemy forts near West Point (more than one hundred miles from the Saratoga battlefield). Burgoyne grabs at this faint hope, cancels his attack, and spends the next two weeks fortifying his position. Maybe Gates will march off to deal with Clinton, leaving the road to Albany open! Maybe pigs will fly!

And what are his enemies doing during those weeks?

"We're doing something basic to Americans," Hughto said. "We're fighting with each other."

The intramural clash, at least as the tale is usually shorthanded, began with a self-serving report Gates sent Congress in which he failed to mention Arnold or note that Arnold's division had done most of the fighting on the nineteenth. Learning of this, Arnold marched over to Gates's headquarters, and a shouting match ensued. ("Matters were altercated in a very high Strain," as one observer put it.) He came back and wrote Gates impassioned letters that can be summed up as: "You've ignored me and disrespected me and I'd rather go work for George." Gates wrote terse replies that added up to: "Don't let the door hit you on your way out." Acolytes of both men poured fuel on the fire. In the end, Arnold decided to stay, but was left, as the story went, with no troops to lead.

"He's sort of relegated to a command of one: himself," Hughto said. "It's a very strange situation."

I found it hard to root for either side.

Why *did* Gates send that Arnold-free letter? Did he feel dissed because his subordinate ignored his protest against sending more men forward? Should we think of him, from a behavioral perspective, as a fifty-year-old journeyman with his first shot at fame and no interest in sharing it? As for Arnold: Even if he was in the right, why couldn't he take a deep breath and walk away instead of publicly calling out his boss when both men should have been focused on the common enemy?

Short answer: Because then he wouldn't have been Benedict Arnold.

"He's a confrontational person," Arnold biographer James Kirby Martin told me later. "He doesn't take slights easily, and he will always challenge you." Martin's book is an original, carefully researched attempt to understand who Arnold was without always seeing him through the frame of his future treason. He thinks his subject's combativeness flowed out of a hatred for arbitrary authority acquired early in life.

Still, if he could go back and give Arnold advice about the blowup with Gates, he would say: "Calm down! You can't personalize every situation. You have to let some of this stuff go."

* * *

Burgoyne and his generals, meanwhile, are hardly acting like a big happy family, either. Hughto picked up their story as we walked a lovely green trail in the woods toward where the next battle will break out.

It's two weeks after the first one, with no word from Clinton, supplies low, desertion up, and the rebels getting stronger daily. Fraser and Friedrich von Riedesel, the German commander, argue that it's time to retreat, but Burgoyne won't hear of it. "He proposes an all-out attack against the American left. *Still* doesn't know where it is." The generals talk him out of this, but agree to an almost equally iffy compromise. They will send a smaller "reconnaissance in force" (upwards of 1,500 picked men) in the same direction, with Burgoyne promising to fall back if good things don't happen. Good things almost certainly will not. The force in question is "too large to be undetected and too small to be effective," Hughto said, before describing a scene that seemed surreal.

By this time, we'd arrived at a broad expanse of open ground less than half a mile south of Freeman's farm. On October 7, 1777, Burgoyne's grenadiers—"they're the best soldiers in the world"—march out into this field and sit down. Why? "Because there's wheat growing here," Hughto said. "They're hungry. They've sent back for foragers to gather the wheat." It's a window on the precarious state of Prong One: Some of the world's best soldiers are marching into unknown territory, against long odds, with stomachs so empty they can be distracted by a field of wheat.

"Do they know the Americans are here?" I asked.

They do not. But they're about to find out.

When the attack comes, it's led in part by the same tough New Hampshire men who fought in the first battle. "The grenadiers blast away," expecting the rebels to turn and run. It doesn't happen. "Boom! The psychological advantage switches—and now the grenadiers are second-guessing themselves." Both sides have bayonets, "and it's hand-to-hand right here where we're standing." Other rebels have attacked other parts of the British line, so far with mixed results.

But here come Daniel Morgan and Henry Dearborn.

Morgan and Dearborn are on a wooded hill, Hughto said, overlooking the British right. "They consult with each other and say, 'Gee, what will happen if we just come running down this hill yelling and screaming?'—and it's kind of like, 'Hey, let's try it.'" Down they come, then. The British don't fire a shot; they just run." Now "the right is collapsing, the left is collapsing," and the Germans in between have to pull back, too.

Running, collapsing, pulling back: It sounds like the end.

Burgoyne's generals, however, including Riedesel and Phillips, do their best to rally the men, "and then you have Fraser, and he's trying to stabilize the right. It works!" Briefly. "But now Fraser is being pretty conspicuous, and he's attracted the attention of Daniel Morgan," who puts some riflemen in trees.

Fraser goes down with a wound that will kill him.

A granite marker near where Hughto and I were talking commemorated the moment. On its top, someone had placed six pennies in the shape of a cross. "Here Frazer fell," the text began, misspelling his name and getting the place wrong. In reality, he was shot "about three hundred yards in that direction," Hughto said, pointing down the road we would walk to the site of the Second Battle of Saratoga's dramatic finale. Which happened to be in the same place the First Battle of Saratoga had begun.

Confusing. Except that by this time, I understood more or less what was going on.

Among the fortifications Burgoyne built after the first battle were two redoubts at Freeman's farm. Nothing remains of them, but the locations are marked. The larger and more formidable was to our right as we approached. The smaller, farther on and to our left, wasn't as strong. Known as the Breymann Redoubt, after its German commander, it was really just a log wall "open in the back." It was these redoubts toward which Burgoyne's men retreated, with the rebels in pursuit.

"And now we're going to pick it up with our friend Mr. Arnold," Hughto said.

The way this part of the story has usually been told, Arnold starts out back in camp, forbidden to command any troops—but look, here he comes, spurring his horse into the thick of the action! He leads a charge against the stronger redoubt (which does not succeed), then gallops through a hail of bullets to lead an attack on the weaker one (which does). In a related version, Arnold rides out of camp and orders that first, failed attack but doesn't lead it, because he rides off before it begins. Nor does he lead the attack on the weaker redoubt: He simply joins what Morgan and others have already begun. But in both versions he's the first American to ride into the open back of the Breymann Redoubt, and no one disputes what happens next. He takes a bullet in the left leg, the same leg as in Quebec, and his horse crashes down on him. One bullet and multiple fractures add up to a gruesome wound.

Standing at the site of the redoubt, Hughto takes off the ball cap he is wearing.

"You're not going to see me doff my hat too much to Arnold," he said, "but Benedict, that was a brave thing to do."

The fight continues and the redoubt falls. With rebels now behind their lines, the British abandon the stronger one. They finally retreat, but don't get far: Gates sends troops up the east side of the Hudson to stop them from recrossing the river. On October 17, 1777, ten days after the second battle, Burgoyne hands Gates his sword. And 110 years after *that*, the weirdest Revolutionary War monument ever created goes up a few yards from where Hughto took off his cap. It's the size and shape of a gravestone. Engraved text names the donor but not the honoree, describing him only as "the 'most brilliant soldier' of the Continental Army who was desperately wounded on this spot" while "winning for his countrymen the Decisive Battle of the American Revolution." Sculpted on the other side is a boot topped by an epaulette and a hero's laurels.

The message comes through loud and clear, Hughto said: "Benedict Arnold, the Hero of Saratoga! Crown him with laurels!"

By now, my guide had put his cap back on. It stayed on as he laid out the details of Arnold's treason and summed up what he had come to believe, after years of study, about the man's leadership in the fall of 1777.

"We'd have won here without him," he said.

* * *

Hughto's tour was a revelation to me. It enriched the Saratoga narrative in ways I couldn't have done on my own, and it left me full of questions we didn't have time for. But here are two I didn't even dream of asking: Could new evidence appear that would rewrite the story of the most important turning point of the Revolutionary War? And if it did, might Hughto's boss find himself smack in the middle of that rewriting?

Yes and yes. But nobody had a clue this would happen when I dropped in at the visitor center, shortly after the tour, to see Eric Schnitzer.

Intense, fast-talking, and not quite forty at the time, Schnitzer is widely recognized as a leading expert on the battle. He started working at the park in his early twenties, and as one of the historians who vetted Hughto and the other authorized guide, he confirmed that the two have wildly different takes on Arnold's role. "We encourage that," he said, as long as they can "back up what they say with evidence."

One question I needed help with was about Jane McCrea: Had her death, as I'd read in Fort Edward, truly roused the countryside to help defeat Burgoyne?

It had not, Schnitzer told me. And his explanation was illuminating.

A good number of militiamen did come out eventually, and they did bolster the army at the second battle—but the connection between "the outpouring of militia and McCrea's death" is a myth. "Militia were only ordered out by government, either the state or the county," he said, and if you look at militia orders from 1777, McCrea's killing is never mentioned. "They're simply looking to stop this British invasion."

Really? Then what took them so long?

Well, as long as Burgoyne stayed east of the Hudson, many in New England "were convinced his destination was the Connecticut River Valley" and wanted to keep their men home. After he crossed to the west side, it was safe to release them.

Another question: How had Arnold's image come to change, in the twentieth century, from pure evil traitor to someone who could even *begin* to be seen as a hero?

Schnitzer's answer: Kenneth Roberts did it.

The novelist didn't invent the New Arnold by himself, he said, but 1933's *Rabble in Arms*, along with its predecessor, *Arundel*, brought this rehabbed character before a wide audience. *Rabble* leaves no doubt of its Manichean view of Arnold vs. Gates, contrasting the former's near-godlike Saratoga performance with the charge that no one "came closer to bringing about our overwhelming defeat" than the latter.

Schnitzer did not share this view, and he brought up one point in favor of Gates that I'd never considered. Saratoga's importance doesn't lie just in the battles, he said, because what happened *afterward* was crucial. If Burgoyne's army had been allowed to straggle back north instead of being forced to terms, "you don't have the turning point of the Revolutionary War. You don't have the French alliance." No British army had ever surrendered before—"I don't mean just in the Revolution; I mean ever"—so this got Paris's attention big-time. And deciding to force the surrender, of course, had nothing to do with Arnold, who was "down in hospital being operated on."

That said, the Americans had to win the battles before the surrender could happen. Who did *he* think deserved credit for those victories?

Schnitzer took it one battle at a time.

"Arnold was brilliant in the Battle of Freeman's Farm," he said, while Gates "was for all intents and purposes of no consequence, for good or ill." It was Arnold who suggested that the army leave the security of its fortifications to attack the British. And yes, he knows Hughto thinks this was too risky, but he doesn't agree.

And the second battle?

"Gates gets the strategic plus, because it's his decision alone that sent out the troops to attack." As for Arnold's heroics, it's tempting to think they were important—"how can you not give wonderful credit to this guy who is once again putting his life on the line?"—but in reality, they were "almost irrelevant" to the result.

So the score was Arnold 1, Gates 1.

I left with no reason to disagree.

The next time I saw Eric Schnitzer, however, he would be standing in front of a couple hundred Revolutionary War obsessives telling them that the history of Saratoga had changed, and laying out precisely how—along with almost every other historian for two centuries—he had come to be so terribly wrong.

\* \* \*

The change arrived in his inbox in the form of an email from Larry Arnold (no relation), the second of the two official Saratoga Battlefield guides. The email included a link to an eBay sale of a letter dated October 9, 1777. The sale had ended, but the letter was still available to viewers online, so Schnitzer took a screenshot and started to read.

"I remember getting up out of my chair," he said, "and thinking: This is one of those moments in life that you'll always remember."

He was telling this story in Colonial Williamsburg at the seventh annual Conference of the American Revolution. Run by a husband-and-wife enterprise called America's History, LLC, these gatherings draw an impressive mix of public and independent historians, academics, and serious amateur students of the war. This year's most riveting talk was Schnitzer's, and it included a review of what he called the "historical orthodoxy" about the October 7 battle, including the Gates-Arnold explosion that preceded it.

"These guys apparently were still not on speaking terms," he said. "According to various versions of this story, Benedict Arnold has been relieved of *command*; Benedict Arnold was under *arrest...*" He hears the sound of battle, knows his men are being sent to fight, and decides to go out there with them. "Again, according to variations of the story, he steals a horse; he's hatless; he clocks one of his own officers on the head, apparently accidentally. One of my favorites is that he gets drunk before the fighting—dipper full of rum, quote unquote...And obviously, as you all know, Benedict Arnold was famously wounded in the left leg near the ankle while assaulting the Breymann fortification."

Two days later, Nathaniel Bacheller sat down and wrote the letter to his wife that so stunned Schnitzer when it came to light.

Bacheller was a staff officer in one of two New Hampshire militia regiments that had recently joined Gates's army. On October 2, he had written a more prosaic letter home that historians already knew about. Now Schnitzer walked us through key parts of Bacheller's October 9 letter, a transcript of which had been handed out. Erratic spelling and punctuation make it hard to read, so what follows are four points I've condensed and neatened up considerably, with some of Schnitzer's explanations added. Only the italicized part of the last line is an exact quotation.

- On the afternoon of the battle, the newly arrived regiments were ordered to join Arnold on the left of the rebel defenses (where Arnold's headquarters were).

- From there, Arnold and an aide rode into the woods to view the enemy, who were then engaged with the riflemen (Morgan's guys).

- Gates soon arrived at our lines, inquired for Arnold, and was told he was out viewing the enemy.

- Returning, Arnold told Gates that the enemy plan was to take possession of a hill about a quarter of a mile to our west... The cannon began to sound in our ears, along with small arms. Arnold said to Gates, *"it is Late in the Day but Let me have men & we will have some Fun with them Before Sun Set,"* upon which the brigades began to march.

Schnitzer scarcely needed to point out how all this disrupts the established story line. "No account we have ever heard of," he said, talks about Arnold and Gates having "a determined conversation, a *sane* conversation—they're not yelling and screaming at each other—about the strategy with regard to the battle."

Now all he had to do was decide whether it was true.

He found three other eighteenth-century sources, all "people who were actually there in the camp who wrote about it." The first was Brig. Gen. Oliver Wolcott, who in a letter three days after the battle mentioned that "Arnold came up with a reinforcement" at about 4 p.m. ("He's not joining the reinforcement," Schnitzer emphasized. "He commands it.") Next was Benjamin Lincoln, the second-ranking officer on the field that day, who wrote in 1799 that Gates "ordered General Arnold to advance with the left, where he commanded." Finally, there was James Wilkinson, at the mention of whom some in the audience began to laugh.

On October 7, 1777, Wilkinson was a twenty-year-old aide to Gates. Nearly four decades later, he published a detail-rich memoir that was and remains catnip for historians, despite being widely mistrusted today. "Take James Wilkinson's *Memoirs of My Own Times*," Jim Hughto had advised me, "and if it's not a rare book, start a fire with it." Schnitzer had a more positive take on the man's indisputable unreliability, however—because it ended up proving his case.

As Wilkinson worked on his 1816 memoir, Schnitzer said, he wrote to officers with whom he'd served, saying, "Hey, could you give me a narrative of events that you participated in along with me?" Then he incorporated what they sent into his book. This wasn't a problem in itself; at the time, it was "something authors did." But the way Wilkinson used the material sent by Henry Dearborn was something else.

What he got from Dearborn included this statement:

"As usual the light troops advanced and soon received orders from General Arnold to file to the left," to "a semi-eminence" from which they were to "advance in a direction to meet the enemy."

Schnitzer underlined why the statement mattered:

"We have Henry Dearborn giving Arnold direct credit for the specific deployment of Morgan's corps, which is the riflemen and the light infantry, to that high ground."

And what did Wilkinson do?

He deleted Arnold from this part of the narrative and replaced him with . . . James Wilkinson! He claimed to have scouted the British position himself; reported what he saw to Gates; and been sent on to tell Morgan "to begin the game." He couldn't ignore the presence of Arnold on October 7 entirely, of course—but he could make stuff up, claiming that the sidelined general rode around camp "betraying great agitation and wrath"; that he "was observed to drink freely"; and that he showed up "on the field of battle exercising command, but not by the order or permission of General Gates."

Wilkinson's readers, in 1816 and beyond, had no trouble believing a notorious traitor could have run amok this way. Historians didn't, either, over the following two centuries.

Schnitzer, his time nearly up, left us with a few thoughts about the way the Bacheller letter changed history. I'll mention two that particularly struck me:

First, Arnold and Gates *both* look better now. The letter doesn't prove they were friends. "Absolutely not." But it does show that they could behave like grown-ups "with the enemy on their proverbial doorstep."

Second, he could declare a winner—finally!—in the Hero of Saratoga Bake-Off.

His scorecard used to read "Arnold 1, Gates 1." No more. Without Arnold in the field to orchestrate the aggressive attack that would cripple Burgoyne, he said, "I have to wonder what Horatio Gates would have done."

# CHAPTER 11

# "We Didn't Mean *You*, Mr. Marquis!"

The young couple with the foreign accents and the cute little girl sat across the room at Philadelphia's City Tavern, too far away for me to eavesdrop on what they said. The menu promised a meal "inspired by the customs and foods of 18th century Colonial America," and I did overhear a question about what this thing called a "pot pie" might be. Then the girl, who looked about four, made her first audible contribution to the conversation. "Un, deux, trois," she counted in a cheerful singsong, and I thought: "Oh my God, they're French! *Do they know they're eating lunch in the same place Washington met Lafayette?*" I'll never know; there was no chance to ask. But my own reason for being at City Tavern—a Park Service replica of the city's revolutionary social hub that has closed since my visit, alas—was to think about Marie-Joseph Paul Yves Roch Gilbert du Motier, Marquis de Lafayette, and how an adventurous, naïve teenager came to embody the foreign entanglement that would turn a colonial rebellion into a world war.

Lafayette was nineteen when he showed up in Philly.

What the heck was he doing there?

Sarah Vowell once took this question from Jon Stewart on *The Daily Show*, and the author of *Lafayette in the Somewhat United States* answered with deadpan economy. "The British had killed his dad," she said, "so he had a grudge. He wanted to get away from his in-laws. And he believed in Enlightenment ideals of freedom and liberty." Oh, and "He also wanted glory—that was number one."

To add a few details:

Lafayette's father had been wiped out by a cannonball during the Seven Years' War, when the boy was two. The in-laws came along fourteen years later, after he'd moved from the provinces to Paris, lost his mother and an extremely rich grandfather, and become the most eligible orphan in France. His father-in-law got him a commission in an elite French regiment, but a reorganization of the army, not to mention peacetime, stalled his military career. He caught the fever for the American cause that was infecting France; fell in with a group of more experienced officers who were looking to cross the Atlantic to fight—some had delusions about taking command of the rebel army, though Lafayette seems not to have known about that part—and wangled an appointment as a major general from an American representative in Paris. Silas Deane had been handing out such appointments like Halloween candy, but in this case, at least, he knew what he was doing. The marquis was "a young Nobleman of great Family Connections here, & Great Wealth," he and his colleague Benjamin Franklin advised Congress, and making nice to him "will be serviceable to our Affairs here."

The young nobleman, meanwhile, bought a ship; defied his in-laws and King Louis XVI, who tried to stop him; left his pregnant seventeen-year-old wife and not-yet-two-year-old daughter; and sailed west with his new friends.

They landed in mid-June 1777 on a marshy, lonely stretch of South Carolina coast sixty miles northeast of Charleston. The first Americans they encountered were Black men harvesting oysters. The men led Lafayette and some companions to the house of their master, rice planter and militia major Benjamin Huger. Waking the next morning, the marquis recalled, the novelty of everything he saw—the mosquito netting on the bed; the Black people materializing "to ask my commands"; and "the strange new beauty of the landscape outside my windows"—combined "to produce a magical effect."

Magic moments were hard to come by on the next legs of his

journey. He moved on to Charleston with a small cohort, mostly on foot, having been able to rustle up just three horses. "Some of us were wearing riding boots, but we were not able to walk in them," one cranky officer wrote, so they finished the trek barefoot, "on burning sand and in the woods."

Still, the new world enchanted Lafayette to the point of blindness. "In America," he wrote from Charleston, "there are no paupers, or even the sort of people we call peasants. Every individual has an adequate amount of property, and the same rights as the most powerful proprietor in the land." Shazam! In two sentences, he had magicked away both the obvious class distinctions among South Carolina whites and the fact that over half the state's population was enslaved.

He bought horses and fancy carriages for the six-hundred-plus-mile slog to Philadelphia. The carriages broke, horses went lame or died, baggage was abandoned or stolen, dysentery struck. Even the marquis admitted to finding it all "a bit fatiguing." From Annapolis, he wrote home with worse news—"Ticonderoga, the strongest post in America, has been taken by the enemy"—then added some characteristic, cheerful optimism: "We must try to make up for that."

But first, he had to survive an ordeal by friendly fire.

Even the most cockeyed optimist would have been depressed by the way Lafayette's party was received in the American capital. The same French officer who had grouched about having to walk barefoot on hot sand wrote an acid account of this reception, which I've paraphrased and tightened up a little. The dramatis personae are John Hancock, president of Congress; Robert Morris, an important congressman; and a less important congressman with useful language skills:

**Hancock:** *Can't help you. Go see Robert Morris.*

**Morris:** *Talk to this guy here, who speaks French.*

**Guy who speaks French:** *We have enough of you French dudes already. Besides, what if you turn out to be like that horse's ass du Coudray? Go away!*

Apparently, it wasn't the best time to show up.

By July 27, 1777, Congress was beyond cranky about how the war was going. Burgoyne was invading, the northern army was in shambles, and by the way, some sixteen thousand troops under Howe had just sailed off from New York, probably headed for Philadelphia. In other news, an experienced but snotty Frenchman named Philippe Charles Tronson du Coudray had showed up recently waving a paper, signed by candy man Silas Deane, that promised him command of the army's artillery. Three top generals, including Knox and Greene, told Congress they would quit if he were given Knox's job. Congress demanded apologies from the generals, in the name of civilian control, but didn't get them. Eventually du Coudray took a different assignment, and there would be few regrets when he resolved the dispute for good by accidentally drowning in the Schuylkill River.

The coolness of Lafayette's reception, however, didn't last. The next day, not one but two French-speaking congressmen knocked on his door. Overnight, someone had figured out that he was in the top .0001 percent of rich, influential Frenchmen, and the new message was: "We didn't mean *you*, Mr. Marquis! Our bad!"

Three days later, a congressional resolution took note of "his zeal, illustrious family and connexions" and made him an official major general. A few days after that, he got invited to a City Tavern dinner where he met his new boss.

Back at the rebuilt tavern, I finished my eighteenth-century lunch—the cornmeal fried oysters were excellent; Alexander Hamilton's Treasury Ale was a bit thin—then walked upstairs to the elegant Long Room, where I tried to imagine the commander in chief and his latest headache eyeing each other across the green tablecloths.

Lafayette would gush about his first impressions of the gracious, physically imposing man who welcomed him to his "military family," but we don't know what Washington was thinking that night. Two weeks later, though, in a private letter, he expressed considerable irritation at the way Congress had saddled him with the boy. Was his rank just window dressing or did he have to be treated like a real major general?

"I know no more than the Child unborn," he wrote.

In the late summer of 1777, though, he had bigger things to worry about than babysitting an underage marquis. Howe and his sixteen thousand men were in fact heading for Philadelphia, and it was Washington's job to stop them.

Wish him luck. He was going to need it.

\* \* \*

The Battle of Brandywine was fought on September 11, 1777, over ten square miles of land in and around what's now Chadds Ford, Pennsylvania, twenty-five miles west and a bit south of Philly. Some thirty thousand troops took part and the fighting lasted twelve hours, making Brandywine the longest, largest single-day battle of the Revolution. Given what was about to happen at Saratoga, the stakes were high. If Washington won decisively, the combined victories could have ended the war. But in the more likely event that his army was smashed, with the bad news reaching Paris before the news of Burgoyne's surrender— well, you can see where this is going.

Yet as huge, important revolutionary battles go, Brandywine doesn't get much respect.

Nobody knows this better than Michael Harris, author of a richly detailed recent history of the battle, with whom I signed up to drive those ten square miles. How could I go wrong, I figured, with a man who had named his son after Nathanael Greene?

A trim-bearded thirty-six-year-old with a quotation from Jefferson on his T-shirt ("I cannot live without books"), Harris fit the well-informed-with-strong-opinions mold I'd come to value in battlefield guides. He had grown up vacationing at historic sites ("We weren't a shore family or a mountain family"); started Civil War reenacting with his dad at fifteen; and found grown-up work at, among other places, Virginia's Fredericksburg Battlefield and Pennsylvania's Daniel Boone Homestead. Moving to Brandywine's small battlefield park, he discovered that he didn't like any of the books on what happened there. A master's thesis expanded to become his own book; layoffs after the 2008 crash turned him into a high school history teacher; and now he was standing in the parking lot of the Brandywine River Museum, ready to teach more than a dozen adults how Washington came to be out-generaled by Howe. But first, he had a trained educator's question:

"How familiar are we with how the armies got here? Anybody need a brief explanation? Be honest!"

"Do it," someone said.

Condensed version: After Sir William finally got his rear in gear, he sailed south to the Chesapeake, then back north up the bay, landing near what's now Elkton, Maryland. Washington decided the best place to fight would be along the Brandywine River, "the last natural defensive barrier" between Howe and Philadelphia except the Schuylkill, and he figured the most likely place for Howe to try to cross would be at Chads Ford, which had one fewer "d" in 1777 because it was named for a ferry operator whose widow lived not far upriver. John and Elizabeth Chads' house still stands, so off we went to see it, with Harris leading a caravan of cars and shepherding us into the yard when we arrived.

The old stone building on the grassy hillside, he told us, had witnessed a scary incident in which George Washington could have been killed.

"There was an artillery position up where these trees are now," he said, pointing. As the battle's morning phase heated up, the guns there began dueling with enemy guns across the river. A loyalist at the enemy position looked through his glass, recognized one of his Virginia neighbors, and told the artillery commander, "You know, that's Washington; you should redirect your fire." As artillery rounds started landing in the yard, the general wisely made himself scarce.

The close call, however, was just a warm-up for the near-death experience of his entire army that day.

He had concentrated most of his troops within a mile of Chads Ford, sending smaller units to a few other fords nearby. Fortunately for him, the river was much deeper than it is now, limiting the number of crossing places he had to guard. And sure enough, here came Howe's attack, right where he expected it, with the first shots fired around 6 a.m., and now the men he'd put on the west side of the river to slow that attack had done their job and were falling back, and now it was about time for the battle to get serious, and now...wait a minute...what was this about a column of British troops kicking up dust in his rear?

Cue the Battle of Brooklyn flashback.

Hadn't Washington learned *anything* since then?

"Keep in mind, this is the sixth time Howe did this maneuver to him," Harris said, listing Brooklyn, White Plains, and four smaller engagements in which the British had turned a Washington flank. "Great organizer, great politically—that's why he made a good president—but he is bad on a battlefield."

Howe's plan was simple in theory but less so to execute. From his camp six miles west of the river, he would send Hessian general Wilhelm von Knyphausen and 6,800 men straight at Chads Ford. Their task: Create a diversion loud enough to hold Washington in place. Lord Cornwallis and Howe himself, meanwhile, would lead 9,600 troops all around Robin Hood's barn—north, east, then south, crossing two branches of the Brandywine at unguarded fords en route—to hit their enemies in the rear. They would march seventeen miles before they fought.

"We're going to drive the whole route," Harris told us. "I like doing the flank drive for you guys because you get a sense of the distances."

I got to ride shotgun in Harris's truck. After some confusing turns, we drove past the kind of upscale suburban neighborhood where the houses all look the same. "So this road we're on, we're in the middle of—where?" I asked.

"Nowhere," he said. "When I came here in 2005, this was a giant apple orchard. Now it's a bedroom community for Philadelphia."

As we drove on, however, long stretches of the flanking route began to look more like an eighteenth-century version of nowhere. Cornfields, baled hay, rail fences, and horse farms lined the narrow, rolling roads. Reaching the west branch of the Brandywine, where those 9,600 troops queued up to cross around 10:30 a.m.—it took them a while—we continued to the east branch, where a one-lane bridge marked the rough location of Jefferis Ford. An old sign noted simply that "Cornwallis crossed here between 1 and 2 o'clock Sept. 11, 1777." Two p.m., as it happened, was about the time Washington realized what was going on.

Harris never actually slapped his forehead and said *"D'oh!"* while talking about the failures of intelligence, communications, and judgment that caused this realization to come so late—but he might as well have. Among the questions raised and answered on his tour and in his book:

*Why did Washington leave those two fords unguarded?*

Two possibilities: Either he didn't know they existed or he thought they were too far north to worry about.

*Why didn't he act on a report he got about the flanking movement— from a trustworthy officer at the northernmost of the guarded fords—that came in at 10 a.m.?*

There is no good answer to that question.

*What did he do instead?*

He waited to hear from a geographically challenged Virginian he'd sent to look around, but received no word from the guy for four hours.

*Did he get other intelligence in the meantime?*

Indeed he did: Another trustworthy officer reported actually skirmishing with a body of troops up north and being informed by locals that Howe was with them. Washington somehow concluded that their target must be one of his supply depots, a considerable distance away. Then he thought: Whoa, that means the Brits across the river at Chads Ford are weaker than I am! I should attack them and worry about those other guys later!

*How did that work out for him?*

Not well. As the attack got going, a militia officer showed up claiming to have ridden the route a flanking march would use—and seen no trace of one. Washington thought: Damn, that flanking thing must have been a feint! Which means Howe's entire army is waiting for me across the river! So he called off the attack.

*What eventually made the scales fall from his eyes?*

Geographically Challenged Virginia Guy finally found the flanking march and relayed the bad news: The enemy was moving around Washington's right flank into his rear.

He had no time to lose.

Our tour picked up the story by following the British from the ford to the crest of Osborne Hill—actually a long, low ridge—where at 3:00, Cornwallis and Howe gave their leg-weary men time to rest and eat. By

4:30, the troops were deployed in a mile-wide line along the ridge, poised to attack. Facing them across the valley, on another long ridge known as Birmingham Hill, were three divisions of the Continental Army rushed there by Washington after Virginia Guy's news woke him up.

The Continentals were outnumbered almost two to one, but at least they had a chance.

Harris has a favorite place to think about the fight that followed. "This is a very cool spot," he said, leading us up a nondescript suburban street where, in 1777, a unit known as the Brigade of Guards formed the far right of the British and Hessian line. Looking south, we had a view across a bigger road to the daunting slope of Birmingham Hill—part field, part forest. But here's the coolest part: Soon after the battle, a British officer who'd taken part in the attack sat down *right here* and painted a watercolor. "The Brigade of Guards are the tiny red brush-strokes," Harris said, pointing to a reproduction on his book's back cover. "They're formed along the fence along the road."

Just after that watercolor moment, they charged.

At the top of the ridge, they smashed into the left end of the rebel line, which—thanks to a pigheaded move by a French officer not named Lafayette—wasn't even in place yet. Separated from the other defenders, under fire from the Guards "at nearly pointblank range," most of these men turned and raced away.

So much for the defenders having a chance.

We stopped at a few more places to talk about the intense combat that nonetheless continued, for an hour or so, as the British and Hessians drove the remaining rebels off the ridge. No matter how strong their position was or how hard they fought, inferior numbers and the French officer's blunder doomed them. "Their flanks keep getting turned," Harris said, until finally "everybody's peeling back and running—down the road, across the farm fields, toward where the last fight is."

Nathanael Greene, for whom young Nathanael Harris was named, helped save what was left of the day.

When the Birmingham Hill fight began, Greene and his division were near Chads Ford; by the time Washington ordered them to go where the action was, things were already out of hand. A kick-ass two-and-a-half-mile march put them in the path of the fleeing defenders and their pursuers just in time. Greene decided to make a stand near what would become, a couple of centuries later, one of the least attractive suburban banks you'll ever see. "Is that a period building?" someone joked as we gathered in the DNB First parking lot. Harris didn't laugh; he was busy explaining why he'd brought us here instead of to one of the other sites where Greene's action has been placed over the years.

The reason is another example of how new discoveries change history. Shortly after the battle, a British engineer made a huge, detailed map of the action. (Harris said it was almost as long as his truck was wide.) The Robertson Map didn't make its way into the Brandywine narrative until the end of the twentieth century, when historian Thomas McGuire unearthed it in the royal map collection at Windsor Castle—but with its discovery, the location of the battle's finale became clear.

"Greene's right flank is where Jimmy John's is—that place with the yellow sign," Harris told us, pointing at a hot dog joint a quarter mile up the Wilmington Pike. The hastily formed American line, which included remnants of the divisions that fought on Birmingham Hill, took the shape of "a big U," descending the gentle slope below Jimmy John's, "curving right around where we're standing" and climbing back toward a barely perceptible ridge that blocked the view of the pursuing redcoats. "The British can't see what's on this side," Harris said, which means that as they approach the U, "they're marching into it blind. And they get fired at from three sides."

It was almost dark. They'd been marching or fighting since 5 a.m.—and now this.

Time to call it a day.

Saved by Greene's stand, enemy exhaustion, a fighting retreat near Chads Ford, and, most important, the setting of the sun, Washington's bloodied army straggled away. "Fugitives, cannon and baggage crowded in complete disorder on the road to Chester," one wounded officer recalled. But at least there still *was* an army—though roughly 8 percent of it (1,300 men) had been killed, wounded, or captured—and it would be ready to fight again in just five days.

Lafayette, however, would not.

The marquis was the wounded officer quoted above. With no command, he'd spent the day as an observer, but when things heated up, he begged Washington's permission to ride to the front. I've read enough conflicting descriptions of what happened next not to trust any details except that a British or Hessian soldier put a musket ball through his leg. Harris pointed out the place this likely occurred. It's in a field a quarter mile west of an elegant terra-cotta column, erected in 1895 to commemorate the wounding.

Brandywine was Lafayette's first battle.

He contributed nothing important, Harris said, but he didn't do anything *wrong*. "He got wounded here trying to help."

* * *

Looking for traces of the next Washington-Howe clash, a dozen miles and five days away, I drove around Malvern and East Goshen without finding much to orient me. Eventually, though, I made my way to a nicely rehabbed house at 606 Swedesford Road—on September 16, 1777, it was the White Horse Tavern—which stood near the center of what could have been a Brandywine-scale battle. Nearby, a marker summed up the stakes:

"A loss here would have been disastrous to the American cause," it said.

Good thing the game was called on account of rain.

Skirmishing left a few men dead and Howe's army poised to strike, but an Arnold-in-Maine-scale deluge made it impossible to continue. Washington's army slogged off to find dry powder. Someone dubbed this near miss "the Battle of the Clouds."

Ten days later, the British marched into Philadelphia unopposed, leaving a hopelessly outmaneuvered George Washington in their wake.

Yet just eight days after *that*—you don't get to be the Father of Your Country by being a quitter—Washington was knocking on Howe's door in Germantown, several miles northwest of central Philly. He managed to surprise a sizable part of the British army there, some of which he forced to retreat. A quick-thinking British colonel and about a hundred men, however, barricaded themselves in a formidable stone mansion known as Cliveden, and the question for the commander in chief became: Must we stop and take the house or should we just go around it? Opinions differed, but Henry Knox's argument that "it would be unmilitary to leave a castle in our rear" prevailed.

It was Knox's biggest mistake of the war.

Touring Cliveden, now a museum run by the National Trust for Historic Preservation, it was easy to imagine the havoc wreaked by defenders firing from second-floor windows. Guides showed me interior walls with patched-up holes made by musket balls; stone steps scarred by cannon fire; a photo of the mansion's battered wooden doors, which survived the battle but not a 1970 fire; and the Plexiglas-covered evidence for a dubious legend about a dying redcoat using his own blood to sketch a woman's portrait.

Germantown isn't an easy battle to understand. An oversized map showing troop movements made my head spin. But I do know that Knox's capture-the-castle foolishness wasn't the only reason the British won. Thick fog and panicky troops are among other factors cited, along with the overly complex plan of attack Washington devised. Still, it was the delay at Cliveden that took away the attack's momentum and gave Howe's veterans the breathing room to organize a counterattack. After that, there was nothing Washington could do to prevent his army's collapse and retreat.

He got credit for trying. Congress even gave him another medal.

Yet by December 19, 1777, when he led his army into winter quarters at Valley Forge, he hadn't won a battle in almost a year—and Horatio Gates had.

# CHAPTER 12

# The Continental Army Does the Wave

Three reasons why everyone's heard of Valley Forge," Bill Troppman was saying. First: "Highest death total of the war's eight winter encampments—by far." Next: "Good news. While the army's languishing here, what country in Europe jumps in on our side?"

"France," one of his listeners replied.

"Oui, monsieur, vive la France!" said the straight-backed ranger-historian in the hunting frock, who was educating tourists in a reconstructed Valley Forge log hut. "So: High death total, French alliance, and finally, this was the birthplace of the United States Army. It's not the birthplace of the *American* army. That's Lexington and Concord. The adjective I inserted is 'united.' You've got four different infantry manuals when you march in here. It's like the umpire at Fenway yelling 'Play ball!' and you've got four rulebooks."

Troppman's personal rules seemed to include an injunction against overlong explanations, for which he kept apologizing. After a quarter century with the Park Service, however, he was fighting a losing battle with his accumulated knowledge and desire to share. "He's Encyclopedia Brown," an awed young colleague told me. "Say one word and he'll give you a whole dissertation."

Take, for example, that high Valley Forge death toll and the word "cold."

"The Victorian artists got it all wrong," Troppman said. "They painted pictures of snow up to men's armpits, thinking they're freezing to death. *AAAANNH!*" He made a noise like the buzzer on a game show. "The second Morristown winter was the coldest winter on record that *century*." Troops there in 1780, two years after Valley Forge, got so hungry they came extremely close to mutiny. "But you know what the death total was that winter? Eighty-seven. Here it was over 1,700."

Why the disparity? The answer brought the words "warm" and "latrine" into play.

"This was the warmest of the encampments. That's not what they wanted. They don't have a germ theory, but they knew if it was too warm a winter—especially when it came to the three-quarter-mile-long slit latrines—the death total would spike. That's what happened here. If you sit around reading about army latrines, you can—I need to get a life, you know. I *do* that. My wife has stopped asking me what my bedtime reading is."

Laughter erupted. Troppman kept explaining.

"So you shovel over the waste with dirt. But what if it's raining? And you're getting ice storms? And then when it dries out, the scabies and lice spread... They wanted it frozen and dry. It's too warm and wet here. That's why the dysentery, then pneumonia, then typhus-typhoid—then in March, a swine flu epidemic went through here. They wanted their winters *frozen*. When there's no wind and it's twenty degrees, you can work all day out here. But what if it's in the high thirties, low forties and raining? They had no problem building cabins, but they have to be outside to survive.

"*That's* Valley Forge."

Valley Forge National Historical Park is twenty miles northwest of Philadelphia, close enough for Washington to keep an eye on the British but a strong enough defensive position to make Howe think twice before attacking. Over its five square miles, multiple story lines converge. To find the next, all I had to do was step out of the hut and onto the Joseph Plumb Martin Trail, named for one of the least known but most important heroes of the war. Lest you doubt the "most important" part, here's how he made his own case:

What could generals do without private soldiers? "Nothing at all."

The quotation is from Martin's memoir, published in 1830. The book's liveliness and candor, plus the author's knack for turning up at key events, make it a gem among the relatively few writings by the war's common soldiers. It went almost unnoticed, however, until the second half of the twentieth century, when historians newly interested in unfamous lives revived it under such titles as *Private Yankee Doodle* and *Ordinary Courage*. Since then, it's become almost impossible to flip through a recent history of the war without encountering one of Martin's yeasty observations. He fought, among many other places, at Kips Bay, Germantown, and the siege of Fort Mifflin, downriver from Philadelphia, where the garrison endured "hardships sufficient to kill half a dozen horses" but attracted little notice, in his view, because no famous general fought there. After marching into Valley Forge, he spent two nights and a day with nothing to eat but "half of a small pumpkin," which he wolfed down as if it were the most delicious pie ever baked.

That said, he had an easier winter than most.

Foraging duties kept him out of the disease-ridden huts and left him relatively well fed. It would be the less deadly encampment at Morristown, mentioned by Troppman, which drove many comrades to the breaking point and Martin to recall their "imbecility" in sticking around to fight for people who didn't care a whit about their travails.

All revolutions are subject to mythmaking. Ours is no exception. Perhaps the most valuable thing about Martin's memoir, then—as one of his editors points out—is that he "had little tolerance for any romanticizing of the allegedly virtuous character of the Revolutionary generation" collectively. He had seen, to his cost, "how few patriots had showed the stamina to stay out for the whole contest."

Meanwhile, speaking of neglected story lines:

Before I started to walk the trail named for the myth-busting private, I met a young woman in a long skirt and a mop cap who was introduced as Ranger Beth. Her task that afternoon was to show children how to play eighteenth-century games, she said, but she also gave talks about women and the army. Some four hundred women walked into Valley Forge with Washington and his troops. Most were probably soldiers' wives, many with kids in tow, who did laundry, cooked, and sewed to earn minimal pay or at least army rations. Some were prostitutes. Like most rank-and-file soldiers at this point in the war, most of the four hundred came from the lowest levels of American society. Couples were "poor to start out with," Beth said, with the men enlisting in return for a signing bonus and the promise of land. But with one fewer adult in the household, many women couldn't make ends meet. "So they packed up everything they deemed essential and followed the army."

"What kind of questions do you get when you're on that topic?" I asked.

" 'There were *women* here?' " she said. "That's the biggest one. People don't even realize—so they don't know where to start."

A mile or so past the cluster of log huts, an equestrian statue caught my eye. It was Brig. Gen. Anthony Wayne, famously—but not yet—nicknamed "Mad Anthony," and he introduced a story line about supplies. A marker titled "Generals and Cattle Raids" talked about how well Wayne had done rounding up beef on the hoof during a food emergency. Why the emergency? "Any number of misfortunes—spoilage, bad roads, or capture by British foragers—could prevent supplies from reaching camp," the marker explained. Which is true, but leaves out the number one "misfortune": the total collapse of the army's quartermaster department and commissary system. Washington's eventual solution would be to ask Nathanael Greene to serve as quartermaster general. He got the job done, protesting all the way. "No body ever heard of a quarter Master in History," Greene wrote, and he was right: It would be 237 years before Valley Forge put up a statue of the most important general not named George to winter there, and at the time of my visit, it was not yet marked on park maps.

Lafayette's quarters were, though.

The marquis bunked down in a small stone house in the park's southwest corner, up a gravel road from a sign proclaiming it "Not Open to Public" and below the trash-strewn verge of the Pennsylvania Turnpike. To be precise, I should say he *sometimes* bunked down there, because he spent a good deal of his winter under orders to…invade Canada.

The orders came from Congress by way of a newly reconfigured bureaucratic entity called the Board of War. The president of the board was Horatio Gates.

Washington was not consulted.

Also not consulted, apparently, was anyone else who might have doubted that marching an army into the teeth of a Canadian winter was the best of all possible ideas.

*   *   *

Lafayette's Brandywine wound had healed quickly, and by late November things had started looking up for him. He'd done well in a New Jersey skirmish, with help from some of Morgan's riflemen. More important, Washington had written Congress, twice, asking that he be given a command. The letters credited the marquis with many virtues— among them bravery, discretion, and rapidly improving English—but as historian Stuart Leibiger writes, Washington's main point was that "the United States could not afford to let Lafayette go back to France in disappointment and disgust." Bringing the French into the war was too important.

Point taken. Before long, the young Frenchman was commanding a division of Virginians. But then came those bizarre orders from the Board of War.

Lafayette, Gates wrote in late January, was to proceed to Albany, where troops were gathering for a Canadian invasion. He should "lose no Time," never mind that he knew squat about what was expected of him: His second-in-command, whom the board had already named, would hand over its instructions when the marquis showed up.

His response was a mix of dreams and doubts.

How glorious would it be for him to lead an army that liberated the former New France? Very! Was he qualified to lead such an army? Not at all! The invasion, he wrote his wife, would be "a terrifying task, especially with so few resources. As to my personal resources, they are practically nonexistent for such a position; at twenty, one is not prepared to be at

the head of an army." Next question: Were Washington's enemies playing him for a fool? He had reason to think so. One of the most visible of
those enemies, though not the most important, was Thomas Conway—
the general the Board of War had made his second-in-command.

Lafayette asked for advice and took it. Declining to go north without
solid information, he went first to York, Pennsylvania, where Congress
had relocated after fleeing Philadelphia. There he extracted actual orders
from Gates and demanded changes, notably that he would continue to
report to Washington and not to the board.

Not bad for an unprepared twenty-year-old. But what he discovered
in Albany filled him with rage and despair.

"Why am I so far from you," he began a February 19 letter to Washington, "and what business had that board of war to hurry me through
the ice and snow without knowing what I schould [sic] do, neither what
they were doing themselves?" His army was half the size he'd been
promised; the troops hadn't been paid in "an immense time"; and their
clothing was so scanty that most "would be naked even for a summer
campaign." Oh, and the highest-ranking, most experienced generals in
the area—Philip Schuyler, Benjamin Lincoln, and yes, Benedict Arnold,
still in Albany recovering from that gruesome Saratoga wound—had
proclaimed the invasion completely nuts. Even Conway had told him
it now looked "quite impossible." Lafayette's great fear, he wrote plain-
tively, was that "I schall [sic] be laughed at."

Washington needed to reassure his anxious protégé, and he did.
Yet it's possible to imagine him laughing—quietly, to himself—not
at the marquis, but at the men who dreamed up this wild Canadian
goose chase. After all, they were the same men who'd spent the past few
months busting their butts to diminish his authority over the army.

This anti-Washington power play, known to future generations as
"the Conway Cabal," is one of those historical rabbit holes down which
it's easy to fall without achieving enlightenment. I'll suggest just a couple of its complications here:

First, calling it the *Conway* Cabal is misleading.

A more accurate name would be "the Conway, Mifflin, Gates &
Co. Cabal." Historians often peg Thomas Mifflin, a formerly valuable

general who fell out with Washington and became the most influential member of the Board of War, as its linchpin.

Second, even the word "cabal" isn't right.

In the words of Mark Edward Lender—who went down that rabbit hole so we wouldn't have to—a better way to describe what those men attempted would be an "administrative coup." But don't be fooled: Whatever you call it, Mifflin, Gates, et al. were aiming high. "They sought control of setting military policy and strategic goals; determining vital training, organizational, personnel, and logistical functions; and even the assignment of theater commanders," Lender writes. "Had Washington lost control of these areas his title of commander in chief would have been utterly hollow."

In short, the Hero of Saratoga and his allies posed a real threat to a bad tactical general on a losing streak. And in fending it off, which took a while, Washington showed more political savvy than all his opponents combined.

Command central for the defense effort was another stone house, a couple of miles north of Lafayette's. If you don't count its kitchen wing, Washington's Valley Forge headquarters is almost as small. On the ground floor is a room filled with tables where something like nine Washington aides worked, though not all at the same time. (One was Alexander Hamilton, a man we last saw firing cannons in New Jersey.) Up two flights of stairs is a garret some of those aides used as a bedroom. "There is an account of aide-de-camp John Laurens rising in the morning and hitting his head on the low ceiling," a sign by the door informed me.

"What can you tell me about Laurens?" I asked the ranger on duty when I got back downstairs.

"He's an aide-de-camp, one of Washington's main ones," she said. "His dad, Henry, is the president of the Continental Congress during this period. So good job, George, having your boss's son working for you."

Good job indeed. Letters between the Laurenses gave Washington a back channel that helped him turn away the long knives of domestic enemies. One more key story line at Valley Forge, in fact, is how much the commander in chief learned—in more ways than I can detail here—about controlling the political environment in which he had to function.

Now all he had to do was learn to beat the British.

Fortunately, the Patron Saint of Résumé Enhancers showed up to help.

* * *

Supersized in bronze, he stands more than eight feet tall atop a six-foot pedestal. A thick coat hangs to his booted ankles, while his bicorne hat and the arm held horizontally across his chest make you wonder, just for a moment, why there's a statue of Napoleon Bonaparte at Valley Forge.

But it's not Napoleon, of course; the future emperor was eight years old in the winter of 1778. It's Friedrich Wilhelm, Baron von Steuben, who showed up here in late February claiming to have served as a lieutenant general under Frederick the Great, king of Prussia, the greatest soldier of the age. A brazen enhancer of credentials—as even a hero-worshipping biographer admits—the forty-seven-year-old Steuben (pronounced SHTOY-ben) had charmed and lied his way into endorsements from Franklin, Hancock, Robert Morris, and Henry Laurens en route. His self-presentation was not all false: He had learned a great deal in Frederick's army during the Seven Years' War, though when abruptly discharged in 1763, he was only a captain. The title "baron" ("Freiherr" in German) got tacked on years later by a perpetually broke princeling he served as a civilian. Jobless again, broke himself, and out of European options, Steuben sailed west, hat in hand and fictitious autobiography at the ready.

None of which would matter if he could take a poorly trained army, instill a modicum of discipline, and make sure everyone was on the same page when it came to marching and maneuvering on a battlefield.

The American fighting force Steuben set out to improve, with Washington's blessing, had been a work in progress ever since it was created. Yes, in theory, Congress had authorized longer enlistments, but in practice the Continental Army was still bedeviled by what Joseph Ellis calls a "turnstile problem." Desertion, severe wounds, death or debilitation from disease, and the expiration of previous enlistments meant that even if it regained its numerical strength, the ratio of raw recruits to veterans would be high, and those four conflicting rulebooks Troppman mentioned wouldn't help.

So Steuben wrote a whole new rulebook.

Being short on time, he kept it as simple as possible.

Speaking little English, he wrote it in French.

Hamilton, Laurens, and others translated it.

And before it was done, he started drilling the men.

Officers of Steuben's alleged seniority *never* did this themselves, but he needed to show Washington's officers not only how it was done but that it was important. To that end, he drilled a model company on the encampment's parade ground. His audience included carefully chosen deputies, who would go on to instruct the rest of the army, as well as anyone else who was free to watch the show. It was a good one: Given the language barrier, Steuben's performance included animated pantomime and hilarious bursts of cursing in German and French with an occasional "goddamn" thrown in.

Would the army really fight better after this?

The jury was still out. But soon, the newly Steuben-ized troops would be given an extraordinary, peaceful opportunity to strut their stuff.

Early in May, a messenger rode into Valley Forge with the long-hoped-for news that a treaty of alliance had been signed in Paris. Word of Burgoyne's surrender certainly influenced the French decision, and it's been argued that portrayals of Germantown as a "near victory" helped, too. But it's also clear that Louis XVI's powerhouse of a foreign minister, the Comte de Vergennes—under whom crucial funds and arms had already been funneled to the rebels, and who surely deserves his own statue at Valley Forge—saw Saratoga as a useful pretext for doing what he needed to do. "Vergennes had already decided," as historian Larrie Ferreiro writes, that "the insurgents were still likely to lose the war without direct intervention." And the possibility that his nation's mortal enemy might get its valuable colonies back was "too dangerous to contemplate."

Vive la France!

Lafayette hugged his normally unhuggable boss. Washington declared May 6 a day of celebration.

And Inspector General Friedrich Wilhelm, Baron von Steuben—goddamn! He had a new title!—orchestrated a celebratory firing of muskets by the entire army. The troops formed two long lines, beginning from where the drillmaster's statue now stands, and performed what was called a feu de joie, a "fire of joy." The first two men from each line fired, then the next two, then the next, producing a steady roar. "Remember the crowds in baseball where they have the wave and you stand up?" Bill Troppman told me, trying to explain. The feu de joie ran down those lines of troops just like a stadium wave.

The celebrating didn't stop afterward, either.

"It was a party—they put up poles, they were dancing," another ranger said. Rum flowed freely. "Washington had a shot with all the different brigade commanders. There were sixteen brigade commanders here."

* * *

Twelve days later, the British were dancing and drinking, too. And if you could win wars by throwing ridiculously inappropriate bashes with weird names, this one would have ended on May 18.

The party in Philadelphia was called the Mischianza, which has been described as a blend of the Italian words for "mix" and "mingle." It was thrown in honor of William Howe, who was going home. Howe had submitted his resignation in late October, around the time rumors of Burgoyne's surrender reached the city, and George III had recently gotten around to accepting it—having noticed, perhaps, that Sir William had failed to suppress the rebellion before the French made the task a lot harder.

But forget that for now! Think of all the fun the chief party planner, Captain John André, had lined up—including a mock medieval joust! Two teams of seven knights would face off to decide which team's ladies, dressed "in gauze turbans and Turkish outfits," were the prettiest and wittiest. The knights would meet "at full gallop, each shivering his spear against his opponent's shield," according to an *American Heritage* account by a professor of romance literature. (Party-pooping scholars say only the leaders of each team squared off.) After the joust, it was time to move inside. André had filled the ballroom of a country house with eighty-five mirrors so guests could check out their dance moves, and he'd assembled "twenty-four black slaves in oriental dress, with silver collars and bracelets" to serve them supper, after which the heartiest drank and danced till dawn.

The hangovers must have been brutal. But they didn't stop the British from tearing out after Lafayette when they learned he was within their reach.

Why the marquis chose to spend two nights camping out at Barren Hill—on a ridge above the Schuylkill, twelve miles from Philadelphia— has puzzled inquiring minds ever since. "We halted here, placed our guards, sent off our scouting parties, and waited for—I know not what," recalled the ubiquitous Joseph Martin, one of 2,200 men along for the ride. Lafayette's orders don't exactly clear things up. Washington assigned him multiple tasks, among them protecting Valley Forge and disrupting enemy communications. He was to recruit "trusty and intelligent spies" and report back if they sniffed out anything about the British leaving Philly. Above all, the boy general was to be careful out there: His detachment was "a very valuable one" and he was to "use every possible precaution" to keep it safe, including not staying in the same place too long.

Lafayette ignored the warning.

Early in the morning on May 20, half the British army showed up with a burning desire to make a captured Frenchman the main attraction at their *next* big party.

Lafayette Hill, as Barren Hill is now called, will never be a Top 10 Revolution Destination. St. Peter's Lutheran Church, which dominates the ridgetop, was at the center of the action. The church has been rebuilt more than once since 1778, and the steeple I saw was hardly original. Still, it was easy to picture the startled marquis scrambling up it to see two enemy columns coming at him from the direction of Philadelphia, with a third sweeping around to take him in the rear.

He had one chance to escape and he seized it.

Unknown to the British, who thought they were about to bottle him up completely, more than one road led down from Barren Hill to a Schuylkill ford. Lafayette hustled his men toward the road his attackers couldn't yet see, while at the same time creating distractions. He wound up getting his whole force across the river (at what's now Conshohocken) with only a few casualties, leaving those British columns to bang into each other, empty-handed. It was a near thing, however. And if someone were leading a staff ride to the Battle of Barren Hill—an unlikely possibility, but maybe it shouldn't be—there would be plenty to discuss.

Modern historians I've read or talked with are united in their view that marching a couple thousand guys out of Valley Forge to scope out what the Brits were up to was "foolhardy," "bizarre," "as useless as it was perilous," and "an invitation to the British high command." Lafayette's detachment, like Burgoyne's at Second Saratoga, was "too large for a scouting expedition and too small to face a major attack." So why did Washington commit this act of folly? Was it *only* because he was a bad tactical general?

Nope. Politics and diplomacy were involved. Lafayette still felt terrible about his Canadian embarrassment, and the brand-new French alliance made keeping him happy more important than ever.

Another argument to assess would be that sure, Lafayette got himself in trouble, but he did a nice job getting out of it, and by the way, he couldn't have done this if his troops hadn't had the benefit of Steuben's training.

The Steuben part would make great staff-ride fodder, because the question is complex. Yet if you frame it in a less friendly way, it becomes: Sure, he did a nice job escaping the mess he got himself into, but what if James Grant—the general commanding the British column in his rear—had moved a bit faster and eliminated all hope of retreat?

Answer: The marquis would have been dead or attending that party in Philadelphia, his career in ruins; the disaster would have left Washington's army severely weakened and demoralized; and Henry Clinton would have been a happier camper as he took command of the British army in America.

Happier, but not *happy*: That was not Clinton's default emotional state. And even if Sir Henry had been a more cheerful human, he'd have been upset about the situation in which he found himself.

The French alliance had changed everything. The war had gone global, with France (and later Spain) threatening British interests in India, the Mediterranean, and especially the Caribbean, which was more important economically than the thirteen North American colonies combined. England itself was now vulnerable, too, leaving its navy stretched impossibly thin. Clinton's superiors wasted no time driving these points home. They told him to ship five thousand troops to the Caribbean; abandon Philadelphia; and get the army back to New York in a hurry. Knowing he'd never get the kind of resources Howe had wasted, Clinton, too, had submitted his resignation. It had not been accepted.

On June 18, he began marching his men through New Jersey. Ten days later, he fought a battle near the village of Monmouth Court House, aka Freehold, where he would be overshadowed, historically, by the far more famous Washington, the soon-to-be infamous Charles Lee, and a woman said to have done something heroic involving a cannon.

\* \* \*

The first thing I did, when I got to the battlefield, was look for the spot where a legendary encounter between Washington and Lee shaped the destinies of both. It was surprisingly hard to find. An online map pointed me to a dirt parking lot on Wemrock Road, but nothing there told me what to do next, unless you count the hand-lettered sign offering Giants and Jets tickets. A hundred yards up the road was a mown path that disappeared around a grove of trees. It, too, had no visible historical signage, but I followed it anyway. Bingo. On the grove's far side stood a rock with an inset plaque and some text dating from 1928. It lauded the valor of those who fought " 'at the Turn of the Tide' in the American Revolution" and summed up the action: "Near this spot Washington checked Lee's retreat and brought victory out of confusion." A more recent marker offered useful detail but the same basic theme: Lee bungled badly and Washington saved the day.

If you think the story was that obvious, I haven't been doing my job very well.

When last we set eyes on Lee, he was being taken prisoner by those enterprising dragoons at Basking Ridge. A year and a half later, exchanged for a British general, he regained his post as Washington's second-in-command and resumed his incurable habit of pissing people off. Who writes a plan for reorganizing the whole army, then gives it to Congress without telling his boss? What can you do with a guy like that?

Not much—at least with the British gearing up to march. The commander in chief rapped Lee's knuckles and moved on to bigger problems. When Clinton hit the road, Washington put some units in motion immediately and led the rest of his army out of Valley Forge the next morning.

He hadn't decided what to do, but he knew he had to do *something*—and that meant getting closer to the enemy.

None of his generals thought an all-or-nothing battle would be a good idea. He didn't either. But could he hit at least part of the enemy column, show some fight? From Hopewell, New Jersey, on June 23, he sent Daniel Morgan and 600 men to get on Clinton's tail, joining militia who had already done so. Then he sent another 1,500, and then 1,000 more. Next problem: Who should have overall command of these "forward elements"? Lee was the obvious choice, but he didn't think the job was big enough for a Number Two Guy, or that taking on the British right now was a good idea. So Washington tapped Lafayette, who proved once again that enthusiasm is no substitute for experience. The marquis outran his supply line, leaving his men half starved. Worse yet, he moved past the point where the main army could support him if he got in trouble.

What if Clinton had figured this out?

But he didn't. And meanwhile, Lee had changed his mind. He wanted that forward command after all.

Annoyed by the flip-flop but worried about Lafayette, Washington found a graceful way to make the switch. So it was the forty-six-year-old veteran, not the novice, who led 4,500 men toward Clinton's camp at Monmouth Court House on the morning of June 28. Lee's orders were to—well, we don't know exactly what they were because the commander in chief delivered them orally. What we do know, from the evidence carefully assembled by Mark Lender and Garry Stone in *Fatal Sunday*—by far the best book on the battle—is that those orders were discretionary. Yes, Washington badly wanted Lee to strike the British if possible. But he left his subordinate to decide how, and even whether, the strike should actually be made.

Off Lee went, sometime around 6 a.m. Right away, he encountered friction. Not the kind that sets sparks flying between individuals, but what Lender and Stone define—echoing military theorist Carl von Clausewitz—as "the accumulation of unanticipated mistakes, bad weather, difficult terrain, misunderstandings, conflicting intelligence, and other complications" that screw up combat operations. All these factors came into play before the serious fighting began. The day was killer hot; treacherous ravines cut through the rolling landscape; and egregious failures to communicate (a repeated theme at Monmouth) kept Morgan's men from even reaching the battlefield. Friction or no, Lee got his troops into position for the kind of attack Washington wanted. The British had resumed their march to New York, but left a gap in their column; Lee thought he could exploit it to cut off Clinton's rear guard.

Sir Henry had other ideas.

This time, he *did* figure out what was happening.

He turned thousands of men around, with the total eventually reaching ten thousand, and sent them after Lee, who had no reasonable option but to fall back and look for a place to make a stand. A couple of hours later, Lee was working to get part of his scattered command safely across one of those problematic ravines when Washington rode up— this would have been near where I found the Turn of the Tide marker behind the grove of trees—and asked him what the heck was going on. "Sir, sir," was all Lee could say at first. He had expected to be praised for his efforts.

There wasn't much time for explanations, however. The Brits were fifteen minutes away.

\* \* \*

A lot was going on at Monmouth Battlefield State Park the day I was there, much due to a reenactment that happens every year. Outside the visitor center, boys and girls lined up to learn their drill. Inside, I got hooked on an old-fashioned battlefield model, the kind where pushing a button gets you a thirteen-minute narration with sound effects—the drumming of hooves, say, as "a disturbed Washington" gallops off to look for Lee—and tiny blue and red lights that show the troop movements.

I'd have pushed that button again if it hadn't been time for the Molly Pitcher show.

Not long before, I'd bought a copy of *A Molly Pitcher Sourcebook*, David Martin's impressive compilation of sources and commentary on the war's "most famous female warrior." Now here was Martin himself, introducing the program in the auditorium. "In the midst of one of the fiercest artillery duels of the American Revolution," he told us, "a woman was observed to do something unusual—help fire a cannon. From this event has spun the legend of Molly Pitcher." Some parts of the legend "have a degree of truth, others are fanciful—and still others confuse the story of Monmouth's Molly with another woman of the Revolution, Margaret Corbin."

I had run into Corbin's story already. A plaque on Upper Manhattan's Margaret Corbin Drive gave the basics. During the attack on Fort Washington in 1776, Corbin's husband was killed while loading a cannon. She took over for him, making her "the first woman to fight as a soldier in the Revolutionary War," and was badly wounded. In 1779, Congress voted her a pension. And in the 1930s, as I was lucky enough to discover online, a muralist named Stuyvesant Van Veen painted Corbin into a wonderful, time-warping vision of the battle. The mural is in the lobby of an apartment building at 720 Fort Washington Avenue, and it shows British and Hessian troops marching uphill with the George Washington Bridge in the background. Redcoats kneel and aim their muskets in front of the Cloisters museum. Defenders kneel and take aim, too. Among the latter is a young woman in a yellow dress, red apron, and white mop cap with industrial smokestacks behind her head and a dead man at her feet.

It took me a while to realize that the mural had no cannon, but it's still pretty great.

Back in the Monmouth auditorium, Stacy Flora Roth, who was also wearing an apron as part of her period costume, stood next to a piece of field artillery and held a ramrod that looked like a seven-foot bottle brush. Martin introduced her as an improvisational storyteller who uses historical sources to create a "conjectural portrait" of the woman behind the Monmouth legend: Mary Hays, the wife of William Hays, a gunner in an artillery regiment.

"You can all call me Molly if you like," Roth said, then explained how she'd come to take part in the battle.

"I'd never thought of bein' a woman of the army," she said, until one day her husband came home and told her he wanted to sign up. "I said, 'I'll support you in it. But you know, William, if you go off to join the army, how am I going to pay the rent? And how am I going to buy food and firewood on a soldier's pay?' And you know what me husband said to me? He said: 'I hadn't thought of that.'"

A woman in the audience laughed.

"Oh, you're married to someone like that yourself, are ye?" said Molly.

Thinking it over, she told William she'd had an idea: They could sell their scant possessions and "I'll come *with* ye. And I'll take care of ye." A recruiting sergeant warned that she'd have to make herself useful if she followed the army.

Not a problem.

In June 1778, Molly and William found themselves headed toward Monmouth. And now came the part that would eventually make Molly Pitcher—though not Mary Hays—a household name.

William's artillery company ended up on "a ridge across Mr. Henry Perrine's field," about a mile northwest of where Washington and Lee had their confrontation. Her husband's job was to oversee the firing of one cannon. "And on the front of the cannon there always hangs a bucket of water. Why? It's for swabbing out the cannon between rounds." After you've fired the gun, "a bit of fabric from the powder bag" might stay in the barrel, "and if it's smoldering and you load another round, what can happen? Boom! It would blow the ramrod right out" and maybe take an arm off the person using that ramrod. "So me husband picked up the bucket and he said to me, 'Well, Molly, you know how you always like to make yourself useful? Will you take this bucket and fill it with water?' " She walked off the farm field and down a steep slope to a spring. Before she started, however, she asked William for his canteen, because she'd noticed how red and hot he was, and grabbed a couple of other men's canteens as well.

"I wasn't carryin' a *pitcher* on the battlefield," she said. "But how does Molly Canteen sound?"

The rest of her story got a bit blurry, as stories from the thick of battle tend to do. Before long, the artillery opened up, and British gunners followed suit. At some point, she saw a man fall near her husband's gun. Was it William? She ran to see, but it turned out to be another crew member who had collapsed in the nearly hundred-degree heat. His job had been "fetching cartridges from the bombardier and running them up to the gun and passing them to the loader and running back for more." Now someone else would need to do it.

So she did.

\* \* \*

Mr. Henry Perrine's field, or Perrine Hill, as it's now called, seemed like the perfect place to think about the rest of the battle—not just because of Molly Pitcher and the artillery, or the hill's sweeping views of where some of the key action took place, but also because of its role in the continuing saga of Washington and Lee.

The clash between the two generals is "part of the folklore of the Revolution," Lender and Stone point out. In a version that still shapes too many retellings, the commander in chief denounces Lee as a "damned poltroon" for retreating, curses him "till the leaves shook on the trees," and orders him immediately to the rear. Yet what really happened in the minutes before the British showed up seems to me more astonishing than the fable.

Washington's first decision, once he got an idea of the real situation, was to send Anthony Wayne and a couple of battalions to disrupt Clinton's right flank. Then he turned to Lee with a question. One of them, he said, needed to ride back and take charge of the main part of the army, just now approaching the battlefield. The other needed to stay right here and rally the retreating men, buying time for the main army to get into position.

*Which job would Lee prefer?*

Think about this. Not only did Washington put aside his frustration and anger (whether justified or not) because he needed help, but he gave his difficult subordinate a choice. If he was looking for buy-in, he got it. Lee chose to stay, promising to be "one of the last to leave the field." Washington galloped off in the direction of Perrine Hill.

I climbed up the hill from another dirt parking lot, this one on County Route 522, a quarter mile west of where an eighteenth-century bridge had crossed an especially marshy ravine. The afternoon was blue-skied and hot, though not one hundred degrees. A split-rail fence divided lush farmland from a scruffier but still gorgeous part of the cleared ground. The slope was gentle, but I could see why an officer whose family farmed nearby had told Washington that Perrine Hill would be a great defensive position.

Wandering the hillside for a couple of absorbing hours, I wished some clever person would project blue and red lights across the fields and orchards so I could see where different actions took place. I also tried, with the usual mixed results, to connect the beauty of a preserved battlefield with what took place there. Trailside markers with quotes from participants helped. "The dust and smoke would sometimes so shut out the view," reported a doctor named William Read, "that one could form no idea of what was going on—the roar of cannon, the crackling of musketry, men's voices making horrible confusion; then the groans and cries of the wounded."

The afternoon's fighting had three main phases: First came an intense half hour during which Lee, Wayne, and the determined men they commanded did their high-risk jobs, buying Washington the time he'd asked for. Next, the guns on Perrine Hill dueled for two hours with British artillery across the marshy ravine, creating the chaos Read would recall but with neither side gaining a military advantage. At this point, Clinton—who had jumped at the chance to destroy a sizable portion of the rebel army, and nearly succeeded—knew it was time for Phase Three. From his point of view, this meant pulling back to rejoin the rest of his army on the road to New York, preferably without interference. Washington had a different notion, and sent just enough men on a late offensive to show that the Continentals had some fight left.

Indeed they did. Phase Three would turn unexpectedly savage before sunset finally drew the curtain, though it would not affect the military outcome.

What it *did* do was help create the politically useful illusion that Monmouth was a glorious win, not a hard-fought stalemate. The illusion was enhanced by the quiet British departure for New York early the following day (Sir Henry had no reason to stick around) and promoted by Washington when he wrote Henry Laurens of having "forced the Enemy from the Field." It was amplified by relentless spin from Washington partisans (notably Hamilton and John Laurens) and by the scapegoating and self-destruction of Charles Lee, of which more later. And while I don't recall seeing the cliché "good optics" used in *Fatal Sunday*, Washington's need for them is at the heart of its argument for the battle's significance. After Clinton's offensive stalled, Lender and Stone write, "the Americans responded with brilliant military theater. The spectacular cannonade, the small detachment actions to harass the British withdrawal, followed by moving forward to occupy ground that the British had abandoned all seemed the stuff of victory."

Six days after the battle, the army got to do the wave again. Washington rested his men in Brunswick, that place of unhappy memories, and ordered up a July 4 celebration capped by another feu de joie. Steuben had reason to be pleased. Though historians still debate how much his training helped at Monmouth—most of the American infantry fighting was "defensive and from cover," not the kind of drill the baron had taught—there's no doubt it helped some. Steuben being Steuben, he lied shamelessly about his role in the battle itself. "I was fortunate enough to decide the day to our advantage," he wrote a friend, and "every soldier wished that he was under my command."

\* \* \*

The first Franco-American military collaboration of the Revolutionary War was a perfect storm of a disaster that threatened to sink the alliance.

This, of course, was no reason to skip the Rhode Island campaign, which took place two months after Monmouth—but it did lower my expectations as to how much commemoration I would find.

British troops had occupied Newport since December 1776, when William Howe sent a frustrated Clinton to take it instead of having him cut off Washington's New Jersey retreat. But in July 1778 a French fleet under the Comte d'Estaing showed up, and by the end of the month there was a plan for d'Estaing and the French troops with him to collaborate with an American force under Maj. Gen. John Sullivan and recapture the city. Alas, when Howe had sailed home in May, his brother the admiral had stuck around, and now here he came with a British fleet to mess things up. D'Estaing hustled back to sea on August 10, and the two fleets were getting ready to slug it out when they were blown to hell and gone by what was probably a hurricane. D'Estaing straggled back to Rhode Island and told Sullivan he wouldn't be helping take Newport after all: His battered ships needed to go to Boston to refit. Sullivan, who hadn't had a great war and probably shouldn't have been put in charge in the first place, blew multiple gaskets and informed d'Estaing—in a letter signed by every general in the vicinity except one—that the French were dishonorable, lying, cowardly, expletive-deleted scum whose mothers all wore combat boots.

Okay, not his precise words, but you get the idea.

Lafayette, who had not signed the letter, spent a few days wondering how many duels he'd have to fight to preserve French honor. Then he galloped off to Boston to mollify d'Estaing, throwing away another shot at glory by missing "the largest Revolutionary War battle fought in New England."

I found some traces of that battle, but not many.

One was a beautiful but obscure park on Turkey Hill in Portsmouth, eight miles north of Newport. At least I think it was Turkey Hill: The mud-encrusted marker that made the largest-battle claim was only partly legible, but did lay out some basics. Sullivan knew he couldn't take Newport without help, so he pulled back to a defensive position at the north end of Aquidneck Island, on which both Newport and Portsmouth are located. The British commander sent redcoats and

Hessians tearing after him on August 29, with the Hessians coming up West Main Road to the hill where I now stood.

And here's where things got unusually interesting.

The Hessians would soon attack the American right wing, in what would prove the decisive part of the day's action. Among the defenders were more than a hundred members of the First Rhode Island Regiment, many of them recently enslaved men who had earned their freedom by signing up to fight.

The First Rhode Island would go on to win fame as "the Black Regiment," though its officers were white and its rank and file included a complex mix that's been described as "predominantly blacks and Indians, both free men and those recently freed."

The Battle of Rhode Island was their baptism of fire.

Many details of the fight on the right wing remain murky, but the outcome is clear: The Hessian attacks were repulsed, the battle ended in a draw, and Sullivan's army made it off Aquidneck Island before a British force led by Clinton could trap it there.

Half a mile north of Turkey Hill, I found Patriots Park, which honors the First Rhode Island and memorializes the battle as a whole. Its centerpiece is a freestanding wall with text and graphics that tell the twinned stories. What kept me staring at it, though, was the frieze running across the top, on which there were hundreds of names:

Sharper Almy, Thomas Amos, Primus Angell…
Ebony Bullock, Africa Burke, Cudjo Burrell…
Cuff Greene, Jack Greene, James Greene…
Peter Mohawk, Lewis Molier, Henry Morris…
Joseph Nocake, Robert Nokeheg, Negro Norsa…
Nathan Pero, Narragansett Perry, Prince Perry…
Freeborn Sweet, Isaac Sweet, Querry Sweeten…

Not all these men fought in the Battle of Rhode Island: The wall lists African Americans and Native Americans who "served as Rhode Island soldiers in the Continental Army and the state militia" at any time during the war.

Some did fight here, though, and some died, and in any case I found it impossible not to be moved.

Yet it was also hard to forget that the First Rhode Island Regiment was an exception to the revolutionary rule—paradoxical, embarrassing, and largely ignored by historians for two centuries—that when enslaved Americans sought freedom between 1775 and 1783, a majority believed that siding with the British was their best hope.

# CHAPTER 13

# "Which Side Would You Join?"

I bet you believe the Revolution was fought for freedom, don't you?" the man in the blue-and-white uniform asked the crowd. "That's what they *said*."

Algernon Ward had just finished taking part in a small reenactment of the Battle of Brooklyn, held near the entrance to Green-Wood Cemetery. Now he and some comrades from the First Rhode Island Regiment were hanging around to talk with spectators, and I was hanging around to listen. That's because I knew that the story of the original First Rhode Islanders—from whom these Black reenactors took their name—was only one chapter in the long, complex, often heroic, far too often tragic story of how African Americans dealt with the Revolutionary War.

"Let me ask you a question," Ward continued.

"You're alive in the time of the Revolution and you're a Black person in America." The British say: "If you take the king's shilling and stay with the strongest army in the world, you will have immediate emancipation." Your option: "Go with George Washington, a Virginia slave owner, who took a slave *with* him, by the way," when he went to war and who said, early on, that "he didn't want any mulattoes or negroes" in his army.

"Which side would you join?"

A few yards away Joseph Becton, another First Rhode Islander, was holding court—loudly and theatrically, while adding some nuance—in front of a homemade sign he had filled with relevant documents and images.

"The British said anybody who came to fight with them against Washington who was *NOT* owned by a loyal British citizen could be free," he told a woman who'd asked a question I didn't hear.

"Ohhhhh," she said, taking his point.

"So we're not looking at something that's done because you want anybody to be free. We're looking at something that's done to hurt the American army."

A conspicuous figure in weathered white period clothing with a white circle beard to match, Becton brought passion, humor, and decades of experience to his historical show-and-tell. A Marine Corps veteran and retired Park Service ranger, he had cofounded the First Rhode Island group and started Joe Becton Tours & Historical Services in Philadelphia, where he was known to enhance history lessons with poetry and live music.

"I want to talk to you about that sign," said an inquisitive twelve-year-old named Arielle, walking boldly up to Becton's display.

"Oh, well, step right up!" he said, and pointed to the best-known document there. "People say the Declaration means freedom. But when you look at it closely, it says things like 'We hold these truths to be self-evident, that all men are created equal.'"

"Not 'all men and women,'" Arielle said.

"Not 'all men and women.' And guess what? Not even all *men*. Because an African like me couldn't be free. 'We can't let Africans get free! Who's going to grow the sugar? Who's going to grow the tobacco?'"

He pointed to a picture: "A lot of times we say the Boston Massacre was the first battle of the Revolution."

"Not officially," Arielle said.

"Oh, I like that! This was in 1770. Five guys gave their lives that day. Crispus Attucks was one of them. But the Revolution didn't start until 1775."

More pictures: Here was Alexander Hamilton, whom Arielle's nine-year-old sister identified instantly, and Phillis Wheatley, who famously published a book of poetry while enslaved, and the Declaration of

Independence's principal author, who, as Becton put it, owned "slaves and slaves and slaves and slaves." And here was the Liberty Bell, named by nineteenth-century abolitionists and silenced by a crack usually dated to February 1846.

"They were celebrating Washington's birthday, and then it cracked," Arielle said. "Abolitionists thought it cracked because he owned slaves and was not for all liberty."

"Whooo!" said Becton, clapping his hands. "Abolitionists said the bell is cracked because America is cracked. The story of freedom is cracked—which is what you were just saying! Just wonderful! Did your parents teach you these things?"

One of the items on Becton's sign was a copy of a November 1775 proclamation by Virginia's royal governor, Lord Dunmore. It declared, as Becton had pointed out, that any enslaved man willing to fight on the British side *and owned by a rebel* was free. As it happened, I knew about Dunmore's Proclamation already, though not from my parents, or any formal education, or, until recently, from histories of the Revolution. Nope: I first learned about the governor—and, more important, about the enslaved people who ran to join him—from a wildly original, two-volume, nine-hundred-plus-page novel for teenagers whose author I had been lucky enough to interview almost a decade before.

With my own book approaching Lord Dunmore territory—including the horrific, surprisingly important little battle that doubles as a key part of the wartime history of African Americans—it seemed like a good idea to sit down with him again.

* * *

Ask Matthew Tobin Anderson what got him going on the Revolution and he'll start by telling you that he grew up in the small Massachusetts town of Stow, from which men had marched off to neighboring Concord to fight, and that on April 19, 1975, when he was six, his parents woke him at 4 a.m., put him in a canoe, and paddled down the Concord River to the Old North Bridge to hear the president (Gerald Ford) give a bicentennial speech. Later, watching a reenactment in the same location, he found himself thinking, "Omigod, if this had been 225 years ago, it would have been my father or me standing there with our fowling pieces," poised to take on the British Army.

Ask Anderson how he ended up writing *The Astonishing Life of Octavian Nothing: Traitor to the Nation*, however—as opposed to something like *We Were There at the Battle of Lexington and Concord*—and he'll toss a few unusual elements into the mix.

We met for dinner in Cambridge, at a restaurant just north of the Common. He sported what looked like the same three-day beard I recalled from years before, and filled his conversation with the same enthusiastic eclecticism. In addition to his history-tinged childhood, he said, a second element that shaped the novel was his longtime fascination with the eighteenth century, especially the clash between its sophistication and its brutality. A third was a story he'd heard in England about a free Black youth whose university education was said to have been an experiment to test the intellect of Africans. A fourth was the strange phenomenon of "pox parties," at which eighteenth-century physicians infected (or "inoculated") revelers with a mild dose of smallpox (this was before a vaccine was developed) and kept them in isolation for a month, hoping they'd emerge alive and immune. What if he sent some characters to a pox party in April 1775, he wondered, "and when they come out, the world has changed," leaving them with a decision to make.

*Which side should they join?*

Amalgamating these notions, he had his title character grow up in a Boston house surrounded by high walls. Within those walls, a cadre of eccentric scholars seeks to determine whether Octavian can soak up knowledge as readily as a person of European origins. The boy is not told that he is an experimental subject, or that he and his African-born mother are owned by the scholars. He figures these things out, survives a pox party gone wrong, runs away, gets recaptured, and escapes again— at which point yet another unusual element takes over the narrative.

Anderson has the pioneering Black historian Benjamin Quarles to thank for this one.

"There's a book called something very 1950s like *The Negro in the American Revolution*," he told me, correctly recalling the title. Quarles's second chapter, "Lord Dunmore's Ethiopian Regiment," amazed him.

It told a "fundamental American story of heroism and tragedy" that he had never heard.

A condensed version might begin like this:

Two days after Lexington and Concord but before the news made it to Virginia, Dunmore, the royal governor, seized the colony's powder supply. Amid the outcry that followed, he threatened to free enslaved Virginians to fight for the Crown against their masters. On June 8, 1775, lacking enough troops to ensure his safety, he fled the capital and took refuge on a warship in the York River. The arrival of a few Regulars who had been in Florida emboldened him, as did a victorious skirmish with rebels at Kemp's Mill, and in mid-November he issued a proclamation in which he declared martial law and included words, as Quarles wrote, that were "destined to be quoted far and wide":

> I do hereby further declare all indented Servants, Negroes, or others, (appertaining to Rebels,) free, that are able and willing to bear Arms, they joining His Majesty's Troops, as soon as may be...

George Washington's reaction to the Dunmore threat, expressed in a letter to a fellow Virginian, echoed the fears of slave owners throughout the South:

> If my Dear Sir that Man is not crushed before Spring, he will become the most formidable Enemy America has—his strength will Increase as a Snow ball by Rolling; and faster, if some expedient cannot be hit upon to convince the Slaves and Servants of the Impotency of His designs.

Washington wasn't kidding. A good number of enslaved people within reach of Dunmore's coastal base had run to him without prompting; his proclamation set many more in motion. Rebel authorities warned that "the time-honored penalty for a slave insurrection was death without benefit of clergy" and the best that slaves "taken in arms" could hope for was to be sold to a West Indies sugar plantation, itself a virtual death sentence. Still, they kept running—women and children among them—if they could.

"When Patrick Henry delivered his immortal demand for either liberty or death," as another historian points out, "he was not speaking to slaves. No matter; they heard him anyway."

But we can't hear *them*, Anderson thought.

Every single runaway, he told me, must have had "a story of escape, and of aspiration, and all the things that make American stories so powerful"—but almost all of those stories are lost. Not without some trepidation, he decided that by imagining a few of them, he might help "fill in what would otherwise be blank."

Octavian's flight takes him south from Boston in the fall of 1775. News of Dunmore's Proclamation sends him to Norfolk, a growing port and Virginia's most prosperous town, where he signs up with the governor's new "Ethiopian Regiment" ("Ethiopian" being a misnomer, at the time, for anyone of African origin). Refusing to give his slave surname, he enters the regiment's books as Octavian Nothing. Issued a musket, he spends more time shoveling than learning to shoot.

His educated speech sets him apart from his untutored fellows, which embarrasses him. But he is greatly drawn to their stories and writes some down.

Anderson's fictional characters converge at a real battle fought a dozen or so miles south of Norfolk on December 9, 1775. To say that Octavian and the others were on my mind as I set out to explore the battlefield would be an understatement: What took place there shattered the hopes of the freedom-seeking Blacks and marked the beginning of a desperate endgame for most.

Yet history, like fiction, depends on point of view.

And the Battle of Great Bridge turned out to be a powerful reminder of how extremely different stories about the same slice of history can both be true.

\* \* \*

"It was one of the earliest, shortest, smallest, least known battles of the Revolution, and yet one of the most important," the evening's speaker began.

I'd been invited to continue my Great Bridge education at a meeting of the American Revolution Round Table of Richmond. The battlefield itself was about a hundred miles farther to the southeast, and when I toured it, I would be much better prepared thanks to Norman Fuss. A retired chemical engineer and management consultant who had studied the revolutionary era for decades, Fuss called himself an "avocational historian"—a term I wish I'd invented—and as part of his Richmond talk, he deployed a homemade 3D map that helped listeners visualize how the 1775 landscape had shaped the battle.

Here's some of what I learned:

- At his Norfolk base, Dunmore had enough ships to fend off attacks from the sea, but not enough men to do the same on land. Luckily for him, most of the area to the south "was covered by the Great Dismal Swamp." The only practical way to attack Norfolk by land was along a north–south causeway that crossed the southern branch of the Elizabeth River on the Great Bridge. A fort there would be a choke point for attackers, so Dunmore had one thrown up. Its garrison would include a mix of Regulars, white loyalists, and men from the Ethiopian Regiment.

- Sure enough, here came the rebels. They could have reduced the fort to splinters if they'd had cannon, but they didn't. So they put up their own fortification a few hundred yards south of the bridge—a W-shaped breastwork "about 150 feet long, seven feet high, eight feet thick"—and settled in to wait for some big guns to arrive.

- Between the fort and the W-shaped breastwork were three other key points: a small island just south of the bridge, on which the rebels posted sentries; a long, curving chunk of causeway below that, dead-ending at the breastwork; and a little dry land in the marsh west of the causeway, well within rifle range.

"We can *see* where these places were," Fuss said, though there are, as usual, modern distractions.

When I got there myself, no fewer than five people affiliated with the Great Bridge Battlefield & Waterways History Foundation turned out to help me locate the eighteenth century beneath the twenty-first. We met in a parking lot near the Albemarle and Chesapeake Canal, which is part of the Intracoastal Waterway and—along with the five-hundred-ton drawbridge that rises hourly—is one of the main distractions. Executive director Lin Olsen kicked things off by describing the foundation's efforts to put Great Bridge on the revolutionary map. Olsen was in charge of getting an 8,500-square-foot museum and visitor center built with resources that were less than infinite. (It would open in 2020.) "See the pilings there?" she said, pointing to a forest of posts rising from a parcel of soggy land. "They went up early because I was able to get them donated. That was about a $450,000 in-kind donation." Two companies donated the piles. A third donated *driving* the piles. Driving them required that a humongous pile driver be floated up the waterway.

"Can you get us a tugboat?" someone asked.

Yes she could: two tugboats, in fact.

How can you not love someone like that, even if she has it in her head that December 9 at Great Bridge—not April 19 on the Battle Road—was "the first victory for our patriots during our Revolutionary War"?

"Well, it's the first land victory in Virginia," Jon Stull told me after Olsen headed back to work.

"That's just local pride," Richard Fisher explained.

Stull and Fisher were two of the four knowledgeable foundation volunteers who walked me around the site and took turns evoking the deadly drama that played out there. As they talked, I mentally layered Fuss's map over the canal, the drawbridge, and Big Woody's Bar & Grill, from which you could look across the river to where Dunmore's fort had stood. I also kept Anderson's characters in mind, because the story I was hearing now was mainly from the rebel point of view.

"The guys who were in charge knew a little bit about tactical operations," said Stull, who was certainly qualified to judge, having served thirty years in the Marine Corps and taught at the Joint Forces Staff College. The rebel commanders were William Woodford and Charles Scott, each of whom has a county in Kentucky named after him. They ordered up that W-shaped breastwork (near the south end of the drawbridge, someone said) as well as some low earthworks to protect riflemen on that dry land west of the causeway. Now all they needed to break the stalemate were those cannon.

Dunmore, directing operations from Norfolk, soon learned that the guns were en route.

This gave him three choices. He could pull his garrison back, preserving scarce Regulars but losing Norfolk; or have his men stay and fight, hoping they could somehow hold the fort anyway; or attack first, before the artillery came. It would have helped to know that the cannon would prove useless—badly cast and honeycombed, they were likely to blow up if fired—but he didn't, and neither did Woodford and Scott.

He chose the preemptive strike.

The plan was for Black troops to outflank the rebels and create diversions before the main assault. This never happened, for reasons unknown, though why it had occurred to anyone to send raw recruits into unfamiliar swampland in the dark is beyond me.

Never mind: Here came the men and officers of the Fourteenth Regiment of Foot, some 150 strong, crossing the bridge in the first faint light of day.

The rebel sentries did their job, firing a few shots and retreating, with one especially valiant man staying at his post longer than duty required. Down the narrow causeway came the Regulars, six abreast and moving fast. The idea was not to stop and shoot but to drive the rebels from the breastwork using only their bayonets. White loyalists and members of the Ethiopian Regiment halted while the professionals led the attack.

"What were they planning to do, climb *over* the thing?" I asked incredulously.

The only logical answer was that the British hoped the rebels would cut and run, as they had at Kemp's Mill a month earlier.

They did not.

Musket fire erupted from the breastwork. British captain Charles Fordyce cried, "The day is our own!" and went down with fourteen holes in his body. Rifle fire from the west added to the slaughter. Five minutes after the first volley, every Regular still standing was in retreat. A rebel officer summed up the scene they left behind.

"I then saw the horrors of war in perfection," he wrote, with "10 and 12 bullets thro' many; limbs broke in 2 or 3 places; brains turning out. Good God, what a sight!"

Incredibly, most of the roughly eight hundred rebels at Great Bridge had played no part in the victory. Encamped a quarter mile to the south, with only one hundred or so men on the front lines when the British attacked, they simply couldn't get there in time.

* * *

Great Bridge spelled doom for Dunmore and his Ethiopian Regiment. His shattered force retreated to Norfolk that night and the governor prepared to abandon the town. A number of the Black troops had been killed, wounded, or captured during the chaotic retreat (records are inexact at best), but military losses would prove the least of their suffering over the next eight months. Space in Dunmore's fleet was limited, and a careful student of the regiment, Charles Carey, estimates that only half of the remaining three hundred Ethiopians made it on board. Crammed together on the smallest vessels, without adequate shelter or clothing, they were struck immediately by a deadly fever, probably typhus, "as if they wore bulls-eyes on their backs."

Smallpox followed.

Epidemic in North America during the Revolution, the disease was such a threat to the Continentals that Washington would be forced to overcome his concerns about the military risk of inoculation. In 1777, his army would begin a year of what amounted to outsized pox parties, both in the encampments at Morristown and Valley Forge and among enlistees before they joined the veterans. Troops from Europe, where smallpox had a longer history, often acquired immunity through childhood contact—but Dunmore's Black recruits were devastated.

As Elizabeth Fenn writes in *Pox Americana*, the Ethiopian Regiment "brought together in one place a large, vulnerable population. Once the virus gained a foothold...a constant influx of susceptible newcomers kept the contagion alive."

Twice Dunmore tried to establish new bases on the Virginia coast, the first near Portsmouth, the second on Gwynn's Island, fifty miles farther north. Twice he was forced to abandon them, leaving hundreds of dead behind. After he sailed away from Gwynn's, rebels were appalled by the number of bodies they found "without a shovelful of earth upon them." Carey's best guess is that of more than 1,100 enslaved Virginians who joined Dunmore's Ethiopian Regiment, only 220 left the state alive.

It was a dreadful price to pay for freedom.

That said, some *did* achieve it, and many remained willing to take the risk. Three years later, Henry Clinton would issue a variation on Dunmore's Proclamation, in which he promised that slaves of rebels who fled to his army would be protected. As the war moved south, uncountable thousands would run to the British, often providing valuable service. At the same time, the fear of a British-aided slave revolt, first made real by the Ethiopian Regiment, drove many white fence-sitters and loyalists into the rebel camp.

Two more stories before we leave the Battle of Great Bridge behind.

First, there's the one about how the Old Dominion helped its favorite son keep his army in the field. "As a result of that victory, the British were driven out of Virginia and there was no organized British presence in Virginia for the next five years," Fuss said. "So here we have the largest, most populous state of the nascent United States" with "nobody around to interfere with it providing massive support to Washington's army."

Then there's the story of William "Billy" Flora.

Flora was the rebel sentry who stayed at his post the longest when the British attacked. A free Black militiaman, he was probably twenty in 1775. According to the tale a white comrade liked to tell, he fired his musket eight times, then pulled up a plank behind him, in an attempt to delay the enemy, while retreating to the breastwork.

William Flora went on to enlist in a regiment of Continentals, serving, among other places, at Yorktown. Returning from the war, he ran "a successful cartage and livery stable business based in Portsmouth"; bought and sold land and houses; paid substantial taxes; and eventually received a land grant for his army service—all of which Norman Fuss reported in the *Journal of the American Revolution*.

And there was this, too:

"Sometime after 1782, he was wealthy enough to purchase freedom for his wife and two children."

\* \* \*

Washington didn't want anyone like William Flora in his army—at least at first. On July 10, 1775, a week after he took command in Cambridge, orders went out that army recruiters were not to sign up any "stroller, negro, or vagabond." In early October, his generals voted to confirm this policy: No Blacks, whether free or enslaved, were to be enlisted. A few weeks later it was made clear that even Black men already serving were not wanted: Soldiers who reenlisted were to get a new set of clothes, "Negroes excepted, which the Congress do not incline to inlist again." Free Blacks in the army protested, and on December 30, a "sympathetic" Washington changed his mind and let them re-up, explaining to the president of Congress that he feared they would switch sides otherwise. What he didn't mention was that a shocking percentage of his mostly white army planned to go home when enlistments expired at the end of the month.

Congress said fine, he could reenlist those guys, as long as he didn't start accepting *new* Black volunteers.

I can't help wondering what Flora would have thought about this, or Prince Estabrook, Peter Salem, Caesar Bason, Samuel Sutphen, Thomas Lively, and any of the other Black rebel soldiers—some already free, some not—whose stories I ran across in my travels. According to an old but widely cited estimate, "about 5,000 blacks served with the American forces," though more recent research suggests that that figure is too low.

What's undisputable is that Prince Estabrook was there at the beginning.

Prince was about thirty-four in 1775. How he came to be enslaved to the Estabrook family of Lexington (whose surname he bore, as was common) is not recorded. We do know that he trained with Parker's militia; turned out on the Green on April 19; got wounded; recovered; and went on to serve, at various times and places, until the fall of 1783, when he returned to Lexington and went back to work for the same family. That year, as it happens, a state court declared slavery unconstitutional in Massachusetts, though the Revolutionary War's first Black casualty might already have earned his freedom by then.

Precisely how Casey Whitney earned *his* freedom is also uncertain, though a famous Concord writer would record some riveting hearsay about it.

Casey, as mentioned in chapter 2, was the subject of an obscure marker I ran across on a hillside near the Battle Road. "In 1775 Casey was Samuel Whitney's slave," its text read. "When revolution came, he ran away to war, fought for the colonies, and returned to Concord a free man." The story's source turned out to be Henry David Thoreau, who relayed what he'd heard from an older friend. Stolen from his African homeland when he was maybe twenty years old, Casey had left a wife and child there. One day, while he was chopping wood, his master's son started throwing snowballs at him. Fed up, he threw his ax at the kid, hid out in the river "up to his neck," left town, and enlisted.

"Used to say that he went home to Africa in the night and came back again in the morning; *i.e.*, he dreamed of home," Thoreau's friend said. "Lived to be old."

Hoping to learn more, I dropped by a small museum across Monument Street from the Old North Bridge. Opened in 2012, the Robbins House works to "unearth and share the stories of Concord's earliest African Americans," and while it hadn't dug up much on Casey, one document did confirm a small part of Thoreau's version. A "receipt for support of Case Whitney" has someone receiving $52 from the town to cover the period between June 1820 and June 1821, proving that he had in fact "lived to be old."

But the most useful thing at the museum, for my purposes, was a rare print copy of a 260-page National Park Service document called

*Patriots of Color: 'A Peculiar Beauty and Merit'; African Americans and Native Americans at Battle Road & Bunker Hill.*

"Every once in a while a piece of scholarship comes along that changes the way you look at a historical event," wrote historian Alfred F. Young in the preface to George Quintal Jr.'s 2004 report. What Quintal changed was our understanding of how many nonwhite Americans fought on April 19 and June 17, 1775—and by extension, during the rest of the war.

Four decades earlier, Young pointed out, Benjamin Quarles could name only six Black men who fought at Bunker Hill. By the time Quintal had devoted nearly three years to the project, he had revised the number of known patriots of color who served there—including fifteen Native Americans—to 103. This is a cautious figure that left out "probables" and "maybes," so the real number may have been closer to 150.

Quintal got started on large-scale revolutionary research as a member of (drumroll, please) the Arnold Expedition Historical Society. It's a small world, and it got smaller, for me, as I learned things about my childhood home in Massachusetts that I had never known.

*Patriots of Color* lists two Black Framingham residents as having served with the town's minute men on April 19. One, Peter Salem, is known to close students of the war, while the other, Jeffrey Hemenway, is obscure, but I don't recall hearing either of their names during my school days. Nor did I learn that while those men were off fighting, "a strange panic seized upon the women and children" of Framingham, inspired by a baseless rumor that "the Negroes were coming to massacre them all!" And I had no clue that the most famous man of color associated with the Revolution might have been enslaved half a mile from my house.

Crispus Attucks's owner, according to the town historian, was a church deacon whose house on Old Connecticut Path still stands. I must have walked past it five hundred times on my way home from school, or to the mall, or to sneak under the canvas walls of the Carousel Theatre to hear the likes of the Lovin' Spoonful and Peter, Paul and Mary for free.

Attucks was the first man killed in the Boston Massacre, the 1770 confrontation between British soldiers and an angry Boston mob that was given its name (by Sam Adams) for propaganda purposes. We know almost nothing about his life for certain, though the "most widely accepted interpretation suggests"—as the author of a recent book subtitled *Crispus Attucks in American Memory* cautiously puts it—that he was "a large man, over six feet," probably of "mixed African and Native American ancestry," who ran from enslavement in 1750, when he was about twenty-seven, and went to sea. In 2000, Framingham put his name on an insignificant span over a brook that flows past his owner's house. Standing on Crispus Attucks Bridge, I tried to wrap my mind around the idea that such a dramatic break for freedom could have been made in my boring suburban neighborhood.

Then I drove to the Old Burying Ground, on the far side of town, where I found four American flags on the gravestone of Peter Salem.

After joining the Battle Road fight on the war's first day, Salem went on to serve at Saratoga, Valley Forge, and Monmouth, among other places. The date of his manumission is not documented, though it's been assumed he was freed before he enlisted. Quintal thinks he "probably served at the most battles" of anyone in *Patriots of Color*, surely reason enough to honor him. Yet Salem's modest, posthumous fame—his grave went unmarked for six decades—derives from a dubious nineteenth-century theory that he shot and mortally wounded British major John Pitcairn at Bunker Hill. Pitcairn's death carried symbolic significance, because the major was thought (wrongly) to have ordered British troops to open fire on the Lexington militiamen on April 19.

Want to know who really shot Major P? J. L. Bell has a great series of posts in his *Boston 1775* blog that will help. But I need to move on to a few of the other men of color who fought in Charlestown that day.

For starters, confusingly, there was Salem Poor, *also* credited with killing Pitcairn.

In 1769, Poor purchased his own freedom for £27. At Bunker Hill, he fought so well that six months later, more than a dozen of his army superiors lauded him in a petition to the Massachusetts legislature for behaving "like an Experienced officer, as Well as an Excellent Soldier." It was "absolutely extraordinary," Bell writes, "to see high-ranking white

gentlemen in 1775 compare a black man to 'an Experienced officer.'"
The petition is dated December 5, 1775, during the period when Washington was trying to drive Blacks out of the army. It's hard to imagine this being a coincidence.

Quintal's invaluable work turned up dozens of life stories—or skeletons of life stories, really—that I wish it were possible to flesh out further.

Prince Hull fought in the redoubt at Bunker Hill and was wounded at Saratoga; in old age, he had to submit a list of possessions (total value $8.57) to prove he was poor enough to deserve a pension. Plato Lambert, a man "of gigantic stature" born in Framingham, is thought to have been murdered. Barzillai Lew, a talented musician, served at Fort Ticonderoga while Arnold fought on Lake Champlain; Lew purchased his wife's freedom and they had enough children to form "a complete band" that played "all first-class occasions" near their Massachusetts hometown. Silas Royal, a free Black body servant to a Rhode Island general, was kidnapped by men who almost succeeded in selling him. Caesar Bason fought on the Battle Road and Bunker Hill; like many in the redoubt, he ran out of powder and was killed there.

Of the 103 men of color he placed at Bunker Hill, Quintal identified 18 (including Bason) as enslaved and 27 as free; the status of 58 was unknown. All were in integrated units. Among those who served later in the war, more fought at Saratoga than in any other battle, and more died at Valley Forge than anywhere else.

Quintal and others believe that roughly eight hundred men of color fought on the rebel side at Monmouth, an even higher percentage than at Bunker Hill. At the Monmouth reenactment, I looked up at one point to see two guys from a group called Sable Soldiers of the American Revolution, one of whom I had met in Brooklyn and later seen rowing a Durham boat across the Delaware. "We're here to start a relationship," Ludger K. Balan told me. "We think there need to be more of us here at the big encampment."

"If you don't tell your story," added Leon Vaughan, "then who will?"

John Laurens fought at Monmouth, too, though I've seen no record of him paying attention to the Black troops there. At the Battle of

Rhode Island, according to his biographer, he "could not have failed to observe" the men of the First Rhode Island in action, though again, I'm not aware of his writing about it. That said, it would be surprising if their presence hadn't reminded him of a notion he'd pitched to his influential dad from Valley Forge eight months before.

On January 2, 1778, a Rhode Island general named James Varnum had written the commander in chief about the idea of freeing some Rhode Island Blacks to fight as part of the Continental Army. The troop-starved Washington had forwarded Varnum's letter to the state's governor with a brief note, in John's handwriting, implying though not stating his approval. A couple of weeks later, the president of Congress received a startling letter from his son. John proposed to raise his *own* Black regiment and asked Henry to give him the use of some "able-bodied Slaves" to begin that good work "instead of leaving me a fortune." It would be a win-win, he argued: The army would get desperately needed manpower while those "unjustly deprived of the Rights of Mankind" could earn their freedom.

Henry didn't say no.

Their epistolary discussion went on for a while.

And if you're looking to examine the radical dissonance between revolutionary ideals and an economy based on chattel slavery, you will find no better case study than the Laurens family of South Carolina.

\* \* \*

Live oaks draped with Spanish moss lined the grand avenue leading to what was called Mepkin Plantation when Henry Laurens bought it in 1762. A marker at the turnoff from the main road lists his impressive revolutionary credentials, among them president of South Carolina's Council of Safety, president of its Provincial Congress, and of course Continental Congress chief from November 1777 to December 1778. The marker says nothing, however, about how Henry got rich enough to buy thousands of acres here on the Cooper River, twenty miles north of Charleston; to acquire property on the outskirts of the city the same year; and to have elegant houses built in both locations.

At the visitor center, I signed up for a tour, though I knew Laurens would play second fiddle to the place's current occupants—a community of Trappist monks. Which is fair enough: The tale of how the old plantation became Mepkin Abbey is fascinating in itself.

It began, our guide told us, when Henry Luce and Clare Boothe Luce ("I don't know if those names ring any bells") fell in love with Mepkin not long after their 1935 marriage. Henry, the magazine innovator who published *Time*, *Life*, and *Fortune*, snapped it up "as kind of a late wedding gift" for his wife, a playwright and journalist who went on to be a congresswoman and ambassador. The Luces used Mepkin mostly in hunting season; gave it up in 1949; and decided—because Clare "found great solace in the Catholic church" after her nineteen-year-old daughter died in a car accident—to donate it so "a group of religious" could take up residence. Twenty-nine Trappists showed up, and the rest is history I can't dwell on, though it's hard to resist mentioning that the monks supported themselves in part by raising chickens and selling eggs until People for the Ethical Treatment of Animals made a big honking stink and they switched to mushrooms. More seriously and sadly, the guide told us, the number of brothers was steadily shrinking.

Back to Henry Laurens, about whom she did mention a few things. "He was a very wealthy merchant, owned hundreds of slaves," who had "married into a family, the Ball family, that had plantations up and down the river; Eleanor's dad had a little dynasty of plantations." The subject of Henry's political career came up briefly, as did his unusual burial request. "Deathly afraid of being buried alive," he insisted in his will that he be cremated, a rare practice at the time. Why? One of his young daughters, thought to have died of smallpox, had been "laid out in the parlor, as they used to do," but before the coffin was closed, cool air or rain reached her from an open window "and she came to."

After the tour, I crossed a ravine on a footbridge that led me to a secluded family cemetery. A nearby marker shed some light on the enslaved people who worked Henry's fields, noting that some brought with them from West Africa "expert knowledge of tidal river rice farming." The text also used a term more specific than "merchant" to describe his pre-Mepkin occupation.

"Slave-trading merchant," it read.

This was an understatement, as I learned when I got home and read *Slaves in the Family,* an eye-opening 1998 book by Edward Ball.

Ball is a descendant of Henry's dynasty-creating father-in-law. He set out to explore his family's history, he writes, not out of personal guilt—"a person cannot be culpable for the acts of others, long dead, that he or she could not have influenced"—but because "the slave business was a crime that had not fully been acknowledged" and he felt "called on to try to explain it."

Between 1751 and 1761, he reports, Laurens and his partner, George Austin, "brought sixty-one slave galleys to the Charleston wharfs—the largest number of any slave importer in the city, and the heaviest volume in the territory of the future United States." Ball estimates how many people the partners imported in that decade (7,800) as well as what they earned in commissions on the sales ("£156,000, enough to make them and their wives, in only ten years, four of the richest people in America"). Arriving slavers threw the dead overboard, usually far enough out so corpses wouldn't wash ashore. The ships then proceeded to Sullivan's Island, at the entrance to Charleston Harbor, where the living were confined to a "pest house" until certified healthy enough for sale.

Ball homes in on one shipload in particular. "Just imported in the *Hare,* Capt. Caleb Godfrey, directly from Sierra Leon, a Cargo of Likely and Healthy Slaves," read a 1756 ad placed by Laurens's firm. Calling these people healthy was a lie: Henry complained privately that they were "a most scabby flock" afflicted by yaws, a chronic, contagious skin disease. Slave dealers, Ball writes, had an extraordinarily callous term— "refuse Negro"—for sick, old, bad-tempered, or otherwise hard-to-sell captives, and Henry used it in reference to some people on the *Hare.*

I learned more about Henry's wealth building from Ball and other historians. After his partnership with Austin ended in 1762, the year he bought Mepkin, "Laurens would continue to sell people, although fewer than before," as his focus shifted to buying more plantations. As a plantation owner, he's said to have been more lenient than many, a low bar even if true. Still, he "did not flinch" when it came to separating families and doling out punishment.

What I did *not* learn was the answer to the following question:

How does a fifty-two-year-old man who has trafficked in human beings for decades come to write that "I abhor Slavery" and in the same August 1776 letter proclaim that he plans to free many enslaved people on his plantations and, what's more, end "the entail of Slavery"—meaning, as historian Jack Rakove explains, "the hereditary transfer of slave status from one generation to another"?

A year and a half later, the letter's recipient would ask him to put his money where his mouth was.

\* \* \*

John Laurens came into the world during Henry's wildly profitable slave-trading decade and spent half his childhood shuttling between Mepkin and the Charleston house. His mother died when he was fifteen—"I know you Love me, I know you will take care of your Children," Eleanor Ball Laurens told her husband on her deathbed—and a year later, Henry moved with their sons to Europe to better educate them. He sailed for home in November 1774 but John stayed, bowing to his father's wish that he study law instead of medicine, which he'd have much preferred. He was twenty-one and still in London when Henry wrote that bombshell of a letter.

By the time it reached him, in the fall of 1776, he was desperate to ditch his studies and go home to fight.

He had been thinking this way for a while. Months before war broke out, he wrote Henry that if it did, "there is no Man I hope would more gladly expose himself, or hold his Life more cheap." This was hardly a declaration to warm a parent's heart, but John would say similar things many times. It is no contradiction to suggest, however, that another factor influenced his decision to leave England. He had gotten a young woman pregnant; married her, as honor and "pity" decreed; but feared obligations to an unwanted wife and child could interfere with "more important Engagements to my Country."

Cut to the Battle of Germantown, October 4, 1777.

John had joined Washington's staff (thanks, Dad) and fought at Brandywine ("It was not his fault that he was not killed or wounded," reported Lafayette). Now he and several others decided they could solve the problem of Cliveden—that castle-like stone house blocking the

Germantown advance—on their own initiative. Their plan was to stack straw against the front door and burn it down, and from what I can tell it was a miracle Laurens survived.

Valley Forge was next.

I once ran across a five-minute animated Laurens bio that nicely sums up John's winter there. We see him at a crowded table with other unhappy aides, including Hamilton, scribbling away as huge stacks of paper materialize beside them. (*"Their job . . . was to write and translate Washington's correspondence. Washington had a LOT of correspondence."*) Next we see him writing a back-channel letter of his own. (*"Dear father, CONWAY SUX!"*) Then a lightbulb flashes over his head and he writes Henry again, this time to pitch the idea of a Laurens-sponsored Black regiment.

It wasn't just Rhode Island's example that inspired him, though that almost certainly provided a spark.

We can't be sure what John thought of slavery as a boy growing up in its midst. But we do know he was exposed to strong antislavery sentiment in London, where, for example, two of his friends had written an impassioned abolitionist tract in the form of a 435-line poem called *The Dying Negro*. By the time he decided to head home, he had come to believe that Americans "cannot contend with *a good grace*, for Liberty, until we shall have enfranchised our slaves." Most revealingly, he mocked the "absurd" argument to which slavery supporters he knew always seemed to be reduced, which he summarized as: "Without Slaves how is it possible for us to be rich[?]"

Was he talking to his father here?

Yes indeed. Those last words are from John's reply to Henry's announcement that he was doing a one-eighty on slavery. It was a change of heart, John wrote, that "coincides exactly with my Feelings upon that Subject." Yet Henry's letter was marred by self-justification— "I am not the man who enslaved them"; "I was born in a Country where Slavery had been established by British Kings and Parliaments"; and "In former days there was no combatting the prejudices of Men supported by Interest"—that his son chose not to address directly.

Why rub it in when "Without Slaves how is it possible for us to be rich" did the trick all by itself?

Now, in the winter of 1778, John was talking to his father again. I'll paraphrase the back-and-forth, taking a few liberties:

**John:** *Can I have my human inheritance now? They can fight for our freedom and earn theirs. Win-win! Or win-win-WIN, because I'll lead them in battle and earn eternal fame.*

**Henry:** *Has it occurred to you that our slaves might not WANT to leave their happy home to be cannon fodder?*

**John:** *Has it occurred to YOU that they were stolen from their real homes to toil for the luxuries of merciless tyrants? Or that serving in the army might help them adjust to life after slavery?*

**Henry:** *Well, if freedom is theirs by natural right, what's your moral justification for withholding it? Try setting them free BEFORE you address them in the language of a recruiting officer: You'll be lucky if four sign up. And hey, if what you really want is your own command, why not go down to South Carolina and recruit a few white guys?*

**John:** *Low blow, Dad. Let's table this idea for now; I can see you're not buying it.*

If you're getting the idea that Henry might not be quite ready to start freeing the enslaved—despite having said he was—your skepticism is justified.

Meanwhile, fortunately for John's mental health, he was back on the battlefield a few months later. On that day of hot and heavy action at Monmouth, he narrowly escaped being captured, had a horse shot from under him, and received a slight wound he neglected to tell Henry about.

Then he helped destroy the reputation of Charles Lee.

In fairness, Lee did a lot of the heavy lifting on that front. Not long after the battle—already aware that his performance was being derided within an army he thought he had saved from disaster—he fired off an angry letter to Washington. Lee accused his boss of "an act of cruel injustice" toward him; demanded a public apology; and went on to say that he knew George would never have dissed him so badly unless egged on "by some of those dirty earwigs who will forever insinuate themselves near persons in high office." Prominent among those earwigs, as Lee knew, were Hamilton and John Laurens.

Washington fired back, taking exception to Lee's tone and denying he'd said anything unwarranted on the battlefield. By the end of June, Lee had asked for a court-martial to clear his name; Washington had filed three charges against him; and he was under arrest.

Cut to December 23, 1778, and cue up "Ten Duel Commandments" from *Hamilton* as a soundtrack.

The court-martial had gone poorly for Lee. Accused of disobeying orders by not attacking; making an "unnecessary, disorderly, and shameful retreat"; and disrespecting the commander in chief, he was convicted on all counts. While he was clearly guilty on the third charge, the first two were highly problematic. The officers judging him seemed to acknowledge this, deleting the word "shameful" and merely suspending him from command for a year, a sentence too light for a man who'd really done what Lee was accused of. But what were those officers to do? As John Shy explains: "An acquittal on the first two charges would have been a vote of no-confidence in Washington"—something neither the army nor the country could afford.

Lee did not go quietly, spewing anti-Washington vituperation in all directions. But Congress, his last hope, sustained the verdict. And in December—angered by the attacks on the man he served and revered— John Laurens challenged Lee to a duel. The two met at the edge of some woods in what's now North Philadelphia. Hamilton served as Laurens's second and wrote about it. Firing pistols from "within five or six paces," Laurens gave Lee a superficial wound sufficient to satisfy both men's sense of honor.

Also on December 23, 1778, as it happened, a British fleet showed up off the Georgia coast.

Six days later, Crown troops waltzed into Savannah, thanks to an enslaved guide who showed them how to take the defenders in the rear.

Seven weeks after *that*, what John Laurens called his "black project" was on the table again. Before long, that project would be blessed by both Congress and his father.

And by April 1779, Henry Laurens's "idealistic and vainglorious son"—as one historian described him—was galloping south to win eternal fame and change the world.

# CHAPTER 14

# The British Were
# Coming—Again

It was time to dive into the Deep South myself, not just to keep up with John Laurens—though I planned to do that—but because the confusing, murderous, heroic, game-changing campaigns there were the part of my subject I knew least well when I started my Revolution travels.

Fortunately, a better-informed friend fixed me up with some expert help.

"These are guys you *really* need to know," he said, naming three men connected to a loosely organized, nearly indescribable group (I'll try later) called SCAR. Not long afterward, I found myself at a noisy Saturday night dinner in Rincon, Georgia, where the Revolutionary War talk never stopped. At one end of a long table, I lobbed question after question at Steve Rauch, the army historian who ended up letting me tag along on his Cowpens staff ride. Down at the far end, where vigorous debates kept breaking out, were Charles Baxley and David Reuwer, who had teamed up to launch SCAR twelve years before. After dinner, Baxley and Reuwer stayed up way too late telling me how to find out-of-the-way sites ("Don't be confused by Battlefield Road, because the battlefield isn't *on* Battlefield Road") and urging me to give the war in the South the attention it deserves.

I said I'd do my best.

They said they'd help, and they did.

A few weeks later I found myself standing on a windy Charleston seawall as Baxley told the astounding tale of how Henry Clinton and the British Navy had their lunch handed to them by the city's defenders in 1776—delaying the start of the *serious* war in the South for two and a half years.

\* \* \*

This was the first of three times the British would attack Charleston, and the only one of which the city's powers that be would have no reason to be ashamed. The story begins with Clinton sailing out of Boston on January 20, nine months after Lexington and Concord. Henry Knox's teams are still hauling cannon; William Howe hasn't yet brought his armada to New York; and the Declaration of Independence is months in the future. Meanwhile, Clever Henry's London bosses have ordered him south to stir things up a bit.

*Plan:* He'll cruise down to Wilmington, North Carolina; join forces with a squadron carrying redcoats sent from Ireland; and support a triumphant rising of North Carolina loyalists.

*Reality:* The loyalists will rise too soon and get crushed at Moores Creek, a fight as consequential and little known as Virginia's Great Bridge. "I don't know why we're so overlooked," a ranger told me when I dropped by the beautiful national battlefield there.

So: What next?

"The British get to the mouth of the Cape Fear River," Baxley said, "find out that the loyalists aren't coming, land on Bald Head—which is a high-dollar resort island now—and start scratching their collective heads. And they say, 'We're all dressed up for a battle and we know these rebels have *no* way of resisting even a *squad* of British soldiers.'" Charleston seems a tempting target, especially after scouts report that its harbor defenses are "in absolute disarray, which is the truth." So Clinton and his navy counterpart, Sir Peter Parker, decide to sail down and attack a half-finished fort there, because, hey, they might not be able to take the city right now, let alone subdue all of South Carolina, but maybe sometime later the harbor could serve "as a base to occupy the rest of the South."

Wishful thinking on this scale was not normal for Clinton— "Seizing a base on the off chance of its future use was ridiculous," his biographer writes—but still, off they went.

Baxley is a wide, handsome man with a trim white mustache. I once heard Reuwer introduce him by saying, "In case you can't tell Charles and me apart, I'm the light troops and he's the heavy artillery." In Charleston, they took turns telling the story of the wartime city to another group of Revolution obsessives, some of whom were from up north and needed help with local landmarks.

"Fort Sumter was a *sandbar* in the American Revolution," Baxley said, pointing across the harbor to the Stars and Stripes waving over Charleston's most famous historical site. "Fort *Sullivan* was over here on the left." In June 1776, the latter was still under construction on the southwest tip of a three-and-a-half-mile-long barrier island—"you know, the Atlantic is on the front side, and the back side is tidal creeks and salt marshes." Sullivan's Island, as previously noted, was where captive Africans were quarantined before being sold.

Fort Sullivan was meant to have four sides, Baxley continued, but "one had hardly even been started." Basically, the fort was made out of sand, but there was a problem: "If you pile sand up, it just slopes back down. You have to have logs to hold it in place."

This is where the humble palmetto tree comes in.

"The palmetto has a density about like balsa wood. It rots fast, but if you wanted to throw up a fast fortification, you cut the palmetto trees, you make cribbing out of them. And I don't think anyone understood that that was a great military material: It was just the only material they had."

So here comes the British Navy on June 28, 1776:

*Plan:* Most of Parker's squadron will "sail in front of the fort at fairly close range" and give it "broadside after broadside." Smaller ships will sail around to the unfinished part, where the big vessels can't go, "and start shooting from the back side."

*Reality:* "There is this fantastic cannonade, which can be heard probably thirty miles away." But "the result of shooting a heavy British solid shot into the fort is it goes *thud* and pokes a hole in a palmetto log, and the sand just falls down into the hole and patches it." While all this bang-bang is going on, tides are making deep water shallower; the smaller ships never make it to the fort's back side; several run aground; and rebel gunners, aiming with care because they're short on ammunition, wreak havoc on Parker's squadron. At dusk, Sir Peter—a brave man who has had his britches blown off by a cannonball and has watched one of his frigates wedge itself so firmly onto a sandbar that it will have to be abandoned and burned—decides enough is enough.

And what is the British Army doing all this time?

Just north of Sullivan's is another barrier island, today known as Isle of Palms and full of pricey real estate. But when 3,500 British troops landed there in 1776, Baxley said, "It was the most miserable place. There were no trees, and they had alligators and snakes and sand fleas and mosquitoes, no potable water—it was *terrrrrible.*" Still, Clever Henry has a plan. While the navy is doing its thing, his troops will cross Breach Inlet—the narrow channel separating Isle of Palms from Sullivan's—then cakewalk down to the unfinished back of the palmetto fort and take the place.

Clinton, however, has been told that Breach Inlet is eighteen inches deep at low tide. In fact, the depth is closer to seven feet. Whoops! Can he put his men in longboats and flatboats and get them across that way? No he can't: Charleston's defenders send nine hundred guys with rifles, muskets, and a couple of cannon to the inlet to make sure.

Campaign over.

Time for the (very cranky) navy to haul the (very cranky) army back north, where Clinton has a date to help Howe fight the Battle of Brooklyn. Time, too, for me to try to explain SCAR—full name Southern Campaigns of the American Revolution—as promised. But first a word about Charles Lee, whose role in the battle Baxley didn't get around to mentioning.

In June 1776, Lee was still riding high. No dragoons had yet caught him basking in Basking Ridge; no "dirty earwigs" had helped plot his post-Monmouth disgrace. Instead, Congress had sent him south to save the day.

Up north, he would get credit for doing so.

In Charleston—not so much.

Lee had taken one look at the palmetto fort, called it a "slaughter pen," and urged that it be abandoned—not an unreasonable view, given what would have happened if the British had gotten around to its unfinished side. But South Carolina's chief executive, John Rutledge, and the fort's commander, William Moultrie, had demurred, and Rutledge had sent Moultrie a three-sentence order to make sure there was no misunderstanding:

> General Lee wishes you to evacuate the fort. You will not without an order from me. I will sooner cut off my hand than write one.

After the battle, the fort would be renamed Fort Moultrie, and Lee would be gracious about its stubborn defenders. As for John Rutledge, the next time he comes into our story, he will behave... differently.

\* \* \*

When Charles Baxley was in the fifth grade, his family moved to the foot of Hobkirk's Hill in Camden, South Carolina. The hill had historical markers on it, he recalled, "so I knew vaguely that there was a battle there, and I *might* have known that it was in the Revolution—but I did not know who was there, why they were there, or which side won. I was always confused about that."

A couple of decades later, back in the Camden area and practicing law, he set out to learn more.

I had asked him to tell me how SCAR came to be—and, in the process, what the heck it was—over lunch after a conference we'd both attended. His wife, Judy, joined us, along with Steve Rauch, which meant there was a lot of institutional history around the table.

For starters, Baxley said, he didn't use "the method normal people use" to study something like Hobkirk's Hill. "I used what I call the concentric method."

Meaning?

"You start at a spot. What happened in *this* spot? Well, you want to understand that, then you have to understand what happened at *that* spot." So "I just started reading about the Revolutionary War in the context of trying to understand first the Hobkirk's Hill battle and then the Battle of Camden."

How far was the latter from his central spot?

"Eight miles. But the Battle of Camden is pretty complicated, and it's part of a larger campaign"—which means that if you set out to understand how Horatio Gates and Lord Cornwallis ended up facing off in 1780, "it just takes you on a trip."

Had his trip taken him into Virginia yet?

"A little. Not much. And if you want to talk about New England, you know, I'm vaguely aware of that, but I don't understand how it relates."

This sounded familiar, and no wonder: It's a mirror image of the standard northern view of the war. To some of us, I said—not telling Baxley anything he didn't know—the war was Lexington and Concord and Bunker Hill, then Washington crossed the Delaware and Saratoga happened and poof! Cornwallis surrendered at Yorktown and we won.

"Well, no, that's magic," he said. "That's, Captain Kirk and the *Enterprise* picked Cornwallis up out of the Carolinas, and because he was a wuss—he was just a *wuss*—they landed him at Yorktown and he gave up. Didn't have anything to do with anything else."

After I stopped laughing, he told me the next part of his SCAR backstory. It had to do with cowboy movies.

He had a friend, he said, who put out a monthly newsletter about B-Westerns called *The Old Cowboy Picture Show*. The friend started out using a mimeograph machine, "and he got up to about four hundred people who were interested, and he had good writers and stories that would be submitted and it took off."

Lightbulb time.

By now, the Baxleys had met David Reuwer, also a lawyer in town, who "had been a Revolutionary War historian since he was a child. And so I was talking to David one day and I said, 'You know, my friend is doing this newsletter that is a model and we might be able to connect to some other people if we *knew* some other people.'" Soon they were sitting at Reuwer's kitchen table with twelve sheets of paper in front of them—one for each month—"and we started writing down what on earth would we put in it."

Reuwer wasn't with us at lunch. Earlier, though, he'd told me about the kitchen-table moment. "You know, we're *fairly* intelligent," he'd said, "but we didn't know much about the Revolution. We were trying to focus on South Carolina and we couldn't fill twelve pages. I don't mean fill them *up*—I mean we had blank ones!"

In 2004, they started their newsletter anyway.

Vol. 1, No. 1 (all fourteen pages of it) led with its ambition: "We want to encourage the exchange of information on the Southern Campaigns' battle sites, their location, preservation, historic signage and interpretation, artifacts and archaeology, as well as the personalities, military tactics, units, logistics, strategy and the political leadership of the region."

The second issue was already starting to feel more like a magazine than a newsletter. It featured a closely argued contrarian take on a bloody turning point around which myth and misinformation swirl to this day. And things just got more interesting from there.

What SCAR's founders were really doing was creating a network for the South's Revolution-obsessed. "There were plenty of people out there doing stuff," Baxley said—amateur and professional historians, archeologists, and more—but "they generally didn't know each other." Before long, SCAR was putting together symposia on the likes of Thomas Sumter and Nathanael Greene; organizing daylong events at which people could share research; consulting with governments about preservation; supporting archeology; and orchestrating excursions to sites where the cooperation of private landowners was often required. ("Charles would basically get us into people's backyards," Steve Rauch said.) It also functioned as an informal clearinghouse, encouraging scholarship and preventing duplication as more and more people wrote in to say things like, "I'm now interested in the Battle of Camden, please send me everything you know."

The heyday of SCAR-the-publication ended after five years. You can still get the original issues online, Baxley said, and he still published a trimmed-down version ("one meritorious article at a time"), but not on a schedule. SCAR-the-network, however, is alive and well—even though "network" doesn't get to the heart of what it really is.

"Let me tell you the rest of the story," he said. "Over the years, many of these people have become close friends. SCAR started off with email addresses and post office addresses and has wound up being a fellow-ship. It's informal, there's no rules, there's no bylaws, there's no formal members—it's a *fellowship*." Also, importantly: "I don't want to make it sound like this is my doings." Because "there's other people like Steve, like David"—here he threw out several more names—"who do things independently."

All true, Rauch said.

And yet: "Without Charles, what would there be?"

"He's the ringmaster," Judy Baxley said.

"He's the ringmaster, or whatever you want to call him," Rauch said. "And when Charles calls you up and says, 'Hey, can you help me out,' you *want* to do that. It's not like you *have* to."

I am not at all cynical about this. If Charles Baxley asked me to do something, I'd probably do it, too. Asked to explain why, though, I might mention a scene I witnessed during a break between speakers at the conference. Baxley sat down at a table and drew a crowd. I had questions for him (I always do) but knew I'd never get to the head of the queue in time. Just then Rauch, who was standing as far back as I was, managed to get our man's attention.

"I've come to kiss your ring, Godfather!" he said.

Baxley didn't hesitate for a second.

"Kiss my ass," he shot back.

*   *   *

We don't know the exact words Governor Rutledge used when John Laurens showed up in 1779 waving a plan to defend his state by arm-ing thousands of slaves. But "kiss my ass"—or the eighteenth-century equivalent—had to be close to what he was thinking.

With the British sitting just across the Savannah River from South

Carolina, Rutledge had sent an envoy to Congress to ask for help. The problem: More than half the state's residents were enslaved, and most of its white men—as the envoy explained—chose to stay home "to prevent Insurrections among the Negroes, and to prevent the desertion of them to the Enemy" rather than serve in the militia.

Rutledge's idea of a solution was: Send us some veteran Continentals, right now.

Congress's idea was: We'll send young Laurens to help raise you some Black troops.

A congressional vote authorized South Carolina and Georgia to enlist "three thousand able bodied negroes" between them. Congress would pay their owners $1,000 a man; the men themselves, assuming they survived the war, would get freedom and $50 each. Oh, and one other little wrinkle: The states themselves would have to approve this plan before Laurens could implement it.

Rutledge told him "no way." A vote by the governor's privy council formalized the state's rejection. "We are much disgusted here at Congress recommending us to arm our Slaves," one otherwise-radical councilor wrote Samuel Adams; the proposal "was received with great resentment, as a very dangerous and impolitic Step."

Laurens would keep trying. He would still be trying three years later. But in May 1779, he, Rutledge, and the council faced a more immediate crisis.

The British were coming. Again. And the man who was supposed to defend Charleston was out of town.

Benjamin Lincoln was the general who, during the Saratoga campaign, had decided to give stubborn old John Stark his head. Lincoln's presumed ability to "cooperate diplomatically with southerners" was one reason Congress had sent him to command the army's Southern Department. Other pluses included his skill as a military logistician and planner and the fact that Washington thought highly of him. An obvious negative was his disconcerting habit of falling deeply asleep in meetings. (Narcolepsy seems the likely cause.) Much more damaging, however, was his decision in late April—made while awake—to march most of his army to the interior of Georgia.

I could explain (maybe) what Lincoln thought he was doing, but why bother? A bold move by the British commander in Savannah rendered his plans moot.

Out marched Augustine Prévost with upward of two thousand troops, heading north to pillage South Carolina for supplies and perhaps throw a scare into Charleston. Scrambling to stop him were 1,200 men, mostly militia, under William Moultrie, who was again asked to hold the fort—metaphorically—against long odds. Pretty soon the British advance guard showed up outside the Charleston defenses, around where the Citadel is today. Lincoln's army was still missing in action, its commander having assumed Prévost's move was a feint. Worst of all, Governor John "I Will Sooner Cut Off My Hand" Rutledge had changed his tune.

Rutledge asked Moultrie if negotiating surrender terms might be a good idea.

Moultrie said he was sure the city could be held.

The governor sent out a flag of truce anyway.

Back came the British terms: "peace and protection" for those who swore loyalty to the Crown; all others to be prisoners of war; you have four hours to respond.

Time for another meeting of the governor's council.

The councilors voted 5–3 to propose a shocking deal. Under it, Prévost would go away and leave Charleston alone; South Carolina would become neutral for the rest of the war; and the question of "whether the state shall belong to Great Britain, or remain one of the United States" would be left for peace negotiators to decide. Moultrie and his top officers wanted nothing to do with this—Laurens refused a request that he carry the proposal to the British—but Rutledge and the civilians had the final say. The neutrality offer, writes historian John Ferling, mincing no words, was "one of the most dishonorable actions of the war." Its foreshadowing of the state's 1861 secession is too obvious to require comment.

But the union survived—in this case, because the British turned the offer down.

They had no authority to negotiate political terms, Prévost's representative said, and would deal only with Moultrie, not the governor. Thus empowered, Moultrie ended the negotiations, informing Rutledge and his council that "we will fight it out."

The next morning, the British were gone.

Prévost had been bluffing. He didn't have enough men to take the city by storm. And he couldn't afford to be sitting there when Lincoln and his army finally showed up.

\* \* \*

In the spring of 1779, Augustine Prévost was in the twenty-fourth year of his army career. Two decades earlier, a facial wound had left him badly scarred; his men are said to have called him "Old Bullet Head." He suffered from gout, he was tired, and he had asked permission to resign; by September, back at his Savannah base, he was drumming his fingers on the table waiting for a replacement to arrive.

What he didn't know was that a French fleet would get there first.

The Comte d'Estaing had had a full year to recover from being called a dishonorable coward by his finger-pointing allies in Rhode Island. Now here he was in Georgia with thirty-one warships and four thousand troops, hoping to do better.

Alas, he and the Americans—once again—couldn't get their act together.

Among their mistakes: The French should have attacked before Prévost's defenses were finished. Lincoln should have gotten his three thousand men into action faster. After d'Estaing demanded the garrison's surrender, he never should have let Old Bullet Head stall for time. And *somebody* should have kept the eight hundred men the British had left in South Carolina from sneaking back into the city untouched.

At the Savannah History Museum, a display titled "Besieged!" made a strong case that being trapped where enemy artillerymen are trying to kill you 24/7 is a bad thing. The city's war-expanded population included numerous civilian refugees, but not even the women and children were allowed to leave. Why? Well, first Prévost refused, hoping their presence, writes historian David Wilson, "might restrain the allies from bombarding the city." (Translation: He used them as human shields.) Later, with the cannonade at its height, he changed his mind, but d'Estaing and Lincoln said no dice. Hearing this, some women decided to be pawns no more: "Taking their children with them, they marched over the trenches and passed across no-man's-land to the French camp."

But if the siege was awful, the assault was worse.

The British were supposed to have given up by now, but hadn't, and d'Estaing, who was due back in the Caribbean, could wait no longer. The result—thanks mainly to the admiral's incompetence—was "a confused piecemeal attack," focused on the strongest part of the defenses, with "one relatively small battalion after another" attacking without support. Up went French troops toward the Spring Hill Redoubt. British cannon mauled them and British muskets raked them from close range. Eventually Americans joined in, but they, too, arrived piecemeal. Leading one column was John Laurens, whose orders were to attack a *different* redoubt. Seeing the French had been thrown back from Spring Hill, however, he chose to try to succeed where they had failed. The body count mounted.

Before leaving Savannah, I had a more obscure site to visit. A ten-minute walk from the reconstructed redoubt took me under U.S. 17 and up to the Old Jewish Burial Ground. High, decaying walls and padlocked doors kept me from entering, but an old marker explained at least part of its role in the battle. Allied reserves were stationed here, it said, and the burial ground had been named as a rallying place for retreating troops. What it didn't mention—though a twenty-first-century monument downtown does—was that the reserves are thought to have included troops from "the largest unit of soldiers of African descent who fought in the American Revolution."

"Les Chasseurs Volontaires de Saint-Domingue" had sailed with d'Estaing from what is now Haiti. At least five hundred free men of color had enlisted to fight alongside the French and Americans. "Historians have yet to evaluate properly the Haitian role," one historian wrote after examining the documentary evidence, and it's hard to disagree:

Mythic Monmouth: Washington confronts Charles Lee in a dubious nineteenth-century illustration; Molly Pitcher helps fire a cannon in a 1935 post office mural on display at the Monmouth County Library.

African Americans, free and enslaved, worked and fought for both sides during the war, though most freedom-seekers believed their best chance lay with the British. At left is a painting by Don Troiani of a patriot militiaman. Below: If you're looking to examine the radical dissonance between revolutionary ideals and an economy based on slavery, you will find no better case study than John Laurens (left) and Henry Laurens of South Carolina.

Nathanael Greene did much more to win American independence than a simple list of his battles can convey. Sent south to rebuild the shattered forces there after Camden, Greene was on his own—and he knew that losing yet another southern army could doom the Revolution.

Above: "The Morning After the Attack on Sullivan's Island, June 29, 1776," by a British officer who watched the palmetto fort and its defenders foil the first offensive against Charleston. Right: A self-portrait by John André, made the day before his October 2, 1780, execution.

Left: Sir Henry Clinton, the brightest but most socially awkward of the Crown's top generals in America, had fewer resources to work with than his less-talented predecessor. Below: Banastre Tarleton, shown in a romanticized 1782 portrait, was the ultimate weapon for the British in the South—until suddenly, he wasn't.

Right: Lord Cornwallis became the most important British player as the war neared its end, in no small part because he ignored his boss. Clinton wanted Cornwallis to be sure South Carolina and Georgia were secure before moving north, but the strategically challenged Lord C rushed to invade North Carolina and Virginia anyway.

Above: The hardened frontiersmen Patrick Ferguson challenged, portrayed here on a marker at Kings Mountain National Military Park, proved more than he could handle. Right: Sunset at the Waxhaws memorial in Buford, South Carolina.

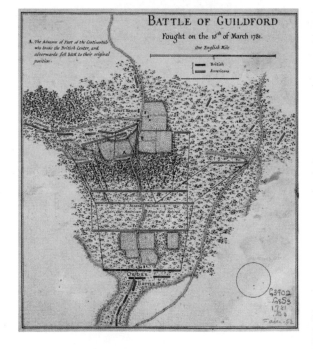

Top: At Cowpens, a misunderstood American order resulted in a reckless British charge. Bottom left: Thomas Sumter, with Francis Marion and Andrew Pickens, was one of the partisans who helped change the course of the war. Bottom right: A British map of Guilford Courthouse shows Greene's defensive lines.

If you want to understand how the United States became independent, you can't leave Robert Morris, the superintendent of finance, out of the picture. And you certainly can't leave out the Comte de Rochambeau (below left) and Admiral de Grasse, without whom Yorktown wouldn't have happened.

The Battle of the Capes, imagined: Onshore at what's now Virginia Beach, you'd have heard the British and French broadsides, seen nothing, and not learned the outcome for days. Right: Rochambeau, Washington, and De Grasse share a Yorktown stamp. Below: The British surrender, as painted by John Trumbull.

That evidence is scant and contradictory. Still, some of it suggests that the Haitians fought right here, near the ground on which I stood, helping cover the retreat of the devastated attackers.

There would be no second try.

The French packed up and sailed away.

And Sir Henry Clinton, in New York, took the news as his cue to head down to Charleston again.

# CHAPTER 15

# The Drunken Bash That Saved the Revolution

Clever Henry wanted nothing to do with Sullivan's Island or the Isle of Palms this time, and who could blame him? After putting 8,700 troops aboard ships in New York in late December (more would come later) and enduring the kind of voyage you wouldn't wish on your worst enemy, he landed twenty miles down the coast from Charleston. In the eighteenth century, the city occupied only the southern end of the peninsula bounded by the Ashley and Cooper Rivers; Clinton's plan was to sweep around it to the west and attack it from the north. To do so, he'd have to get his men across the Ashley someplace, and the place he chose was near a spectacularly beautiful brick plantation house that still stands on the riverbank today.

Drayton Hall is worth a visit even if you don't give a damn about the Revolution—which is a good thing, because it's possible to tour the mansion and hear barely a word about 1780. I learned about the sixteenth-century Italian architect Andrea Palladio, from whose designs some of the house's clean lines were borrowed ("Palladio was all about ratio and proportion"); about mahogany balustrades and limestone columns ("it took twenty-six men to get one of these into an upright position"); and about how the Drayton family measured children's height on doorframes (a childless woman measured her dogs). Our guide also warned against imagining the wrong kind of dancing in the elegant but not overly large rooms. "If you have a picture of women twirling around a room in hoop-skirted dresses to a Viennese waltz, we need to turn the history meter back," she said. "Switch out Margaret Mitchell for Jane Austen and you'll have a better idea what was going on socially when the house was built."

What didn't change, in those years, was the slave-based economy that made Drayton Hall possible. Enslaved people built it; hauled food and chamber pots up and down its back stairs; and worked the thousands of hugely profitable acres the Draytons had under cultivation in rice and indigo. I learned a fair amount about this part of Hall life, too, much of it at a separate thirty-minute presentation, including the fact that the field hands' tools were taken away at night lest they be used as weapons or to sabotage dams in the rice fields. Still, the percentage of architecture talk seemed a bit high.

As for that unheralded river crossing:

To get his army across the Ashley and in position north of the city, Clinton needed the navy's help. To get that help, he had to bite his nails until Admiral Marriot Arbuthnot—not his favorite naval colleague, assuming Sir Henry could be said to have one—thought conditions were right to risk crossing a long sandbank in Charleston Harbor known as the Bar. By the end of March, however, both bar and river had been safely crossed; Drayton Hall was in Clinton's rearview mirror; and his troops were encamped near where Old Bullet Head's had been the previous year.

This was no bluff, though. On April 1, he ordered the digging to start.

To get a feel for where the armies faced off, I dropped by the Charleston Museum at 360 Meeting Street and asked if the director, Carl Borick—author of the best book on the Charleston siege—might have a few minutes to talk. He had five, and he made good use of them.

"In 1780, this was the outskirts of Charleston. You wouldn't have had any buildings or *anything*," Borick said, walking me out to the museum's front steps. But had we been standing here during the siege, "we'd have been in a no-man's-land" between the armies.

Just south would have been the city's defenses. Just north, British lines would have been moving closer. Clinton used standard eighteenth-century siege techniques, as had d'Estaing: First you dig a trench parallel to the enemy defenses but a relatively secure distance away. Then you dig "approach trenches" (also called "zigzags" or "saps") designed to protect the diggers as they push forward to start a second parallel, then a third. Each parallel sprouts artillery batteries, which wreak havoc as the range diminishes.

His five minutes up, Borick sketched out a siege walk I could take in the immediate neighborhood. "You're not going to see any lines," he warned—just topographical hints at where they were.

A hundred yards south I hit Wragg Square, which looked about four feet higher than the street beyond it. The rise was part of a long, low ridge along which Charleston's defenders built their main line of batteries and redoubts. Heading back north, I saw Elizabeth Street drop down slightly, then rise. Near the drop-off, defenders used a tidal creek to create another obstacle by digging a canal across the peninsula. Two minutes later, I was in enemy territory. The Aiken-Rhett House Museum stood roughly where the British third parallel ended, and Elizabeth Street soon ran into Mary Street, where the second parallel had been.

What did I learn? Before the walk I'd had no sense of how extremely close the two armies had been. Now I did. I had also discovered that a person could stroll through the geographic heart of "one of the critical points in the military history of the American Revolution," as Borick calls the siege, and find no historical markers about what happened. The only such marker I would see was a quarter mile south, closer to the headquarters of Benjamin Lincoln.

For whom, it must be said, absolutely nothing had gone right since he crossed the Mason-Dixon Line.

After Savannah, Lincoln knew more trouble was coming and begged for help. Washington sent upward of three thousand Continentals, which was good, though it took a while for them to arrive. Congress sent three of the navy's frigates, which could have been good, if only their commander hadn't been risk-averse. Meanwhile, South Carolina, as usual, raised far too few troops of its own. The latest excuse was a rumored smallpox outbreak in Charleston, but all the old excuses still applied. Desperate for manpower, Lincoln went so far as to raise with Rutledge—again—the verboten idea of arming Blacks. Not only did he lose that argument, he couldn't even get the state to send as many enslaved laborers as he needed to shore up the city's fortifications.

Still, Lincoln retained hope.

A siege isn't guaranteed to work if the besieged city can be resupplied and reinforced, as Charleston still could from across the Cooper River. What's more, if your besieger's objective isn't just to take the city but to eliminate the army defending it, as Clinton's certainly was, all you need is an escape route, right?

Welcome back to the limelight, Banastre Tarleton.

\* \* \*

Tarleton was fighting in America because he'd been bored in school. Also because he started his army career on April 20, 1775, the day after the war began.

Young Banastre got his first name from his maternal grandfather and his money from his father, a Liverpool merchant who, like Henry Laurens, built the family fortune through the slave trade. At Oxford, he rode, boxed, and played cricket. In London, after his father's death, he pretended to study law while pissing away his inheritance. Fortunately, his mother forked over the cash to buy him an army commission, which was how you got to be a British officer in those days.

His first taste of war came during Clinton's 1776 Charleston expedition, though his thoughts on that debacle are not recorded. Six months later, he was writing his excited letter home from New Jersey:

*Hey, Mom! I bagged Charles Lee!*

The Tarleton correspondence soon got more prosaic. In May 1777, Banastre thanked his mother for the bottled beer she'd shipped across the Atlantic and asked her to forward "a few shirts & Stockings" as well. Before long, however, he started gambling heavily, losing, and sending debts home for payment. Still, by August 1778, Tarleton—who had entered the officer corps at the lowest possible rank—had risen to become lieutenant colonel of the British Legion, a loyalist regiment made up of both cavalry and infantry. In late December 1779, he took ship with Clinton's army in New York and sailed south.

The winter storms hit almost immediately.

Ships were dismasted and sunk. The voyage took five weeks instead of ten days. Supplies of water and food ran low for both men and horses—but the horses could be thrown overboard, and most were. "It must have been a scene out of Hades," writes historian John Buchanan, with "men struggling on pitching decks to heave over the side panicked, kicking horses, the screams of animals with broken legs."

Once ashore, Tarleton purchased or seized all the horses he could find. Then he used them to win one of the least-known crucial battles of the war.

Moncks Corner was a tiny crossroads nine miles upriver from Mepkin Plantation. Lincoln had pulled almost all his troops into Charleston by the time the siege began, but he had sent four cavalry units to Moncks Corner to stop the British from reaching the far side of the Cooper, where they could threaten his lines of supply and retreat. This was a smart move, but there were a couple of problems:

First, Clinton knew perfectly well that he needed to cut those lines, and he wasted no time getting started.

Second, he chose the right man to take the lead.

On the night of April 13–14, Tarleton and his Legion, with others under his command, were moving quietly north when they captured an enslaved man carrying a message from Isaac Huger, the general in charge of those four cavalry units. This gave Tarleton a detailed picture of how Huger's men were deployed at Biggin Bridge, near the Moncks Corner crossroads. He knew his enemies would be better mounted than his troops, with their hastily acquired replacement nags, which meant taking those enemies by surprise would give him his best shot at victory. At about 3 a.m., he sent his men straight at the only patrol they met, barely outside the rebel camp, and went on to shatter the main body of Huger's unprepared force in minutes.

Thundering cavalry charges were fearful things, and the surprise of this one, while perhaps not total, was close enough so the distinction didn't matter. "Sabers thudded sickeningly into heads and shoulders,"

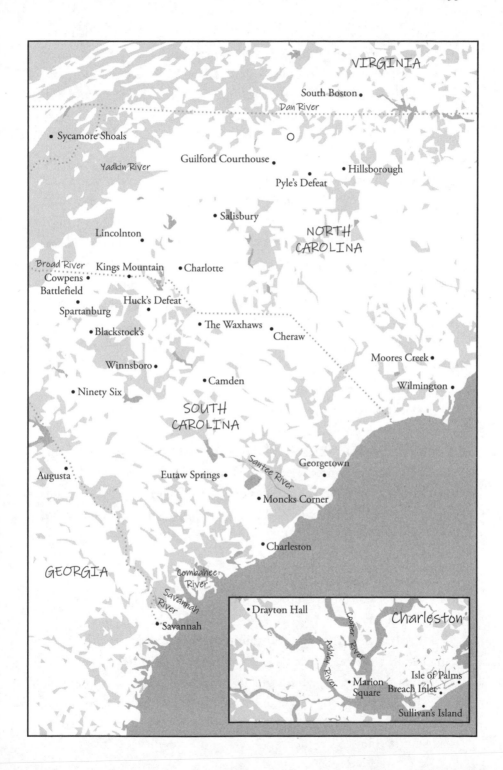

writes Borick, "while men shrieked in agony and fear." Many fled into swamps, but 15 were killed and 63 captured, including 18 wounded; more than forty wagonloads of supplies and ammunition were lost; and a great number of trained cavalry horses changed hands. Tarleton had only a few men wounded. Most importantly, he and the British were well on their way to cutting Charleston's lifeline to the north.

You won't be surprised to hear that I had trouble locating the Battle of Moncks Corner, aka the Battle of Biggin Bridge—a relatively small encounter that didn't go well for the home team. Still, I expected to find a marker for it somewhere.

And why not? Didn't I own a copy of *Parker's Guide to the Revolutionary War in South Carolina*, a three-pound doorstop that rode shotgun with me as I drove the Palmetto State? Hadn't John C. Parker Jr. spent eight years locating and describing five hundred–plus "battles, skirmishes, ambushes, murders, assaults and other documented acts of war"? And wasn't there a map on page fifty-six showing where Biggin Bridge had been?

Yes, yes, and yes. But . . .

Following that map, which I probably read wrong, I found a boat landing where it seemed as if one end of the eighteenth-century bridge must have been. Nada. Lunch at Gilligan's, a nearby seafood restaurant, proved just as unenlightening. No one I spoke with had ever heard of the battle, though the she-crab soup was delicious. After lunch, I spent more time than I could spare cruising a nearby commercial strip; it had more chain restaurants than I could count, but I saw nothing Revolution-related and gave up.

A week later, I was back, armed with information from conversations with several SCAR folks, including Drew Ruddy, who lived in Moncks Corner.

I'd been warm! Though I was cautioned that the real detective work remained to be done, it seemed likely that Tarleton had charged somewhere uphill from Gilligan's, right in the area I'd been checking out. More specifically, Ruddy had said, it might be worth taking a look at the high ground where a Walmart stands today. So I drove to the far corner of the parking lot, turned my back on the store itself—it's not easy to imagine galloping cavalry if you're staring at a herd of riding lawn mowers—and saw how the land dropped off to the north and east.

As for that elusive marker, there turned out to be one after all. It was a small hunk of aging granite beside Route 52—at ground level, in front of the Auto Mart, just a few yards north of Kentucky Fried Chicken. Not only was it effectively invisible, but it gave no hint of why the action on April 14, 1780, was important. So let me suggest some additional text for a new Battle of Moncks Corner marker, should one ever be created:

"Tarleton's small but smashing victory," it might read, "was a giant step toward cutting off Lincoln's army from the possibility of reinforcement, resupply, or escape. And what happened to that army a month later could have changed—and nearly did—the whole trajectory of the Revolutionary War."

* * *

As far as I know, the only physical remnant of the Revolution's longest siege is a weird, boulder-like object in Marion Square, a few acres of green space just south of where the main American line had been. "Remnant, of Horn Work," reads a cryptic sign on the black metal fence enclosing it. South Carolinians sometimes call it "the tabby structure," further confusing out-of-town visitors.

Tabby, in this case, has nothing to do with felines. It refers to a concrete-like material made by mixing lime, sand, oyster shells, and water. The hornwork was a fortified gate, built of tabby long before the war, which became part of the city's 1780 defenses. Lincoln set up his command post there. Late in the siege, he ordered additions built with the idea of making the hornwork a citadel-like "place of retreat" for his army in case the British broke through the outer defenses.

Where better, then, to think about the worsening prospects for the general and the city he was trying to defend?

The news from Moncks Corner forced Lincoln to reassess his position. The main thing now keeping his supply lines open, as well as his only possible escape route, was an artillery battery across the Cooper east of Charleston. The existence of that battery (at Lempriere's Point, now called Remley's Point) had kept the British from sending ships upriver to complete the city's encirclement. "I need not remind you that your post is critical," Lincoln wrote the officer in charge, but he might as well have spit in the wind: On April 27, when that officer got a false report that he was about to be attacked, he panicked and abandoned the battery.

Goodbye, possible escape route.

Yet as I had learned from Borick's book, a more disturbing type of shameful behavior had already foreclosed the possibility of saving the army.

A couple of weeks earlier, with British siege lines moving closer and shot and shell raining down on the city, Lincoln had urged Governor Rutledge and some of the privy councilors to get out while they could. The idea was to preserve the state's executive authority if Charleston fell. Rutledge took that advice, leaving Lt. Gov. Christopher Gadsden and the remaining councilors to function as the civilian authorities. That same day, after laying out a detailed assessment of the odds against a successful defense, Lincoln asked his officers to consider "the Propriety of evacuating the Garrison." Some, notably Lachlan McIntosh of Georgia, argued for withdrawing across the Cooper as soon as possible, but with the officers urgently needed on the lines, the discussion was tabled. A week's delay didn't change McIntosh's mind, though he admitted that the difficulty of a retreat "appeared much greater" since the British had put troops across the river themselves. Others, however, thought it was time to negotiate surrender terms, and their argument won out.

Until the civilians went berserk, that is.

First, Gadsden showed up midmeeting with or without an invitation. The lieutenant governor "appeared surprised & displeased" that surrender or retreat would even be discussed, and he rushed off to consult the available privy councilors. That evening, he came back with four councilors in tow. Lashing out at Lincoln and the officers, Gadsden told them that "the Militia were willing to Live upon Rice alone rather than give up the Town upon any Terms" and that even "old Women" weren't afraid of British artillery. Then a councilor named Thomas Ferguson weighed in with a threat. Citizens of Charleston "would keep a good Watch," he said, and should Lincoln's army try to withdraw by boat, they would "open the Gates for the Enemy and assist them in attacking us before we got aboard."

Civilian control of the military was a crucial principle in the new republic and remains so today. Washington adhered to it throughout the war and Lincoln followed suit—but this was not its finest hour. Could a retreat have saved the army at such a late date? That's unknown. Yet attempting it could scarcely have produced a worse result than the one dictated by Gadsden, Ferguson, et al., who, in Borick's words, "were willing to sacrifice the security of the rest of the state, and possibly of the entire south, for the security of Charleston"—a false hope, as it turned out, that would vanish in weeks.

On May 12, 1780, the defenders marched out of the hornwork—not far from where that fenced-off chunk of tabby stands today—to lay down their arms.

\* \* \*

I spent several days exploring Charleston with a checklist of revolutionary sites in hand. Mostly I walked, which is the best way to see this low-rise gem of a city. In the old residential district below Broad Street, I found myself crossing and recrossing streets to read the markers attached to what seemed like every second house. Many offered more architectural detail than I wanted, but some told—or hinted at—amazing tales.

Take the jumbo-sized Georgian at 27 King Street, which Clinton used as his headquarters after the surrender. "Built between 1765 and 1769 by Miles Brewton, revolutionary patriot," read its marker. "Inherited 1775 by Brewton's sister, Rebecca Motte, revolutionary heroine, in whose family it has remained." The British, I later learned, let Motte retain a few small rooms; eventually, she moved to a country house, only to have it, too, taken over by the enemy, who turned it into a fort. The Americans who came to recapture it decided it would have to be burned, at which point Motte told them—at least according to Henry "Light Horse Harry" Lee, Robert E. Lee's dad, not always a reliable source—that she'd be delighted to see Fort Motte destroyed for the good of her country. Then, Lee wrote, she produced "a bow and its apparatus imported from India" suitable for firing flaming arrows into her own home.

Great stuff. Yet some other things about the Miles Brewton House are worth mentioning.

First, Miles Brewton built it with the fortune he made as a slave trader on the scale of Henry Laurens. Second, the fence in front is topped by a terrifying array of long iron spikes—they look like barbed wire on steroids—put up in the 1820s, a time when the owners of such mansions were especially fearful of slave revolts.

That said, the biggest story in the neighborhood, for my purposes, was the Drunken Bash That Saved the Revolution.

The party most likely took place at 106 Tradd Street. "The house is a rare example of a colonial side-passage plan," a marker informed me, also mentioning that its owner, a loyalist who had supervised southern Indian affairs for the Crown, had fled during the war and his property had been confiscated. It said nothing, however, about some dude trying to exit the place through a second-floor window and breaking his ankle.

Okay, actually he wasn't just *some* dude.

The ankle-breaker was a Continental Army officer who, while "an amiable man," didn't drink. He went out the window because his bibulous host had locked the doors to keep guests from escaping "till each individual should be gorged with wine." Because the injured officer couldn't walk, Benjamin Lincoln ordered him out of town along with other officers unfit for duty. And because our hero didn't become a prisoner of war when the city fell, he was free to reinvent himself as a key leader of South Carolina's partisan resistance, which prevented the British from—well, you can see where that "saved the Revolution" idea comes from, however grandiose.

His name was Francis Marion. I would run into him again soon, but not before contemplating one of the most distressing stories of the war.

Magazine Street is less than half a mile north of Tradd, but had a more unmanicured feel. Broken shutters and peeling paint marred some houses; laundry dried on lines behind public housing units; and saplings sprouted from cracked walls at the former Charleston District Jail. No marker alerted visitors that anything worth remembering had taken place on its two narrow blocks. Yet in recording what he saw there three days after Charleston surrendered, Johann Ewald—a thirty-six-year-old Hessian officer and Revolutionary War diarist who had served in armies more than half his life—wrote that he had never "witnessed a more deplorable sight."

Ewald was looking to find muskets for his men from among the thousands captured when the city fell. He headed for "the building or magazine" where he'd been told the guns were, but a chance encounter sent him into a house a few hundred yards short of his destination. Then came a deafening blast and a scene straight out of Hieronymus Bosch. Running outside, he saw that the magazine had "blown up with all the people who worked in and around it." Perhaps sixty people lay in the streets, "burnt beyond recognition"; other bodies hung from houses far enough away to have survived.

No one knows what caused the blast, but the "general consensus" is that careless handling of loaded muskets near kegs of black powder was the culprit. (Reading this made me think of the redcoats who took off hobnailed boots before entering the stone tower in Somerville, back in 1774, lest a spark set off powder there.) The exact site of the exploded building is uncertain as well. But we do know that somewhere on Magazine Street was the Work House, which Edward Ball describes as a place where civil servants "administered floggings for a fee" when slave owners didn't wish to dirty their own hands. What happened to anyone inside that day, we can only imagine.

\* \* \*

On June 8, 1780, as Sir Henry Clinton boarded the ship that would carry him back to New York, he had every reason to be proud. Hadn't he avenged his most embarrassing personal defeat, won the biggest British victory of the war, captured the wealthiest city in North America, and eliminated the only significant rebel army in the South? And what was to stop his successor from finishing the good work of the Southern Strategy—first by pacifying the rest of South Carolina with help from hordes of eager loyalists, then by sweeping north to retake North Carolina and Virginia for the Crown?

Clinton still wasn't happy, though.

He had been longing to leave the whole of the American war behind. Almost a year earlier, when his superiors blew off a plea for more troops, he had submitted his resignation. On March 19, he had finally gotten a reply: The king was "too well satisfied with your conduct," wrote Lord Germain, "to wish to see the command of his forces in any other hands." So what if Clinton's number two—long poised to step into the top job—might not take the news graciously?

Lt. Gen. Charles, Earl Cornwallis could scarcely have been more different from Sir Henry. He was confident where the commander in chief was neurotic, socially adept where Clinton was tactless. If the troops had been asked to vote using that dopiest of modern character tests, in which we choose people for high office by deciding which we'd rather have a beer with, the noble earl would have won hands down. Yet when it came to skill at strategy and planning, there was no contest: Cornwallis was at his best leading men on a battlefield and at his worst when he had to think ahead.

You could call them polar opposites and be done with it, except that human lives are rarely so simple, and these two had a personal tragedy in common.

Both married for love, not for social standing or money. Both wives died young. Both husbands were devastated. And there's also a poignant what-if that hadn't occurred to me before I learned about Cornwallis and the former Jemima Tullekin Jones.

They married in peacetime, in 1768. Three happy years later, Sir Joshua Reynolds painted Jemima as "an elegant woman with long limbs and an impossibly long neck." When war broke out, she tried hard to stop her husband from going. For two years, he played major supporting roles under Howe and Clinton, doing well except for the time he let Washington's army slip away after Second Trenton—a whopping blunder that kept the rebellion alive. By late 1778, though, he was worried enough about his wife's failing health to sail home and resign his position in America. Exactly what was wrong with her isn't known. But her death in February 1779, he wrote, "destroyed all my hopes of happiness in this world" and made the thought of staying in England unbearable.

So back across the Atlantic he went, where he would become—as he would not have otherwise—the most important British player as the war neared its end.

Still heartsore, he found himself outside Charleston in 1780, doing his best to get along with his awkward boss. Clinton consulted his second religiously as the South Carolina campaign began, which was his duty—his resignation could have been accepted any day—though he also wanted the help. Then came the bad word from London, and a fuming Cornwallis told him to start making his own bloody decisions. Their relationship was a train wreck after that: Clinton sent Cornwallis to take over operations north of the Cooper River, then settled in to finish up the siege on his own.

The earl's new assignment wasn't unimportant, but Tarleton had already done the heavy lifting at Moncks Corner, and Cornwallis wouldn't see much actual fighting himself. Soon after Charleston surrendered, however, he would have the opportunity to send the hyperaggressive cavalryman tearing off toward another smashing, savage victory. The shock of what happened in a backcountry settlement called the Waxhaws on May 29, 1780, would reverberate through the South—and this time, I would have no trouble finding where its ground zero had been.

\* \* \*

The Buford Variety Stop Cafe offered chicken salad, potato salad, mac and cheese, and other tempting homemade food, but starving or not, I had to pass it by. A rusty roadside marker, erected the same year as Pearl Harbor, had just informed me that "Buford's Bloody Battleground" was a short distance south on Highway 522, and I needed to see it before darkness fell. Minutes later I stood gazing at a ten-foot marble obelisk with an inscription rendered almost illegible by time and souvenir hunters.

"Nearly the entire command of Col. Buford were either killed or wounded," it read in part. "Gallant soldiers are buried in this grave."

Light-colored rocks in the shape of a rectangle extended the memorial to the west, marking a mass burial site. Four small American flags stood propped among the rocks. There was modern signage as well: Visitors reading twenty-first-century markers nearby could piece together much of what's now understood about what took place here. They still wouldn't know everything, though—because no one does.

The story begins with a two-part task Cornwallis gave Tarleton on May 27. Task One was to eliminate a force of some 350 Virginia Continentals under Col. Abraham Buford that had been headed for Charleston but was now retreating toward North Carolina. Task Two was to bag South Carolina governor-in-exile John Rutledge, if possible. He was on the run in the same direction. Both were long shots, but there was no harm trying.

The fastest-moving man in the British Army rode north from Nelson's Ferry (on the Santee River) with 170 cavalrymen and 100 mounted infantrymen. Some of the latter rode solo, others doubled up. Most of the troops were loyalists from the British Legion, though some were Regulars from another unit. Their commander drove them to exhaustion and a number of their horses to death. Still twenty miles or so behind his quarry, he sent a messenger ahead to demand Buford's surrender, offering the same terms Lincoln's army received at Charleston. Buford said no and kept moving.

Tarleton caught up with the Virginians sometime after 3 p.m. Immediately, he formed his men to attack. The infantry, dismounted now, were to charge from each flank with bayonets. Between the flanks, three groups of cavalry would charge as well. Facing them were most of Buford's troops, deployed in a single line two rows deep. They were infantrymen with muskets, and while they were Continentals, not militia, most were recent recruits. For some reason, they had been ordered to hold their fire until the enemy was ten yards away.

Ten yards! With cavalry charging straight at you!

If any serious historian thinks this was a good idea, I'm not aware of it. A single volley couldn't begin to stop a cavalry charge allowed to get so close. Once Buford's men had aimed (hastily) and fired, Tarleton's riders would have been among them in slightly less than one second, assuming, as a close student of the battle has, that the horses were "galloping at about 25 miles per hour." Picture that single second in slow motion, with justifiably terrified soldiers trying any way they could— including throwing away empty muskets and starting to run—to avoid being sabered to death. Picture Tarleton's cavalrymen reining their horses around to make "pass after pass" through the shattered rebel ranks. Now put these images together with a point made in *With Zeal and with Bayonets Only*, historian Matthew Spring's examination of British Army operations and tactics during the war, and you'll have at least some notion of the horror that ensued:

In "warfare of any age," Spring writes, "prodigious slaughter was inevitable once cavalry got in among disordered enemy infantry."

Prodigious is right: Tarleton reported 113 of Buford's men killed outright; 150 more wounded so badly that they were "unable to travel"; and 53 taken prisoner. He gave his own losses as 5 killed and 12 wounded, not counting the horses, among which the casualty rate was higher. These wildly disproportionate numbers, which we have no reason to doubt, lead straight to a contentious historical question:

Are we talking battle or massacre here?

"Massacre or Myth?" a marker at the memorial asked as a way to start this discussion. After the fight, it went on, "reports spread that many were stabbed and killed as they tried to surrender." Historians "continue to debate" what happened, not to mention what to call it, yet at least one essential thing is clear: "Tarleton's actions, here and elsewhere, stirred and angered the backcountry settlers into action." Stories were "told and retold of the slaughter at the Waxhaws" and "the phrase 'Tarleton's Quarter' became synonymous with cruel treatment and the execution of prisoners."

All true—and a masterpiece of careful wording.

In trying to weigh the evidence, I would again find a SCAR connection helpful. Jim Piecuch published a detailed massacre-or-myth article in an early newsletter; later, it became a small book. Here's a condensed sample of what I learned, from it and other sources:

Buford galloped away early enough to survive, reporting that "we were completely surrounded by four time [*sic*] our numbers," claiming to have sent out a surrender flag and adding that "many" of his men "were killed after they had lain down their arms." Tarleton's horse was killed before he reached the rebel lines and, in his words, "slaughter was commenced" before he could mount another. Rebel casualties were so high, he explained, due to his cavalry "so effectually breaking the infantry"; also because a report of his death "stimulated the soldiers to a vindictive asperity not easily restrained"; and finally, as a result of Buford's mistakes, notably the hold-your-fire order. The story of the truce flag, meanwhile, reads like a case study in how hard it is to turn chaotic events into accurate history. Two eyewitness accounts have been used to support Buford's claim. Each first saw print more than four decades afterward and they're wildly conflicting.

The more I learned, the longer my list of questions grew. I'll mention just a few, along with some educated guesses about the answers.

*Why did Buford claim to have been outnumbered four to one?* He was either traumatized, covering his ass, or both.

*What did Tarleton mean by "slaughter"?* The same thing Matthew Spring means, I believe: a bloody and utterly one-sided defeat.

*What about that phrase "a vindictive asperity not easily restrained"?* It's code for out-of-control behavior, and I think—along with most everyone who's written about the Waxhaws—that it proves *some* men trying to surrender were killed.

*Okay, but how MANY men trying to surrender were killed?* Now we're at the heart of the matter, and the deeply unsatisfying answer is: We can't know.

In a field beyond the memorial, the setting sun turned a farm pond crimson. Bare trees stood silhouetted against a darkening sky. Lingering in the dusk, I thought about the men who lay beneath that rectangle of rocks. They had been brave, or maybe not. They had signed up to fight for a cause they believed in, or because the army was their best chance to get ahead, or both. Might they have been comforted to know that the ghastly chaos of their last moments would be described, centuries later, on a marker just yards from their graves, as "a crucial turning point in American history"?

Mulling the unanswerable, I got back in the car and drove to Camden, where I had a date to talk about the next rebel disaster of the year 1780.

\*   \*   \*

If you were putting together a list of Revolutionary War historians with unusual career paths, Jim Piecuch might top it—unless, of course, you can think of anyone else who spent thirteen years as a New Hampshire firefighter before writing a fat book challenging the assumption that Britain's Southern Strategy was doomed from the start. But before we get going on that, it would be good to know how the man pronounces his name.

"Yeah, that's tough," he said when I asked. "PIKE-itch. Just think of the ancient weapon and the itch you scratch."

We met not far from his home in Camden, the same small city where Charles Baxley grew up clueless about revolutionary history. A fit-looking fiftysomething with graying hair and faded jeans, Piecuch had his own tale of youthful ignorance. As a boy, he got only "the high school version" of the Revolution: "Americans didn't want to pay taxes so they threw some tea in the harbor and Washington came and captured the British army at Yorktown and that was it." The University of New Hampshire offered more complexity, but his father, who worked at the post office, made him quit after a year. "He said, 'Your college education will never earn you back the money you would earn if you stopped going to school.' And he was very old-fashioned and demanding," so his word was law.

Manchester Fire Department, here we come.

Fast-forward more than a decade. Piecuch liked firefighting, but had begun to wonder how long he could keep doing it. ("Going out at 3 a.m. in the middle of January isn't too bad when you're twenty-five, but...") Should he maybe finish college and switch to the school department? Intrigued by history and encouraged by professors, he wound up getting both a BA and a master's degree from UNH. Next unforeseeable stop: Williamsburg, Virginia, for a PhD program at William and Mary. By now he was hooked on studying the war he'd known so little about, and his new profs had some advice for him:

The North had been done, they said.

Find something to do about the *South*.

The result was *Three Peoples, One King*, a deeply researched dive into the argument that the British not only mismanaged their relationship with *white* loyalists in the South but failed to capitalize on the potential of Indians and especially enslaved African Americans to bolster their cause.

But to get back to the subject of Revolutionary War ignorance: It was time to deal with some of my own.

I had come to Camden to learn more about the what-are-the-odds occasion when Horatio Gates and his army ran smack into Lord Cornwallis and *his* army in the middle of the night. And I'm ashamed to say that much of what I knew, or thought I knew, about that Gates-Cornwallis collision—which occurred a few miles north of Camden, then a key link to the backcountry and a well-manned British post—came from *The American Heritage History of the Revolution*, a gripping narrative I had admired when I was fourteen.

"Cheerfully, Gates pushed south, piling blunder onto blunder," the relevant passage began, wearing its disdain for the Hero of Saratoga on its sleeve.

*Blunder No. 1:* He picked "the shorter but more barren" of two routes to Camden, ensuring that his men wouldn't have enough to eat. *Blunder No. 2:* He didn't know how many men he actually had. Told that the number was more like three thousand than the seven thousand he'd been guessing, "he exclaimed dramatically, 'Sir, there are enough for our purpose.'" *Blunder No. 3:* He ignored warnings that more than half of those men, far from being battle tested, were "barely capable of marching in formation." All of which brings us to *Blunder No. 4:* "With his green command, he decreed a night march and a surprise attack on the British."

I haven't mentioned Gates for a few chapters, and with good reason. His most memorable act after the Board of War lost its power struggle with Washington was to refuse command of an expedition against the Iroquois. But now fate and Congress had sent him south to pick up the pieces after Lincoln surrendered at Charleston, and now here he was, moving half-starved men down the road toward Camden at 2 a.m. on August 16, 1780, and now here I was in Piecuch's GMC Envoy, heading up the modern equivalent of that road for another tutorial on the intersection of history and myth.

"Here's Sanders Creek," Piecuch said as we crossed a small stream six miles north of town. "This is what Gates is aiming for."

Wait—I thought he was aiming for Camden! Did this mean he *wasn't* planning a surprise attack on the British troops there?

"Gates has no intention of attacking Camden. Many of his officers write that later because he kept his plans to himself," sharing them only with his chief aide and with the engineer he sent ahead to scout out a good defensive position.

A defensive position? *Here?*

"The creek's been dammed, but there's a lot of water. He wants to use the low, marshy ground as a barrier and take a defensive position on the high ground"—fortifying it and inviting the British to attack *him*.

And why does he want that?

"Because he basically wants to replicate Saratoga: Take a strong position, wait to be attacked, and cut off their supply lines as he did at Saratoga with the militia."

Interesting! Yes, there are plenty of questions about other Gates decisions and whether this one would have worked, but still, it makes him look less like a total doofus than my *American Heritage* book did—not to mention numerous other histories that take the same line. The reason Gates never got to test his Saratoga-at–Sanders-Creek theory, however, is undisputed:

A general faster than John Burgoyne got there first.

Cornwallis was in Charleston, 130 miles away, when informed that Gates seemed headed for Camden. Four days later, on the night of August 13–14, he rode into town with a few aides and took command of the Camden garrison. ("Contrary to popular belief, he does not bring reinforcements; he just shows up.") On August 15, he, too, ordered a night march. The idea was to surprise Gates in camp at dawn. He was already past Sanders Creek when the armies' advance guards ran into each other and started shooting. But neither side wanted to risk a night battle, so they stopped.

"And the Americans now had to decide what they were going to do."

By this time Piecuch and I had stopped, too, parking near a sign reading "Battle of Camden National Historic Landmark." We were the only ones there. Most of the battlefield was open pine forest, as it had been in 1780. "This is the actual roadbed," Piecuch told me, pointing to a one-lane track with patches of sand showing through pine needles. "It was part of the old wagon road that came all the way down from Pennsylvania." Why the sand? "This used to be the beach. Between ice ages, maybe we're talking millions of years ago, this part of South Carolina was the coast."

The decisive part of the battle, by comparison, took just hundreds of seconds.

Cornwallis was eager to fight. Though he was outnumbered—he had 2,200 men and thought Gates had 5,000—he knew his troops were superior to most of his enemy's and that swamps on both sides of the field would keep him from being flanked.

Gates was less eager, but had no real choice, Piecuch said. "To try to turn around an army, at night, at three in the morning when first light is about four thirty, and get your wagon train turned around, and try to escape in column formation—how do you do that with the British right behind you?"

As for the fight itself:

Piecuch led me down trails he'd helped seed with evocative markers ("Attack at Dawn," "Panic and Valor," "Driven from the Field") and offered commentary that could have filled a dozen more. We talked about the raw Virginia and North Carolina militiamen Gates placed east of the road, and how they dropped loaded muskets and ran the instant yelling British Regulars came at them with bayonets. ("Most of them didn't stop until they got home.") We talked about the shameful behavior of the few cavalrymen Gates had. ("They saw the militia go, so *they* fled—then stopped to loot their own army's wagon train.") And we talked about the fierce, stubborn stand made by some of the best troops in the whole American army. Continentals from Maryland and Delaware, they'd been sent to help at Charleston, but way too late, and were led by Baron Johann de Kalb, a veteran European officer who'd crossed the Atlantic with Lafayette. The Continentals fought for almost an hour after the militia fled. De Kalb finally went down, wounded eleven times. He would die three days later and his heroism is so obvious, Piecuch said, that historians overlook a serious mistake. Caught up in the back-and-forth struggle west of the road, he "forgot that he was in charge of *all* the Continentals," including some men still holding out to the east.

Time for those few hundred decisive seconds.

"Cornwallis is going to try to break the stalemate; he's not going to slug it out all day," Piecuch explained. The bad news for him: He was down to his last reserves. The good: Those reserves were Tarleton's cavalry. Now here they came, splitting their attack in two parts. One hit the flank of the remaining Continentals east of the road while the other showed up behind de Kalb's command to the west. The Continentals there, caught up in their own struggle, had no notion of the disaster on the far side of the field until they turned and saw Tarleton's dragoons charging them. Some were killed, some surrendered, and others ran into the swamp, where the undergrowth was so thick—and still is—that no horseman could follow. "I tried going in there with the dogs sometimes," said Piecuch, who used to bring his huskies with him when he walked the battlefield. "Even on foot, you can barely move."

And where was Horatio Gates while his army was being crushed? A marker titled "General Gates's Disgrace" addressed this question. "When the militia fled before the initial British charge," it began, "Gates tried to rally them. However, the throng of panicked militiamen swept him up in their northward flight."

Swept him up? So he couldn't turn *around*?

If you're not buying this excuse, you're not alone.

Piecuch tends to be more sympathetic than many. "Physically, if they wanted, they could have turned their horses around," he agreed, referring to Gates and the militia generals who galloped north with him. "But they're trying to get the militia back in action, and the militia simply aren't listening." The longer they try, the farther away they get, "and of course Gates compounds his mistake." Hearing no firing, he assumes the battle is over and thinks, "I'd better go to Charlotte and reorganize the defense." Finding no defenders there to reorganize, "he gets a bright idea that *really* sinks him." The North Carolina legislature is at Hillsborough, 180 miles from the battlefield: Why not head there and ask for help, leaving whatever was left of his army behind?

The ride took him three days. His enemies would mock him relentlessly for it.

Yet after nearly a year of debilitating losses—at Savannah, at Charleston, at the Waxhaws, at Camden—even his friends had no time to worry about one man's lost reputation. While Gates was still on his way to Hillsborough, 170 fast-riding troops led by (who else?) Banastre Tarleton surprised and routed a much larger partisan force under Thomas Sumter at Fishing Creek. Sumter escaped only by leaping half-naked onto a horse and galloping away bareback. Meanwhile, another soon-to-be-well-known partisan leader won a victory that proved more discouraging than Sumter's defeat. Not long after the Camden rout, Francis Marion learned that Cornwallis was sending prisoners to Charleston. Specifically, he learned that 150 of those prisoners, Continentals from Maryland and Delaware—some of the best troops in the American army, remember—were close enough for him to attack their guards and free them.

So he did.

But more than half of them didn't *want* to be freed.

They had been starved, betrayed by cowardly militia, and abandoned by the Hero of Saratoga. They told Marion they would just as soon go to Charleston and rot in a prison ship, thank you very much, as be forced to keep fighting a hopeless war.

# CHAPTER 16

# Down the Benedict Arnold Escape Path

Perhaps you're wondering, despite the advantages of hindsight, how the American rebels in the South could even begin to dig themselves out of the mess Gates made. But we need to set that question aside for now and shift our gaze seven hundred miles to the northeast, to the banks of the Hudson River below West Point, where another Hero of Saratoga was doing his damnedest to make sure his countrymen lost the war.

The best place to meditate on how close he came, I decided, was a short trail in the woods known these days as the Benedict Arnold Escape Path.

I had read that it was just off Route 9D on Glenclyffe Road, named for a nineteenth-century mansion once owned by Governor, Senator, and Secretary of State Hamilton Fish, who was himself named after Alexander Hamilton. Passing a sign for the mysterious-sounding Garrison Institute (motto: "Timeless Wisdom, Timely Action"), I pulled up beside a map that showed the path but confused me about where it started. Luckily, a couple of returning hikers stopped to help.

"I'm trying to do this Arnold Escape thing," I said.

"Oh, that's where *we* were—the historic overlook," one replied, and I soon had good directions.

Then came a cautionary note: "Just so you know, if you go that way there's, like, a silent meditation retreat going on. Which is fine, you're totally allowed down there, but there will be all these weird people walking like zombies and not talking."

I saw no zombies, but did run into six characters from the Arnold drama—or pictures of them, at least—pinned behind Plexiglas at an isolated kiosk in the woods.

There was Arnold himself, in an image based on the only known portrait made from life: a powerful-looking, middle-aged man in profile, staring intensely at something outside the frame. There was his second wife, Peggy, half his age, with hair so big it seemed to tug her eyebrows into a permanently raised position. There were Washington leaning on a cannon, and Hamilton and Lafayette, striking battlefield poses as well. Finally, there was handsome John André, who'd been promoted to major since he staged the Mischianza. On September 25, 1780—the day Arnold galloped down more or less the route I was to walk—André had a week left to live.

Off I went, in a cloud of mosquitoes.

The woods were thick enough that it was tough to imagine a horse galloping, but in Arnold's day, the trail would have been a wider cart track. It also would have ended at a boat landing instead of at a wooden platform overlooking power lines and a railroad cut. Yet from that platform I could see the Hudson through the trees, and by the time I'd crossed the tracks and bushwhacked over to the misty riverbank, where a startled heron flapped off at my approach, it was easier to picture the sudden arrival of a panicked thirty-nine-year-old who knew his treason was about to be discovered. American soldier-oarsmen awaited him at the dock. They thought they'd be rowing him up a bit and across the river to the fortress at West Point, which was under his command. Instead, he ordered them downstream. After twenty miles or so, they sighted the British sloop of war *Vulture*. Raising a makeshift white flag, Arnold went on board.

The question that still bedevils us is: Why?

* * *

I've read too many different answers to believe we can know for sure. Yet there are strong clues to be found in chronology, and as good a place as any to start—though there are earlier options—is the afternoon of October 7, 1777, when Arnold lay on the ground at Saratoga, his left leg gruesomely shattered, and told his old comrade Henry Dearborn that he "wished the ball had passed his heart."

He spent five months in an Albany army hospital. Surgeons kept asking permission to amputate; he kept saying he'd rather die. To straighten the leg, writes James Kirby Martin, "the doctors could offer only a wooden fracture box," a "crude cast" that required him "to lie fully immobilized—endlessly and uncomfortably—on his back." In March, still not able to walk, he had himself hauled to Connecticut in a cart.

Meanwhile, he had endless time to brood about how he never got enough respect.

On November 29, for example, still immobilized in Albany, he got a letter from the president of Congress conveying news that an average human in good health would have considered positive. The story is complex, as are so many involving Arnold. Nine months earlier, Congress had denied him a promotion—this was still well before Saratoga—that he and Washington, who hadn't been consulted, thought he obviously deserved. Arnold saw the denial as a "way of requesting my resignation," but promised his boss he wouldn't act hastily. Soon afterward, he fought with such obvious valor during a British raid on Connecticut that Congress made him a major general after all. But was he satisfied? No. Five less-qualified men (in his not-unreasonable view) had achieved that rank at the time he was initially rejected, which made them senior to him. Feeling dishonored, he had nonetheless agreed to help with the Saratoga campaign. Now Henry Laurens was writing to tell him Congress had fixed the seniority problem. It had done so by kicking the decision back to Washington, who backdated Arnold's appointment.

So did *this* satisfy him?

It did not. Having "previously pursued this outcome with a persistence that bordered on obsession," writes a recent biographer, Stephen Brumwell, he "seemed indifferent."

Six months later, another well-meaning personnel move helped pave his road to hell.

In the late spring of 1778, as the British pulled out of Philadelphia, Washington named him the city's military commandant. It was a job a nonambulatory man could handle physically, but it required the kind of people skills the short-fused Arnold lacked while offering numerous temptations to use public office to recoup his finances. By 1779, these and other factors had begun to converge.

In February, Pennsylvania's civilian government declared war on Arnold, making eight public accusations against him. Among the most serious was that "he had used state wagons" to transport private property from a ship called the *Charming Nancy*. Early in April, Congress told Washington to have him court-martialed on four of the charges.

On April 8, Arnold married into a family with apparent loyalist sympathies. During the British occupation, Margaret "Peggy" Shippen's home had been "a magnet for young British officers," including John André. At the wedding, the groom, barely able to stand, needed a soldier's support to make it through the ceremony.

Not long afterward, he pleaded for his court-martial to be scheduled soon. Washington told him it would begin May 1, but then, whoops, it had to be postponed.

On May 5, he sent the commander in chief an exceptionally agitated letter. "If Your Excellency thinks me Criminal For Heavens sake let me be immediately Tried and If found guilty Executed," he wrote. "I have nothing left but the little reputation I have gained in the Army"— so "Delay in the present Case Is worse than Death."

Five days later, a Philadelphia shop owner arrived at Henry Clinton's New York headquarters and conveyed a verbal message to André, whose duties included vetting intelligence: Maj. Gen. Benedict Arnold was ready to turn traitor.

I'm shorthanding here, of course. No one involved would have been gauche enough to use the T-word.

A great deal happened during the following one year, four months, and fifteen days before Arnold's gallop down the Escape Path. There was the decision, easily made, that he would be worth way more if he stayed put than if he defected right away. There were negotiations about price. (He had big money problems, which some think were the whole answer to the "why treason" question.) There was his much-delayed court-martial, at which he defended himself with breathtaking hypocrisy. ("Is it probable," he asked his fellow officers, "that after having acquired some little reputation...I should all at once sink into a course of conduct equally unworthy of the patriot and soldier?") There was the shocking (to Arnold) verdict, which convicted him on two counts, one being the use of the wagons for private gain; and the humiliating if minor sentence "to receive a reprimand" from Washington; and the birth of a son. Sir Henry, meanwhile, with André in tow, was busy taking Charleston. After the surrender, they sailed back to New York, where in June, they received one of the most valuable pieces of intelligence Arnold would ever supply. Acted on, with some luck and the navy's help, it could have destroyed the French alliance.

That story will have to wait a few chapters, though. Because right now I need to drive twelve miles down the Hudson to the beautifully situated hamlet of Verplanck, where the future grandfather of women's rights pioneer Elizabeth Cady Stanton—a man who knew zilch about the treasonous plot unfolding in his vicinity—made a random decision that hopelessly screwed it up.

Might I find a heroic statue of him, perhaps?

Alas, no. Though I did see a marker at Steamboat Riverfront Park that mentioned what he did without explaining its true significance or giving his name.

Still, Col. James Livingston ranks high on my list of Unknown Dudes Who Accidentally Saved the Revolution. So let me introduce him and start lobbying for that statue. It could go either at Verplanck or at my next stop, ten miles farther south.

\* \* \*

We've met James Livingston before, actually. He's the guy who led the failed diversionary attack at Quebec right before Arnold's first wound. Of American parentage though a longtime resident of Canada, Livingston raised a regiment there and led it south, where he and his men helped Arnold relieve Fort Stanwix and fought at Saratoga. In August 1780, he was commanding at Verplanck—which guarded Kings Ferry, a crucial Hudson River crossing point—when once again he found himself reporting to Arnold.

By this time, Clinton and Arnold had agreed to aim high. Arnold would help the British take West Point, fulfilling their long-frustrated goal of controlling the Hudson. To do so, he would need to return to active duty and get himself put in charge of the Continental Army's Hudson Highlands Department.

No problem. Except—whoops!

On August 1, Washington welcomed Arnold back by announcing he would command the Continental Army's left wing. He had to say: Sorry, my leg isn't *that* much better. Two days later, he got what he wanted. Seven weeks after that, the betrayal plan was in its late stages. André and Arnold just needed to meet in person and nail down the details. On the night of September 21, a small boat appeared alongside the *Vulture*, the aforementioned British sloop of war, and picked up André. Wearing a blue cloak over his scarlet uniform coat and going by the name "John Anderson," he was rowed to an isolated spot near an Arnold-friendly house on the Hudson's west bank. The idea was that the men would have a chat and André would return to the sloop, but they talked until it was almost daylight.

Problem.

André would need to wait till nightfall to leave.

Meanwhile, the Unknown Dude had sent a four-pound cannon and a howitzer to Teller's Point, part of a peninsula jutting out from the river's east bank. Around dawn, the guns opened fire on the *Vulture*. Lack of wind or a favorable tide made the sloop an easy target, and it sustained some damage. When its captain—his own nose slightly wounded by a splinter—was finally able to get it underway, he sailed it downriver and out of sight.

No one had ordered Livingston to do what he did.

The usual explanation is that he was "irritated" or "exasperated" by having the *Vulture* hang around his neck of the woods, which might well be the case. So I was surprised to discover that an old marker at today's Croton Point Park—508 gorgeous acres of which Teller's Point is the southwestern tip—named two *other* unknown dudes who might have played a part in Livingston's decision. From the marker's vague text and two snippets of local history I'd picked up, all problematic, I learned that Jack Peterson ("a negro") and George Sherwood, militiamen employed at a local farm, were said to have fired "shot guns" at one of the *Vulture's* boats the day before André came ashore. What's more, "realizing that the *Vulture* was in cannon range," they "reported their observations to Colonel Livingston."

If this is true, I should be lobbying for three statues, not one. I hadn't wrapped my brain around that concept, however, before it was time to drive south once more: through Ossining, home to Sing Sing prison; past the Rockefeller State Park Preserve, formerly the country estate of the Republic's first billionaire; through Sleepy Hollow, where the fictional Headless Horseman chased a terrified Ichabod Crane; and a few yards into Tarrytown, where I knew there really *was* a statue honoring some dudes who helped foil Arnold's plot.

Why there?

Bad luck, bad planning, and naïve incompetence all played a part. It's tempting to use the term "comedy of errors," except that no one on either side was laughing.

After the rattled conspirators watched the *Vulture* sail away, the decision was made—it's not clear how, though André said he was unhappy about it—that the major would have to return to the British lines by land. So he changed out of his uniform (necessary though extremely risky) and, at Arnold's urging, stashed West Point documents in his riding boots (unnecessary and stupid; most were in Arnold's handwriting, and André could have memorized the important stuff). Escorted by the owner of the Arnold-friendly house, who seems to have swallowed a cover story but in any case acted as if lives were not at stake, "John Anderson" made his way across the Hudson at Kings Ferry, turned south at Verplanck, and headed for the dangerous no-man's-land between the armies. Partway through this "Neutral Ground," his escort turned back, leaving him to ride on alone.

Uh-oh.

A bas-relief on the base of the Tarrytown statue picks up the story. André sits on a rock with one boot off, an anxious look on his face and his arms outstretched as if in supplication toward three young men in front of him. One holds a document as another leans forward to read it. By capturing the disguised Brit, a nearby marker states, "three honest militiamen" had prevented "disaster to the American cause."

Tarrytown, it needs to be said, didn't look a bit like it does today. By 1780, the war had made much of Westchester County devastatingly unlivable. Foraging parties from both armies wreaked havoc on families by confiscating grain and livestock, while roving bands of freebooters, as one historian put it, "deliberately robbed and plundered noncombatants." What John Paulding, David Williams, and Isaac Van Wart were actually doing in that lawless landscape when they jumped out of the bushes and nabbed "John Anderson" remains a mystery. But never mind that: It made them stars in our ongoing miniseries about Revolution-saving accidents.

They turned their captive over to a clueless Continental colonel. The colonel sent messages to his boss (Arnold!) and to Washington, who was traveling but due at Arnold's HQ for breakfast on September 25. Arnold got his message first.

"Gotta go!" he told his wife and galloped down the Escape Path.

Actually, he probably told her a little more, because after Washington showed up and got around to reading his mail—it took a while—a partially clothed Peggy greeted him with a convincing hysterical fit, raving that someone was planning to kill her son, denying that Washington was really Washington, and so on. Alexander Hamilton, meanwhile, tore off to Verplanck on the slim chance Arnold might be intercepted there.

No such luck. But he didn't quite return empty-handed. Aboard the *Vulture*, Arnold had written Washington a letter, and he had sent it to Verplanck to be passed on.

"I have ever acted from a Principle of Love to my Country," it reads, and the same principle "Actuates my present Conduct, however it may appear Inconsistent to the World: who very Seldom Judge right of any Mans Actions." Also: "I have no favor to ask for myself," because "I have too often experienced the Ingratitude of my Country to Attempt it." Yet

Arnold *did* have a favor to ask for Peggy, who is "Inocent [*sic*] as an Angel, and is Incapable of doing Wrong." Could Washington please take her under his protection, lest "the mistaken fury of The Country" cause her harm?

He was lying about her, of course.

British intelligence documents that surfaced in the twentieth century make it "impossible to doubt," Carl Van Doren writes, "that she was perfectly aware of the conspiracy from the beginning." Still, it's easy enough to forgive a man for trying to protect his wife.

What's most shameless about that letter, it seems to me, is Arnold asking for help from a man he had done his best to betray in the most personal way possible. Earlier in the month, as the West Point plot thickened, Washington had decided to cross the Hudson to confer with French officers in Hartford. Told the details of the commander in chief's travel plans, Arnold alerted the British—and he did the same a week later, as Washington headed back.

Possible twofer! Crucial fortress falls! Indispensable Man captured!

It didn't happen. But it came way too close.

\* \* \*

An unlovely cube-shaped hunk of granite marks the spot where John André died. It's on secluded Andre Hill Road in Tappan, New York—west of the Hudson and north of the Jersey line—near where, on October 2, 1780, the Continental Army was encamped.

Three days earlier, Washington had appointed fifteen generals to sit in judgment on the prisoner. Among them were Lafayette, Knox, Stirling, Glover, and Steuben. Nathanael Greene presided. It was not a show trial, exactly, but there was little chance these men would spare an enemy officer who'd been caught inside American lines wearing civilian clothes, using a false name, and with documents passed to him by a traitor on his person. Hours before his execution was scheduled—though it would end up being postponed a day—André sketched a heartrending self-portrait and gave it to one of his guards. Only as he approached the gallows did he learn that his request to be shot like "a Man of honour" rather than be hanged had been denied.

He was buried where he died, though his remains would end up in Westminster Abbey. Tappan's memorial went up around the centennial of his death, and the most intriguing part is a short quote, in Latin, from Virgil's *Aeneid*. I'm no classical scholar, but its translation moved me:

> *They weep here*
> *For how the world goes, and our life that passes*
> *Touches their hearts.*

In the midst of the Arnold-André turmoil, Greene wrote his much-loved wife, Caty, with the awful news. A few days after André's death, though, he had something happier than treason to report. He'd been tapped to take over at West Point, and it looked as if she could join him there for the winter!

Then the commander in chief dashed this hope.

Asked by his civilian bosses to make his own decision about who should take over what was left of the southern army—Congress's last choice not having worked out—Washington told Greene: You're the man.

Spoiler alert:

He would have more success in the Carolinas than his predecessors. A great deal of it would come because he was an infinitely better general. But he would also get a whole lot more help from militia—much of it before he even arrived.

# CHAPTER 17

# Over the Mountains, Kings of the Hill

The first part of that militia help came in a tiny South Carolina engagement that would prove significantly more important than its small scale and weird name suggest. The Battle of Huck's Defeat was fought on July 12, 1780—before Gates had even left his army behind at Camden—and it served to disabuse Cornwallis of his belief that the British had "put an end to all resistance" in the state.

That said, you could walk the battlefield in ten minutes if you didn't stop to read the marker texts or admire the paintings that help magnify its story.

Christian Huck was a captain in a unit of so-called "provincial" troops—loyalists, mainly from the North, who signed up for the long haul and got trained like British Regulars—that ended up attached to Tarleton's Legion. Sent west of the Waxhaws to harass rebel sympathizers in and around what's now York County, Huck earned a reputation as a foulmouthed hater of Presbyterians (who made up most of the local population) and a disdainer of nonprofessional fighting men. At one point, or so the story goes, he harangued captive listeners about why the rebels could never win.

"We have driven the Regulars out of the country," Huck said, meaning the Continental Army, "and I swear that if it rained militia from the Heavens, I would not value them."

That same night, a number of local militia leaders agreed on a plan of attack. Moving quietly toward the farmhouse around which Huck's force had camped, they surprised their enemies at daybreak. One of the paintings on the battlefield trail—it's part of a larger county site called Historic Brattonsville—captures the chaos as rebels fire from behind a split-rail fence; provincials go down; and a shirtsleeved Huck tries to rally his men. Another shows him throwing up his arms and falling backward, shot dead while trying to gallop away. Three different militiamen would claim credit.

"Lucky shot," Michael Scoggins told me, laughing.

Scoggins, who I'm sad to say died in 2019, was the author of *The Day It Rained Militia* and the world's leading expert on the Battle of Huck's Defeat. When I asked him to highlight some of what he'd learned, one of the first things he mentioned was the effect of the carnage at the Waxhaws.

More than a hundred of Buford's men ended up at the Presbyterian meetinghouse there, he said, where those tending them got a close look at their wounds. The news "sent a shock wave through people" and jarred Scotch-Irish Presbyterians into thinking: "This is the same kind of thing that used to happen back in the old country." He was referring to the centuries-old culture of violence on the border of England and Scotland, and to the flood of emigrants—many coming by way of Northern Ireland—who carried that culture with them to the southern backcountry.

"They really were border clans," he said. "You back them in a corner, they're going to fight. That's what they do—and they're pretty damn good at it."

In truth, it didn't rain *many* militia on July 12, 1780. The total that actually made it to the battlefield is most often given as 133, a few more men than Huck had with him. But never mind the numbers. The Battle of Huck's Defeat proved "for the first time that local militiamen could fight and win"—in the right circumstances—against better-equipped, better-trained professionals. And less than three months later, some of the same men who took down Huck would join a far larger force of fron-tiersmen to win one of the pivotal victories of the war.

Except for their scale, Scoggins said, the two battles were strikingly similar:

"Once again, you have an enemy commander who comes into the area, pisses a lot of people off, and makes boastful claims about how the British are going to defeat the rebels. And once again, in a very short period of time, a coalition of local militia commanders comes together, puts together a strike force, surrounds his position, and wipes him out."

\* \* \*

That second victory took place on October 7, 1780, at Kings Moun-tain, some twenty-five miles northwest of the Huck's Defeat battle-field. Despite its name, there was no actual mountain nearby: The fight Thomas Jefferson once called the "turn of the tide of success" took place on a section of ridge whose crest runs southwest to northeast for six hundred yards and has been described as being shaped "like a human footprint." It rises maybe 150 feet above the surrounding countryside, though lower numbers are often given.

Still, it looked plenty high enough for Maj. Patrick Ferguson's purposes.

Until all of a sudden it didn't.

At thirty-six, Ferguson, an aristocrat Scot and firearms expert, had already had an eventful military career. Four years earlier, he'd found himself flat on his back near London, in the pouring rain, showing off a breech-loading Ferguson rifle—his improved version of a French design—for a gaggle of army muckety-mucks. A year after that, if his story is to be believed, he was at the Battle of Brandywine, before it really heated up, aiming one of those specially designed rifles at none other than George Washington. The two were one hundred yards apart, a distance at which Ferguson had "seldom missed." Yet "it was not pleas-ant to fire at the back of an unoffending individual who was acquitting himself very coolly of his duty so I let him alone."

Was it really Washington he had in his sights?

Possibly. The debate is way complicated. But hands up, please, if you find the notion of Horatio Gates as commander in chief comforting.

Shortly after Ferguson failed to change history (maybe), a bullet smashed his right elbow, making him in essence a one-armed man. Sidelined for months, he learned to ride, shoot, and wield a sword left-handed. He also helped out with intelligence work, forging a strong connection with Henry Clinton while he was at it. When Clinton took his army to Charleston, Ferguson went with it. And just before Sir Henry headed back north, he gave his protégé an impossible-sounding new job. As inspector of militia, Ferguson's orders were to use his "best Endeavors, without Loss of Time, to form into Corps all the Young or unmarried Men of the Provinces of Georgia and the two Carolinas as Opportunity shall offer"—all while reporting to Cornwallis, whom Clinton hadn't bothered to consult.

Organize Georgia and the two Carolinas! With an angry boss!

It was a tall order. And threatening a bunch of hardened frontiersmen that if they didn't stop being rebellious, he would "march his army over the mountains, hang their leaders, and lay their country waste with fire and sword" was not going to help.

* * *

The mountains (real ones) over which Ferguson threatened to march against those frontiersmen were the Appalachians, and one of their leaders was Isaac Shelby, the man to whom the threat had been delivered.

Shelby, at twenty-nine, had been a scofflaw long before he was a rebel. That's because after the British won the French and Indian War, they banned white settlement west of the Appalachians. The idea was to keep costly frontier warfare from further depleting the treasury. On this side of the Atlantic, however, the Proclamation Line of 1763 was anathema both to speculators (among them the future Father of His Country) and to impoverished pioneers. Predictably, few were deterred—least of all the evocatively named "over-mountain men" who, with wives and children if they had them, settled along the Watauga, Holston, and Nolichucky Rivers in what is now East Tennessee.

By 1780, Shelby was making his home on the Holston. In May,

when Charleston fell, he was off surveying for land grabbers in Kentucky, but that summer, he was mainly a warrior. Answering a call from Carolina partisans, he and a band of over-mountain men had already helped win a fierce fight with provincials and loyalist militia at Musgrove's Mill. Afterward, he had a suggestion to make: Why didn't leaders on both sides of the mountains stay in touch and figure out how to make their Ferguson problem disappear?

Meanwhile, the inspector of militia and his impatient superior were doing some planning themselves.

On fire to lead the main British army into North Carolina—because South Carolina was in the bag, right?—Cornwallis ordered Ferguson to help out by multitasking.

His jobs: Keep recruiting loyalists, keep "overawing the disaffected," and, in his spare time, function as the invading army's left wing.

*  *  *

My Kings Mountain visit didn't get off to a great start. For one thing, there was a storm brewing. Also, the woman at the visitor center told me—after asking if I had an umbrella—that the park didn't offer guided tours on weekdays. But there was good news, too: "The trail is made out of recycled tires, so it's easier on your feet and legs."

Hoping to beat the rain, I followed that trail around the base of the ridge. For a long time I didn't see or hear another human, just red flashes of cardinals in flight and the reet-reeting of frogs in a nearby stream.

The trailside markers, unsurprisingly, slowed me down. "Unrelenting civil war had scourged the South with partisan plundering, bushwhacking, and brutal massacres," one noted, pitting "neighbor against rancorous neighbor, and fathers against sons." Another, titled "Fighting in a Forest Primeval," explained that the woods I was seeing were "only a shadow of the mature forest that stood here in October 1780. Hardwood trees like oaks, hickories, and chestnuts covered the slopes of Kings Mountain, their great trunks massive by today's standards." Looking up at the ridgetop now, through the scrubbier modern forest, made me wonder what Patrick Ferguson thought he was doing up there.

Yet Ferguson himself appears to have been doubt-free.

Not long after his meeting with Cornwallis, he'd made his way into western North Carolina with a force that by the time of the battle would consist of fewer than a hundred veteran provincials plus roughly a thousand barely trained local militia. By mid-September, he'd fired off his hang-your-leaders-lay-your-country-waste threat to the over-mountain men, sending it north with a prisoner of war released for that purpose.

Receiving it, Isaac Shelby wasted no time.

First, he rode forty miles to consult John Sevier, another formidable over-mountain fighter, speculator, and partisan leader. Sevier agreed that Ferguson had to go, right now, and the two men divvied up the job of contacting partisans in western North Carolina and southwestern Virginia. Shelby's next move was to seek help from William Campbell of Washington County, Virginia (yes, there were already counties named after George). Some four hundred Washington County men showed up at the most celebrated of several anti-Ferguson rendezvous.

That gathering took place at Sycamore Shoals on the Watauga River, in what's now Elizabethton, Tennessee. More than a thousand men with horses and long rifles milled around the flats by the river, saying goodbye to wives and children and preparing to cross the mountains. The next morning, according to "the tradition of the country," a Presbyterian clergyman sent them off with a rousing battle cry from the Old Testament.

"The sword of the Lord and of Gideon!" he called out.

"The sword of the Lord and of our Gideons!" came the response, and away they rode.

Each man carried his own blanket and provisions, mostly parched cornmeal mixed with maple sugar. The first day they tried driving cattle, but no quick-strike force has time to deal with stampedes, so they butchered a few and left the rest. After climbing to the gap below Yellow Mountain, where their route crossed today's Appalachian Trail, they noticed that two of their number had deserted and had to assume the enemy would soon know their plans. Descending into North Carolina, they joined forces with backcountry partisans from that state—and had a critical decision to make:

Who should have overall command as they pursued Ferguson and, with luck, brought him to battle?

The politics were tricky, but Shelby achieved his goal, which was to keep the job away from a leader viewed as "too inactive." It went instead to Campbell, though he was to be "regulated and directed" by the group as a whole.

Plot lines now began to intersect.

Cornwallis, proceeding with his North Carolina invasion, reached Charlotte, where determined rebels outside the town made it hard for him to communicate with his left wing. Ferguson made it even harder by moving west in pursuit of a Georgia partisan leader he'd been told was out there. And now those two deserters from the over-mountain men showed up, bringing him bad news.

If you were Ferguson, what's the first thing you'd have done when you heard about the threat headed your way? Your choices are (a) ask your boss to send professional help, or (b) issue a proclamation impugning the manhood of every potential loyalist recruit who didn't run to your aid right now. Hint: The last line of that proclamation read: "If you choose to be pissed upon by a set of mongrels, say so at once, and let your women turn their backs upon you, and look out for real men to protect them."

He did eventually ask for help, but no message got through before it was too late. He also began moving toward Charlotte, but didn't seem in much of a hurry. Why? We don't know. Yet it seems fair to suggest, among other reasons—ambition, lust for glory, unwillingness to relinquish independent command—that the author of that macho proclamation couldn't bear to let "a set of mongrels" send him running to the protective arms of Daddy Cornwallis, even if that was the right thing to do.

In any case, there he sat on the top of that foot-shaped ridge at three o'clock on the afternoon of October 7, 1780, about to engage in a deadly game of King of the Hill.

\* \* \*

The trail would take me to the ridgetop before too long. Already I'd glimpsed a tall gray monument above me, blending in with the trees and dark clouds. But for now I was still wending around the base of the slope, thinking about what Shelby told his men before the fight, especially the part used as a title on a trailside marker:

"Be Your Own Officer," it read.

The over-mountain men and their allies had split their force in half, sending the strongest fighters on the fittest horses ahead. Shortly after sunset on the sixth, they reached the Cowpens—still just a way station for cattle drives, not yet the most famous cow pasture in revolutionary history—where a party of South Carolina militia joined them. There was time to eat but not to sleep. At 9 p.m., more than nine hundred men rode east toward Kings Mountain, which was still thirty-three miles away.

Naturally, it poured rain half the time.

At one point, some leaders proposed a rest halt.

Shelby would have none of it. They rode on.

By the time they reached their destination and dismounted, the rain had stopped. Their plan was simple. Each commander and his men would take an assigned position at the base of the ridge, surrounding it completely, then all would charge up the slope. Once the fight began, no single leader would be able to coordinate the whole force; in fact, it would be nearly impossible for a commander even to control his own unit. That was why Shelby's advice to his men, as quoted in the text of that marker, made such good sense:

"When we encounter the enemy, don't wait for a word of command. Let each of you be your own officer, and do the very best you can."

They were almost but not quite in position when sentries noticed them and the shooting began. Campbell's and Shelby's units, at the heel of the ridge, started up first, emitting shrill, eerie whoops. Up they climbed, advancing from big tree to big tree. They fired the same rifles they used for hunting, with which they could hit targets at two hundred yards, but which took sixty seconds to reload. Down charged the loyalists, led by Ferguson's veteran provincials. They carried muskets with which they couldn't be sure of hitting anything at more than fifty yards, but which could be loaded three times as fast as hunting rifles, and unlike those rifles, were equipped with bayonets.

"Charging Cold Steel—Three Times" read the next marker title I saw. It might just as well have read: "Running Away Because, Gosh, Why Wouldn't You—But Then Coming Back for More." Each time the provincials charged, a few rebels would be bayoneted or shot, but most just fired their rifles and decamped downhill. Ferguson would then call his provincials back to meet another threat—signaling with blasts on the silver whistles he learned to use after his Brandywine wound—and the rebels who had retreated would pull themselves together and rejoin the battle. Be your own officer! It's worth pointing out that their actual officers *encouraged* them to return. Yet encouragement was rarely enough when ordinary militia confronted bayonets. Which goes to show that whatever you want to call the kind of fighter willing to start up that slope again and again, "ordinary" is the wrong word.

Could the loyalists have won? Sure, if those first assaults they broke had stayed broken. But they didn't. As one historian describes the action, "unit formations broke into pockets of small teams and individual assaults, which created a swarming effect." All around the ridge, men worked their way up, "supporting one another as they moved."

I worked my way up, too. On a side path, I learned that seventy thousand people had jammed this hillside in 1930 to hear President Herbert Hoover say Kings Mountain had been dissed. "History has done scant justice to its significance, which rightly should place it beside Lexington and Bunker Hill, Trenton and Yorktown," he told them.

Seventy thousand people! I'd met just one so far.

Now the clouds let loose and a hard rain lashed the trail. I hustled on to where the first riflemen gained the rocky crest, then jogged past two tall monuments, one an obelisk that looked like a scale model of Bunker Hill's. Rain or no rain, though, I needed to pause at the hunk of rough-hewn stone marking the spot where Ferguson fell.

As the hourlong battle drew to a close, chaos broke out on the ridgetop. Riflemen swarmed up from all sides, catching their enemies in a crossfire. Some men knew how to pick out Ferguson in a crowd, because a loyalist messenger, captured earlier, had told them he wore "a checked shirt, or duster" over his uniform. No one seems to know why, but it remains part of Patrick Ferguson's legend that he wore a red-and-white garment that looked like an Italian tablecloth—at least if the reenactment photo on the park marker is any indication—when at least seven bullets cut him down.

My last stop of the day was his grave, a few yards farther down the trail, where visitors still add rocks to the rough cairn that rises above it.

* * *

Jefferson was right to declare Kings Mountain a turning point. The out-of-nowhere victory stopped Cornwallis's 1780 invasion of North Carolina and drove a stake through British hopes of mobilizing loyalists to win the war. It had more strategic impact than the strong-willed men who fought it could have imagined. Yet we also need to remember its aftermath, which showed how hard ending civil strife in the South was likely to be.

After Ferguson went down, his second-in-command tried to surrender. It took far too long. Shooting continued for "some time," Shelby wrote, for two reasons: Some latecomers to the ridgetop simply took a while to grasp what was happening, but others didn't *want* to stop the killing. Angered by what they believed Tarleton had done at the Waxhaws, they "were willing to follow that bad example."

More than 150 loyalists died at Kings Mountain; upward of 160 were too seriously wounded to move, while nearly 700 became prisoners. Total rebel casualties were in the high double digits. The next morning, as one witness would recall, loyalist wives and children arrived to find that their "husbands, fathers, and brothers lay dead in heaps, while others lay wounded or dying." The victors, meanwhile, fearing a Tarleton pursuit, beat a quick retreat. Three days in, Campbell had to order "officers of all ranks" to "restrain the disorderly manner of slaughtering and disturbing the prisoners."

What followed, on October 14, was worse.

Charging thirty or forty loyalists (accounts vary) with crimes ranging from parole-breaking to house-burning to assassination, the partisans held a "trial" and began to hang the accused—at night, by torchlight, three at a time. Nine died before the leaders somehow concluded that enough was enough.

The underlying cause—as the latest Continental general ordered south would see almost as soon as he took command—was a civil war in which the cycle of atrocity and retaliation raged out of control.

# CHAPTER 18

# "A Sweeping Guerrilla War of Movement"

Beneath the statue of Nathanael Greene on his most important Carolina battlefield—quick, can you name it? If not, we'll get there—is a list of nine battles in which he played a significant role. Harlem Heights, Trenton, Princeton, Brandywine, and Monmouth date from his northern service; Guilford Court House, Hobkirk's Hill, Ninety Six, and Eutaw Springs represent his southern campaign. The general gazes across his horse's mane toward a smaller statue of Athena, goddess of wisdom and war, who appears to be leading him forward toward glory.

Yet there's something wrong with this picture, as I realized when I thought about those nine names. It's that Greene did so much more to help win the war than a simple list of battles can convey.

He'd always been a quick study, but like Henry Knox, was forced to educate himself. His father, a well-off Rhode Island Quaker of what Greene called "the most Supersticious sort," thought sons destined to work in the family business—which included a foundry and a mill—need learn only to read and to do sums. Nathanael rebelled, as children of domineering parents have been known to do. He read everything he could get his hands on, eventually rejecting his father's religion as well. And like Knox, he became fascinated with military history.

Not that this kept him from being humiliated by the first military organization he joined.

Looking backward from the day he rode south, it's tempting to see Greene's career as a series of tutorials designed to prepare him for the Mission Impossible he would end up taking on. This is a stretch, but I'm going to do it anyway—starting with the moment on October 25, 1774, two months after the Powder Alarm roiled New England, when members of a militia unit Greene had been instrumental in founding told him he was "a blemish to the company" and could not be one of its officers. The problem? He'd had a slight limp since childhood, and a limping lieutenant would look bad on parade. He almost quit, but swallowed his pride and served in the ranks. Seven months later, when the Rhode Island assembly needed a brigadier general to command the force it was sending to Boston, it chose Pvt. Nathanael Greene.

*Suck it up and persevere* is the lesson here—though book learning and family connections surely helped.

Greene's next big lesson emerged from the Battle of Brooklyn, even though he wasn't there. By August 1776, he was the Continental Army's youngest major general—a man with zero combat experience who had so impressed his commander in chief that he'd been entrusted with the defense of Long Island. Could his mastery of the terrain have made a difference? We'll never know, because on the night the British waltzed through Jamaica Pass, Greene was recovering from a violent fever that almost killed him. Still, I'm guessing he made a couple of mental notes on Washington's narrow escape:

*Don't get pinned against a river. But if you do, be sure to have enough boats.*

The most painful lesson came in November, when he watched Fort Washington fall: *Never, ever, risk losing 2,800 men to hold a position you don't need.* A devastated Greene took that one to heart. But if you're wondering why his boss kept him around, the answer suggested by Arthur Lefkowitz, author of *The Long Retreat*, is illuminating. Well before the debacle, Greene put together a proposal to stash supplies along the route the troops might have to take if retreating through New Jersey. As a result, "the rebels never faced critical shortages of ammunition or food."

So many lessons: At the Delaware, he learned about necessary bold-ness (and, once again, about boats). At Brandywine, he helped stop defeat from morphing into disaster. At Valley Forge, he took on the thankless job of supplying the army—which Washington trusted no one else to do—and ended up serving as quartermaster general for more than two contentious years. He still got to wear his major general hat on a few battlefields, notably Monmouth and Rhode Island, learning plenty there as well. But by the summer of 1780, sick of quartermaster-generaling and under fire from Congress (it's complicated), he quit that part of his job.

Then Cornwallis crushed Gates at Camden.

Alexander Hamilton reacted instantly: "For God's sake," he wrote an influential congressman, "overcome prejudice, and send Greene."

Washington was more cautious, waiting till Congress told him to pick Gates's replacement himself. Then he ordered Greene to waste no time and put his right-hand man's task in context in a letter to a South Carolina ally. "I think I am giving you a General," he wrote, "but what can a General do, without men, without arms, without cloathing, with-out stores, without provisions?"

Great question. No obvious answer. But one thing was clear to Greene as he set off for Charlotte, North Carolina, to take over the shat-tered southern army. Fighting big battles—let alone winning them—would not be at the top of his to-do list. Instead, one of his first official acts in Charlotte would be to ask the Swamp Fox for help.

\* \* \*

Francis Marion is a character so cloaked in hagiography and Hollywood that when discussing him, it's useful to keep a few facts in mind. For starters, no one called him the Swamp Fox when he was alive. The term "vile swamp fox" attached itself to him in a dubious biography published fourteen years after his death; two more decades would pass before the nickname acquired its capital letters and "positive connotation." Also, despite the soulful portrait I saw in a Charleston museum, no one ever painted him from life.

We know, however, that he didn't look anything like Mel Gibson.

In the summer of 1780, he was around forty-eight years old, a little over five feet tall, not much over a hundred pounds, and walking "with a pronounced limp," a recent biographer writes, because the ankle he broke at the Drunken Bash That Saved the Revolution hadn't fully healed. But when Greene sat down to write him on December 4, he didn't know or care what his new ally looked like. "Until a more permanent Army can be collected than is in the Field at present," he observed, "we must endeavor to keep up a Partizan War and preserve the Tide of Sentiment among the People as much as possible in our Favour."

This, of course, is what Marion and other southern partisans—including the Kings Mountain heroes, about whom Greene knew far less—had been doing for months.

I once had the good fortune to hear John Buchanan, then eighty-seven years old and sharp as ever, explain how crucial those months were. After the British took Charleston, Buchanan said, they established a chain of bases across the backcountry, brushed Gates aside, and prepared for "a triumphant sweep northward." Then "the unexpected happened: The majority of rebels in that area rose in revolt, mounted their horses, waged a sweeping guerrilla war of movement, and stymied the British pacification effort.

"The rising was fundamental," he said. "It changed the course of the war."

Marion's area of operations, unlike that of most South Carolina partisans, was the low country, not the backcountry, mainly between the Santee and Pee Dee Rivers. He depended on his knowledge of its swamps and byways to keep one jump ahead of his enemies. Like the backcountry partisans, though, he and his men were mounted, allowing them to appear suddenly, attack, and just as quickly disappear. Within weeks, his small band had alarmed Cornwallis, who had supply lines to protect as he prepared to invade North Carolina. Lord C sent Maj. James Wemyss to terrorize the rebels in the area. This he did, burning and hanging as the outmanned Marion made himself temporarily scarce.

Eight days after Wemyss boasted that his mission was accomplished, the Swamp Fox was back, routing some loyalist militia near Black Mingo

Creek. By early October, he was parading through Georgetown with too few men to threaten its British garrison, but enough to send a message that someday he might. Shortly after *that*, he surprised a party of well-equipped King's Friends around midnight and sent most fleeing into Tearcoat Swamp. Small victories all—but collectively, they mattered.

Banastre Tarleton was up next.

By November, Kings Mountain had forced Cornwallis to abandon Charlotte, postpone his North Carolina invasion, and hole up in Winnsboro, South Carolina, to wait till next year. Yet the British still had supply lines to protect, and Marion remained a problem. Why not use their ultimate weapon? "I am always sanguine when you are concerned," Tarleton's boss told him.

He shouldn't have been.

True, Tarleton almost lured his quarry into a trap. But Marion—outnumbered, outgunned, and warned at the last minute—galloped off unscathed. Tarleton pursued with his usual vigor, but a daylong, twenty-six-mile chase proved fruitless. Frustrated, he destroyed the property of the family whose warning foiled his plans; burned some thirty other houses for good measure; and, in a November 11 letter to Cornwallis, reported failure and declared victory in the same sentence. "I had the Mortification not to fight them, but I had the Pleasure in a great Measure to disperse them," he wrote.

Three days later he received an urgent summons. Thomas Sumter had struck again—and Cornwallis needed Tarleton back to deal with this bigger threat.

*  *  *

Sumter was only two years younger than Marion, and he, too, was on the small side. But in other ways the Gamecock—a nickname by which he actually *was* known during the war—was about as unlike the Swamp Fox as a fellow partisan could be.

He was "not a sympathetic character," as Buchanan writes in *The Road to Guilford Courthouse*. "Wearing his ego on his shoulder, he had few peers as a prima donna and could spot a slight, intended or not, around a corner. He was careless with security and lives. His penchant for bloody and repeated frontal assaults was unnecessarily costly" and his notion of working for the common good didn't include cooperating with others unless he was in charge. All true, but here's the thing: "Generals are like artists—one does not have to like them, only to respect what they do when they do it well."

And what Sumter did better than anyone, during those first crucial months of the rising, was inspire men in the backcountry to come out and fight.

He grew up poor in Virginia, and two tales from his young manhood show the range of his experiences. In one, he traveled with three Cherokee chiefs to England, where he translated between them and George III. In the other, jailed for debt, he escaped and fled the colony. Nothing if not resilient, he remade himself as a South Carolina merchant and planter, marrying money and "participating in the great American game of land speculation." When rebellion broke out, he served in a number of capacities, ultimately raising a regiment of riflemen that became part of the Continental Army. He resigned his commission in 1778, however, and chose not to join the struggles for Savannah or for Charleston. Still, he had enough of a name that on May 28, 1780, Tarleton—hotfooting it toward the Waxhaws—dispatched some cavalry to bring him in.

Sumter didn't wait for them. With "no rank, no men, no prospects"; with his home about to go up in flames; and with only his enslaved body servant, Soldier Tom, for company, he rode north to organize resistance. A gathering of backcountry leaders soon chose him as South Carolina's overall militia commander.

That summer, he and many hundreds of recruits fought at Rocky Mount (an impressive near victory) and Hanging Rock (a real victory, not quite completed because too many of Sumter's men got drunk). After Camden, as we've seen, he was forced to flee for his life, bareback, half-naked, and alone. Yet less than two weeks later, Cornwallis wrote that "the indefatigable Sumter" was "beating up for recruits with the greatest assiduity," and by August 30, according to one report, he'd "encreased his Corps to upwards of 1,000." Kings Mountain was fought without him—he was too busy fending off a challenge to his authority—but some of his militia joined in to help crush Ferguson.

This brings us to the climactic month of Thomas Sumter's partisan career.

Early November found him and several hundred men within thirty miles of Cornwallis's Winnsboro camp. While no threat to the main British force, they made a tempting target, so Cornwallis sent James Wemyss to surprise them. Wemyss added his own wrinkle: As his attack began, a few picked men were to dash into the enemy camp, "find Sumter, and either kill or capture him." At about 1 a.m. on November 9, however, as Wemyss approached Fish Dam Ford on the Broad River, alert rebels shot him down, wounding him so badly that he had to be left behind when his command was forced to retreat. Sumter, meanwhile—who'd been asleep in his tent when the British showed up—had evaded his would-be assassins by leaping over a fence and dashing naked through a briar patch.

That's right. For the second time in three months, the man had cheated death while not fully clothed.

Surely one can be forgiven for thinking he had nine lives—especially given what happened next.

* * *

"Don't be confused by Battlefield Road, because the battlefield isn't *on* Battlefield Road," I remembered Charles Baxley saying, and it was good advice. Monument Road—south of the Tyger River, at the border of Union and Spartanburg Counties—is what takes you to the site of the rematch between the Gamecock and "Bloody Ban" Tarleton.

Ten days after Fish Dam Ford, Sumter had more than a thousand "mostly seasoned" militiamen, thanks to the inspiriting win over Wemyss. Tarleton had half as many, but all were veteran provincials or Regulars. He was moving fast, and the rebels didn't know he was coming—until one person's choice changed that. "Sometime in the early morning hours of 20 November, a British soldier deserted from the 63rd Foot, stole a horse, rode to Sumter's camp, and revealed Tarleton's location, strength and mission."

Decision time. If they retreated, Sumter and his officers knew, they risked attack while crossing a river or "strung out on the road." Besides, they didn't *want* to retreat. Instead, they agreed to find a good defensive position and fight. Someone suggested William Blackstock's farm—or "plantation," as modest backcountry holdings that looked nothing like Tara were called.

With an hour of daylight left, Tarleton showed up on top of a hill across from the farm. Now it was his turn to make a decision.

He had just 270 men, having pushed so hard he'd had to leave most of his infantry behind. Ideally, he'd wait for them to catch up, but he feared the rebels might escape across the Tyger during the night. Sumter, meanwhile, knew Tarleton wasn't at full strength, because Mary Dillard—a local woman who'd seen the British go by—had ridden six miles to give him the news. It's unclear who started the fight, but whatever Tarleton's intent, he deployed his men in a way that prompted a reaction.

Down the hill toward Blackstock's field marched eighty dismounted Regulars with bayonets fixed. Down the opposite slope, with orders to confront the Regulars, came four hundred of Sumter's men. Possessed of the militia's usual fear of Brits with bayonets, they stopped too soon, shot from too far away, and retreated. So far, so good, from Tarleton's point of view, but then the Regulars advanced too impetuously, bringing them within range of riflemen hidden in some outbuildings. Deadly fire forced Tarleton to bring his Legion to the rescue. "The attack," he wrote after the war, "was attended with immediate success. The cavalry soon reached the houses, and broke the Americans, who from that instant began to disperse."

Except that wasn't really what happened.

"Tarleton lied," Buchanan writes. "He lied in his battle report to Cornwallis, and he lied in his *History*." Yes, he extricated what was left of the eighty Regulars, displaying plenty of personal courage. "But he did not reach the buildings, he did not break the American center or any part of its line, he did not cause the Rebels to immediately disperse, he inflicted minimal casualties on them, and he lost far more men than he admitted," because rifle fire from the buildings, a fence, and the woods wreaked havoc. Of the 270 men Tarleton brought into action, 92 were killed and 76 wounded. Total rebel casualties were in the single digits.

What Tarleton *did* do was make Sumter one of those casualties.

As he and several officers rode forward to observe Tarleton's retreat, the British rear guard fired a volley. Five buckshot entered Sumter's chest; another "hit him under his right shoulder, kept going and chipped his spine, and finally came to rest under his left shoulder." He gave no sign of being hit until someone noticed blood streaming down his back. From a farmhouse bed, he finally admitted—to Soldier Tom, but no one else—that he needed a doctor right away. With the most dangerous shot removed, he was carried across three rivers to safety while Col. John Twiggs of Georgia wrapped up the day's work and sent the victorious militia home.

It would take Sumter months to get back in action.

Still, Nathanael Greene sought him out. On December 8, two and a half weeks after the battle at Blackstock's Plantation, the new commander of the southern army rode ten miles to the Catawba River, where Sumter was convalescing. There was no meeting of the minds. Sumter's big strategic idea was that Greene should instantly attack Cornwallis, which was just silly. But Greene did his best to conciliate his wounded ally without letting on what he was really thinking.

Eight days later, he divided his small force and ordered Daniel Morgan to lead the stronger half into South Carolina west of the Catawba— right in the middle of Thomas Sumter territory.

* * *

The text on the statue of Daniel Morgan in Spartanburg, South Carolina, makes no mention of any place he fought in the North. Erected in 1881 to celebrate the centennial of his most notable southern accomplishment—which took place less than twenty miles from what's now called Morgan Square—it's all about Cowpens, not Saratoga.

Which seems fair enough: The man starred in more than one Revolutionary War turning point, did he not?

The statue itself, however—influenced by the Beaux Arts style— doesn't look a bit like the fiercely determined man who, by 1781, had already survived hundreds of British lashes during the French and Indian War, a starved trek through the Maine wilderness, and a furious attempt to wrest victory from defeat in Quebec, plus those two war-changing struggles in upstate New York. Nor is there any sign of the angry pride that led Morgan to quit the army in 1779 after a lesser man got a job he believed he'd earned.

The job was commanding a light infantry corps. The lesser man was Anthony Wayne, whose career could have ended when his men were surprised and slaughtered at Paoli in 1777, but didn't. Morgan's experience was more relevant and his accomplishments far greater, but as a colonel, he had an insurmountable disadvantage: His rival was a brigadier general. Still, feeling dishonored, he resigned and rode home to Virginia.

A year and a half later, all that had changed.

January 15, 1781, found him camped twelve miles east of where his statue would someday rise. Horatio Gates had called him out of retirement, though Morgan hadn't gotten to South Carolina in time for Camden; Congress had made him a general, though a bit grudgingly; and now Gates's successor had entrusted him with the cream of his army—exactly the kind of light troops he had wanted to lead.

So why was he so pessimistic when he sat down to write Greene that day?

Well, Banastre Tarleton had something to do with it, but Thomas Sumter had more.

The essence of Greene's orders to Morgan before they set off in different directions—they would end up 140 miles apart—can be summed up as *I trust you, but be careful.* Yes, he was authorized to fight if necessary, "either offensively or defensively, as your own prudence and discretion may direct," but the key was "prudence," and Greene emphasized that Morgan was to use "every possible precaution" to avoid being surprised. Meanwhile, he was to focus on a few things besides conventional battles. Simply by showing the flag, he could influence the political struggle for hearts and minds, and by keeping provisions and forage away from the enemy, he could help win the war for stomachs. And in doing all these things—including fighting if it came to that—he was to rely on support from backcountry militia, notably "the militia lately under the command of Brig. Gen. Sumter."

Sumter's militia, however, refused to help.

As Morgan wrote Greene on January 15, the Gamecock had instructed his subordinates "to obey no orders from me, unless they came through him."

The consequences were grave. With barely enough provisions for his immediate needs, Morgan told Greene, he worried that "no part of this State accessible to us can support us long." And with only a few hundred non-Sumter militiamen to augment his six hundred light infantry and cavalry, he was vulnerable to attack. The rewards of staying where he was weren't worth the risks, he concluded, so he asked Greene to recall him.

But his request came too late. Even as Morgan composed his letter, he knew Tarleton was heading in his direction. Just before he sent it off, a new report caused him to add a sentence. "We have just learned that Tarleton's force is from eleven to twelve hundred British," he wrote, meaning Regular troops, British or provincial. He had half that many Continentals. It would take a *whole* lot more militia to even the odds—and Sumter's selfish obstinacy stood in the way of his getting them.

This was where Andrew Pickens came in.

Of the three most important South Carolina partisan leaders, Pickens is the least known. He lacks a catchy nickname, as I heard Clemson historian Rod Andrew Jr. point out in a talk titled "Not the Swamp Fox," and his only full portrait shows a lean, thin-nosed man staring at us with what looks to be disapproval. Andrew drew laughter with the tale of his own mother reacting to that image on the cover of his Pickens biography ("'Do you think you could have found a nicer picture of him?'" she said, "and I said, 'Mom, that's Pickens *smiling*'") and more laughter when he cited a quip about his subject's legendary taciturnity ("Before he uttered a word, he would take it out of his mouth between his fingers and examine it"). But that was it for the jokes, and pretty soon he was arguing that Morgan's high-stakes victory at Cowpens wouldn't have happened without Mr. Not the Swamp Fox and the militia Pickens ended up commanding there.

He rode into Morgan's camp at the end of December with sixty or seventy followers from the Long Cane settlements in southwestern South Carolina. A devout Scotch-Irish Presbyterian and community pillar, he was also, at forty-one, hardened by battles with both Cherokees and loyalists—the kind of leader who drew men to him. After Charleston fell, with the rebellion looking hopeless, he had accepted parole and "taken an oath to support British government in exchange for protection" for his family and property. Until recently, he'd still felt bound by that oath. When and why he changed his mind remains unclear, though the generally accepted story is that in late November, with Pickens away from home, loyalists "plundered his plantation and mistreated his family."

Whatever happened, Pickens renounced his parole and started filling the leadership gap left by Sumter's wounding.

Before long, his men were the eyes and ears of Morgan's army, serving as "a screen and early warning of the enemy's approach" while foraging for themselves and recruiting among local sympathizers. On January 12, Pickens sent word that Tarleton was moving north fast. Morgan moved north in response, establishing a new camp near what's now Thicketty, South Carolina. It was from there he wrote Greene to say he didn't have enough militia.

The next morning's news was worse.

Tarleton was camped six miles away.

Time to go. Never mind that unfinished breakfast.

The hungry redcoats ate the leftovers when they arrived.

By now, Morgan knew he had to fight. He hoped to cross the Broad River and pick a battleground in some rugged country on the other side, but ran out of time. A torturous slog up a muddy road left his army far from the Broad as daylight faded, with the river running high. A night crossing would be too risky. Better to stop now, feed his men, and prepare to greet Tarleton whenever he showed up.

The good news: They were at the Cowpens, a landmark that would make it easier for Pickens and others to gather militia who hadn't yet come in.

Militia movements during the thirty-six hours after Morgan sent his pessimistic letter are impossible to track fully. But by the morning of January 17, as exhaustive work by historian Lawrence Babits has shown, he had far more men than early histories would report. In addition to

Pickens and numerous South Carolinians, there were militia from North Carolina, Virginia, and Georgia, as well as a number of "state troops" enlisted for longer service. Some had joined the column on the march, but all night, as one Continental officer remembered, more militia kept showing up, "calling on Morgan for ammunition, and to know the state of affairs." Seeing the increase in numbers, Morgan adjusted his battle plan. He spent the rest of the night going from campfire to campfire, joking, exhorting, raising spirits, and making sure the militia understood—very clearly—what his plan asked them to do and what it did not.

It's unlikely that he slept. Pickens probably didn't, either.

Both were awake before dawn in any case, riding the camp to trumpet the news a scout had just delivered. "Boys, get up, Benny's coming!" Morgan shouted, or so a militia officer reported years later. When Benny himself arrived a little before 7 a.m. with his exhausted, hungry, but always dangerous veterans, Morgan, Pickens, and their rested, well-fed men were waiting, with Pickens commanding—as Steve Rauch told the officers on his Cowpens staff ride—"a thousand militia in a line."

\* \* \*

"Here's the thing about Pickens: He's a regional leader," Rauch had said that day. "*Morgan* can't call out the militia. They don't know him; he's from Virginia." But if Pickens tells you to show up at Cowpens and you don't, you've got to live with him and the rest of your community afterward. "So are there places in the world today where you've got to work with local leaders to get things done?" They have various titles, but all of them are "the guy you've got to go to because nobody else is going to do anything until they get the word from *that* guy. Right?"

Right. But getting militia to turn out was one thing, and figuring out the best way to use them was another. It was Morgan who did that part.

"The profession of arms does not often attract innovative minds," Buchanan writes. "On rare occasions, however, the uncommon man appears who solves a serious problem with a method untried yet on the face of it so simple that afterward others wonder why it took so long to discover." And what was Morgan's simple-seeming thought? Well, militia had proved again and again that they would run if you asked them to withstand a bayonet charge. So why do it? Go ahead and put them in your front line, where they can do damage as the enemy advances—but don't ask them to stay there. Put the regulars behind them, not off to one side, and tell the militiamen you just need them to get off two or three good shots, then retreat in an orderly fashion. Or in the colorful words attributed to Morgan as he went campfire to campfire the night before the battle: "'Just hold up your heads, boys,' he would say, 'three fires, and you are free! And then, when you return to your homes, how the old folks will bless you, and the girls kiss you, for your gallant conduct.'"

Which is what happened, as we've seen—though not quite according to script.

Walking the battlefield after the staff ride, and many times later in my head, I tried to wrap my brain around the notion that Morgan, the war's most charismatic leader and original tactician, might have done so much great work at Cowpens and still lost.

Yes, the militia did what he asked, except that most didn't have time to get off two shots, let alone three. Yes, they retreated without running, but no one knew if they would come back. Yes, the Continentals held the line, until a misunderstood order made them retreat. And yes, John Eager Howard, their commander, coolly helped rescue the situation, but that might not have been possible if British discipline hadn't broken down.

With victory in the balance, then, here came the Seventy-First Highland Regiment, ordered forward by Tarleton at the crucial moment, charging the Continentals' right flank. The Highlanders were starving, sleep-deprived, and eager to get this Morgan thing over with. And as Jim Piecuch had startled me by pointing out, if the two companies on Howard's flank had *understood his order properly and turned to face their attackers instead of retreating*, they'd likely have been overwhelmed, after which the rest of the line would have been rolled up, the militia would have fled, and Cowpens would have been a catastrophe. When I got a chance to ask Rauch about this scenario, he agreed.

"The Seventy-First were no-shit guys. I don't care how tired they were," he said.

Instead, thinking they had won, they broke ranks and rushed like a mob toward their enemies. Steadied by Morgan and Howard, the Continentals turned around, shocked the Highlanders with a close-range volley, and followed up with a bayonet charge. Now here came Morgan's cavalry under William Washington—George's distant cousin, and a Cowpens hero I haven't given his due—and here, too, came Pickens's revitalized militia, and now both British flanks were under attack. The fighting wasn't quite over, but the casualty figures, inexact as they are, show how one-sided it became in the end. Morgan reported his losses as "12 killed and 60 wounded," though as Babits notes, he didn't include the militia, so his real killed-and-wounded total may have been closer to 150. Tarleton lost more than 800 men, with close to 600 of them becoming prisoners.

The battle probably lasted less than an hour. Tarleton fought bravely, then galloped to safety at the last minute. This meant he got to tell Cornwallis the terrible news in person.

But Morgan didn't wait to see how His Lordship would react. He knew.

By midday, he had most of his army on the road, getting a jump on the inevitable pursuit.

# CHAPTER 19

# "Across the River, Just in Time"

Now it was North Carolina's turn to be the white-hot center of the war. First up was the epic 250-mile chase scene known as "The Race to the Dan"—a soggy, frozen, high-stress retreat that could have ended in disaster many times but instead frustrated Lord Cornwallis, screwed up Britain's Southern Strategy, and kept Americans' hopes alive near the climax of their marathon struggle for independence. And hey, that was only the opening act of a fourteen-week spectacle that featured Greene commanding a battle more important than any Washington had fought in years and Cornwallis making a hugely consequential decision in April without consulting his boss.

But speaking of Cornwallis's decisions, let's begin our tour of those fourteen weeks with the *first* startling one he made.

Lincolnton, North Carolina, is a modest-sized county seat forty-five miles northeast of the Cowpens battlefield. Its most visible claim to revolutionary fame is as the site of the 1780 Battle of Ramsour's Mill, a bloody, neighbor-against-neighbor clash between militias. Knowing that Cornwallis had set up camp on the same ground, I drove to Battle-ground Elementary School ("Site of the Past; Home of the Future"), contemplated a haunting rectangle of grass beneath which many Ramsour's Mill dead are buried, and started looking for traces of what the British did in January 1781.

If those traces were visible, I missed them. But here's the story I wanted them to tell.

Cornwallis got off to a slower start than he wanted after Cowpens—bad intelligence sent him in the wrong direction at first—and it took him a week to reach Ramsour's Mill. By then, Morgan had crossed the Catawba, which was now in impassable flood. Lord C mulled his options. Then he ordered his army to burn its baggage.

Audacious? Insane? Both?

It was too early to tell, though it's safe to say such a move would never have occurred to Howe or Clinton. But Cornwallis with his blood up was more aggressive than those two combined. And if he wanted to bring his enemy to battle—as he was desperate to do—he had to move faster than an army with baggage could. Into an enormous bonfire, then, went "tents, excess clothing, anything deemed not vital to the army's functioning." The rank and file would carry what they needed on their backs; officers put a few things on packhorses. The only wagons not burned were reserved for ammunition, salt, medical supplies, or the sick and wounded.

Greene's half of the army received the Cowpens news near Cheraw, South Carolina, more than one hundred miles southeast of Lincolnton. Joyful drinking and a feu de joie ensued, but soon Greene was making his dangerous way to Morgan's Catawba camp with just a tiny escort. By January 31, with the British still waiting to cross the flooded river, he was sitting on a log on the opposite bank, making plans with Morgan, William Washington, and William Lee Davidson, a key North Carolina militia general. Afterward, Davidson said Greene knew more about the Catawba "than those who were raised on it." Yet that knowledge couldn't save the man for whom Davidson College and Davidson County are named. Tasked with defending multiple fords on February 1, he had only eight hundred men to work with, and at Cowan's Ford, now obliterated by Lake Norman, Cornwallis's troops shot him dead.

My next stop was Salisbury, an important backcountry town where the race got even scarier. A famous story about Greene's desperate straits took root there, and it goes like this: With the British across the Catawba, he made his way to Salisbury alone and entered a tavern run by a widow named Elizabeth Maxwell Steele. Someone asked how he was. "Fatigued—hungry—alone, and penniless" came the reply, which Steele overheard. Soon she was discreetly handing him two bags of hard currency.

"Take these," she said, "for you will want them, and I can do without them."

At Salisbury's Rowan Museum, alas, I found no support for this uplifting tale. "That's a legend," said the man who greeted me. "It was written down in the 1840s, like all the great legends," though "Steele really *was* a patriot."

Yet there's no question Greene had reasons to be distressed that day.

His baggage-free enemies were coming fast. His half of the army, which he had ordered to join Morgan's at Salisbury, hadn't showed. Morgan himself was ill and could barely ride. With Davidson dead, North Carolina's militia had scattered. And Greene, who really did know a lot about Carolina rivers, was frantic to get across the next one before it, too, became impassable and the British pinned Morgan's vital force against its south bank.

Approaching that river, the Yadkin, I found myself in what looked like a war zone—but not because of what happened in 1781.

Just south of the bridge on Route 29, a pair of rusty water tanks marked "North Carolina Finishing Company" loomed above acres of brick-strewn rubble. A *Salisbury Post* article filled me in. "For someone who wants to know what the world might look like years after human civilization has ended, this place seems fitting," reporter David Purtell wrote, then launched into a too-familiar-sounding narrative. A textile plant dies...Hundreds lose their jobs...An investment banker buys the property...The banker announces "grand plans"...The mill buildings are torn down without permits...A lawsuit by a defrauded investor, among other things, puts an end to this fantasy.

The ruin is a mile and a half upriver from the ford where Greene and Morgan had to cross. Looking east from the bridge, I saw white smoke rising from a power plant. To see the crossing place, I'd either have to get permission or trespass on Duke Energy land, which I wasn't brave enough to try.

The two generals didn't need anyone's permission. All they had to do was get to Trading Ford in time to deal with a rain-swollen river that was almost—but not quite—too high to cross even in boats. Once again, Cornwallis's intelligence was bad. The idea that his enemies might already have boats at the Yadkin was news to him. When his vanguard got there, it found the Americans safely on the other side.

Fifty miles or so north, in what's now Greensboro, the two halves of Greene's army reunited at last. But its leaders—meaning Greene, really, but with support from his officers—decided it was still too weak to fight. That meant it would need to get across yet another river, the Dan, which winds along the North Carolina–Virginia border. And this time, they'd have to do it without Morgan. Weeks earlier, he'd warned Greene that his body was betraying him. A combination of rheumatism, "ciatick pain in my hip," and hemorrhoids (no joke for a man on horseback) would keep him from finishing the race his spectacular victory had set in motion.

So Daniel Morgan set out for home in a carriage on February 10, just as Nathanael Greene divided his army once more.

\* \* \*

The river greeted me with snow flurries, freezing temperatures, ankle-deep mud, and a current so strong it couldn't be crossed in boats, or at least in boats with reenactors in them. I had timed my visit to coincide with the annual Crossing of the Dan commemoration, which usually draws a crowd to the slice of riverbank on which I stood, but most of the year's event had been moved indoors—a decision whose wisdom became clear when I tried to tiptoe over to read the text on a small obelisk near the shore.

Still, twenty minutes spent scraping mud off walking shoes seemed a small price to pay for even a hint of what Greene's men endured on their last, sleepless, foul-weather sprint toward Virginia.

Cornwallis finally made it across the Yadkin, some twenty-five miles above Trading Ford. This put him in good position to cut off his enemies before they reached the shallow upriver fords that were the easiest way to cross the Dan. But Greene, knowing the British would expect him to use them, instead chose a couple of more difficult downriver options, Boyd's Ferry and Irwin's Ferry, in what's now the town of South Boston, Virginia. For his plan to work, he needed Cornwallis to stay fooled, so he sent seven hundred men—Morgan's old command, plus some needed reinforcements—to play decoy.

Nearly six years after someone fired that first shot at Lexington, it seemed, the fate of the Revolution might come down to a single question:

Would Greene and his guys make it across?

A few hundred yards' walk uphill took me to South Boston's cultural center, the Prizery, which at the time featured a beautifully done exhibit that helped visitors grasp both context and details of that question. My eyes were soon drawn to a blown-up map with three colored lines superimposed on it. Two blue lines showed Greene's army separating as it headed northeast; the lower line was the main army and the one above it represented the decoy force, commanded by Col. Otho Holland Williams. A red line farther north showed the British being decoyed—until suddenly all three lines converged on the downriver ferries.

It's hard to imagine anyone, even Morgan, doing a better job in these circumstances than Otho Williams. He had joined a Maryland rifle company in 1775, been taken prisoner at Fort Washington the following year, and served with distinction since being exchanged. Now he led his seven hundred men on what the exhibit called a "March of Misery." It consisted of nineteen-hour-a-day trudges on dirt tracks "thick with mud by day, sharp with frost by night," keeping just ahead of the likes of Banastre Tarleton, then tearing off toward the lower crossing places as the British finally realized what was up. Frayed nerves were inevitable. On the morning of February 13, Greene wrote his subordinate an unhelpful note. "You have the flower of the army," he admonished Williams, so "don't expose the men too much, lest our situation should grow more critical."

The tone of Williams's reply has been characterized as "dejected and demoralized," but I suspect he was really thinking: *Oh please—tell me something I don't know.*

Fortunately, by the end of the next day, everybody's moods had improved.

"Across the River, Just in Time" read the exhibit type below an image of four men sharing a late-night moment on February 14. Greene and Williams wait on the Dan's north shore at Boyd's Ferry as two other officers on a flatboat move toward them. One is Light Horse Harry Lee, who had taken on the scary task of bringing up Williams's rear and done it superbly. The other is Edward Carrington, Greene's quartermaster general. It had been Carrington's idea to use the downriver ferries instead of the upriver fords, and he'd also rounded up the necessary boats.

Virginia hospitality was just what Greene's exhausted men needed. But a little over a week after the army's just-in-time escape—rested, fed, and somewhat stronger, though more reinforcements were expected—Greene was ready to lead it back across the Dan. "It was necessary to convince the Carolinians that they were not conquered," as he put it, and to keep loyalists from reinforcing Cornwallis.

To that end, he'd already sent Lee back to North Carolina.

Learning what Light Horse Harry did there would force me to consider—once again—how thin the line between combat and murder can be.

\* \* \*

Pyle's Defeat, Pyle's Massacre, or Pyle's Hacking Match, as the macabre event in question is variously known, took place in or near what is now Burlington, North Carolina, some sixty miles southwest of Boyd's Ferry. I found myself thinking about it on a quiet stretch of Old Trail Road that runs between a small manufacturer called Splawn Belting and the Rock Hill Mobile Home Park. The road might or might not be overlaid on the eighteenth-century track where the action took place; the specific location has been disputed, but the dispute doesn't change what's important about the story.

On the afternoon of February 24, 1781, several hundred mounted loyalists led by Dr. John Pyle crossed Great Alamance Creek, less than a mile from where I stood, and began riding up the road. They were headed for Lord Cornwallis's camp in Hillsborough, twenty miles east, where the British, also exhausted, had gone to recuperate. Pyle's

approach was good news for Cornwallis, who, like Greene, needed reinforcements. He sent Tarleton and 450 men to escort the loyalists into
camp.

Lee and his troops, by now, had joined forces with Andrew Pickens
and seven hundred militiamen. Outnumbering Tarleton, Lee and Pickens set out to find him, failed, but found Pyle instead—which is when
the color of everyone's clothes became decisive.

Both Lee's and Tarleton's troops, for reasons having to do with their
units' elite status, wore green uniform coats. When two of Pyle's scouts
ran into green-clad horsemen, the scouts assumed they had found Tarleton. Light Horse Harry did not disabuse them of this notion. Instruct-
ing Pickens to get his men (who were *not* dressed in green coats) out
of sight, he sent word to Pyle to move his force to the side of the road
because "Tarleton's" tired troops were in a hurry to reach "their night
position." Leading his cavalry past the compliant loyalists, who called
out greetings, Lee reached the end of the column, where Pyle himself
was stationed.

Then the killing began.

There are many versions of exactly how it started, none definitive.
Lee always denied planning an attack. He wrote Greene that he'd had
his men pretend to be Tarleton's so they could get by the loyalists fast
and keep chasing the *actual* Tarleton. Changing his story in his memoirs, he wrote that he'd been about to tell Pyle his real identity—and
would have offered the loyalists a choice of switching sides or "returning
to their homes"—when an outbreak of fighting behind him took the
matter out of his hands.

Whatever happened, in ten minutes at least ninety loyalists were
dead, with the majority of the survivors wounded. None of the men
with Lee died, though one did lose a horse.

Pickens viewed the slaughter with cold-blooded pragmatism. "It has
knocked up Toryism altogether in this part," he wrote. Greene showed
more humanity, but not much. He mentioned a "dreadful carnage"
among the loyalists before reaching his bottom line.

"It has had a very happy effect on those disaffected Persons," he
wrote, "of which there are too many in this Country."

* * *

Greene worked out a careful plan for the first battle at which he was ever in full command. Still, despite his well-earned reputation for anticipating nearly everything, he ended up with less time to get ready than he could have wished.

Since recrossing the Dan, he'd been playing mouse to Cornwallis's cat, applying yet another lesson learned up north—*Don't be like Lafayette at Barren Hill*—by keeping constantly on the move. The idea was to avoid battle until he had enough militiamen to improve his odds, but their tendency to come and go as they pleased infuriated him. Eventually, however, enough showed up that he decided he could fight.

On March 14, the army was at Guilford, home to a wooden courthouse that served as the hub of a tiny farming community. Greene had been here on his way north and thought the ground well suited for a defensive stand. But now, with well over four thousand men under his command, he wanted to attack.

Cornwallis beat him to it.

His Lordship was twelve miles away down the New Garden Road. He had fewer than half as many men, just under two thousand, but every one was a British or Hessian veteran. Learning Greene's position, he marched them off without breakfast, hoping to catch his quarry unprepared. Light Horse Harry prevented that. Sent by Greene to guard the approach to the camp, Lee learned in the early hours of the fifteenth that the British were about to move and sent his boss a heads-up. He then skirmished with advance elements of Cornwallis's army, led by Tarleton, for more than two hours while Greene organized his defenses.

Would they hold? Three metal silhouettes outside the Guilford Courthouse National Military Park visitor center didn't bode well. One was a Brit with a bayonet. The others were militiamen, running away. I headed off on a self-guided tour to learn more.

Greene had borrowed a good deal from Morgan's innovations. His version of a defense in depth included two militia lines, not one—because he had more men and his battlefield was bigger—as well as other changes. But the main idea was to replicate the Cowpens triumph, and who could argue with that? Now more than a thousand North Carolina militiamen, whom Greene had put in his first line, stood behind split-rail fences watching the enemy advance. They were about to go down in history as cowards, though the judgment continues to be debated.

As it happened, I had recently been introduced to that debate. At the Race to the Dan commemoration, I'd heard a Virginia participant chaff two North Carolina reenactors about their state's Guilford Courthouse performance. "You know, North Carolina license plates say 'First in Flight,'" he said, "and that's not about the Wright brothers." Silence. After the guy left, a reenactor made sure to point out that the most thoroughly researched recent book on the battle—*Long, Obstinate, and Bloody* by Lawrence Babits and Joshua Howard—tells a more nuanced story.

"The North Carolina militiamen were justifiably nervous," Babits and Howard write, as bayonet-wielding veterans came at them. But the attackers had jitters as well: A British sergeant recalled the daunting sight of a long row of muskets and rifles "resting on a rail fence" as the defenders took aim, and reported that it led to "a general pause."

Urged on by their officers, the attackers kept coming.

As for the defenders: They hadn't been told to stay and face those bayonets forever. Greene, like Morgan before him, had said they need only "fire two volleys and then retire." The idea that everyone would get off two shots was wishful thinking, but a Virginian who climbed a tree to watch the fight start saw *some* North Carolinians fire twice, and other witnesses confirmed that the Carolinians' initial volley did serious damage. What came next was predictable, given that most had no experience with this kind of battle. The bayonets got too close; many men ran, especially in the center; and Cornwallis's troops charged through the gaping hole.

Next up: the second line, some four hundred yards away.

The second-line defenders were Virginians, and there is no doubt most fought courageously. Yet their courage was just part of why a very different story unfolded here. The other part was trees. "Firing from behind thick trunks of the ancient forest," a marker text informed me, "Virginia militia exchanged heavy fire with advancing British infantry," which found it impossible to stay in formation. The assault morphed into multiple engagements, "with clusters of troops trading shots with other small units." On the northern half of the second line, some Virginians did run, though unlike most of the Carolinians, they didn't flee the field entirely. On the southern half, they gave as good as they got for a while, though they were eventually forced to retreat.

Now it was the Continentals' turn.

Greene had placed his third line five hundred to six hundred yards behind the second, curving along relatively high ground above a creek. Emerging from the woods, Cornwallis's men—thinned, tired, starving, and with their own line so broken up that they would arrive at different times and fight as separate units—would need to cross the creek and climb out of the valley to attack. Facing them would be some of the best troops in the Continental Army, but also some barely trained recruits.

The first British regiment out of the woods attacked without bothering to find out where the rest of their army was. A storm of rebel fire drove it back. Next up was a battalion of the elite Brigade of Guards. The Guards, too, advanced without support, but at first fared better. That was because their opponents were the newly recruited Continentals of the Second Maryland Regiment, scarcely superior to militia and just as quick to flee. Charging after them, the Guards found themselves behind the American line. This might have been a good thing, except now they had to deal with a far better Continental regiment—the *First* Maryland, confusingly enough—which turned to face them. The Marylanders' commander went down. Cowpens hero John Eager Howard took over. Now here came another Cowpens hero, William Washington, with his cavalry, and the Guards didn't know what hit them.

We've seen this horror show before. Washington's men "rode directly into the Guards' formation, hacking the terrified foot soldiers," as another historian of the battle writes. "The wild horsemen attacked through the disorderly Guards formation at least once more, perhaps twice," after which fierce hand-to-hand infantry fighting continued between Howard's Marylanders and the Guards, who were "pushed back toward the woods from which they had recently arrived."

By this time, Cornwallis had arrived in those woods as well. He had thought he was winning the battle, and knew he couldn't afford to lose it. What would he do?

The shocking answer I'd had in my head since I first read about Guilford Courthouse, and had seen repeated often, was that he ordered his field artillery to fire canister or grapeshot into the struggling mass of men, mowing down the rebels and his own Guards alike. His Lordship "did what he had to do," as Buchanan puts it. "What he did was terrible but what choice had he?"

And yet...

Babits and Howard make a strong case that "the incident as it has come to be described" never occurred. No one in position to be a witness, they point out, ever wrote about it. Lee's memoirs are its source, but Light Horse Harry was "more than a quarter mile away" at the time. They suspect the tale began as "either a rumor that Lee had heard or something that he developed in the interest of a good story."

Whatever happened, however, Greene had already done what *he* had to do.

We don't know exactly when, but sometime earlier in the third line fight, he made the decision that earned him a heroic equestrian statue on the battlefield. And there he sat, when I got to the last numbered stop on the park's tour, with all those battle names spelled out beneath him and Athena seeming to lead him toward a winner's rightful laurels. Yet it was just as easy to imagine the goddess of wisdom leading him *away* from Guilford Courthouse, leaving his enemy to claim the field and the victory, because that was the right thing to do. *Never risk your men to hold a position you don't need* was the lesson Fort Washington had taught, and as Morgan wrote him before the battle, having the core of yet another southern army cut to pieces would mean "losing all our hopes."

Wisely then, Greene had ordered a retreat.

That doesn't mean he was happy about it. He *wanted* those laurels. Not for the last time during the war in the South, he resorted to some frustrated scapegoating.

Victory would have been "certain," he wrote George Washington, if only North Carolina's militiamen had fought. "But they left the most advantageous position I ever saw with out scarcely firing a gun."

* * *

If Greene could have wandered through the British camp on the night of March 15, his concern with lost glory would have vanished, driven out by horror, pity, and the knowledge that his enemies would be in no shape to fight again soon.

"I never did, and I hope never shall again, experience two such days and Nights, as these immediately after the Battle," Gen. Charles O'Hara would write. The troops "remained on the very ground on which it had been fought, cover'd with Dead, with Dying and with Hundreds of Wounded, Rebels, as well as our own—A violent and constant Rain that lasted above Forty Hours made it equally impracticable to remove or administer the smallest comfort to many of the Wounded." The men's last meal had been more than a day before. When numbers could be tallied, they would show that Cornwallis had lost 93 killed and 413 wounded, more than a quarter of his already diminished force. None of this stopped him from proclaiming that he had "totally defeated the rebel army." Then, actions speaking louder than words, he left his most severely wounded to be tended locally; condemned others who couldn't ride (O'Hara among them) to bounce torturously along in wagons; and headed for the coast. The wounded men who *could* ride included Tarleton, shot through the right hand and with two fingers amputated.

Greene's army, meanwhile, was hardly unscathed. Having suffered perhaps three-fifths as many killed and wounded as the British, it was also down a thousand militiamen, who had gone home. Still, Greene had no fear Cornwallis would attack again, and before long, was cautiously pursuing his battered enemies. No battles ensued, though, and by the end of March, he had decided that chasing the Brits all the way to Wilmington—where they had a fortified base and access to the sea—would be pointless.

Why not do the unexpected and head back to South Carolina instead? Never mind if it was risky and unconventional to leave an enemy in your rear.

"I shall take every measure to avoid a misfortune," he wrote

Washington, but "I trust my friends will do justice to my reputation if any accident attends me."

Washington, in turn, had to trust Greene to do the right thing. The southern campaign was too distant to micromanage. Besides, ever since the year began, he had been neck deep in troubles of his own.

\* \* \*

On January 1, two weeks after Greene sent Morgan off toward Cowpens, roughly 1,500 Pennsylvania Continentals decided they'd had enough. Unhappy with broken promises about "food, clothing, quarters, pay, bounties, and terms of enlistment," they shouldered muskets, commandeered some field artillery, and set out to march from Morristown, New Jersey, to Philadelphia. "Officers who tried to intervene," Edward Lengel reports, "were shoved aside and told that the soldiers' quarrel was with the civil authorities and not with them." At Princeton, the mutineers halted and opened negotiations, mainly with Washington's former aide Joseph Reed, now president of Pennsylvania's Executive Council. One part of the resulting deal settled the terms-of-enlistment question: Men who argued that they'd signed up for three years, not the duration of the war, essentially won their case. Another part guaranteed that the mutineers would not be punished. But it took weeks to dot the i's and cross the t's—during which time *another* unit mutinied.

Washington knew he couldn't let this go on.

He had stayed out of the first negotiations, but when some New Jersey Continentals followed the Pennsylvanians' lead, he sent five hundred troops and ordered the general leading them to "instantly execute a few of the most active and most incendiary leaders."

He also knew that the mutinies, dangerous in themselves, were symptoms of a larger crisis that threatened the Revolution. Congress had no power to pay for an army through taxation. The paper money it printed was almost worthless. Support from individual states was erratic at best. The only answer was more help from abroad, and someone needed to cross the Atlantic, in the middle of winter, to push for it.

Which was how John Laurens ended up with what his biographer calls "the most important assignment of his public career."

Out of action since May 1780, when Charleston fell, Laurens was one frustrated young man. As a prisoner on parole, he'd been barred from returning to the fight until he was exchanged. This took until November. Soon afterward, Congress tapped him to go to France. Laurens didn't want the job and wasn't suited for it—no candidate had a less diplomatic temperament—but the delegates couldn't agree on anyone else. His dad might have untangled this knot, except that Henry had already set off to negotiate with the Dutch; gotten captured by a British frigate; and been thrown into the Tower of London.

John's crossing, believe it or not, was almost worse. His ship ran into what a traveling companion, Thomas Paine, called "a tumultuous assemblage of floating rolling Rocks," and this near-*Titanic* experience included an iceberg smashing into a part of the vessel on which Laurens had been standing moments before. By March 9, though, he was safely ashore, ready to press the French to provide—right now!—the extra cash, supplies, and military support his country so desperately needed.

Meanwhile, back in South Carolina, no enslaved men were being promised their freedom to bear arms.

Slavery was still practiced throughout the new nation (Vermont had banned it but not yet closed all loopholes). The South, however, had built an entire economy and social structure around keeping hundreds of thousands in bondage—John Laurens, as you may recall, summed up his peers' self-justification as "Without Slaves how is it possible for us to be rich"—which meant that slavery played a larger role in the war there than it did up north. Months before Clinton left New York for South Carolina, he issued a Dunmore-like proclamation aimed at encouraging the labor force of his southern enemies to flee. In it, he promised that no "Negroe, the property of a rebel" who joined the British would be sold, and that such a fugitive would have "full Security to follow within these Lines, any Occupation which he shall think proper."

This sounds simple, but what happened was not.

From the beginning, writes historian Gary Nash, enslaved people "took advantage of wartime disruption to obtain their freedom in any way they could." Some, even in the South, managed to join rebel armies. Others fled west. But most often, those who sought freedom did so "by joining the British whenever their regiments were close enough to reach." Running was not an easy choice: If fugitives were caught, punishment could be severe or fatal. Still, many thousands of African Americans seized the chance "to stage the first large-scale rebellion of American slaves—a rebellion, in fact, that was never duplicated during the remainder of the slave era."

As for the Brits saying they'd welcome only Blacks owned by rebels, forget it.

Fugitives from both sides flooded in, sparking a predictable backlash in a white population terrified of slave revolts. Yes, the army got a great deal of help from liberated men and women who built fortifications, cooked, drove wagons, did washing, cut firewood, foraged, and so on. Many would have run to the British anyway, proclamation or no proclamation. But to openly invite a disruption of the slave system while counting on white loyalist support was going to be problematic—at least if you weren't planning to give large numbers of Black men muskets and turn them loose to fight.

Which in the end, neither side was willing to do.

Washington argued privately that arming slaves would be counterproductive because it would lead to an arming-slaves race his side could not win. Worse, freeing some men to fight could produce "discontent" in those who remained enslaved. What he meant, as Lengel makes clear, was that "arming blacks on a large scale would spur an exodus from the plantations that might destroy the institution of slavery altogether."

Individual Black men, nonetheless, kept fighting in rebel armies as the war moved south. To dig up even fragments of their stories takes extraordinary effort. But some historians have made that effort, and from them, I learned many names I hadn't seen on battlefield markers. Here are a few:

Drury Harris was shot and bayoneted during the failed Franco-American attack on Savannah; supporting his pension application, a comrade wrote: "I saw no man, officer nor private, more Activer nor braver" on that day. Thomas Lively, who had already lost an eye at Monmouth, suffered a leg wound at Charleston and survived fourteen harsh months as a prisoner of war. Andrew Pebbles—whose story eventually intersected with John Laurens's—endured Valley Forge, fought at Guilford Courthouse, and would later be wounded three times at the last major battle in the South.

As for those on the other side: Harry Washington ran from Mount Vernon in 1776; three years later, as a free man, he took his famous surname south with a corps of Black laborers who supported Clinton's artillery. Peter Anderson fought at Great Bridge in Dunmore's Black regiment; captured and condemned to hang, he escaped, hid in the woods, and made his way aboard a British warship; according to historian Cassandra Pybus—my source for the stories in this paragraph—he likely was at the siege of Charleston as well. Scipio Handley, a free South Carolina fishmonger who was "caught carrying messages for the embattled royal governor" in 1775, also escaped prison and a death sentence. Helping defend Savannah in 1779, he made grapeshot, carried it out to the redoubts, and took a musket ball in one leg, which he almost lost to gangrene.

And then there was Thomas Peters, who, in the spring of 1776, found himself in Wilmington, North Carolina, with a life-changing choice to make.

Details are scarce, as Nash points out, "because nobody recorded the turning points in the life of slaves." Born in what's now Nigeria, Peters, whose African name is lost, was kidnapped at twenty-two and shipped to French Louisiana. Ten years into captivity, he was sold to "a leading member of Wilmington's Sons of Liberty" for whom he worked as a millwright. By then he had tried to escape three times, with the usual consequences. But when Henry Clinton's fleet showed up at the mouth of the Cape Fear River, en route to humiliation at Charleston's palmetto fort, he chose to try again. The British took him along when they returned to New York, and his post-Wilmington life included five years with a company of Black support troops, two wounds, and a promotion to sergeant.

We already know what Cornwallis had been up to during those same five years.

Now he, too—like Thomas Peters—found himself in Wilmington, faced with a choice upon which a great deal would depend.

\* \* \*

A lovely old Georgian mansion at 224 Market Street seemed a good place to consider that fateful choice. Could I check out the very room, I wondered, where Cornwallis wrote a notoriously frustrated letter to an old friend? Or walk the same floors he walked while wrestling with the question of what to do next? Alas, I had timed my visit wrong, arriving in Wilmington on a Sunday when the Burgwin-Wright House was closed. I did get to see an old marker that said he'd occupied the building, but otherwise all I could do was wander the rest of the historic district, where I learned that Whistler's mother was born here, as was a Confederate general who went on to serve in the Egyptian Army, and that a souvenir shop blocks from the Cornwallis marker sold signs that read, "Support Our Troops / We'll Need Them to Overthrow Our Government."

Nonetheless, I was very glad to have seen Wilmington—which hadn't been on my radar screen before I'd asked Jim Piecuch a question about turning points.

Suppose he could pick just two, I inquired, one for the war as a whole and the other for the South: What would they be? "For the whole Revolution, I have to go with the traditional one," he said, ticking off reasons Saratoga fit the bill. No surprise there. For the South, though, I was expecting Kings Mountain, Cowpens, the Race to the Dan, or Guilford Courthouse. Good cases can be made for each, but Piecuch didn't mention them.

"It's Cornwallis's decision to go to Virginia from Wilmington rather than back to South Carolina," he said.

After he finished explaining, I revised my travel plans. Still, it wasn't until I'd had more time to digest what he told me—as well as to study a private letter Cornwallis wrote to Maj. Gen. William Phillips from Wilmington and to learn what Greene and Washington were doing and thinking at the same time—that I fully grasped the case for April 1781 as a capital-letter Turning Point of the Revolutionary War.

By then, as we know, Greene had decided it would be dumb to attack Cornwallis on the coast. "Don't be surprisd if my movements don't correspond with your Ideas of military propriety," he wrote a militia colonel, and sure enough, by April 6 he was leading his men south again.

Three days later, on April 9, Washington sent an exceptionally gloomy letter to John Laurens. "I give it decisively as my opinion," he told his protégé, that without the help Laurens had braved the Atlantic to seek, "our present force (which is but the remnant of an Army) cannot be kept together this Campaign," let alone be made ready for another. In short, "we are at the end of our tether" and "now or never deliverance must come."

And the day after *that*, April 10, Cornwallis—at the end of his own tether, apparently—wrote a letter that's made some historians rub their eyes in disbelief.

"Here I am, getting rid of my wounded and refitting my troops at Wilmington," he told Phillips. "Now my dear friend, what is our plan? Without one, we cannot succeed, and I assure you that I am quite tired of marching about the country in quest of adventure. If we mean an offensive war in America, we must abandon New York, and bring our whole force into Virginia. We then have a stake to fight for, and a successful battle may give us America."

On April 10 as well, he floated his Screw-New-York-It's-Virginia-or-Bust strategy to his boss.

This letter—yes, it was a bit more politely worded than my summary—took ten days to reach Manhattan. But His Lordship had no intention of waiting for Clinton to reply. He marched north on April 25, leaving a talented but undermanned subordinate in South Carolina to try to cope with Greene. And in one of those irresistible coincidences eagerly seized upon by writers like me, when Lt. Gen. Cornwallis arrived in the Old Dominion, he would be greeted by perhaps the only general officer in the British Army more aggressive and offensive-minded than he was.

That would be Brig. Gen. Benedict Arnold, his coat now red instead of blue.

# CHAPTER 20

# The Midnight Ride of Jack Jouett

I don't often compare myself with Lord Cornwallis, yet we do have at least two things in common. We both planned to end our Revolutionary War adventures in Virginia, and neither of us knew much about what it would take to achieve that goal. Heck, when I started out, I didn't know Benedict Arnold had even set foot in the state, let alone how his successes and failures had foreshadowed those of Lord C.

Luckily, a trained professional was available to give me a crash course.

Mark Lender was one of two historians who signed on to guide an Arnold Raids Richmond tour for some of Virginia's most committed Revolution obsessives. I'd met Lender only briefly, but his work on Monmouth, as readers may recall, was a revelation, and as our bus headed southeast from the capital, he gave us the necessary background.

For some time, he said, Henry Clinton had wanted to establish a base in Virginia that the Royal Navy could use for regional operations. From it, as well, the army could disrupt the state's economy, limiting its support for rebels elsewhere. Sir Henry had tried once, sending a general to fortify Portsmouth, but the shocking news from Kings Mountain had disrupted that attempt. Now, late in 1780, he sent the World's Most Famous Traitorous Scumbag—my words, not Lender's—sailing down from New York to try again. Arnold's orders "were first to secure Portsmouth," but they also allowed him to attack rebel supply depots if he could "do so without undue risk."

Arnold thought he could. He also thought fortifying Portsmouth could wait. Up the James he went, landing at Westover Plantation before Virginia's governor, the distinctly unmilitary Thomas Jefferson, could wrap his mind around the threat.

Westover remains in private hands, so we didn't go inside. Instead, we gathered in front of one of the earliest, finest examples of Georgian architecture in America and wished we could look in some of its too-high windows as Lender pointed toward "the dining room in which Arnold and his officers had breakfast."

Breakfast? Really?

Who offers breakfast to a traitor who just landed a thousand troops on your lawn?

Mary Willing Byrd, that's who. The widowed mistress of Westover, a Philadelphia native, happened to be a cousin of Peggy Shippen, aka Mrs. Benedict Arnold. Did Mrs. B have advance word that Cousin Benedict would drop by? We don't know, but we can guess. After the raid, "she had to do a little backpedaling with the patriot authorities," but being in "the highest strata of Virginia social and political society," she got off easy.

As for the Virginia militiamen in the area, they might as well have offered Arnold a nice meal themselves. It would have slowed him down more than what they actually did.

He departed Westover on January 4, the same day he arrived. The next morning found him near the base of what's now called Libby Hill, in modern Richmond's East End, wondering how many defenders were on top. "If there was going to be a defense of Richmond," Lender said when we reached the high ground ourselves, "this would have been the place," but the militia lacked leadership, numbers, and time to dig in.

Understandably, if not heroically, they fled before a shot was fired.

Following the raid's path through Richmond, we got to see a "very historic empty lot" where Arnold made his headquarters (he stayed in town just one day) and "the location of many tobacco warehouses

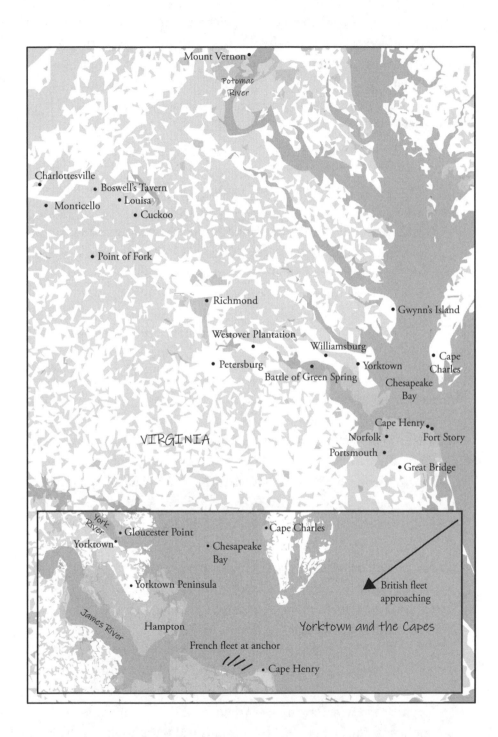

Yorktown and the Capes

Arnold's people burned" (because tobacco profits supported the fighting farther south). A few miles west, we peered across the James to where the raiders destroyed a munitions manufacturing facility. As a bonus, they got to burn most of the capital's public papers, which the governor had sent there for safekeeping. "Poor Jefferson," Lender said, laughing. "He just couldn't catch a break in this whole thing."

Two days later, Benedict Arnold was enjoying Mary Byrd's hospitality again.

Two weeks after that, he was in Portsmouth, getting ready to fortify the town.

Before long, however, Richmond would be threatened again. Defending it this time would be the Marquis de Lafayette, who'd been ordered south by Washington with some blunt instructions for dealing with Arnold. Lender paraphrased them for us:

"If you catch him, you hang him from the nearest tree."

* * *

The boy general was twenty-three now. In theory, he was a veteran, but in practice, not so much. His last major campaign season, in 1778, had offered teachable moments at Barren Hill and Monmouth, but who knew how much he'd really learned? Nobody made the Great French Hope stay after school and write "I will listen to my boss's advice" on the blackboard five hundred times. And after that season's fiasco of a finale in Rhode Island, where he didn't even get to fight, he was so eager for action that he tossed around half-baked ideas like an adolescent with ADD.

*Couldn't I have another whack at invading Canada?*

Not a good idea right now, Washington said.

*Or spend the winter fighting Brits in the Caribbean?*

Don't even think about it, Washington said.

*How about if I go back to France and make my peace with the king?*

Now you're talking, Washington said, and sent him to ask Congress for a leave.

Granted. He sailed for home in January 1779 bearing a letter to "our great, faithful, and beloved friend and ally, Louis the Sixteenth" in which Congress praised the "zeal," "courage," and "prudent conduct" of the marquis. Translation: Forgive the boy for dissing you; don't be mad about that Rhode Island kerfuffle; and please send more help.

Lafayette promised to lobby for that help, and did. But during his yearlong stay in France, there were a few distractions.

He'd barely landed when celebrity washed over him. "I had left as a rebel and fugitive," he would write, "and returned in triumph as an idol." The king rapped his knuckles and forgave him. His wife got pregnant with a son they named George Washington Lafayette. The marquis made friends with Benjamin Franklin, and along with their meat-and-potatoes political consultations, the two collaborated on some unusual extracurricular projects. Take the illustrated book for American schoolchildren Franklin recruited Lafayette to help with, in which he planned to publish thirty-five images of what one Lafayette biographer describes as "horrors inflicted by the British upon the Americans during the Revolutionary War." (They only got up to twenty-six.) Or take the daring raids on the English coast in which the marquis was to team up with Franklin's friend John Paul Jones. The raids were to be self-funding, with cash extorted from towns like Liverpool by threatening to burn them, but this plan, too, never came to fruition. It was canceled in favor of a Franco-Spanish invasion of England that also fell through. (Have I mentioned that Spain officially entered the war in June 1779 on the side of the French? Or how crucial this alliance would prove, despite the failed invasion plan, because it gave the combined French and Spanish fleets naval superiority, at least numerically?)

More distractions ensued. But in early 1780, it was time to get serious about sending troops across the Atlantic—and by the way, the marquis explained, his friends the Americans would be *very* upset if he were not put in charge.

The French minister of war had his own ideas about that. He chose the Comte de Rochambeau, decades older and far more experienced, sending the marquis ahead to deliver the news. In May, Lafayette told Washington what he knew, which didn't yet include where his countrymen would land. Before long, though, word came that they were headed for Newport.

Unfortunately, thanks to Arnold, that word soon reached the British as well.

What might have happened if Clinton had been able to act on this intelligence when he got back to New York from Charleston, three weeks before Rochambeau showed up with many of his roughly six thousand men incapacitated by scurvy? Anyone who thinks "nothing good" will get no argument from me. As for why Sir Henry couldn't make an attack happen, a dysfunctional relationship between the navy and the army didn't help.

Lafayette was at Washington's side that autumn when the thunderbolt of Arnold's treason struck. He sat in judgment on John André and watched him hang. A few months later, he was off to Virginia at the head of 1,200 Continentals.

The plan was to trap the traitor in Portsmouth. It relied heavily on the medium-sized fleet that had come to Rhode Island with Rochambeau. Two previous attempts at cooperation with the French Navy had ended in disaster, but might the third time be the charm? Down sailed Adm. Charles Destouches, intending to cut off Arnold's escape by sea and drop off a thousand French infantrymen to do the same by land, aided by some Virginia militia and Lafayette's Continentals if they arrived in time. Now down sailed Adm. Marriot Arbuthnot, with a similar-sized British fleet, hoping to intercept the French. Arbuthnot's ships were faster—they all had copper bottoms; some French ships did not—and when the fleets ran into each other near the entrance to the Chesapeake Bay, Destouches figured his mission to get Arnold was over. How could he land his troops with the British Navy hanging around?

He had no option but to fight, though—and much to the surprise of knowledgeable students of naval warfare, then and now, he won.

But did he follow up the next day, perhaps destroying Arbuthnot's fleet completely? Nope. He sailed right back to Newport, content, as one apologist put it, to "retreat with honor after punishing the enemy's arrogance and establishing the reputation of French arms in the eyes of the people of America."

You can run what-ifs off this stupid decision six ways to Sunday. But here's what actually happened.

Arnold, who according to the Hessian diarist Ewald, "always carried a pair of small pistols in his pocket as a last resource to escape being hanged," got a reprieve. Clinton, who saw how vulnerable Arnold was, sent more than two thousand additional men under William Phillips his way. With Phillips in overall command, the British went on offense: waltzing into Williamsburg, taking Petersburg, and moving, once again, toward Richmond.

Lafayette, meanwhile, was yo-yoing back and forth between Maryland and Virginia. He had dashed south, ahead of his troops, hoping to be in on the Portsmouth kill; headed north in a funk, intending to retrieve his men and rejoin the main army; and then—whoops!—had to turn right back around. Washington was in a worse funk, but knew he couldn't let Phillips join Cornwallis without sending a few more regulars to oppose him. Which was why, in late April, the marquis found himself and most of his Continentals atop the very same Richmond heights the militia failed to defend in January. Below him, across the James, were more than twice as many men, led by Phillips and Arnold.

His cannon hadn't caught up yet, but his enemies didn't know that.

They chose not to press their attack.

It was a nice start to his first independent campaign. But with Cornwallis pushing north from Wilmington, the odds were about to get worse.

* * *

Phillips was a skilled artillery officer who'd fought well on the Saratoga campaign. By 1781, he seems to have been the only general capable of maintaining friendships with both Sir Henry *and* Lord C, so it's easy to imagine how his rendezvous with the latter—scheduled to take place in May—might have improved communications all around.

It was not to be, however.

Early that month, Phillips had turned his army back toward Petersburg to meet Cornwallis's, but he died from a fever a week before his old friend showed up. The location of his grave was kept secret; an old marker close to the city's Blandford Church tells us merely that his remains "lie buried in this church-yard." If Lord C dropped by to pay his respects, as he might well have done, I've not seen it mentioned.

Then again, he was only in Petersburg four days.

Just as Arnold had been, he was eager to do damage right away. By May 26, he'd led most of his army across the James to Westover. "I shall now proceed to dislodge La Fayette from Richmond," he wrote Clinton from Mary Byrd's place.

Lafayette knew enough to dislodge himself without waiting for assistance.

It was a maneuver the marquis would repeat many times, according to the author of a book that traces his path during this overlooked phase of the 1781 story. "Okay, so this is the number-one-selling book on Lafayette's campaign in Virginia," I once heard John Maass joke as he introduced a lecture. "Also the *only* book on Lafayette's campaign in Virginia." Maass, an army historian, said the subject drew him because so many writers covered it "in two or three sentences, or maybe two paragraphs"—and because Lafayette "really did not get any other major opportunity like this" during the war.

Had his on-the-job training been enough?

Abandoning Richmond was a no-brainer. He couldn't have defended it against Cornwallis, and there wasn't much left to defend anyway; the state government had decided that relocating to Charlottesville, seventy miles to the west, would be the better part of valor. But what should he do now? Go north again, he figured. There was an iron foundry and arms factory near Fredericksburg he wanted to protect (or at least try to). There were reinforcements heading south under Anthony Wayne with whom he was anxious to hook up. Most of all, he needed to stay out of harm's way.

"Lafayette's goal was to keep some kind of geographic feature between him and Cornwallis," Maass said, "which in this part of Virginia was almost always a river. If you plot out where Cornwallis crossed a river, Lafayette got north of the *next* river."

At first, His Lordship moved north in pursuit. (Arnold, superseded, was off to rejoin Clinton in New York.) Early in June, Cornwallis found himself not far from where the Kings Dominion amusement park would open in 1975—and where he, like his quarry before him, had a what-now question to decide. The answer was: Stop chasing the damn boy and head west. He gave troops under John Graves Simcoe and Tarleton separate targets. Simcoe's was a supply depot at the confluence of the James and Rivanna Rivers, known as Point of Fork. Tarleton's was the entire government of Virginia.

This made my own what-now decision an easy one.

My first stop was a place Tarleton doesn't mention in his history of the southern campaigns. Why should he? He had no idea, while passing through the oddly named community of Cuckoo in Louisa County, that he had just alerted the Paul Revere of the South, who would jump on a horse and try to reach Charlottesville first. Here's how Henry Wadsworth Longfellow might have kicked off his story:

> *Listen my children while I review it*
> *The midnight ride of John "Jack" Jouett,*
> *On the third of June, in Eighty-One:*
> *Hardly a human beneath the sun*
> *Recalls how Jefferson almost blew it.*

Sorry, couldn't resist. Still, as a Richmond editor once wrote: "If you mean to be a historical figure, it is a good idea to get in touch with a leading literary figure—a Longfellow, a Homer, a Virgil. Paul Revere, Odysseus, Aeneas—they all took this precaution. Poor Capt. Jack Jouett didn't. And as a result this six-foot-four, two-hundred-pound giant from Virginia, who saved the leaders of the American Revolution from a disheartening and possibly disastrous reverse, has been left out of practically all the history books."

Jouett shows up in more books today, and I've read that if you visit the Jack Jouett House in Kentucky, where he ended up, a guide might inform you that Revere was the Jack Jouett of the North. But let's get back to Cuckoo, where in the lush grass near the intersection of Routes 33 and 522 a marker asserts that a "tavern that stood here" was where the midnight rider first saw Tarleton's 250 horsemen and guessed their destination, forty miles away. Off he rode, using obscure trails and byways to stay out of sight.

The race was on.

Tarleton didn't know he was in a race, but he was still no slouch when it came to moving fast. At the town of Louisa, I picked up his trail on a marker by the police station; he rested men and horses for a few hours at a nearby plantation. Eleven miles west in the rolling country-side, I pulled up in front of Boswell's Tavern, built in 1735 and now a private residence. Here Tarleton burned twelve wagons filled with sup-plies bound for South Carolina, which slowed him a bit. Seven miles beyond Boswell's, a twentieth-century marker for a house called Castle Hill said Tarleton "stopped here for breakfast," creating a delay that "aided the patriots to escape"—a delay which, as implausibly claimed elsewhere, was prolonged by "potent mint juleps" he was persuaded to sip after his morning meal.

Shades of clever Mistress Murray and her beautiful daughters! But Tarleton's real problem wasn't devious rebel hospitality. It was Jouett, who won his race by a good margin, rode to Monticello—where Jeffer-son is said to have offered him a glass of Madeira—and continued on to Charlottesville to warn the legislators.

Jouett soon faced the same problem that vexed Revere: The peo-ple he'd risked his life to warn were slow to react. And now here came Benny, charging across the Rivanna River below the town, still hoping to bag Virginia's leaders, and here came a detachment of green-coated cavalrymen climbing the road to Monticello, which the principal author of the Declaration of Independence—and wouldn't he look good along-side Henry Laurens in the Tower of London?—had not yet left. True, he'd sent his wife and kids off in a carriage, but it would take a second warning, this one from a young officer en route to join Lafayette, to get him out of his beloved house. No more than ten minutes later, the offi-cer would recall, Monticello was surrounded "by a troop of Light-horse."

The legislators were sluggish also. Seven were captured. The other thirty-plus fled across the Blue Ridge Mountains to Staunton, where they would elect a new governor—Jefferson's term mercifully having expired.

Tarleton didn't linger in Charlottesville. His orders were to go help Simcoe as soon as possible. Before he left, however, he spent a night within what are now the city limits, which made me want to go have a look. On East Jefferson Street, two miles from the Jefferson-designed heart of the University of Virginia, I was rewarded with one of the more unusual revolutionary landmarks I'd seen. Set back from the street, out of scale with its neighbors, stood an elegantly proportioned brick mansion with Tuscan-columned porticos and a lawn dotted with non-Tuscan metal sculptures. A name-dropping marker assured me I was in the right place, mentioning not just Tarleton but Meriwether Lewis and George Armstrong Custer as being connected to the place, though failing to note that a famed frontiersman slept here, too. Daniel Boone was one of the seven legislators nabbed by Tarleton's men (Kentucky being part of Virginia then), and as I'd learned from Maass, Boone had been "held overnight in a nearby coal shed" before being released.

At Tarleton's next destination, Point of Fork, he learned that Simcoe hadn't needed help capturing the stores there, unless you count Friedrich Wilhelm, Baron von Steuben's decision—after being duped into thinking he was facing Cornwallis's whole army—to abandon them. Steuben was in Virginia because Greene needed someone to gather supplies and recruits for the southern army. But the baron had achieved mixed results at best, and by now he and the state's leaders were furiously pointing fingers at each other.

Lord C, meanwhile, wasn't far away.

He'd settled in at one of Jefferson's smaller estates, Elk Hill, which, unlike Monticello—unaccountably spared by Tarleton—would end up trashed. Cornwallis "destroyed all my growing crops," Jefferson would report, "burned all my barns," used "my stocks of cattle, sheep, and hogs for the sustenance of his army, and carried off all the horses capable of service," killing the rest. Also carried off, as their owner put it, were numerous enslaved people, though that description is at odds with what we know happened in the South whenever British armies appeared nearby.

But all good things must end someday, and for Cornwallis, who despite his earlier protestation appeared to love "marching about the country in quest of adventure," that day had come. His Lordship needed to go east, pick up his mail, and find out what his nominal boss, Sir Henry, wanted him to do. And no sooner did he head in that direction than here came Lafayette—having finally been joined by Wayne—on his trail.

Well, sort of on his trail.

"We make it seem we are pursuing him," Lafayette wrote, for political reasons. The idea was to encourage Virginians by giving Cornwallis's movements "the appearance of a retreat. Would to God there were a way to give him the appearance of a defeat."

A few weeks later, he decided this second possibility might be worth a try.

* * *

The short, sharp, near disaster that erupted late in the afternoon of July 6, 1781, is known—to those who know it at all—as the Battle of Green Spring. Needing someone to show me around, I asked the president of the American Revolution Round Table in Richmond if he knew anyone who could help.

"Me," Bill Welsch said, and organized a tour.

How did part of Lafayette's small army and most of Cornwallis's big one end up squaring off? Well, Lord C's mail had put him in a Washington-like funk. Opening it at Williamsburg in late June, he'd learned, though he could hardly have been surprised, that Clinton didn't agree with his Virginia-centric plan for ending the war. Sir Henry, as Welsch told the dozen or so enthusiasts he'd assembled, was "convinced that the allies were planning to attack *him*" and he wanted Cornwallis to send thousands of troops to New York before taking up a defensive position on the Virginia coast. His Lordship wrote back to call this plan a crock of horse manure, or words to that effect, then got ready, for once, to do what he'd been told. This involved marching six miles or so from Williamsburg to the James River, which he would need to cross on the way to Portsmouth, where the New York–bound troops would embark.

The vicinity of that crossing site was where Welsch was taking us now.

I'd met him at Fort Ticonderoga and can't begin to list all the ways he'd been helpful since. His dive into the American War of Independence, he told me, had begun with a fifth-grade trip to Valley Forge and continued (while he earned an adult living as a college administrator) with him turning himself into a guide and leading groups all over Pennsylvania and New Jersey. Retirement took him to Virginia, where he plunged into the war in the South, though on the day of our tour, his attire—a red Valley Forge ball cap and a blue shirt touting Samuel Adams Boston Lager—hinted at divided loyalties.

Back to that river crossing:

Lafayette had continued to do his nip-at-the-heels thing, when possible, but kept hoping for more. He was the same young man, after all, who had crossed the Atlantic with glory as his number one object. Maybe, finally, this was his chance! "He thought he might catch Cornwallis crossing the James," Welsch said, and be able to wipe out His Lordship's rear guard without too much risk.

Shouldn't he send Anthony Wayne to take a look?

Mad Anthony was the wild card in the Green Spring deck. He had acquired his famous nickname by now, for noncombat reasons nobody seems quite sure of, though his men have been said to think it "described their commander pretty well." Wayne had a couple of notable things in common with Lafayette: No one questioned his bravery, and he, too, had made a horrible rookie mistake by camping in the same place too long. Wayne's was at Paoli, and unlike Barren Hill, had proved a true disaster, not just a near one—but neither man would commit the same blunder again.

No indeed. On the afternoon of July 6, they teamed up to commit a different one. And it was time to get out of our cars and see where it happened.

Driving down today's Greensprings Road, we had found ourselves in a wide, flat landscape with a horse farm on the right and many acres of open land on the left. Through the latter ran a fifty-mile bicycle trail that passed within a foot or so of a marker we needed to see, and our guide warned us that we could be maimed or killed by cyclists.

"Please, please, be careful," he said. "They generally show no mercy, okay?"

Which is exactly the same advice Wayne could have given his guys about the British, if he'd known what was about to hit them.

The action started slowly that July afternoon. Advancing roughly the way we'd just driven, Wayne and some five hundred men spent a long time skirmishing with British pickets and cavalrymen—troops who had been assigned, he assumed, to help guard Cornwallis's river crossing. At this point, Lafayette was six miles farther back with his main force, though he would later send perhaps four hundred more men ahead to join Wayne. "Anybody who does any of these tours knows you never find two sources that agree on the numbers," Welsch said, and with Green Spring, other key facts are missing as well. We don't know if Wayne's orders were simply to do a reconnaissance or if he'd been told from the start to attack the enemy's rear guard. Nor are we sure just where he was when the excitement began, though it was most likely left of the modern road. But we do know that "about five or five-thirty" Wayne formed his men in a line and sent some forward to take charge of a seemingly abandoned British cannon.

But now—wait, what?—thousands of enemy troops emerged from the woods ahead of them and quickly formed lines of their own.

Cornwallis hadn't crossed the James after all. He'd sent his baggage across, with a unit to guard it, while hiding his main force in what Welsch called a "wonderful defile" not far from today's Jamestown Settlement—tourist trap or living history museum, take your choice, but not the real thing—which couldn't be seen from where we stood. The skirmishing had been designed to lure Lafayette into a trap. The cannon was a decoy. And now Mad Anthony faced what he called "a choice of difficulties."

He chose to order a bayonet charge. Why not?

"He figures: If I just turn around and start to retreat, this is going to turn into a rout, but if I attack them, it's going to momentarily stop them—which it did," Welsch said.

No guts, no getaway: Wayne, Lafayette, and most of their men could now pull back to safety, and with night coming on, Cornwallis did not pursue.

Still, it gives one pause to think what might have happened if Lafayette's irreplaceable little army had stuck its head farther into the British trap; or if Wayne's men hadn't fought and died so heroically during his improvised attack; or if Lord C had ordered his troops out of the woods with an hour more daylight left. The marquis, for one, knew he'd survived another near-fatal misstep.

"This campaign is a good school for me," he wrote three days later. "God grant that the public does not pay for my lessons."

\* \* \*

The Comte de Rochambeau turned fifty-five the year he crossed the Atlantic and landed in Newport, Rhode Island. To start thinking about his unheralded impact on the war, I crossed the Claiborne Pell Bridge for a first-time visit myself. Coming into town I passed a sign for the Newport Yachting Center Marina; saw a Newport Storm truck with a slogan ("One Airport, One Area Code, One Beer") that made me nostalgic for the more downscale Rhode Island brew of my youth ("Hi-Neighbor! Have a 'Gansett"); and drove out of my way to glimpse two of the obscene mansions that came to define Newport in the nineteenth century: Chateau-sur-Mer, whose "grand scale and lavish parties," its modern custodians say, "ushered in the Gilded Age of Newport," and the Breakers, "the grandest of Newport's summer 'cottages.'" The latter was built for railroad czar Cornelius Vanderbilt, possibly the first American to whom the term "robber baron" was applied.

Had Rochambeau lived to see this Newport, he wouldn't have liked it. He earned "promotions, distinctions and rewards not at the court of Versailles, but on the battlefield," as one historian points out, and while never an enemy of the monarchy, had "no inclination for the frivolous and dissipated life" that came with it. Nonetheless, Newport has done him proud. There he stands on a pedestal in King Park, presumably, though not certainly, near where he first set foot in Rhode Island on July 13, 1780.

Who was this man chosen to lead the French in America? How had he earned the job? And what would he do with it?

Getting a sense of the count's early life and career isn't easy. His memoir has been described as "written with military brevity and soberness" by means of which the author "severely suppressed his emotions, opinions and even his own personality." As a younger son, he'd been on his way to becoming a churchman when his elder brother's death sent him into the army instead, but details of the impressive on-the-job training that followed—at Maestricht, Port Mahon, Krefeld, Kloster Kamp, and a host of other places—soon began to blur together in my mind. I knew almost nothing about eighteenth-century land wars in Europe and was eager to get my newest character across the ocean. Still, it was good to know that when he landed, he had decades of high-level experience he could use to help the Americans win the war.

Especially because for a year after that, he and his army looked to be no help at all.

Almost as soon as the French showed up, Washington began urging a joint attack on New York. This was unrealistic, to say the least, and the count let it be known that "he did not wish to suffer another debacle such as the failed siege of Savannah." After that it was wait-till-next-year time. The two generals met near Hartford in May 1781 to plan the campaign, but uncertainty haunted them, as did secrecy and mutual mistrust. Shortly before the meeting, a French source wrote Washington to tell him that a large fleet had left France (first stop: the West Indies) but that he mustn't let Rochambeau know he knew. The count had already learned this and more, of course, but he, too, chose not to share everything. It would have been rude to mention, for example, that he had been ordered to head for the Caribbean himself should Washington's army "disintegrate and cease to exist."

They had to decide something, though.

And when they did, George seemed to get his way.

"Fixed with Count de Rochambeau upon a plan of Campaign—in Substance as follows," he wrote in his diary on May 22. The French army would march from Newport to the Hudson, join the Americans there, and "commence an operation against New York." That operation, "it was thought," would cause the city to fall, or at least make the British pull troops out of the South to reinforce it. True, he and the count could "extend our views to the Southward as circumstances and a Naval superiority might render more necessary & eligible"—bypassing New York for Virginia—but the diary lists many sensible arguments against this option.

Two months later, Washington and a polite but still skeptical Rochambeau found themselves wandering around what's now the Bronx with four thousand troops in tow.

Their object was to check out New York's defenses and decide whether throwing men at them would be worth the cost. At one point, the generals ascended high ground where cannon fire from enemy batteries was so thick their guides refused to follow. This Grand Reconnaissance, as it's known, took them as far as Throgs Neck, where Howe's men had landed in 1776 before moving on to Pell's Point. How often, while reconnoitering some of the same territory now, did Washington's memory throw up unwanted images from his thrashings at Brooklyn and Kips Bay; his near-fatal delay leaving Manhattan; or the fall of his namesake fort, where his failure to overrule Greene had cost the army nearly three thousand men? "More than once" seems a fair guess. It's also reasonable to speculate, as historian Robert Selig has done, that part of his obsession with New York rose from the need for "an act of redemption" for that "humiliating defeat."

Yet here's another unanswerable question:

How could Washington not have known that the fortifications in New York would be formidable? The British had been occupying the place for five years!

The Grand Reconnaissance ended on July 23, and the following three weeks were bad ones for the American commander in chief. By then he knew he'd been dreaming. Without "massive reinforcements" and "the assistance of a powerful fleet," as Selig writes, the odds against taking New York were way too long. And not even Rochambeau, who still wasn't telling all he knew, could say when or where that fleet might turn up.

Worst of all, the Revolution was running out of time.

Yes, those January mutinies had ended, but the army's problems had only worsened since. Washington had begged the states to send sufficient recruits for this year's campaign, to no avail. Congress was too impotent to raise troops itself; it still couldn't tax anyone, and the worth of its paper currency continued to trend toward zero. The French, who had financial issues of their own, were tired of pouring cash down the

North American drain. Word had reached Washington of a proposal that European powers convene a peace conference to mediate the end of the war; the idea was serious enough that John Adams, summoned by foreign minister Vergennes to discuss it, feared the end had come for his country's independence.

The reason can be summed up in the Latin phrase "uti possidetis." It refers to a kind of diplomatic freeze tag—a game in which each side got to keep the territory it controlled "at the moment the armistice that preceded the conference took effect." Yikes. The threat passed this time, but Washington had no trouble grasping its magnitude. Had uti possidetis been imposed that summer, it would have weakened the fragile new nation, perhaps fatally, as well as leaving Mount Vernon in British hands.

Small wonder he seemed agitated as July turned to August. Everything he'd fought for in the course of six long years was at risk—and he didn't know what to do. "The Genl is exceedingly anxious & finds himself in a most perplexing & ridiculous situation, not being able to determine on any fixed plan of operation," an aide wrote.

Then a courier arrived at a four-room farmhouse in what's now Hartsdale, New York—and everything changed.

# CHAPTER 21

# A Battle You Could Hear
# but Couldn't See

The awkwardly named Odell House Rochambeau Headquarters was a construction site when I showed up to check it out. "This Area Under Video Surveillance" warned a sign on the chain-link fence surrounding it. Behind the fence I saw a backhoe, a portable restroom from Got To Go, and a battered eighteenth-century dwelling with a tarp over its roof and gray metal rectangles dotting its shingled walls.

"The room where it happened," Susan Seal said, pointing, "is right in the front section there. Bottom floor, left window—those gray things are windows." The originals, alas, were removed in the 1970s.

Seal, who had volunteered to meet me at the house this Saturday morning, was president of the Friends of OHRH. A seventysomething woman with white hair and a sharp sense of humor, she had the mix of determination and collaborative skills that gets things done, even if it takes a while. When she started living in Hartsdale, she told me, she was unaware of its French connection: "I moved to Rochambeau Drive in 1998 and said to myself: *Why is this street named for a French general?*" In answering that question, she learned about the house at 425 Ridge Road, not far away, and soon committed herself to saving it. More than twenty years would pass before the town of Greenburgh, of which Hartsdale is a hamlet, negotiated a contract to take ownership. I can't go into the details of this perversely fascinating saga, so I'll just quote Seal on the state of play a few years before my visit.

"The house had become an absolute safety hazard," she said. "It was vandalized. Kids were hanging out in it. There was a huge hole in the roof, and it was going to collapse!"

What I was seeing now was the late stages of the house being shored up so full restoration could begin. The state and town had provided considerable funding; more was needed. As I listened to Seal tell her story, though she emphasized the involvement of many others, I found myself wishing she could be cloned and put to work on a few additional neglected revolutionary sites. "Somebody once said to me, 'What do you do?'" she said, and she told them: "I make sure the grass gets cut and then I try to raise a million dollars. Other than that, it's a piece of cake."

But about that courier mentioned above:

The man galloped in from Newport on August 14, 1781, which Robert Selig—who knows as much as anyone about the allied encampment that began here in early July—calls "The Day That Would Shake the World." Rochambeau received the courier and read the letter he'd brought in the front room Seal had pointed out. In that letter, Adm. François Joseph Paul, Comte de Grasse—who commanded the much-anticipated French fleet—wrote that he was sailing to the Chesapeake from what's now Haiti; expected to arrive before September; and would need to be back in the West Indies by mid-October.

Rochambeau dashed off to look for Washington. The meeting that followed—we don't know whether it took place at the OHRH or at Washington's headquarters, half a mile away, in a house that has not survived—is said to have lasted "several hours."

There are competing versions of what happened.

The more familiar comes from Washington's diary entry that night, in which he wrote that he'd been "obliged"—because de Grasse couldn't stay long, and the French Navy didn't like the idea of attacking New York's harbor, and by the way, the states hadn't sent him anywhere near enough men—to change his plans and head for Virginia.

The French version is more revealing. Cobbled together from several sources, notably the recently translated journal of an aide who was likely at the meeting, it has Washington pushing the New York plan until Rochambeau "told him that matters were too far advanced to back out, that he was determined to march, come what may."

Come what may, I'm marching! "This sounds as if Rochambeau is putting a pistol on Washington's chest," Selig told an audience in 2021. Despite being "nominally the commander in chief," the American general "was also, militarily, the weakest link" in the triumvirate formed by de Grasse, Rochambeau, and himself—"and they all knew it."

In any case, they made a decision. But it was one that carried enormous risks.

Washington and Rochambeau couldn't know when, or even if, de Grasse would actually show up. The Brits had a pretty decent navy themselves, after all. Also, the Continentals would be unhappy about marching south: They feared (rightly) that the summer climate in Virginia was unhealthy, and they hadn't been paid (as usual) for a long time. A third risk was that the allies planned to leave fewer than four thousand troops behind, so if Clinton (who had many more) decided to march out of New York, no one could stop him. Finally, when the two generals made their August 14 decision, they had no idea where Cornwallis—whose army they were heading off to confront—even was.

On August 15, Washington fired off a letter to Lafayette.

Keep your eye out for a ginormous French fleet, he told the marquis. And whatever you do, don't let Lord C escape to the Carolinas.

\* \* \*

Five months earlier, with that ginormous fleet less than two weeks from leaving France, John Laurens had had a stroke of diplomatic luck. No sooner had he disembarked at Lorient, having survived the Attack of the Killer Icebergs, than he learned that the French naval minister was coming through town. Target of opportunity! Laurens did his best to convince him that the American Revolution was on the verge of collapse, and apparently he did. "It is almost certain," writes Jonathan Dull, an expert on the eighteenth-century French Navy, that the minister—who was en route to meet with de Grasse—conveyed Laurens's urgency to the admiral.

Did this matter? The minister's boss, after all, was the man making foreign policy decisions, and while Vergennes had been pushing a strategy in which "major blows should be landed less in Europe than in America," that didn't necessarily mean *North* America. As we've seen, Europe's combatants viewed the wealth-generating Caribbean as the more important battleground, which was why de Grasse was being sent there. True, he'd been authorized to swing north at some point, but that wasn't the priority.

Yet there would come a time when he would need to sort through all the information he had, from all sources, and make up his own mind what to do. Surely Laurens's sense of urgency could have played a small part in his decision.

De Grasse was fifty-eight when he took command of the fleet in Brest, but he'd been in training for this opportunity since he was eleven. The bulk of his education came during six years with the Knights of Saint John, a militant religious order based on Malta that had its own navy. In 1747, at twenty-four, he barely survived the most horrific battle in which he ever fought. A British cannonball decapitated his captain; de Grasse, standing nearby, received a severe head wound; seventy-five shipmates died; and he ended up a prisoner.

Flash-forward thirty-four years. He was Admiral de Grasse now, having risen steadily without achieving unusual renown. But on March 22, 1781, he was bound for glory—assuming, of course, that he could get to the Chesapeake in time to be useful. An incredible number of things had to go right for that to happen, which is a part of the story of achieving independence that Americans *really* don't grasp today, so I'll mention a few:

*De Grasse had to get safely out of the harbor in Brest.* He could do so only because the British—obsessed with resupplying Gibraltar—assigned their entire home fleet to that task rather than stopping him from sailing or attacking him as soon as he did.

*A talented British admiral had to screw up.* For complex reasons, among them greed and ill health, George Rodney failed to attack de Grasse's fleet when it got to the Caribbean. Then, just as Rodney was about to sail home to England, he learned that the French were headed for the Chesapeake in force. Inexcusably, he waited *two weeks* before sending a note to a New York colleague about this development.

*Rochambeau had to nudge de Grasse in the right direction.* The count wrote the admiral about Washington's preference for New York, then mentioned *Virginia* as the place "where we think you may be able to render the greatest service." Later he asked de Grasse to bring as many troops from the Caribbean as possible (because Washington had so few) and requested that he rustle up a few tons of hard cash as well.

*Spain needed to help—big-time.* After de Grasse read his mail, he met with Spanish envoy Francisco Saavedra, who suggested he take his entire fleet north because, hey, the Spanish Navy could hold the fort in the Caribbean. Also, there were 3,400 French troops waiting to take part in a Franco-Spanish operation that wouldn't happen for a while— why didn't de Grasse take them, too? Nathaniel Philbrick calls Saavedra "indispensable" to de Grasse's efforts, which is no exaggeration.

*De Grasse had to make a high-risk choice by himself.* He decided to go to the Chesapeake—with as many ships as possible—because this looked like France's best chance, and maybe its last, to help the Americans win their part of the war.

*Finally, the French fleet had to remain unseen en route.* De Grasse sailed north on August 5. The admiral who took over from Rodney, Samuel Hood, sailed in the same direction on the tenth. Hood's fleet was half the size of de Grasse's—mainly because it never occurred to British decision-makers that the French might be in all-or-nothing mode—but its copper bottoms made it faster.

What would have happened if the two fleets had run into each other?

The question can't be answered. But you can safely use the words "something different" if you want to give it a try.

\* \* \*

On August 16, two days after Rochambeau said he would march south "come what may," a letter from Lafayette arrived. The room where it happened, this time, would have been in Washington's vanished head-quarters, near where a huge radio tower now rises above Hartsdale's

Secor Road. Across the road is Ferncliff Cemetery, where a surprising number of twentieth-century notables are buried—James Baldwin, Judy Garland, Malcolm X, Thelonious Monk, and Ed Sullivan among them, as well as Harold Arlen, composer of "Over the Rainbow."

Had Washington wished upon a star?

Probably not, but Lafayette's news really was a dream come true. Cornwallis had chosen to occupy York and Gloucester, on opposite sides of Virginia's York River not far from where it emptied into the Chesapeake Bay. "Should a fleet Come in at this Moment," the marquis wrote, "our Affairs would take a very Happy turn."

How did His Lordship end up there? Let's start with a brief recap.

Crushing Gates at Camden had been the last major thing to go right for Cornwallis. Kings Mountain and Cowpens had shocked him and, with the Race to the Dan and Guilford Courthouse, cost him the greater part of his army. His move to Virginia, without orders, had left his commander in chief infuriated, the hard-won British holdings in South Carolina and Georgia at risk, and all semblance of a coherent strategy in ruins. Since then, he'd kept himself busy trashing rebel stores and shadow-boxing with Lafayette—arguably not the best use for a force that was now (thanks to Clinton, who'd sent so many men south with Arnold and Phillips) more than seven thousand strong.

In fact, that was what Sir Henry did argue. But the bitter back-and-forth between the generals is hard to follow without footnotes, so here's what we need to know:

Clinton gave up on getting Cornwallis to send troops to New York, thanks to Germain and the king, who loved Lord C's aggressiveness and completely failed to grasp its downside. But Sir Henry also refused to authorize his alleged subordinate to return to Charleston, despite Cornwallis having informed him—infuriatingly—that he was now "willing" to do so. Instead, Clinton ordered him to establish a coastal base in Virginia at all costs. Portsmouth, the site of Arnold's close call and a breeding ground for disease, had proved a bad choice, so he offered Cornwallis two alternatives. One was the tip of the peninsula between the James and York Rivers. His Lordship rejected this as unsuitable for protecting a fleet or blocking the entrance to the James.

The other was Yorktown. And when Washington and Rochambeau got their armies on the road, Yorktown was their destination.

They worked to keep this secret as long as possible. Only a few in the high command were told. Most of the troops marched north to Kings Ferry, then turned west to cross the Hudson. When they turned south again, Washington did his best to make it look as though they were targeting New York via Staten Island, ordering boats gathered, bake ovens built, and deceptive letters sent in the hope they would be intercepted. Late in August, with the troops in New Jersey, he and Rochambeau rode ahead to Philadelphia, where they had innumerable tasks to perform before the march could continue.

High on Washington's list was getting his army paid. And to do that, he was going to need Bob Morris.

\* \* \*

"Are you admiring Robert Morris?" asked a woman with a Christ Church name tag.

It was a reasonable guess: I was standing in the churchyard staring at the man's tomb. Above us rose what's been called America's Steeple, said to have been the highest structure on the continent for fifty-six years. Built in 1754, it had recently been discovered to be tilting two feet northwest. Jokes about the Leaning Tower of Philly were made.

"This is the Morris who was the financier?" I asked.

"Absolutely. That's him. Yup—the big guy!"

"It doesn't say anything about that on the plaque."

"Well, there are so many things you could *put* on the plaque that it's hard to know where to begin."

I had dropped by the church, a ten-minute walk from Independence Hall, to see the final resting place of Charles Lee—"Knight Errant of Liberty" is what *his* plaque says—without knowing Morris was there. My bad. Because if you're looking to understand how American independence was won, you can't leave the big guy out of the picture.

As a teenager, Morris swept floors and clerked for a Philadelphia shipping firm. At twenty-three, he was a partner. At thirty-five, under that not-yet-leaning steeple, he married into the city's elite. At forty-two, as a member of Congress, he opposed declaring independence but stepped out of the room before the 1776 vote, not wanting to flout the will of the majority. He signed the Declaration in the end and did his best to save the Revolution during the soul-trying months that followed. Most of Congress fled Philadelphia that December, fearing that Washington couldn't keep the British out of the city. Not Morris, though. As his biographer, Charles Rappleye, explains, he and two colleagues were authorized to stay behind, and he ended up—not for the last time— "essentially serving as chief executive of a beleaguered government facing its most severe trial."

Fortunately, the British didn't come that year.

Unfortunately, Washington—who was on the bank of the Delaware planning a desperation move—needed muskets, lead, gunpowder, and other supplies that were tied up in the chaos on the Philadelphia docks. Could Morris fix this, please? Yes he could.

Off went George to surprise the Hessians at Trenton.

A week later, the Second Battle of Trenton loomed, the one where a loss would have made us forget the first. But Washington couldn't fight without men, and most of his men's enlistments expired on New Year's Day. So on New Year's Eve, as you may recall, he promised $10 in hard cash to any soldier who would stay another month.

Problem: He didn't actually *have* that cash.

Solution: You guessed it.

Over and over, Morris would have chances to help out this way. But we need to jump ahead to 1781, when Congress threw up its hands at its own inability to govern and named him superintendent of finance.

That newly created job, for which he was the only viable candidate, "is generally compared to the modern secretary of the treasury," Rappleye notes, yet the analogy understates its importance. As the nation's "primary administrator," Morris "would be responsible for every aspect of governance but the disposition of the army in the field. At a time when the central government was comprised of a single legislative house, he would fill the role later reserved for the president of the United States." Still, when de Grasse's bombshell blew up everyone else's plans, it exploded his as well.

Morris was in Hartsdale when the letter arrived. He'd ridden up hoping to persuade Washington that the army's budget for 1782 should shrink. Hah! Instead, he would need "all his energy and available funds" to help that army get to Virginia right now.

It wouldn't be easy.

"I have already advised your Excellency of the unhappy situation of money matters, and very much doubt if it will be possible to pay the Detachment a months pay," Morris wrote Washington on August 28, "therefore it will be best not to raise in them any expectation of that kind." Ouch. But then came a consolation prize: He invited the general and his aides to stay at his Front Street house when they got to Philadelphia. There weren't enough beds, but the aides could have mattresses on the floor.

Heck, nobody had much time to sleep anyway—except perhaps Sir Henry Clinton.

What had Clever Henry been *thinking* as his enemies marched south unopposed? We don't actually know, despite the fact that he's been repeatedly excoriated for not attacking them. The simplest answer may be that Clinton was still thinking what he'd been thinking for months, with good reason—that the Americans and the French were focused on New York—and was way too slow to change mental gears. By the time he got contrary intelligence he couldn't ignore, on September 2, it was too late.

That same day, Washington confessed his greatest fear to Lafayette. "I am distressed beyond expression, to know what is become of the Count de Grasse," he wrote from Morris's house. On September 4, he wrote Greene that "the present Time is as interesting & anxious a Moment, as I have ever experienced." This was saying something: Think how many such moments he'd experienced in his forty-nine years. On September 5, still with no word from de Grasse, he rode south to keep doing what he had to do. If he left a note saying *Dear Bob: Find the damn cash*, it did not survive, though he later wrote: "I wish it to come on the Wings of Speed."

Could Morris—somehow—get the troops paid?

He was still trying, but his options were limited.

Already, he was using his personal credit—in the form of promissory notes known as "short Bobs" and "long Bobs" depending on the terms of redemption—to help the army buy such necessities as flour, horses, wagons, and boats. But those notes were paper money, and the troops demanded specie. In desperation, he turned to Rochambeau, "the only man in the city who could access substantial quantities of hard money," who stalled. The count wasn't sure of the state of his treasury, and his treasurer was on the road south.

Morris recruited a traveling companion and rode off to find the man.

Rochambeau went by water. Briefly setting aside current business, he played historical tourist, stopping with some of his officers to see the Delaware River forts that had been part of the 1777 campaign. Later, continuing downriver, he came upon a fantastic scene. As described by historian Barbara Tuchman, it starred "a tall man acting as if he had taken leave of his senses. He was jumping up and down and waving his arms in sweeping circles, with a hat in one hand and a white handkerchief in the other."

Bob Morris pleading for cash, perhaps?

Nope. It was George Washington, who'd gotten word that de Grasse had sailed into the Chesapeake and was eager to give Rochambeau the news himself. "His features, his physiognomy, his deportment, all were changed in an Instant," recalled a French officer who'd known the general only as a man of solemn gravitas. "A child, whose every wish had been gratified, would not have experienced a sensation more lively."

Washington Waves His Hat is a Revolutionary War moment that remains shamefully uncommemorated. Perhaps that's because we don't know where it occurred.

Chester, Pennsylvania, gets the most votes from historians, but Marcus Hook, three miles south, gets a few, too, and it happened to be the first place I looked. "Weapons, Firearms, Ammunition, Explosives and Incendiary Devices Are PROHIBITED" read a sign at the Marcus Hook Industrial Complex, a former Sunoco oil refinery turned transport hub for liquefied natural gas. The town itself (population roughly 2,300) looked tiny by comparison. At Mickey Vernon Park, on Market Street, I admired a statue of the two-time American League batting champ, but found no trace of Washington. At a second park, right on the riverbank, I watched tankers make their way toward Philadelphia. The Delaware is more than a mile wide here, as opposed to less than three hundred yards where the Continentals crossed en route to Trenton in 1776.

Still, I found no mention of George. And on the afternoon of September 5, 1781, there was not yet any assurance that the troops would get paid.

Then, somewhere north of Chester, Morris and his companion ran into "a lone rider, making haste and raising a cloud of dust." He was looking for Robert Morris, he said. Opening the packet the man handed him—it was from Washington—Morris learned that de Grasse's fleet had arrived. Was the hard cash Rochambeau had asked the admiral to bring on board? It was indeed.

A French loan should be easier to negotiate now.

"This was the first that could be called money, which we had received as wages since the year '76," recalled Joseph Plumb Martin, describing its disbursement, "or that we ever did receive till the close of the war, or indeed ever after as wages."

Washington didn't stick around to watch.

Confident his men would be paid (thanks, Bob) and aching to see Mount Vernon for the first time in more than six years, he left his army at the northern tip of the Chesapeake and headed for Baltimore. Early on the morning of September 9, the day after most of the pay was doled out, he set out to ride the last sixty miles home. With him were William Lee, the enslaved man who'd been by his side throughout the war, and a single aide-de-camp. They arrived at dusk. Martha was there to greet them, as were four step-grandchildren George had never met, all born since he rode north in 1775. When he left, there had been no guarantee that he would see Mount Vernon again. In the spring of 1781, British raiders had sailed up the Potomac; taken aboard seventeen of his enslaved workers, who had made a break for freedom; and threatened to burn his house unless given livestock and other supplies. Washington's caretaker, his cousin Lund, had complied, only to be harshly reprimanded by George, who thought Lund had dishonored him.

"It would have been a less painful circumstance to me," he wrote, "to have heard, that in consequence of your non compliance with their request, they had burnt my House, & laid the Plantation in Ruins."

Still, here he was now: happy to come home to an unburned house, looking forward to a few nights in his own bed, but not ready for the news a messenger would bring shortly after he resumed his journey.

A British fleet had appeared at the Chesapeake.

The French had sailed out to fight it.

And nobody knew yet what had happened.

\* \* \*

"Victory in Defeat" proclaims a marker at the site of Nathanael Greene's last major battle. It took place at Eutaw Springs, twenty-five miles northwest of Moncks Corner, on September 8, 1781, a few days before the scary news about the French and British fleets caught up with Washington. But put all that navy stuff out of your mind for now, because if you've been wondering what Greene had been up to since leaving Cornwallis to his own devices and heading back to South Carolina, "victory in defeat" sums things up pretty well.

Here's another way to say it: He'd been losing his battles and winning his war.

To see how this trick was done, the place to start is at Hobkirk's Hill, a battle Greene had lost back on April 25. If the name sounds familiar, it may be because Charles Baxley mentioned it while explaining his "concentric method" of studying the past. But for me, Hobkirk's Hill carries an association with another historian as well. Jim Piecuch drove me through the battlefield on our way to walk the better-known Battle of Camden (aka "Gates's Disgrace"), and if I could have a do-over, I'd pay more attention.

"It's pretty much developed," Piecuch told me, "but there's one area that's parkland where you can get a sense of what it looked like." Pulling over at the top of a house-free slope, he pointed to something I couldn't make out and said, "There's the pond where the Americans were doing their laundry when the British started coming out of the woods."

If your army gets attacked while washing its socks, you've been surprised. Not good.

Greene had showed up at Camden two weeks earlier, eager to pick off the garrison at this link between Charleston and the backcountry. The fortifications proved too strong to assault, so he set up on the low ridge of Hobkirk's Hill, hoping his opposite number—the young but talented and experienced Lord Rawdon—would march out and attack *him*. The outnumbered Rawdon did precisely that, but not where he was expected, and eventually Greene found himself retreating—just as at Guilford Courthouse—because he couldn't risk the destruction of his army. Frustrated and depressed, he publicly criticized a subordinate whose mistake he believed responsible for his defeat.

But then the victory part kicked in.

Two days before the battle, it turned out, Francis Marion and Light Horse Harry Lee had teamed up to cut the British supply line between Camden and Charleston. On May 9, Rawdon, knowing his position was now untenable, began pulling back to the coast, which left Greene free to go on offense.

One more consequence of this pullback deserves attention. As we know but tend to forget, Greene's campaign took place amid a murderous civil war. "In our time," Buchanan writes, "we have become all too familiar with the plight of civilian refugees fleeing war zones," and the loyalists who fled Camden with Rawdon "were no different. They had good reason to fear what Rebel militia bands would do to them if they stayed," and they ended up near Charleston in what we'd now call a displaced persons camp.

Greene's next move was to attack a vital base in the far South Carolina backcountry.

His target was the oddly named Ninety Six, eighty miles south of the Cowpens. Central to its defenses was an earthen fortress, shaped like an eight-pointed star, from which defenders could fire on attackers from multiple angles. Greene decided taking the fort by siege would be the smart choice, which it was, except for one little problem: Neither Greene nor his chief engineer had experience with siege warfare. They ordered a trench dug too close to the walls and were driven off. They didn't fully block enemy access to water from a nearby stream. Other difficulties presented themselves and before long, Rawdon marched out of Charleston intent on rescuing the defenders. By mid-June, Greene was out of time. If you think back to the siege of Savannah, you can guess what came next: a failed assault, too many brave men dead, and a humiliating retreat.

But then—here we go again.

Rawdon couldn't *hold* the isolated base he'd saved. By July, he was headed back to Charleston, along with another column of homeless refugees. Later that month, Greene moved his own army to the High Hills of Santee in what's now Sumter County, looking to rest his exhausted troops and escape the killer heat of a South Carolina summer.

He couldn't exactly zone out, though.

Uti possidetis haunted him.

And it was in no small part his fear of a mediated peace—which could leave the South in British hands—that led to his last big fight at Eutaw Springs.

He had a new opponent this time, Col. Alexander Stewart, because Rawdon had sailed home to recover from what was probably malaria. Historians argue about the strength of the two armies, but agree (I think) that while Greene had more men, Stewart had a higher percentage of veteran Regulars. Nonetheless, Greene tapped the militia to lead his attack—and they fought extremely well.

Militia had fought well before, but almost always from defensive positions. Now they advanced "steadily and without faltering," as one of Greene's officers recalled. Credit goes to the men themselves, toughened by the partisan wars, and to leaders like Pickens and Marion, whom they trusted. Inevitably, though, their attack slowed. Greene sent some recently recruited Continentals to help. They, too, fought well before faltering. Some of Stewart's men smelled victory and charged without orders. Not smart: Now here came Greene's *veterans* to sweep them from the field.

And they would have, too, except...

Unpredictable things, as they always do, began to happen. There were cavalry charges that failed for lack of proper leadership. There was the confusion created as the Continentals charged into the British camp, perhaps because they stopped to loot it (long the standard narrative) or maybe for less disgraceful reasons. And there was a huge X factor in the form of a brick plantation house whose windows commanded the heart of the battlefield. Before the fight began, Stewart had the sense to order that it be occupied should things start going wrong, and this was done with devastating effect.

If the result didn't remind Greene of Germantown, it should have:

Given some breathing room, the British counterattacked, forcing him to pull his exhausted men back from the exceptionally bloody four-hour battle they had come so close to winning decisively. Roughly 20 percent had been killed or wounded. Pickens, shot off his horse and presumed dead, was dragged off the field, surviving only because the musket ball hit a buckle on his sword belt. Cowpens hero John Eager Howard, also badly wounded, would not fight again.

Stewart, however, ended up as Greene's ultimate Victory-in-Defeat victim.

He had lost close to 40 percent of *his* men, including hundreds who had been captured, leaving him no choice but to retreat toward Charleston—from which, once he arrived, no sizable British force would emerge to contest control of the state.

\* \* \*

To get within hailing distance of the Revolutionary War's most important battle, I first had to get myself past a gate at Joint Expeditionary Base Little Creek–Fort Story in Virginia Beach. It was a bit harder than zipping through a tollbooth with an E-ZPass.

The base, better known simply as Fort Story, describes itself as "the country's premier installation for housing and training the nation's Expeditionary Forces" and, in an unexpected burst of military lyricism, "The Pearl by the Bay and the Emerald on the Ocean." I was there because it seemed a good place to contemplate what happened when de Grasse's fleet sailed out of the Chesapeake Bay into the Atlantic Ocean on September 5, 1781, with the fate of the Revolution hanging in the balance. Guards checked my license, registration, and insurance card, then told me to get out of the car, open all five doors, and raise the hood.

"Any alcohol?" one asked.

"Couple of beers in the cooler."

"Are they open?"

I said no. They checked anyway. Inspection complete, they offered some useful advice. My specific destination, they knew, was the Cape Henry Memorial, a tiny National Park Service site within the base that was less than a quarter mile away. After that, a guard told me, I would see a fire station and some flashing lights.

"Go past those," he said, "and you don't want to deal with what happens."

Reaching the memorial—trust me, I didn't drive an inch farther—I pulled into an empty parking lot. At one end stood a statue of a tall man in a naval uniform. Erect and appropriately sea green, thanks to the oxidation of bronze, de Grasse had his legs spread wide for balance and his eyes turned toward the dunes that blocked his view of the ocean. A path led over those dunes to a small platform overlooking the Atlantic. On it were some rusty, coin-operated binoculars, which mostly served to make seagulls look bigger, and a weathered marker titled "Battle of the Capes," which was more helpful. Among other things, it said that by the time the British and French fleets began firing at each other, late in the afternoon of the fifth, they were out of sight of the land.

For two hours, then, if you'd been standing here, you'd have heard their broadsides.

Then it would have gotten quiet, and you wouldn't have learned the outcome for days.

Gazing into the offshore haze, I wondered how to evoke an unwalkable yet immensely critical turning point that had by no means been guaranteed to turn the way it did. Then I went home, read more about the Battle of the Capes—aka the Battle of the Virginia Capes, the Battle of the Chesapeake Capes, or just the Battle of the Chesapeake—and began to indulge in a bizarre fantasy:

What if historical tourists could see that invisible battlefield from a helicopter? Better yet, what if it were a *time-traveling* helicopter, so it could fly us around the bay and the ocean as they would have appeared when the battle was actually happening?

It's nuts, I know. But humor me.

Sometime after dawn, we would pick up the British fleet under Adm. Thomas Graves as it sailed south toward the Chesapeake from New York. We'd see that it consisted primarily of ships of the line: hulking wooden arsenals, some close to two hundred feet long, each with two or three tiers of cannon. The first thing we'd want to do would be to count those behemoths, because in eighteenth-century naval battles, the side with the most ships of the line usually won. Graves had nineteen of them. But a couple of frigates would also catch our eyes, because before long, we'd see those faster, more maneuverable vessels—the fleet's "scouts, messengers, and mounted cavalry," as James Nelson calls them—detach themselves and head for the mouth of the Chesapeake. That's because the British didn't yet know what they were going to find there.

Next, we'd fly off to see for ourselves.

Just inside the entrance to the bay, defined by Cape Henry on the south and Cape Charles a dozen miles to the north, we'd count twenty-four ships of the line. Soon the two frigates would hightail it back with the shocking news. It was shocking because precisely none of the relevant decision-makers—not George Rodney, who had gone home; not Samuel Hood, who, following Rodney's orders, had brought only fourteen ships of the line with him from the Caribbean; and certainly not Thomas Graves or Henry Clinton in New York, who depended on the others for intelligence—had dreamed de Grasse would roll the dice and sail north with almost his entire fleet.

Farther inside the bay, however, a short copter flight up the peninsula between the York and James Rivers would reveal disadvantages that evened things out.

Look, there sat three *more* French ships of the line, sent to the York to keep an eye on Cornwallis. They would stay there. And look, there was another, near the mouth of the James, helping with the process of landing the three-thousand-plus troops de Grasse had brought—a job that involved rowing them miles upriver and required well over a thousand sailors and officers from the fleet. Most of them wouldn't make it back for the battle.

Another problem would show itself as de Grasse scrambled out of the Chesapeake.

Ships of the line were built to fight as part of a "line of battle" (hence their name), with one following another, in a prearranged order, against an enemy similarly arrayed. Usually, it took these cumbersome, wind-dependent vessels considerable time to arrange themselves properly, but on September 5, de Grasse didn't have that kind of time. Instead, he told his captains to form a "line of speed" or "ligne de vitesse," with its order to be determined by how quickly each captain got out of the bay. This would have serious consequences, as we'll see, but right now, it really livened things up. "Since the ships that sailed out of the bay the fastest would have the honor of leading the fleet into battle," Philbrick explains, the result was "an exhilarating race. Making it all the more exciting, if not downright terrifying, was the challenge of maneuvering a ship of the line at close quarters without her full complement of crew."

Worse, once de Grasse's ships did get out of the bay, they formed a line with holes in it. Most dangerously, the French vanguard was so far ahead that the British—whose own ships were upwind and in good order—had a chance to sweep down and destroy it before the rest of de Grasse's fleet could get close enough to help.

Why didn't Graves seize that chance?

Short answer: He wasn't a chance-taking kind of guy.

Longer answer: In fairness, most British admirals of the era were similarly conservative. This was by design. Their London bosses wanted them to follow the damn rules, and those rules said: Form a line of battle and stick with it. Also, Graves had never commanded a fleet in battle and wouldn't have been commanding this one if Rodney had been there or if Hood had had more seniority. Finally, the rule-obsessed British Navy (go figure) allowed different fleets to use different signaling systems. As a result, the signals used by the fourteen ships from the Caribbean differed enough from those used by the five from New York to make intricate maneuvers hard to coordinate.

Good reasons all, perhaps. Still, as Hood saw it—and he wasn't alone—"a most glorious opening" had been ignored.

Instead, Graves wasted much of the afternoon executing various steps of a mystifying nautical dance. Eventually he noticed that just a few hours of daylight were left. Blimey! Time to attack! Due to a combination of intent, signal flag confusion, and a shift in the wind, however, only the front part of the British line wound up seriously engaging its French counterpart. The British bore down at an angle, Nelson writes, with the converging lines "resembling a chevron of geese" as they came together.

What followed were those two intense hours in which broadsides could be heard, though not seen, from the shore.

Exhaustion and darkness ended the fight for the day. Both admirals assumed it would resume, possibly as soon as the next morning—but it never did.

Four more days of nautical dancing brought a return engagement no closer. On September 9, de Grasse realized—much later than he should have—that he had more important things to do than chase the Brits around the Atlantic. Back to the Chesapeake he sailed, where a welcome sight met his eyes. In late August, a smaller French fleet under the Comte de Barras had set out from Rhode Island to join the allied forces. Graves had hoped to intercept de Barras, but failed. Now here he was, having waltzed into the bay with eight ships of the line while the big fleets were otherwise occupied.

With him, soon to be unloaded, were siege guns big enough to give Lord Cornwallis nightmares.

CHAPTER 22

# "Little Short of a Standing Miracle"

W hen I set off on the one-man staff ride that would take me so many unexpected places—starting with that bullet-shaped stone tower where the dress rehearsal for Lexington and Concord began—I already knew what my last major stop would be. How could I not? Even the most casual students of the Revolution can name the little town where the British lost, the surrender drums beat, and the world turned upside down.

The Yorktown story, however, turned out to be more complex and dramatic than the one I thought I knew.

"Here's your driving map of the battlefield," the ranger at the visitor center said, handing me a copy. "Just remember this is over sixteen miles of tour road and you're going to be on over four thousand acres."

I made it around those sixteen miles eventually, stopping at markers for old friends along the way. There was Benjamin Lincoln, who'd had to wait six months after surrendering Charleston to be exchanged; he was now Washington's second-in-command. There was Lafayette, of course, who'd tried and failed to nab that number two job for himself, and Steuben, still in the commander in chief's good graces despite the debacle at Point of Fork. There was artillery maestro Henry Knox, who hadn't had a chance to show what he could do since Monmouth, and there was—oh, come on. Did I *really* need to stop at a marker called "Headquarters Site of the Quartermaster General"? Yes. Keeping the army supplied, as Nathanael Greene had proved, could be at least as important as leading it in battle. But the intriguing thing about that marker, to me, was its mention of the officer whose dog met a sad fate on the march to Quebec and whose Saratoga memories would be twisted into falsehoods by James Wilkinson.

Old friend Henry Dearborn, it seemed, was helping to run the quartermaster department now.

A side road took me to Washington's headquarters. There wasn't much to see, just "a good place to pitch a tent," as someone later joked, though I did learn that it sat at the junction of the American and French forces. (Rochambeau was a five-minute walk away.) By the time my self-guided tour ended, however, I'd also come to believe that a real staff ride might help me braid the familiar and unfamiliar names I'd seen—plus the trenches, redoubts, and artillery positions I'd glimpsed along the way—into a coherent Yorktown narrative.

And to my great good fortune, Jon Stull invited me to join the one he would be leading.

Stull was the retired Marine who'd helped show me around Great Bridge. The staff riders would be from a seminar at the Joint Forces Staff College in Norfolk, where he used to teach. *"Okay, no kidding, working together,"* he said, summing up the JFSC's mission to build interservice teamwork skills. "The seminars are third, third, and third—sea, air, and ground. So unlike going to the Army War College or the Naval War College, you're not getting a dark green or a dark blue solution with 'Oh, there's your token Marine and there's your token Air Force officer.' This is like: 'You're going to have to convince the other *plurality* what makes sense.'"

Fifteen staff riders joined us outside the visitor center. Stull told me they were majors and lieutenant colonels and guessed they were around forty years old. I said they looked younger. "That's why I stopped teaching," he said. "Because they're looking more and more like Cub Scouts to me." The group gathered around as he went into Socratic mode.

Question: Why was Cornwallis in Yorktown and not in Portsmouth, anyway?

A few answers: It was a superior deep-water port, safe from enemy warships if you put guns on both sides of the York River. Higher ground also meant better visibility. "Better drainage, too," Stull said. Malaria was a serious challenge, "and you know about mosquitoes in the Tidewater.

"What else? I've got some army officers here."

"He can canalize his opponents' approach," one said.

The verb was new to me. In the Yorktown context, it meant that two ravines created by swampy creeks, one near each of Cornwallis's flanks, would force any major infantry attack toward his center, allowing the defenders to concentrate their fire.

And speaking of military language: The word "siege" comes from the Latin "to sit," Stull told us. "So you're going to sit out your enemy and he will capitulate." But you can speed things up with cannon. "The defeat mechanism for siege warfare is artillery: It's about making those who are surrounded give up because their position's been pounded, their fortifications are being destroyed, and life inside the works is just intolerable."

From the visitor center, we drove off to see part of the siege line where this mechanism first came into play. But before talking about that, I need to explain what Cornwallis had done to fortify his position during the eight and a half weeks before Washington, Rochambeau, and a force well over twice the size of his showed up in his front yard.

"Not enough" is an obvious part of the answer.

Digging began in early August, north of the river at Gloucester Point. The heat was oppressive. There weren't enough entrenching tools, and it was late in the month before Lord C—still cranky about being ordered to play defense—bothered to ask for more. In the meantime, the earth-moving at Yorktown itself had barely started. The plan called for two defense lines: an inner line around the town plus a ring of outer works.

De Grasse's August 30 arrival greatly increased His Lordship's sense of urgency. But his inner line still wasn't finished on September 28, when the French and American armies—their sweaty trek from Harts-dale finally completed—marched the twelve miles from Williamsburg to Yorktown to begin the siege.

When the staff riders reached their destination, Stull grilled them some more.

*Q: Why does Cornwallis have outer defenses?*

A: To deny the enemy easy access to these approaches.

*Q: Because what happens if I'm an opposing force and I come across a redoubt?*

A: You've got to fight it.

Well maybe you do, or maybe you don't. Washington and Rochambeau spent the day after they arrived figuring out how best to attack the enemy's outer works. But Cornwallis, too, was weighing his options, and on September 30, the allied commanders woke up to find that the British had *abandoned* the outer defenses they'd been worrying about.

Why? Because an express boat had slipped past the blockade and brought him a message from Clinton, which said that five thousand troops from New York—to which Graves and his fleet had returned after the Battle of the Capes—would soon sail to his aid.

"There is every reason to hope we start from hence the 5th October" were Sir Henry's exact words, and Lord C chose to read "every reason to hope" as a firm promise.

Did that make pulling back the right move?

Banastre Tarleton and many others didn't think so. "Great time would have been gained," Tarleton wrote, "by holding and disputing the ground inch by inch" rather than cooping the troops up behind the town's weak inner line. We're deep in what-if territory here, of course. But we do know that the French and American armies promptly moved forward, occupying and revamping the abandoned fortifications they thought useful, and that less than a week later, on the night of October 6, they were digging their first siege line.

Planks had been laid down to show the troops where to dig. "You've got to keep it Marine proof," Stull said. "Give that basic soldier a shovel, say, 'Okay, *this* side of the plank, not *that* side of the plank.'" As he spoke, he stood on a long, linear earthwork above a grass-covered ditch. Like all but one of such works at Yorktown today, this was a Depression-era reconstruction, built with help from the Civilian Conservation Corps.

By October 9, the allies had their batteries built and their guns emplaced. The French, on the left of the siege line, had the honor of firing first, at 3 p.m. A couple of hours later, on the right, Knox's artillery would join in.

If you've read about this moment, you've likely learned that Washington himself lit the fuse to the first American cannon fired. I'm not certain that's true (really long story), but am still fond of a scene a Knox biographer created in which Washington, seeing the guns lined up and ready to go, "felt a great impulse to start the firing" and Knox, "who no doubt wished to do this himself," generously handed his boss a lighted torch.

What I love isn't the author's uncanny ability to channel Washington's feelings or Knox's willingness to let an amateur near an eighteenth-century cannon with a torch. It's that the passage evokes the bond between two men from wildly disparate backgrounds who met just days after one took command of the army, then spent six years fighting a war that could easily have ended badly. In particular, it made me think about the Second Battle of Trenton, in January 1777, where if it hadn't been for Knox's cannon and Washington's just-in-time decisiveness, their cause might not have survived the month, let alone long enough for them to be side by side at Yorktown with victory in sight.

Cornwallis was their opponent in both places. In each, overconfidence helped do him in. Standing on the first siege line, poised to lead the group to the next stop, Stull had a final, related point to make.

Before the allied guns begin to fire, he asked, "What does Cornwallis think Washington has for weight?"

"Light cannon," someone replied.

"Light cannon. It's a field army," Stull said. Armies that move as fast as the allies had en route to Yorktown, Cornwallis knew, bring with them only field artillery—relatively light guns. "So he's saying, 'They've *got* to be light, and trust me, behind my earthworks I can spend all day with them just going boomp, boomp with eight-pounders.' Now on that first day, when the twelve- and twenty-four-pounders go off, he's probably saying, 'Where did *that* come from?' And he's going, '*Where's my Intel Officer?*' "

The staff riders cracked up. I did, too.

But nobody in town, I'm guessing, found much to laugh about on the afternoon of October 9 or during the hellish days that followed.

\* \* \*

Hell took many forms in Yorktown that October, not all a result of fire from the siege guns. Cornwallis lacked forage for his horses, for example, so hundreds of the unfortunate beasts ended up in the river with their throats slit. (Many carcasses would float ashore.) Sickness, meanwhile, laid soldiers low. By one estimate, 1,500 of the British and German troops—around 20 percent of Lord C's total force—became "ineffective due to illness." But African Americans accompanying the army suffered a far worse fate.

Enslaved Virginians had been running to Cornwallis ever since he entered the state. With the army on the move, Cassandra Pybus writes, they proved invaluable as foragers, "driving off livestock, and stripping the fields and storage cellars" as well as liberating a great quantity of still-living horseflesh. ("Nothing but a treaty of alliance with the Negroes," Lafayette complained to Washington in July, would allow him to match the enemy's "formidable Cavalry.") Later, when fortifications were required, these newly free workers helped build them. Yet once again, as with Dunmore's Ethiopian Regiment, bringing together a large population vulnerable to smallpox proved disastrous, and Cornwallis—fearful of further contagion and in any case unwilling to devote scarce resources to feeding his Black allies—ordered them driven out of town. A number of soldiers commented on the appalling result, among them Joseph Plumb Martin. "During the siege we saw in the woods herds of Negroes," Martin reported, "turned adrift with no other recompense for their confidence in [Cornwallis's] humanity than the smallpox for their bounty and starvation and death for their wages."

As for what might be called Defeat Mechanism Hell:

When the allied siege guns opened up on October 10, they made the previous day's bombardment look like child's play. After an hour, as Jerome Greene writes in *The Guns of Independence*, his wonderfully detail-rich book on Yorktown, "British guns ceased to respond at all: the weapons were either too damaged to fire, or the gunners' positions along the works had become too hazardous to maintain."

Of the roughly two hundred buildings in town, many soon became rubble and most sustained serious damage. People who had chosen to stay when Cornwallis's army showed up now sought shelter under sandy cliffs by the riverbank, not always successfully. The troops themselves, according to one account gathered from British survivors, resorted to digging "holes and Pits…with timber in the top edge" in which they could squat if they were lucky enough to see an incoming shell in time. As for Cornwallis, he is said to have taken refuge in "a kind of grotto" built for him underground near the battered house that had been his headquarters, and the record shows that overconfidence was no longer one of his problems. On October 11, three days after the shelling began, he wrote Clinton that "nothing but a direct move to York River, which includes a successful naval action, can save me."

The key word in that sentence is "successful."

And everyone involved knew the odds were long.

All Sir Henry and the navy would have to do would be load up the promised five thousand men, sail down to the Chesapeake, somehow get past de Grasse's superior fleet and up to the river, offload the troops with no interference from their enemies—and then what? Did they expect Rochambeau and Washington to throw up their hands and march away? Was de Grasse supposed to shut his eyes as the British fleet waltzed past him again, on its way back *out* of the bay? And by the way, what would be at risk if anything should happen to go wrong? Oh, just most of the British Army in North America, and with it any chance of hanging on to at least some of the colonies, not to mention Britain's far more valuable holdings in the Caribbean sugar islands, which required naval protection. Admiral Graves, as Clinton's biographer points out, remained the navy's key local decision-maker; he "had in his hands the one British naval force in the hemisphere, and if he lost it in the Chesapeake he would lose the West Indies with it."

Small wonder, then, that no rescue mission left New York on October 5, despite "every reason to hope" it would—or that none was en route by the night of October 14, when French and American troops attacked two redoubts that had to be eliminated before they could complete their second siege line.

Stull took his staff ride to the less famous one.

"Welcome to Redoubt Number Nine," he said. Once again he stood atop a reconstructed earthwork, but this time it was pentagonal in shape, with rows of pointed artificial logs projecting from its sides and an interior that looked way too small for hundreds of men to fight in. Before getting to that part of the story, though, Stull filled in some background. French units were assigned to take the redoubt where we stood. American troops from Lafayette's division, led by Hamilton, were to take Redoubt No. 10. (If you can't recall which was which, Stull told us, just think: "Whose face is on the ten-dollar bill?") The attacks would begin simultaneously after dark. Men with axes would be up front, tasked with hacking passages through the logs while under fire from above.

"So this is not going to be a fun time," he said.

Next he read from a journal kept by a man who confirmed that getting over the wall had not been at *all* fun, but for whom what came next was worse. Furious soldiers jammed together in the dark redoubt, Georg Flohr wrote, couldn't always tell who was who, and " 'our people were killing one another.' "

"Imagine," Stull said, gesturing down at a space that looked smaller than a basketball court. "You've got an assault force of four hundred, a defending force of one hundred forty. This is a relatively intense environment right here—I mean heck, you can't even swing your elbows."

Somehow, the French completed their mission in thirty minutes with a surprisingly moderate casualty count.

\* \* \*

As for Redoubt No. 10: If your bucket list includes walking around on the very spot where Alexander Hamilton made himself a war hero, you're out of luck.

His target sat directly above the riverbank, and most of the original washed away long ago. Yes, there's a twentieth-century reconstruction, at least a partial one: It's a grassy mound featuring a row of those fierce-looking faux logs. But there's also a chain-link fence that keeps Revolutionary War obsessives and/or Lin-Manuel Miranda fans from squeezing through those logs and perhaps sliding down to the river themselves.

That said, you can spend as long as you want *outside* the fence, staring at the re-created No. 10 and marveling at how Hamilton came to be there at all.

Eight months earlier, he'd quit his job in a huff. The specifics of his quarrel with his boss were trivial. The real problem was that Hamilton—who'd begun his war by making himself into an excellent artillery officer and fighting at Trenton and Princeton, among other places—was now so indispensable as an aide that Washington refused his repeated requests to return to the field. So he resigned, stayed a month to ease the transition, then went home to his new wife, Elizabeth Schuyler.

But did he give up trying to get what he wanted?

Of course not: He was Alexander Hamilton!

"If Washington expected relief from Hamilton badgering him for an appointment," writes Ron Chernow, a biographer of both men, "he soon learned otherwise." By July 31, the twentysomething lieutenant colonel, who understood that "battlefield honor...would be a useful credential in the postwar political world," was in command of a light infantry battalion. He hadn't wasted the intervening months, either. Shortly after Robert Morris was named superintendent of finance, to take just one example, Hamilton "sent a marathon letter to Morris—it runs to thirty-one printed pages—that set forth a full-fledged system for shoring up American credit and creating a national bank." Morris, whose own plan for a bank had recently been approved by Congress, was impressed.

Equally impressive is the way Hamilton made sure Yorktown history would keep its eyes on him.

Lafayette was responsible for taking Redoubt No. 10, but not for leading the assault himself. Troops pulled from three regiments would do the fighting; their commanders would be Hamilton, John Laurens—back from France and champing at the bit—and Jean-Joseph Sourbader de Gimat, a Lafayette protégé who had distinguished himself most recently at Green Spring.

One of the three had to be in overall command. The marquis chose Gimat. Hamilton went over his friend's head and changed that.

Nobody knows why Washington overruled Lafayette. But in any event, there was Hamilton on the night of October 14, moving as quietly as possible toward Redoubt No. 10 with four hundred men. No muskets were loaded; it was a bayonets-only attack. The watchword was "Rochambeau," which sounded to Joseph Martin like "Rush on boys"— and rush they did when the time came, scarcely waiting for the ax men to do their chopping. It's been said that Hamilton stepped on the back or shoulder of a willing soldier and sprang atop the redoubt wall, and while I haven't yet nailed down a reliable source on that, it sounds like something the man would have done. Outnumbered more than five to one, the defenders had little chance, and the fight ended ten minutes after it began.

Ten minutes!

If you're feeling snarky, you could call Hamilton the Ten-Minute War Hero—but I'm not on board with that.

Yes, he was lucky; no, he couldn't be sure he would even survive. Before the attack, he sent his pregnant wife a cheerful letter about being home soon. After it, he confessed: "Two nights ago, my Eliza, my duty and my honor obliged me to take a step in which your happiness was too much risked." We can debate whether it was ambition, more than duty and honor, that made him risk Eliza's happiness—and if so, what we think about that—but the risk was real, as the story told by another Redoubt No. 10 attacker makes clear.

Stephen Olney recalled the silent approach march as one in which some men likely thought "less than one quarter of a mile would finish the journey of life with them." He, like Hamilton, made the top of the wall, at which point "I had not less than six or eight bayonets pushed at me." Surgeons were sure one wound would kill him, but it didn't.

Olney, as it happened, was a captain in the only Rhode Island regiment active at the time. In February, what was left of the famed First Rhode Island had merged into it. The merger created some historical confusion: As Judith Van Buskirk writes in her book *Standing in Their Own Light*, "Many historians assume that the Rhode Island Regiment of 1781" was the original Black Regiment, which can lead them to give African American soldiers a "starring role in the taking of Redoubt 10." In reality, while more than a hundred Black troops did serve with the Rhode Island regiment at Yorktown, only a few were among the light infantrymen making the October 14 assault.

The fall of the redoubts shattered Cornwallis's illusions—assuming he still had any—about holding out in Yorktown until rescued.

On October 15, he wrote Clinton to say: Don't come. "I cannot recommend that the Fleet and Army should run great Risque, in endeavoring to save us."

The next night, he tried to send the majority of his men across the York, leaving his sick and wounded behind. A violent storm ended this belated attempt.

On October 17, a drummer boy and an officer waving a white handkerchief appeared on a Yorktown parapet. Luckily, they were not blown to bits by cannon fire.

And around noon on October 18, at an early-eighteenth-century house less than a mile southeast of the redoubt he had helped to take, John Laurens sat down with three other officers—one French and two British—to hash out a surrender agreement.

"Washington wanted these guys to move quickly and produce a draft," said Roger Cubby, the volunteer on duty when I visited the restored Moore House. "He worried about British reinforcements possibly arriving from New York. And his nightmare was that they'd arrive and this thing would still be being negotiated."

* * *

"Go ahead, give it a push," Stull said. The staff ride had reached its final stop, Surrender Field, and while he joked that he was willing to keep talking—"I know you guys want to hear me narrate again"—he preferred to have someone hit the red button below a marker titled "Ground Your Firelocks!" so we could get the park's version. Looking out at an expanse of ordinary-seeming meadow, we heard a slow drumbeat as a man with a made-for-radio voice began to talk about October 19, 1781, when Cornwallis's army came here to lay down its arms.

The Articles of Capitulation were finished that morning and approved by Washington, who had trusted Laurens with the details but naturally retained the final say. Among the terms: British and German troops would march "to a place to be appointed" at 2 p.m. (in reality, they'd be an hour late) and would do so with no flags flying (Americans had been denied what were called "the honors of war" at Charleston, so British protests went nowhere). The commander in chief did agree to a key British demand: Cornwallis could use the sloop of war *Bonetta* to send dispatches to Clinton, and it could sail without being inspected. Why? Because as Jerome Greene explains, giving the enemy a way to ship some loyalists to New York "allowed Washington to retreat gracefully" from his earlier promise "to hang all deserters found in Yorktown."

October 19 was six and a half years to the day after some unknown person at Lexington fired the first shot of the war; after citizen-soldiers marched down a Concord hillside to the North Bridge; and after minute men and militia from all over northeastern Massachusetts converged on the Battle Road to drive the redcoats back to Boston. Now here came Cornwallis's troops down the road from Yorktown—with the French lined up on one side and the Americans on the other—unable to continue the fight.

"Some men bit their lips to hold back tears. Some were sobbing. Some had been drinking," the park narrator said. British bands played "melancholy marches."

Most Yorktown visitors think they know what song those men marched to. But the first suggestion that "The World Turned Upside Down" was on the surrender playlist came forty-seven years after the war, though numerous versions of the tune, with various lyrics, did exist in 1781. "Americans seized on the 'Upside Down' version," historian Thomas Fleming sensibly concluded, "because it so exactly fitted their view of the event."

Whatever those bands played, Cornwallis wasn't there to hear it.

Pleading illness, he had stayed away.

Was he shamming? There's no way to be sure, but here are two things we do know. First, some 1,500 of his long-suffering soldiers were wounded or sick enough to skip the ritual humiliation. Second, His Lordship was sufficiently healthy the next day to write a self-justifying dispatch to Clinton and accept a dinner invitation from the French.

And where was Sir Henry when the surrender took place? On his way! He and five thousand troops had sailed south from New York with the British fleet that very day. All the obstacles to their success remained, but no officer involved wanted to go down in history as the guy who wouldn't even *try* to rescue a trapped British army. It would be five days before they got their first hint of the bad news.

Yorktown was the Revolutionary War's last major confrontation involving Americans—but nobody knew that at the time. Washington didn't think the war was over, and he soon sent a few troops south to help Nathanael Greene. The captured British and Germans didn't think the war was over, and 30 percent of the British POWs would die before they could be exchanged. (As usual, the rank and file had it worse than the officers.) De Grasse didn't think the war was over, but despite pleas that he help take Charleston, he sailed back to fight in the Caribbean "without ever setting foot on American soil." True, when the Yorktown news reached London in late November, the prime minister is said to have exclaimed, "Oh God! it is all over!" multiple times. But George III thought otherwise, and it would be months before peace talks began and almost two years before a treaty ending the war was signed in Paris on September 3, 1783. And it would not be until November 25 of that year that British troops in New York sailed away and Washington, at long last, was able to reenter the city in triumph.

Weeks before, however, he had composed a lengthy farewell to his army. Written in the third person and coming in at about 1,600 words, it served many purposes both personal and public. For one thing, he left no doubt that his commander-in-chief gig was ending. ("The Curtain of seperation [*sic*] will soon be drawn—and the Military Scene to him will be closed for ever.") For another, he underlined his hard-earned belief that without a stronger central government—capable, though he didn't put it in so many words, of raising money to pay its debts and its army—the new nation could not survive.

In reading this document, though, I found myself drawn to the passages in which he looked backward—choosing to "indulge himself," as he wrote, "in calling to mind a slight review of the past."

He noted the "disadvantageous circumstances" in which the war began, and if you think back to when he took command in 1775, you'll see how understated that phrase is. He recalled the "singular interpositions of Providence" without specifying any, though Brooklyn's weather in August 1776 and the timely arrival of de Grasse's fleet five years later spring quickly to mind. He lauded "the unparalleled perseverence [*sic*] of the Armies of the United States, through almost every possible suffering and discouragement," which he judged "little short of a standing Miracle." And before he was done, he threw out a challenge to future historians and historical tourists:

Who "that was not on the spot," he asked rhetorically, "can trace the steps by which such a wonderful Revolution has been effected, and such a glorious period put to all our Warlike toils?"

Not me! I'm not here to argue with the Father of My Country about the American War of Independence!

Well, maybe just a little.

Because after at least trying to trace the steps of so many people who fought that war—with Washington, against him, or without him—I came to understand something he unquestionably knew. Which is that at any number of times and places, a different step could have taken our story down an unknowable path.

# "Let's Take a Ride"

The concept of a historical turning point, of course, can include steps not taken as well as those that were. With that in mind, looking briefly into the future of some characters in this story, it seems fitting to start with John Laurens.

Not long after Yorktown, Laurens went south with two goals. One was to fight under Greene and maybe get a last shot at the glory he craved. The other was to revive his plan to arm and free enslaved men. That plan still faced long odds, and its failure, early in 1782, would prove the opposite of a step forward: South Carolina legislators not only voted it down but endorsed a scheme by which white men who enlisted "would receive one slave for each year of duty."

As for that shot at glory...

Greene, like Washington, didn't think the war was over until it was over, so he kept the pressure on the British in Charleston. This included harassing their foraging parties, and in late August, when one such party sailed up the Combahee River, a feverish Laurens rose from his sickbed to help oppose it. Sent ahead of the main force with fifty men and orders to throw up a breastwork on a sand bluff, he ran into a stronger British detachment and, being John Laurens, attacked without waiting for help.

"Poor Laurens is fallen in a paltry little skirmish," Greene wrote. "This state will feel his loss; and his father will hardly survive it."

Hoping to see where he died, I found myself stumped. The exact site had not been pinned down (it has now) and in any case, it was on inaccessibly private land. Then I read *The Combahee River Raid*, about a far better known event during the Civil War, on the same part of the Combahee, in which Harriet Tubman helped Union troops free hundreds of enslaved people. Realizing that its author, local historian Jeff Grigg, must know the landscape of Laurens's death as well as anyone, I dropped in on him with too little notice.

"Let's take a ride," Grigg said. We got in his truck and headed down a dirt road.

He couldn't show me the skirmish site without permission. But he could show me something else—he wanted it to be a surprise—if I promised to keep the location to myself. I did. Pretty soon he parked and we walked into the woods, where I stared in amazement at the place John Laurens had first been laid to rest.

"He was buried right here, inside this small walled enclosure," Grigg said.

When Henry Laurens died in 1792, his will stipulated that his son's remains be moved to Mepkin and reinterred beside his own. But for ten years, they had lain right next to where we were standing.

I asked Grigg for a few minutes alone and thought about what might have been.

\* \* \*

Moving quickly through some other familiar names:

**Daniel Morgan** lived much longer than his 1781 health would suggest, dying in 1802 in Winchester, Virginia, and being buried there. Nearly 150 years later, a bunch of South Carolinians showed up with shovels, intent on moving his remains to Cowpens. They failed. "I wonder why Quebec doesn't put in a claim for him," said one sarcastic Morgan defender. "After all, he fought a battle there."

As an old man, **John Stark** was invited to a Battle of Bennington reunion. Writing to say he couldn't make it, he added the words "Live free, or die," which became New Hampshire's motto and still grace its license plates, which are made, as he might not be amused to learn, by inmates in the state's prison system.

**Benedict Arnold** sailed for England in December 1781. Shortly before Yorktown fell, he had amplified his reputation as a Traitorous Scumbag—no easy feat—with a raid on New London, Connecticut. Most notoriously, he had sent troops to storm nearby Fort Griswold, where the fighting "was as brutal as any in the war" and most of the garrison's casualties came after a botched attempt to surrender. In England, despite a cordial reception from George III, Arnold never again persuaded anyone to employ him as a soldier.

**Charles Lee**'s treason wasn't discovered until seventy-five years after he died. As a prisoner in 1777, he gave the British a plan for winning the war, justifying it, writes historian Christian McBurney, "as an effort to spare American blood." Reasonable people have bought Lee's argument. McBurney doesn't. I don't, either.

The postwar career of **Henry Knox** included serving as secretary of war and maneuvering to acquire more than a million acres of Maine land, some of which had been confiscated from Lucy's loyalist family. There, as an unsympathetic historian writes, he "courted financial disaster with heedless, ambitious investments in multiple, grandiose, ill-conceived, and poorly managed ventures." **Joseph Plumb Martin**, meanwhile, had been working a tiny portion of the same tract, treating it as a homestead. After Knox required settlers to purchase their lots, Martin begged, unsuccessfully, for extra time to pay. Losing his land, he scraped by on an $8 monthly pension awarded thirty-five years after he left the army.

**Henry Clinton**, as he'd feared, became the war's scapegoat, and he could do nothing to change this, despite spending the rest of his life trying. Alternative scapegoats **William Howe** and **John Burgoyne** were old news, and as for **Lord Cornwallis**, he might as well have been wearing red-coated Teflon. He was the only one of the four to have a notable postrebellion career, serving in top political and military capacities in India and Ireland and being honored, after his death, with an elegant Indian tomb in Ghazipur and a memorial in St. Paul's Cathedral.

"Tarleton's Last Fight," proclaims a marker four miles north of Yorktown, where the most hated man in the British Army briefly battled French troops. Back home, **Banastre Tarleton** changed from villain to hero, began a much-gossiped-about fifteen-year romance with actress Mary Robinson, and won election to Parliament, but was never offered combat command. A feud with the future victor of Waterloo didn't help. "Greene, Sumter, and Morgan may have injured him," one Tarleton biographer writes, "but it was the Duke of Wellington who finished him."

**Light Horse Harry Lee**'s war ended with a bad case of combat fatigue. He went on to serve in Congress and as governor of Virginia, but speculated disastrously in land and wrote his memoirs in debtor's prison. **Robert Morris** also succumbed to land fever, though on a vastly larger scale. He, too, ended up in debtor's prison and would be freed after more than three years, according to his biographer, only because "Congress passed the nation's first bankruptcy law" in 1800.

**The Marquis de Lafayette**'s stint in jail was longer and scarier. To sum up his role in the French Revolution in a sentence is a fool's errand, but here goes: Important in the early going, he tried to remain a moderate, was effectively condemned to die, fled the country, and wound up in an Austrian prison for five years. His wife's grandmother, mother, and sister were guillotined; Adrienne de Lafayette herself came very close. Three decades later, the marquis was invited to tour the United States. He spent more than a year doing so, drew adoring crowds in twenty-four states, and left his name all over the map.

**The Comte de Rochambeau** was arrested and scheduled to be guillotined, but narrowly avoided that fate. **Admiral d'Estaing** was not so fortunate. As for the man who saved the American Revolution by getting to the Chesapeake in time, **Admiral de Grasse** went on to lose a major Caribbean fight, the Battle of the Saintes, to none other than **Adm. George Rodney**, ensuring that Rodney's egregious screwups of the year before would be forgiven.

**Andrew Pebbles**, the free African American wounded three times while fighting under Greene at Eutaw Springs, also fought in the skirmish that killed John Laurens. Decades later, at the time he applied for a pension, his wife and child remained enslaved. **Henry Laurens**, after finally being released from the Tower, learned of his son's death in a letter from John Adams. In the same letter, Adams urged him to join the peace negotiations in Paris "as soon as possible." He did, and as historian Richard Morris writes, "managed to get a clause inserted forbidding the carrying off of Negroes or other property" by the British as they evacuated. **Guy Carleton**, however, who by 1783 had replaced Clinton as commander in chief, rejected as "dishonorable" the idea of betraying those who had trusted British promises of freedom. Among the thousands who sailed off to Nova Scotia as a result were **Harry Washington**, formerly enslaved at Mount Vernon, and **Thomas Peters**, who had run to the British near Wilmington. But Canada proved a nightmare for Black settlers, and to make an astonishing story short, Peters sailed to London, worked on arrangements to start a free Black colony in West Africa, then returned to Nova Scotia to help lead 1,200 African American refugees to Sierra Leone.

Among South Carolina's partisans, the Swamp Fox, **Francis Marion**, got his own Disney TV series; **Andrew Pickens** got the shaft, immortality-wise; and the Gamecock, **Thomas Sumter**, got his name on the fort where the Civil War began and his nickname on the University of South Carolina's athletic teams. Sumter is also remembered, by some, for Sumter's Law, under which men who signed up to serve under him were rewarded with enslaved men plundered from loyalists.

**Nathanael Greene**, three weeks before Yorktown fell, sent a plaintive letter to Knox. "We have been beating the bush and the General has come to catch the bird," he wrote. "The General is a most fortunate Man and may success and laurels attend him. We have fought frequently and bled freely, and little glory comes to our share." The rest of this justly admired general's story is shameful and sad. South Carolina and Georgia, grateful for his service, thanked him with the gift of confiscated plantations. Greene seized on these as a means to ensure both status and financial security. The idea made some northern friends unhappy—"Will you be a Planter with a Retinue of Slaves? Or will you come Northward to enjoy more Ease, but less Splendor?" one asked—but he went ahead and moved his family to Georgia, where a sudden illness killed him in 1786. He was forty-three years old.

\* \* \*

And George Washington? Well, on September 18, 1793, some months into his second term as president, he stood at the southeast corner of what's now the U.S. Capitol and presided over the ceremonial laying of its cornerstone. And that's all I'm going to say about the sixteen years between the end of the war and Washington's death in 1799. Because how presumptuous would it be, really, to try to evoke in a few paragraphs everything he accomplished, or didn't, as the independent nation he'd done so much to create took shape—largely under his guiding hand—during those years?

That said, if you walk into the Capitol Rotunda today and look straight up, you'll see him seated in the center of an 1865 fresco called *The Apotheosis of Washington*. He's surrounded by Roman gods and goddesses; by thirteen happy maidens representing the original states; and by myriad other figures, real or allegorical. A female Armed Freedom, sword in hand, defeats Tyranny and Kingly Power; Vulcan's forge produces a cannon and a steam engine; Minerva appears to be lecturing Benjamin Franklin; and Mercury, weirdly, hands Robert Morris a bag of cash.

"The word 'apotheosis' in the title means literally the raising of a person to the rank of a god, or the glorification of a person as an ideal," explains the Architect of the Capitol's website, and it's true that Washington, in life, seems to have wanted nothing more than historical immortality. Yet he knew he was human, understood both his talents and his flaws, which he worked strenuously to master, and fully realized—as we've seen, over and over—how narrow the line had been between triumph and defeat. I'd love to know what he would have thought and felt if he could have looked up at his image under that Capitol dome.

But then, being George Washington, he probably wouldn't have let on.

# Acknowledgments

One of the pleasures of writing what I call traveling history is the chance to meet so many people who are wonderfully generous with their time and knowledge. This is their book as well as mine, though all errors of fact or judgment are mine alone.

Specifically—and more or less in order of appearance—I want to thank Steve Rauch for his Cowpens staff ride and much more; J. L. Bell for his Powder Alarm walk and fantastic blog; and John Denis for his remarkable ability to separate what we know about April 19, 1775, from what we don't. Steve Clark, Kenny Wing, and the Arnold Expedition Historical Society opened my eyes to the epic they've worked to keep accessible. Barnet Schecter showed me where modern Brooklyn hides traces of a battle that could have ended the war. Al Frazza made himself into the best guide to revolutionary New Jersey you could ask for. Peter Paine, Gordy Hamilton, Pam Mellor, Jim Hughto, Larry Arnold, and Eric Schnitzer enriched the story of the Saratoga campaign in multiple ways, one of which was turning a false account of the final battle on its head.

James Kirby Martin made the pre-treason Benedict Arnold come to life. Michael Harris put Brandywine back in the center of the story. Bill Troppman disrupted conventional wisdom at Valley Forge. Stacy Flora Roth evoked the legendary Molly Pitcher and the real women on whom she was based. Mark Lender brilliantly reinterpreted the myths and politics of Monmouth. Christian McBurney shared his expertise on Charles Lee and the war in Rhode Island. Joe Becton, Algernon Ward, and M. T. Anderson, among many others, helped frame the complex, difficult history of African Americans and the war.

Bill Welsch contributed in more ways than I can count. To name just one, he connected me to Charles Baxley, David Reuwer, and Steve Rauch, who became key guides to the war in Georgia and the Carolinas. The late Michael Scoggins drew revealing parallels between Huck's Defeat and Kings Mountain. Jim Piecuch offered repeated, surprising insights into the southern story. Susan Seal pointed to "the room where it happened" in Hartsdale, New York, and to new information about the Washington-Rochambeau clash in August 1781. Jon Stull invited me on a Yorktown staff ride that allowed me to begin and end *Revolutionary Roads* with a kind of symmetry I never could have planned.

Bruce and Lynne Venter deserve a special shout-out for putting together the annual Conference of the American Revolution, which draws Revolutionary War obsessives of all stripes. The Society of the Cincinnati hosts relevant speakers within walking distance of my house, for which I'm grateful. And my heartfelt thanks go out to the many people encountered on my travels whose contributions I can't specify here. Among them are Larry Aaron, Ludger Balan, Barbara Bass, Carl Borick, Ann Brownlee, Ron Bruno, Nic Butler, Nancy Ceperley, Clay Craighead, Roger Cubby, Chris Davalos, Richard Fisher, Bob Furman, Jeff Grigg, Jason Howell, Teri Jobe, Richard Joly, Willem Lange, Sam Leary, Ed Lengel, Wayne Lynch, John Maass, Charles Macdonough, David Martin, Christine Mitchell, Jane Morse, Lou Mosier, John Murray, Lin Olsen, Paul O'Shaughnessy, Drew Ruddy, Robert Scordia, Tom Spierto, Dael Sumner, Jahzeer Terrell, Carole Troxler, Fred Wallace, Maggie Weber, and Joe Zellner.

For their longtime friendship—not to mention their guest rooms in revolutionary hot spots, occupied at length—I owe a huge debt to Patrice Moskow, Gordon Saperia, Paula Span, Judy Thoms, and the much missed John Thoms. Less tangible but no less important support came from Glenn Frankel, Cynthia Gorney, Bill Sokol, Peter Carlson, Chris Motley, Beth Horowitz, Michael Kazin, Ann Karalekas, Jud Harward, and many more, including a beloved group of college friends who gathered remotely each week throughout the pandemic. Blessings on you all.

My agent, Bob Mecoy, and my editor, Sean Desmond, once again got behind an unconventional venture in historical storytelling. If I owned a tricorn hat, I'd tip it to them for their guidance, skill, and patience. Many thanks, as well, to Zohar Karimy, Carolyn Kurek, Jim Datz, Mark Steven Long, and the rest of the team at Twelve and Hachette—and to my nephew, Pete Thompson, for the author photo.

My father, Will Thompson, earned a Purple Heart fighting in Italy with the Tenth Mountain Division. I kept it pinned to my bulletin board as I wrote. Shot in the foot by a sniper after guiding medics to the front, he played dead for a while, then hopped on one leg over a ridge to safety. As a lifelong mountaineer, he was proud of being in good enough shape to do that hopping. I wish he were around to read this book.

It remains true, as I wrote in my previous book, that Lizzie Thompson and Mona Thompson are the best possible daughters a father could have. Their mother, Deborah Johnson, is—understatement alert—the person most responsible for seeing this new one through to the end. There's really no good way to thank someone who has been your first reader, second reader, third reader, biggest supporter, best critic, and most frequent technical adviser, along with spending way too many dinners across the table from a guy who had no conversational topic beyond whatever historical rabbit hole he'd gone down that day.

Let me try, though. I will love her forever.

# Notes

**Abbreviations Used**

*FO*: Founders Online
https://founders.archives.gov/
*FO/EAD*: Founders Online Early Access Document
https://founders.archives.gov/about/EarlyAccess

\* \* \*

## INTRODUCTION: "Something Different Is Going to Happen"

PAGE

7     *"the roar of musketry"*: John Buchanan, *The Road to Guilford Courthouse* (New York: John Wiley & Sons, 1997), 324.

## CHAPTER 1: "You'll Have Noise Enough Before Long"

PAGE

14     *"the first American Revolution"*: Ray Raphael, *The First American Revolution* (New York: The New Press, 2002).

14     *"at every house"*: Quoted in J. L. Bell, *The Road to Concord* (Yardley, PA: Westholme, 2016), 18.

17     *"a dangerous playground"*: Adamg, "South End Park Will No Longer Do the Wave," Universal Hub, May 11, 2018 (https://www.universalhub.com/2018/south-end-park-will-no-longer-do-wave).

18     *"great joiner"*: David Hackett Fischer, *Paul Revere's Ride* (New York: Oxford University Press, 1994), 27.

18     *"knew everyone"*: Ibid.

18     *"link one group"*: Ibid.

18     *"supremely good"*: Ibid.

20     *"a call to arms"*: Ibid., 331.

20     *"that one man alone"*: Ibid.

22     ***"the British troops":*** "Letter of Elizabeth Clarke: 19 April 1841," courtesy of
       Lexington Historical Society.
22     ***"wringing her hands":*** Ibid.
22     ***"Dolly going round":*** Ibid.

## CHAPTER 2: The Grassy Knoll of the Revolution

PAGE

27     ***"Lay down your arms":*** Deposition of Thomas Price Willard, April 23, 1775,
       quoted in Harold Murdock, *The Nineteenth of April 1775* (Boston: Houghton
       Mifflin, 1925), 33.
28     ***"a stout, large framed man":*** Theodore Parker, *Genealogy and Biographical
       Notes of John Parker of Lexington and His Descendants* (Worcester, MA: Press of
       Charles Hamilton, 1893), 81.
32     ***"Fire, for God's sake":*** Douglas P. Sabin, *April 19, 1775: A Historiographi-
       cal Study* (Concord, MA: Minute Man National Historical Park, 1987), Part
       III, 44.
37     ***"such an incessant fire":*** Ibid., Part VI, 11.
37     ***"within a mile":*** Ibid., Part VI, 12.

## CHAPTER 3: "A Middle Finger Raised to the Powers That Be"

PAGE

43     ***"rabble in arms":*** John Burgoyne to Lord Rochfort, quoted in Edward Bar-
       rington de Fonblanque, *Political and Military Episodes in the Latter Half of the
       Eighteenth Century* (London: Macmillan, 1876), 142.
44     ***"looping":*** J. Anthony Lukas, *Common Ground* (New York: Vintage Books,
       1986), 144.
44     ***"up the long slope":*** Ibid.
45     ***"Looping was an initiation rite":*** Ibid.
45     ***"The Danger we were in":*** Peter Brown to his mother, June 28, 1775, in *The
       Literary Diary of Ezra Stiles* (New York: Charles Scribner's Sons, 1901), Vol. 1,
       595.
45     ***"Hit me if you can":*** Quoted in Nathaniel Philbrick, *Bunker Hill* (New York:
       Penguin Books, 2014), 201.
45     ***"a kind of wood-and-grass sandwich":*** Ibid., 211.
47     ***"the worn, dirty, shirt-sleeved":*** Richard M. Ketchum, *The Battle for Bunker
       Hill* (Garden City, NY: Doubleday, 1962), 106.
47     ***"assault the redoubt":*** Allen French, *The Siege of Boston* (New York: Macmil-
       lan, 1911), 259.
48     ***"until they could see the enemy's half gaiters":*** James Wilkinson, "A Rapid
       Sketch of the Battle of Breed's Hill," in Charles Coffin, compiler, *History of the
       Battle of Breed's Hill* (Portland, ME: D. C. Colesworthy, 1835), 12.
48     ***"quite alone":*** Quoted in Philbrick, *Bunker Hill*, 224.
48     ***"we gave them such a hot fire":*** William Prescott letter to John Adams,
       August 25, 1775, Massachusetts Historical Society.

48  **"great pyramids of fire":** John Burgoyne, quoted in Ketchum, *Bunker Hill*, 118.

50  **"a sight too dreadful":** John Waller letter to a friend, June 21, 1775, Massachusetts Historical Society (https://www.masshist.org/bh/waller.html).

51  **"too dearly bought":** Quoted in Philbrick, *Bunker Hill*, 230.

## CHAPTER 4: "The Difference Between Life and a Frozen Death"

PAGE

54  **"check the AEHS website":** Arnold Expedition Historical Society (https://arnoldsmarch.org/audio-booth/).

55  **"scarcely any personal":** Don Higginbotham, *Daniel Morgan: Revolutionary Rifleman* (Chapel Hill: University of North Carolina Press, 1961), 1.

55  **"sixty crudely built dwellings":** Ibid.

56  **"nothing but wrecks":** Kenneth Roberts, ed., *March to Quebec: Journals of the Members of Arnold's Expedition* (Garden City, NY: Doubleday, 1953), 202.

56  **"mountains begin to appear":** Ibid., 49.

59  **"8 feet perpendicular":** Ibid., 54.

59  **"wandering West Indian hurricane":** Ibid.

60  **"fifteen days' provisions":** Stephen Clark, *Following Their Footsteps* (Scarborough, ME: Clark Books, 2003), 68.

61  **"so small that the men":** Ibid., 75.

61  **"the difference between":** Ibid.

61  **"They ate every part":** Quoted in Thomas A. Desjardin, *Through a Howling Wilderness* (New York: St. Martin's Griffin, 2006), 99.

61  **"a vision of horned cattle":** Roberts, *March to Quebec*, 219.

63  **"to these arguments":** Quoted in James Kirby Martin, *Benedict Arnold: Revolutionary Hero* (New York: New York University Press, 1997), 177.

64  **"scenarios and outcomes":** Clark, 102.

## CHAPTER 5: "Are You Here for the Knox Marker?"

PAGE

66  **"a deadly serious—if somewhat awkward":** Peter Henriques, *Realistic Visionary* (Charlottesville: University of Virginia Press, 2006), 71.

67  **"If Washington had been killed":** David Preston, Society of the Cincinnati lecture, June 15, 2016.

68  **"far from seeking this appointment":** George Washington to Martha Washington, June 18, 1775, *FO*.

68  **"trouble acknowledging":** Joseph Ellis, *His Excellency* (New York: Vintage Books, 2005), 70.

68  **"an essential fabrication":** Ibid., 70–71.

68  **"a trust too great":** George Washington to Martha Washington, June 18, 1775, *FO*.

68  **"that I this day declare":** Washington, "Address to the Continental Congress," June 16, 1775, *FO*.

71  **"large and very elegant":** Advertisement quoted in North Callahan, *Henry Knox: George Washington's General* (New York: Rinehart, 1958), 20.

72  **"the silken lining":** Ibid., 31.

74  **"I christen thee Ticonderoga":** Ticonderoga Historical Society blog post, January 18, 2015 (https://www.tihistory.org/post/in-harm-s-way).

74  **"Stephanie Pell, what have you done?":** Ibid.

74  **"an exceedingly good fire":** Quoted in Wm. L. Bowne, *Ye Cohorn Caravan* (Schuylerville, NY: NaPaul Publishers, 1975), 21.

75  **"a cruel thaw":** Ibid., 42.

75  **"trembl'd for the Consequences":** Ibid., 46.

75  **"by flooding it":** Callahan, 48.

76  **"the good people":** Bowne, 56.

76  **"We are now without":** Washington to Joseph Reed, January 14, 1776, *FO*.

76–77 **"I have often thought":** Ibid.

77  **"improper"… "impracticable"… "too great a Risque":** Minutes of Washington's meeting with his generals, October 18, 1775, quoted in J. L. Bell, *Longfellow House-Washington's Headquarters National Historic Site Historic Resource Study*, 346.

78  **"ominous confusion of mountains":** Callahan, 51.

78  **"arranged for two span":** Bowne, 65.

78  **"A novelist would fill":** Edward G. Lengel, *General George Washington: A Military Life* (New York: Random House, 2005), 119.

78  **"The officers had considered":** Ibid.

78  **"overestimated the capabilities":** Ibid., 120.

78  **"or had ever fired a shot in anger":** Ibid.

78  **"fixed positions":** Ibid., 121.

79  **"sufficient to defend them":** Quoted in Bell, *Historic Resource Study*, 579.

80  **"the honor of the troops":** Quoted in David McCullough, *1776* (New York: Simon & Schuster, 2005), 96.

80  **"the first great strategic success":** Text of National Park Service marker on Dorchester Heights tower.

80  **"seemed to be succeeding":** Washington to Landon Carter, March 27, 1776, quoted in Bell, *Historic Resource Study*, 592.

80  **"remarkable Interposition":** Ibid.

81  **"arrived too late":** Ibid., 595.

## CHAPTER 6: Toward the Gap in That Brooklyn Ridge

PAGE

84  **"The British saw New York as the key":** Barnet Schecter, *The Battle for New York* (New York: Walker, 2002), 2.

84  **"secured one end of the Hudson":** Ibid.

84  **"the largest expeditionary force":** Ibid., 3.

85  **"appearance of riot":** Washington's General Orders, July 10, 1776, *FO*.

85  **"be executed by the proper authority":** Ibid.

85    *"advisable"*: Council of War, July 12, 1776, *FO*.

85    *"lacked even a small hard core"*: James Kirby Martin and Mark Edward Lender, *"A Respectable Army,"* 3rd ed. (New York: Wiley-Blackwell, 2015), 54.

90    *"things had gotten kind of quiet"*: Green-Wood Cemetery historian Jeff Richman, co-leading a tour.

91    *"on what appeared to be"*: Schecter, 150.

91    *"Neither he nor anyone else"*: Paul David Nelson, *William Alexander, Lord Stirling* (Tuscaloosa: University of Alabama Press, 1987), quoted in Schecter, 150.

92    *"one of the nation's"*: EPA Superfund website (https://cumulis.epa.gov/supercpad /SiteProfiles/index.cfm?fuseaction=second.Cleanup&id=0206222#bkground).

94    *"probably would have surrounded"*: Schecter, 154.

94    *"it required repeated orders"*: Quoted in McCullough, 178.

94    *"little inclination to check the ardor"*: Ibid.

95    *"in Howe's position, he, too"*: Ibid., 195.

95    *"risk the loss"*: Quoted in Schecter, 148.

95    *"at a very cheap rate"*: Ibid.

96    *"shipyards and ropewalks"*: Author interview with Barnet Schecter.

97    *"not to speak, or even cough"*: Joseph Plumb Martin memoir, quoted in Schecter, 161.

98    *"I am afraid you have ruined us"*: Quoted in McCullough, 190.

98    *"a very dense fog"*: Quoted in Schecter, 165.

98    *"I think I saw Gen. Washington"*: Ibid.

99    *"Take the walls!...Take the cornfield!"*: Ibid., 185.

99    *"So many stories"*: Lengel, 153–4.

100    *"heart and soul"*: Amy L. Cohn, ed., *From Sea to Shining Sea* (New York: Scholastic, 1993), 68.

100    *"Nothing will give me greater pleasure"*: Ibid., 70.

100    *"a romantic story"*: McCullough, 216.

100    *"an amusing but probably spurious legend"*: Lengel, 154.

100    *"even in the unlikely case"*: Schecter, 190.

100    *"written into Clinton's orders"*: Ibid.

100    *"great numbers of the enemy"*: Quoted in Schecter, 184.

100    *"He who fights and retreats"*: Cohn, 73.

101    *"smart skirmishes"*: Washington to Nicholas Cooke, September 17, 1776, *FO*.

103    *"staggered intervals"*: George Athan Billias, *General John Glover and His Marblehead Mariners* (New York: Holt, Rinehart and Winston, 1960), 116.

103    *"No professional soldier"*: Ibid.

103    *"looked like a half-ruined sand castle"*: Lengel, 164.

104    *"It is said so completely to have overcome him"*: Washington Irving, *Life of George Washington* (New York: G. P. Putnam, 1859), Vol. 2, 398.

## CHAPTER 7: Where the Hell Was Charles Lee?

PAGE

106 *"Never did I need"*: Quoted in Terry Golway, *Washington's General* (New York: Henry Holt, 2006), 103.

107 *"if they had only hurled stones"*: Quoted in Arthur S. Lefkowitz, *The Long Retreat* (New Brunswick, NJ: Rutgers University Press, 1999), 46.

110 *"an ingenious worthy young man"*: Quoted in David Freeman Hawke, *Paine* (New York: W. W. Norton, 1974), 20.

110 *"clerk, or assistant tutor"*: Ibid.

110 *"These are the times that try men's souls"*: Thomas Paine, *The American Crisis* (https://www.loc.gov/resource/cph.3b06889/).

111 *"most miserable of his wretched days"*: Douglas Southall Freeman, *George Washington*, Vol. 4, *Leader of the Revolution* (New York: Charles Scribner & Sons, 1951), 271.

111 *"that rarity in any age"*: John Shy, *A People Numerous and Armed* (Ann Arbor: University of Michigan Press, 1990), 138.

112 *"remarkable for his slovenly"*: Ibid., 135.

112 *"would say almost anything"*: Ibid.

112 *"almost naked"*: Quoted in Lefkowitz, 85.

112 *"fatal indecision of mind"*: Charles Lee to Joseph Reed, November 24, 1776, quoted in Lefkowitz, 91.

113 *"we had not 3,000 men"*: Greene to Nicholas Cooke, December 4, 1776, quoted in Christian McBurney, *George Washington's Nemesis* (El Dorado Hills, CA: Savas Beatie, 2020), 45.

113 *"in the best Order"*: Washington to Richard Humpton, December 1, 1776, *FO*.

113 *"most expeditious Manner"*: Ibid.

114 *"remain in a peaceable obedience"*: November 30, 1776, proclamation by the Howe brothers (London: *Annual Register,* 1777), 294–96.

115 *"to watch the Motions of the Enemy"*: Washington to John Hancock, December 3, 1776, *FO*.

115 *"such Troops as are here fit"*: Washington to Hancock, December 5, 1776, *FO*.

116 *"doubted himself"*: Lefkowitz, 111.

116 *"open controversy"*: Ibid.

116 *"There is no way to tell for certain"*: Ibid., 130.

117 *"An old Woman upon her Knees"*: Banastre Tarleton to his mother, December 18, 1776, quoted in Robert D. Bass, *The Green Dragoon* (Orangeburg, SC: Sandlapper Publishing, 1973), 20–22.

117 *"the only rebel general"*: Quoted in William M. Dwyer, *The Day Is Ours* (New Brunswick, NJ: Rutgers University Press, 1998), 150.

118 *"immediately march into Quarters"*: Quoted in Christopher Ward, *The War of the Revolution* (New York: Macmillan, 1952), Vol. 1, 291.

118 *"It is now very unsafe"*: Quoted in David Hackett Fischer, *Washington's Crossing* (New York: Oxford University Press, 2004), 179.

119 *"we may yet effect"*: Washington to Horatio Gates, December 14, 1776, *FO*.

## CHAPTER 8: The Battle of the Rusty Pole

PAGE

121 *"remains conjectural"*: John Ferling, *Almost a Miracle* (New York: Oxford University Press, 2007), 169.

122 *"the Speedy Inlistment"*: George Washington to Lund Washington, December 17, 1776, *FO*.

122 *"would have been sitting in ice water"*: Fischer, *Washington's Crossing*, 216.

123 *"small icebergs"*: Text of marker at Washington Crossing Historic Park.

124 *"rained, hailed, snowed, and froze"*: Quoted in Fischer, *Washington's Crossing*, 212.

124 *"forgot to mention sleet"*: Fischer, *Washington's Crossing*, 212.

124 *"so benumbed with cold"*: Quoted in Fischer, *Washington's Crossing*, 228.

126 *"through dense clouds"*: Fischer, *Washington's Crossing*, 235.

126 *"the only major offensive action"*: Ferling, *Miracle*, 175.

129 *"an incorrect bit of local lore"*: Al Frazza, Revolutionary War New Jersey (https://www.revolutionarywarnewjersey.com/new_jersey_revolutionary _war_sites/towns/passaic_nj_revolutionary_war_sites.htm).

131 *"about 2,600"*: Fischer, *Washington's Crossing*, 274.

132 *"unaccountably left his post"*: Bicentennial edition of Mark Mayo Boatner III, *Encyclopedia of the American Revolution* (New York: David McKay, 1974), 366.

132 *"We met them, and opened our ranks"*: Quoted in Edwin Martin Stone, *The Life and Recollections of John Howland* (Providence, RI: G. H. Whitney, 1857), 73.

132 *"On one hour, yes, on forty minutes"*: Ibid., 74.

133 *"unless a miracle intervened"*: Ibid.

133 *"with interlocking fields of fire"*: Fischer, *Washington's Crossing*, 302.

133 *"The enemy came on"*: Quoted in Fischer, *Washington's Crossing*, 306.

133 *"We loaded with canister shot"*: Ibid., 306–307.

133 *"was the heaviest"*: Jac Weller, "Guns of Destiny," *Military Affairs*, Vol. 20, No. 1 (Spring 1956), 2.

133 *"We've got the Old Fox safe now"*: Quoted in Fischer, *Washington's Crossing*, 313.

134 *"The situation was strong to be sure"*: Henry Knox to Lucy Knox, January 7, 1777, in Philip Hamilton, *The Revolutionary War Letters of Lucy and Henry Knox* (Baltimore: Johns Hopkins University Press, 2017), 69.

134 *"it would avoid the appearance of a retreat"*: Washington to Hancock, January 5, 1777, *FO*.

135 *"by a single hair with a thousand deaths flying all around him"*: Extract of letter from James Read to his wife, *Pennsylvania Magazine of History and Biography*, Vol. 16, No. 4 (January 1893), 466.

135 *"curiosity-driven basic research"*: Institute for Advanced Study website (https://www.ias.edu/about/mission-history).

135 *"as central to the Battle of Princeton"*: Letter to the National Trust for Historic Preservation, quoted in *Philadelphia Inquirer*, September 1, 2016.

136 *"intense and accurate fire"*: Text of marker at Princeton Battlefield State Park.

136   ***"just enough time"***: Richard M. Ketchum, *The Winter Soldiers* (New York: Henry Holt, 1999), 307

136   ***"If they had known"***: *Diary of Captain Thomas Rodney, 1776–1777* (Wilmington, DE: Historical Society of Delaware, 1888), 36.

## CHAPTER 9: "It Was One Afternoon in August—But It Made a Difference"

PAGE

137   ***"complex man of modest talent"***: Sylvia R. Frey reviewing Richard J. Hargrove Jr.'s *General John Burgoyne* in *William and Mary Quarterly*, Vol. 40, No. 4 (October 1983), 640.

139   ***"give stretch to the Indian forces"***: Quoted in John F. Luzader, *Saratoga* (New York: Savas Beatie, 2008), 42.

140   ***"We are dayly insulted"***: Benedict Arnold to Washington, July 27, 1777, *FO*.

140   ***"in the most shocking Manner"***: Ibid.

140   ***"we should then be in a Condition"***: Ibid.

140   ***"broken and disheartened"***: Commissioners to Canada report to John Hancock from Montreal, May 27, 1776, quoted in Richard M. Ketchum, *Saratoga* (New York: Henry Holt, 1999), 36.

140   ***"could not see, speak, or walk"***: Quoted in James Kirby Martin, "The Northern Theater," in James Kirby Martin and David L. Preston, eds., *Theaters of the American Revolution* (Yardley, PA: Westholme, 2017), 20.

142   ***"come around, and work their way"***: James L. Nelson, *Benedict Arnold's Navy* (Camden, ME: McGraw-Hill, 2006), 296.

142   ***"The object of this fleet"***: Kenneth Roberts, *Rabble in Arms* (Camden, ME: Down East Books, 1996), 279.

143   ***"he had no choice"***: Paul David Nelson, "Guy Carleton Versus Benedict Arnold: The Campaign of 1776 in Canada and on Lake Champlain," in *New York History*, Vol. 57, No. 3 (July 1976), 355.

145   ***"was said to have run into the boudoir"***: Andrew Jackson O'Shaughnessy, *The Men Who Lost America* (New Haven, CT: Yale University Press, 2013), 148.

145   ***"a mere wagon track"***: Hoffman Nickerson, *The Turning Point of the Revolution* (Boston: Houghton Mifflin, 1928), 147.

146   ***"saved the northern Continental army"***: Bruce M. Venter, *The Battle of Hubbardton* (Charleston, SC: The History Press, 2015), 8.

147   ***"with a tenacity that"***: William B. Willcox, *Portrait of a General* (New York: Alfred A. Knopf, 1964), 156.

147   ***"would swallow the army"*** ... ***"had no prospect"*** ... ***"to make contact"*** ... ***"impale Washington"*** ... ***"abandoning"***: Ibid., 154. Quotations are from Willcox's summary of Clinton's argument, not directly from Clinton himself.

147   ***"he would have reached"***: Luzader, 73.

151   ***"and hung onto him"***: Barbara Graymont, in *Dictionary of Canadian Biography*, Vol. 4.

151     *"with intelligence, ability":* Ibid.

151     *"as near to a lecture":* Isabel Thompson Kelsay, *Joseph Brant* (Syracuse, NY: Syracuse University Press, 1984), 173.

155     *"application of psychological warfare":* Luzader, 138.

156     *"contentious, suspicious, opinionated":* Ibid., 98.

157     *"the most difficult tactic available":* Ibid., 105.

157     *"With one hour more of daylight":* John Stark, private letter to Horatio Gates, first draft, quoted in Caleb Stark, *Memoirs and Official Correspondence of Gen. John Stark* (Concord, NH: Edison C. Eastman, 1877), 131.

## CHAPTER 10: The Accidental Battle That Won the Revolution

PAGE

166     *"Matters were altercated":* Quoted in Luzader, 260.

167     *"He's a confrontational person":* Author interview with James Kirby Martin.

167     *"Calm down! You can't personalize":* Ibid.

171     *"came closer to bringing about":* Roberts, *Rabble,* 528.

175     *"to begin the game":* James Wilkinson, *Memoirs of My Own Times* (Philadelphia: Abraham Small, 1816), Vol. 1, 268.

175     *"betraying great agitation":* Ibid., 273.

175     *"was observed to drink freely":* Ibid.

175     *"on the field of battle":* Ibid.

## CHAPTER 11: "We Didn't Mean *You*, Mr. Marquis!"

PAGE

177     *"The British had killed his dad":* Sarah Vowell on *The Daily Show,* July 2, 2015.

178     *"a young Nobleman of great Family Connections":* Benjamin Franklin and Silas Deane to Congress's Committee of Secret Correspondence, May 25, 1777, in Stanley J. Idzerda, ed., *Lafayette in the Age of the American Revolution: Selected Letters and Papers 1776–1790* (Ithaca, NY: Cornell University Press, 1977), Vol. 1, 51.

178     *"to ask my commands":* Quoted in Harlow Giles Unger, *Lafayette* (Hoboken, NJ: John Wiley & Sons, 2002), 32.

179     *"Some of us were wearing":* Idzerda, Vol. 1, 73.

179     *"In America":* Ibid., 61.

179     *"a bit fatiguing":* Ibid., 66.

179     *"Ticonderoga, the strongest post":* Ibid., 67.

180     *"his zeal, illustrious family and connexions":* Ibid., 88.

180     *"I know no more than the Child unborn":* Washington to Benjamin Harrison, August 19, 1777, *FO.*

188     *"it would be unmilitary to leave a castle":* Quoted in Michael C. Harris, *Germantown* (El Dorado Hills, CA: Savas Beatie, 2020), 328.

## CHAPTER 12: The Continental Army Does the Wave

PAGE

191 *"Nothing at all":* Joseph Plumb Martin, *Ordinary Courage*, edited by James Kirby Martin, 4th ed. *(New York:* Wiley-Blackwell, 2013), 2.

191 *"hardships sufficient to kill":* Ibid., 56.

191 *"half of a small pumpkin":* Ibid., 68.

191 *"imbecility":* Ibid., 121.

191 *"had little tolerance for any romanticizing":* Introductory notes by James Kirby Martin in *Ordinary Courage*, xvii.

191 *"how few patriots":* Ibid., xviii.

192 *"No body ever heard of a quarter Master":* Nathanael Greene to Washington, April 24, 1779, *FO.*

193 *"the United States could not afford":* Stuart Leibiger, "George Washington and Lafayette," in Robert M. S. McDonald, ed., *Sons of the Father* (Charlottesville: University of Virginia Press, 2013), 215.

193 *"lose no Time":* Gates to Lafayette, January 24, 1778, in Idzerda, Vol. 1, 249.

193 *"a terrifying task":* Ibid., 275.

194 *"Why am I so far from you"… "I schall be laughed at":* Ibid., 299–301.

195 *"administrative coup":* Mark Edward Lender, *Cabal!* (Yardley, PA: Westholme, 2019), xvii.

195 *"They sought control":* Ibid.

196 *"turnstile problem":* Joseph J. Ellis, *American Creation* (New York: Alfred A. Knopf, 2007), 69.

197 *"near victory":* Orville T. Murphy, "The Battle of Germantown and the Franco American Alliance of 1778," in *Pennsylvania Magazine of History and Biography*, Vol. 82, No. 1 (January 1958), 59.

197 *"Vergennes had already decided":* Larrie D. Ferreiro, *Brothers at Arms* (New York: Alfred A. Knopf, 2016), 99.

198 *"mix" and "mingle":* O'Shaughnessy, 210.

198 *"in gauze turbans":* Ibid., 208.

198 *"at full gallop, each shivering his spear":* Morris Bishop, "You Are Invited to a Mischianza," *American Heritage*, Vol. 25, No. 5 (August 1974), 69–75.

199 *"twenty-four black slaves":* O'Shaughnessy, 209.

199 *"We halted here":* Martin, *Ordinary Courage*, 78.

199 *"trusty and intelligent spies":* Washington to Lafayette, May 18, 1778, *FO.*

199 *"a very valuable one":* Ibid.

199 *"use every possible precaution":* Ibid.

203 *"the accumulation of unanticipated":* Mark Edward Lender and Gary Wheeler Stone, *Fatal Sunday* (Norman: University of Oklahoma Press, 2016), 234.

203 *"Sir, sir":* Ibid., 289.

204 *"most famous female warrior":* David G. Martin, *A Molly Pitcher Sourcebook* (Hightstown, NJ: Longstreet House, 2003), v.

206 *"part of the folklore of the Revolution":* Lender and Stone, 290.

206 *"damned poltroon":* Quoted in ibid., 290.

206 *"till the leaves shook on the trees":* Ibid.

207 *"one of the last to leave the field":* Quoted in ibid., 293.

208 *"forced the Enemy from the Field":* Quoted in ibid., 383.

208 *"the Americans responded with brilliant military theater":* Lender and Stone, 383.

208 *"defensive and from cover":* Ibid., 406.

208 *"I was fortunate enough":* Quoted in Paul Lockhart, *The Drillmaster of Valley Forge* (New York: HarperCollins, 2008), 167.

209 *"the largest Revolutionary War battle":* Text of marker in Heritage Park, Portsmouth, RI.

210 *"predominantly blacks and Indians":* Text of marker in Patriots Park, Portsmouth, RI.

## CHAPTER 13: "Which Side Would You Join?"

PAGE

216 *"destined to be quoted far and wide":* Benjamin Quarles, *The Negro in the American Revolution* (Chapel Hill: University of North Carolina Press, 1996), 19.

216 *"I do hereby further declare":* Ibid.

216 *"If my Dear Sir":* Washington to Richard Henry Lee, December 26, 1775, *FO.*

216 *"the time-honored penalty":* Quarles, 25.

216 *"taken in arms":* Ibid.

217 *"When Patrick Henry":* Charles W. Carey Jr., "Lord Dunmore's Ethiopian Regiment" (master's thesis, Virginia Polytechnic Institute and State University, 1995), 82.

221 *"I then saw the horrors":* Richard Kidder Meade to Theodoric Bland Jr., December 18, 1775, in *The Bland Papers* (Petersburg, VA: E. & J. C. Ruffin, 1840), Vol. 1, 39.

221 *"as if they wore bulls-eyes":* Carey, 56.

222 *"brought together in one place":* Elizabeth A. Fenn, *Pox Americana* (New York: Hill and Wang, 2001), 57–58.

222 *"without a shovelful of earth":* Quoted in Fenn, 60.

223 *"a successful cartage and livery stable business":* Norman Fuss, "Billy Flora at the Battle of Great Bridge," *Journal of the American Revolution*, October 14, 2014.

223 *"Sometime after 1782":* Ibid.

223 *"stroller, negro, or vagabond":* Quoted in Quarles, 15.

223 *"Negroes excepted":* Ibid.

223 *"sympathetic":* Quarles, 15.

223 *"about 5,000":* Gary B. Nash, introduction to 1996 edition of Quarles, xix and xxi.

224 *"up to his neck":* Henry David Thoreau, *The Journal: 1837–1861* (New York: NYRB Classics, 2009), February 18, 1858, entry.

224   *"Used to say that he went home":* Ibid.

224   *"Lived to be old":* Ibid.

224   *"unearth and share the stories":* Robbins House website (https://robbinshouse
      .org/about/).

225   *"Every once in a while a piece of scholarship":* Alfred F. Young, preface to
      George Quintal Jr., *Patriots of Color* (Boston: Boston National Historical Park,
      2004).

225   *"a strange panic":* J. H. Temple, *History of Framingham, Massachusetts* (Fram-
      ingham, MA: Town of Framingham, 1887), 275.

226   *"most widely accepted interpretation":* Mitch Kachun, *First Martyr of Lib-
      erty* (New York: Oxford University Press, 2017), 3.

226   *"a large man, over six feet":* Ibid.

226   *"mixed African and Native American":* Ibid.

226   *"probably served at the most battles":* Quintal, 44.

226   *"like an Experienced officer":* Quoted in J. L. Bell, *Boston 1775* blog post,
      February 12, 2009.

226   *"absolutely extraordinary":* J. L. Bell, *Boston 1775*, ibid.

227   *"of gigantic stature":* Quoted in Quintal, 146.

227   *"a complete band":* Quoted in Quintal, 151.

228   *"could not have failed to observe":* Gregory D. Massey, *John Laurens and
      the American Revolution* (Columbia: University of South Carolina Press,
      2015), 120.

228   *"able-bodied Slaves":* John Laurens to Henry Laurens, January 14, 1778,
      quoted in Massey, 93.

228   *"instead of leaving":* Ibid.

228   *"unjustly deprived of the Rights of Mankind":* Ibid.

230   *"a person cannot be culpable":* Edward Ball, *Slaves in the Family* (New York:
      Farrar, Straus and Giroux, 1998), 14.

230   *"the slave business was a crime":* Ibid.

230   *"called on to try to explain it":* Ibid.

230   *"brought sixty-one slave galleys":* Ibid., 190.

230   *"£156,000, enough to make them":* Ibid., 191.

230   *"pest house":* Ibid., 89.

230   *"Just imported":* Quoted in Ball, 192.

230   *"a most scabby flock":* Ibid., 193.

230   *"refuse Negro":* Ibid, 192.

230   *"Laurens would continue":* Ibid., 194.

230   *"did not flinch":* Judith L. Van Buskirk, *Standing in Their Own Light* (Nor-
      man: University of Oklahoma Press, 2017), 150.

231   *"I abhor Slavery":* Henry Laurens to John Laurens, August 14, 1776, quoted
      in Gabriel Neville, "The Tragedy of Henry Laurens," *Journal of the American
      Revolution*, August 1, 2019.

231   *"the entail of Slavery":* Quoted in Jack Rakove, *Revolutionaries* (New York:
      Houghton Mifflin Harcourt, 2010), 215.

231   *"the hereditary transfer of slave status":* Rakove, 215.

231  *"I know you Love me":* Quoted in Massey, 21.

231  *"there is no Man I hope":* Quoted in Rakove, 213.

231  *"more important Engagements":* Quoted in Massey, 68.

231  *"It was not his fault":* Quoted in Massey, 75.

232  *"Their job":* Eleanor Porter, *Life of Laurens*, video (https://thelittlelionofvalleyforge .tumblr.com/post/177919416251/life-of-laurens).

232  *"cannot contend":* Quoted in Massey, 63.

232  *"Without Slaves how is it possible":* John Laurens to Henry Laurens, October 26, 1776, in *South Carolina Historical and Genealogical Magazine*, Vol. 5, No. 4 (October 1904), 206.

232  *"coincides exactly with my Feelings":* Ibid., 204.

232  *"I am not the man who enslaved them":* Quoted in Rakove, 215.

232  *"I was born in a Country":* Quoted in Neville, "The Tragedy of Henry Laurens."

232  *"In former days":* Ibid.

233  *"an act of cruel injustice":* Charles Lee to Washington, c. June 30, 1778, *FO*.

233  *"by some of those dirty earwigs":* Ibid.

234  *"unnecessary, disorderly, and shameful retreat":* Quoted in McBurney, 169.

234  *"an acquittal on the first two":* Shy, 159.

234  *"within five or six paces":* Alexander Hamilton and Evan Edwards, "Account of a Duel between Major General Charles Lee and Lieutenant Colonel John Laurens, [24 December 1778]," *FO*.

234  *"black project":* Quoted in Massey, 130.

234  *"idealistic and vainglorious son":* Van Buskirk, 142.

## CHAPTER 14: The British Were Coming—Again

237  *"Seizing a base on the off chance":* Willcox, 85.

239  *"slaughter pen":* Quoted in Buchanan, *Guilford Courthouse,* 10.

239  *"General Lee wishes you":* Ibid.

243  *"to prevent Insurrections among the Negroes":* Quoted in Massey, 132.

243  *"three thousand able bodied negroes":* Ibid.

243  *"We are much disgusted here":* Christopher Gadsden to Samuel Adams, July 6, 1779, quoted in Jim Piecuch, *Three Peoples, One King* (Columbia: University of South Carolina Press, 2013), 164.

243  *"cooperate diplomatically":* Carl P. Borick, *A Gallant Defense* (Columbia: University of South Carolina Press, 2012), 9.

244  *"whether the state shall belong":* Quoted in Borick, 12.

244  *"one of the most dishonorable actions":* Ferling, *Miracle,* 387.

245  *"we will fight it out":* Quoted in Borick, 13.

245  *"Old Bullet Head":* Ferling, *Miracle,* 384.

246  *"might restrain the allies":* David Wilson, *The Southern Strategy* (Columbia: University of South Carolina Press, 2008), 152.

246  *"Taking their children with them":* Ibid., 155.

246 *"a confused piecemeal attack"*: Ibid., 162.

246 *"one relatively small battalion after another"*: Ibid.

246 *"the largest unit of soldiers of African descent"*: Text on Haitian Monument in downtown Savannah.

246 *"Historians have yet to evaluate properly"*: George P. Clark, "The Role of the Haitian Volunteers at Savannah in 1779: An Attempt at an Objective View," *Phylon*, Vol. 41, No. 4 (Winter 1980), 358.

## CHAPTER 15: The Drunken Bash That Saved the Revolution

PAGE

250 *"approach trenches"*: Borick, 110.

250 *"one of the critical points"*: Ibid., xii.

251 *"a few shirts & Stockings"*: Quoted in Bass, 33.

252 *"It must have been a scene"*: Buchanan, *Guilford Courthouse*, 27.

252 *"Sabers thudded"*: Borick, 149.

254 *"battles, skirmishes, ambushes"*: Hugh T. Harrington review of *Parker's Guide*, in *Journal of the American Revolution*, March 4, 2014.

255 *"place of retreat"*: Borick, 200.

256 *"I need not remind you"*: Quoted in Borick, 183.

256 *"The Propriety of evacuating the Garrison"*: Quoted in Borick, 139.

256 *"appeared much greater"*: Quoted in Borick, 168.

256 *"appeared surprised & displeased"*: Quoted in Borick, 169.

256 *"the Militia were willing"... "old Women"*: Ibid.

256–257 *"would keep a good Watch"... "open the Gates for the Enemy"*: Ibid.

257 *"were willing to sacrifice the security"*: Borick, 170.

257 *"a bow and its apparatus"*: Henry Lee, *Memoirs of the War in the Southern Department of the United States*, 3rd ed. (New York: University Publishing Company, 1870), 347.

258 *"till each individual"*: William Gilmore Simms, *The Life of Francis Marion* (New York, Henry G. Langley, 1845), 96.

259 *"witnessed a more deplorable sight"*: Captain Johann Ewald, *Diary of the American War*, translated and edited by Joseph P. Tustin (New Haven, CT: Yale University Press, 1979), 239.

259 *"the building or magazine"*: Ibid.

259 *"blown up with all the people"*: Ibid.

259 *"burnt beyond recognition"*: Ibid.

259 *"general consensus"*: Joshua Shepherd, "A Melancholy Accident: The Disastrous Explosion at Charleston," *Journal of the American Revolution*, August 5, 2015.

259 *"administered floggings for a fee"*: Ball, 56.

260 *"too well satisfied"*: Quoted in Willcox, 316.

260 *"an elegant woman"*: Franklin Wickwire and Mary Wickwire, *Cornwallis: The American Adventure* (Boston: Houghton Mifflin, 1970), 39.

260 *"destroyed all my hopes of happiness"*: Quoted in Wickwire and Wickwire, 115.

262 *"galloping at about 25 miles per hour"*: Jim Piecuch, *The Blood Be Upon Your Head* (Lugoff, SC: Southern Campaigns of the American Revolution Press, 2010), 97.

263 *"pass after pass"*: Ibid., 22.

263 *"warfare of any age"*: Matthew H. Spring, *With Zeal and with Bayonets Only* (Norman: University of Oklahoma Press, 2008), 270.

263 *"unable to travel"*: Quoted in Piecuch, *Blood*, 91.

263 *"we were completely surrounded"*: Quoted in Piecuch, *Blood*, 62.

263 *"many"… "were killed after they had lain down their arms"*: Quoted in Piecuch, *Blood*, 62–63.

263 *"slaughter was commenced"*: Banastre Tarleton, *A History of the Campaigns of 1780 and 1781, in the Southern Provinces of North America* (Dublin: Colles, Exshaw, et al., 1787), 31.

264 *"so effectually breaking"*: Ibid., 32.

264 *"stimulated the soldiers to a vindictive asperity"*: Ibid.

266 *"Cheerfully, Gates pushed south"*: Bruce Lancaster and J. H. Plumb, *The American Heritage Book of the Revolution* (New York: Dell, 1963), 303.

266 *"the shorter but more barren"*: Ibid.

266 *"he exclaimed dramatically"*: Ibid.

266 *"barely capable"*: Ibid.

266 *"With his green command"*: Ibid.

## CHAPTER 16:  Down the Benedict Arnold Escape Path

PAGE

273 *"wished the ball"*: Quoted in Steven Brumwell, *Turncoat* (New Haven, CT: Yale University Press, 2018), 111.

273 *"the doctors could offer only"*: Martin, *Benedict Arnold*, 404.

273 *"crude cast"*: Ibid.

273 *"to lie fully immobilized"*: Ibid.

273 *"way of requesting my resignation"*: Arnold to Washington, March 11, 1777, *FO*.

273 *"previously pursued this outcome"*: Brumwell, 119.

274 *"he had used state wagons"*: Ibid., 146.

274 *"a magnet for young British officers"*: Ibid., 127.

274 *"If Your Excellency thinks me Criminal"*: Arnold to Washington, May 5, 1779, *FO*.

274 *"I have nothing left"*: Ibid.

275 *"Is it probable"*: From *Proceedings of a General Court Martial for the Trial of Major General Arnold* (New York: Privately printed, 1865), 106–107.

275 *"to receive a reprimand"*: Ibid., 145.

276 *"irritated"*: Nathaniel Philbrick, *Valiant Ambition* (New York: Viking, 2016), 291.

276 *"exasperated"*: Brumwell, 265.

277 *"a negro"... "shot guns"*: W. J. Kelleher, *History of Verplanck N.Y. 1609–1914* (Peekskill, NY: n.p., 1948), 20.

277 *"realizing that the Vulture was in cannon range"*: Jan Horton, *A Place Set Apart* (unpublished manuscript, 2004), 53.

278 *"deliberately robbed and plundered"*: Sun Bok Kim, "The Limits of Politicization in the American Revolution: The Experience of Westchester County, New York," *Journal of American History*, Vol. 80, No. 3 (December 1993), 877.

278 *"I have ever acted from a Principle"*: Arnold to Washington, September 25, 1780, *FO/EAD*.

278 *"I have no favor to ask for myself"*: Ibid.

279 *"Inocent as an angel"*: Ibid.

279 *"the mistaken fury of The Country"*: Ibid.

279 *"impossible to doubt"*: Carl Van Doren, *Secret History of the American Revolution* (New York: Viking Press, 1968), 200.

279 *"a Man of honour"*: John André to Washington, October 1, 1780, *FO/EAD*.

280 *"They weep here"*: Virgil, *The Aeneid*, translated by Robert Fitzgerald (New York: Vintage Books, 1990), 20.

## CHAPTER 17: Over the Mountains, Kings of the Hill

PAGE

281 *"put an end to all resistance"*: Quoted in Michael C. Scoggins, *The Day It Rained Militia* (Charleston, SC: The History Press, 2005), 92.

281 *"We have driven the Regulars out of the country"*: Quoted in Scoggins, 114.

282 *"for the first time:"* Scoggins, 13.

283 *"turn of the tide of success"*: Thomas Jefferson to John Campbell, November 10, 1822, *FO/EAD*.

283 *"like a human footprint"*: Boatner, 579.

283 *"seldom missed"*: Patrick Ferguson to Dr. Adam Ferguson, January 31, 1778, quoted in Hugh F. Rankin, ed., "An Officer Out of His Time: Correspondence of Major Patrick Ferguson 1779–1780," in Howard H. Peckham, ed., *Sources of American Independence* (Chicago: University of Chicago Press, 1978), Vol. 2, 300.

283 *"it was not pleasant"*: Quoted in ibid.

284 *"best Endeavors, without Loss of Time"*: Quoted in ibid., 358.

284 *"march his army over the mountains"*: As recalled by Isaac Shelby, quoted in Lyman C. Draper, *King's Mountain and Its Heroes* (Cincinnati: Peter G. Thomson, 1881), 562.

285 *"overawing the disaffected"*: Quoted in John S. Pancake, *This Destructive War* (Tuscaloosa: University of Alabama Press, 1985), 116.

286 *"the tradition of the country"*: Quoted in Draper, 176.

286 *"The sword of the Lord and of Gideon!"*: Ibid.

286 *"The sword of the Lord and of our Gideons!"*: Ibid.

287 *"too inactive"*: As recalled by Shelby, quoted in Draper, 564.

287 *"regulated and directed"*: Ibid.

287   *"If you choose to be pissed upon"*: Quoted in Buchanan, *Guilford Courthouse*, 219.

289   *"unit formations broke into pockets"*: J. David Dameron, *King's Mountain* (Boston: Da Capo Press, 2003), 60.

289   *"supporting one another as they moved"*: Ibid., 61.

290   *"a checked shirt, or duster"*: Draper, 233.

290   *"some time"*: As recalled by Shelby, quoted in Draper, 566.

290   *"were willing to follow that bad example"*: Ibid.

290   *"husbands, fathers, and brothers"*: Quoted in Buchanan, *Guilford Courthouse*, 236.

290   *"officers of all ranks"*: Quoted in Draper, 531.

290   *"restrain the disorderly manner of slaughtering"*: Ibid.

## CHAPTER 18: "A Sweeping Guerrilla War of Movement"

PAGE

292   *"the most Supersticious sort"*: Quoted in Golway, 20.

293   *"a blemish to the company"*: Quoted in Buchanan, *Guilford Courthouse*, 264.

293   *"the rebels never faced critical shortages"*: Lefkowitz, 58.

294   *"For God's sake"*: Alexander Hamilton to James Duane, September 6, 1780, *FO*.

294   *"I think I am giving you a General"*: Washington to John Mathews, October 23, 1780, *FO/EAD*.

294   *"vile swamp fox"*: Quoted in John Oller, *The Swamp Fox* (Boston: Da Capo Press, 2016), 87.

294   *"positive connotation"*: Oller, 87.

295   *"with a pronounced limp"*: Ibid., 3.

295   *"Until a more permanent Army"*: Greene to Marion, December 4, 1780, quoted in John Buchanan, "'We Must Endeavor to Keep Up a Partizan War': Nathanael Greene and the Partisans," in Gregory D. Massey and Jim Piecuch, eds., *General Nathanael Greene and the American Revolution in the South* (Columbia: University of South Carolina Press, 2012), 120.

295   *"a triumphant sweep northward"*: Buchanan, speaking at the eighth annual Conference of the American Revolution, March 23, 2019.

295   *"the unexpected happened"*: Ibid.

295   *"The rising was fundamental"*: Ibid.

296   *"I am always sanguine"*: Cornwallis to Tarleton, November 5, 1780, quoted in Bass, 110.

296   *"I had the Mortification"*: Tarleton to Cornwallis, November 11, 1780, quoted in Bass, 113.

296   *"not a sympathetic character"*: Buchanan, *Guilford Courthouse*, 115.

297   *"Generals are like artists"*: Ibid.

297   *"participating in the great American game"*: Ibid., 119.

297   *"no rank, no men, no prospects"*: Ibid., 120.

297   *"the indefatigable Sumter"*: Cornwallis to Henry Clinton, August 29, 1780, quoted in ibid., 249.

297   *"encreased his Corps":* Horatio Gates to Washington, August 30, 1780, *FO/ EAD.*

298   *"find Sumter, and either kill or capture him":* Buchanan, *Guilford Courthouse,* 250.

298   *"mostly seasoned":* Ibid., 253.

298   *"Sometime in the early morning":* Ibid., 252.

298   *"strung out on the road":* Ibid., 253.

299   *"The attack":* Tarleton, *History,* 182.

299   *"Tarleton lied":* Buchanan, *Guilford Courthouse,* 256.

299   *"But he did not reach the buildings":* Ibid.

300   *"hit him under his right shoulder":* Ibid., 257.

301   *"either offensively or defensively":* Greene to Daniel Morgan, December 16, 1780, quoted in James Graham, *The Life of General Daniel Morgan* (New York: Derby & Jackson, 1856), 260.

301   *"every possible precaution":* Ibid.

301   *"the militia lately under the command":* Ibid.

302   *"to obey no orders from me":* Morgan to Greene, January 15, 1781, quoted in Graham, 285.

302   *"no part of this State":* Ibid., 285–86.

302   *"We have just learned":* Ibid., 286.

302   *"Not the Swamp Fox":* Rod Andrew Jr., speaking at the eighth annual Conference of the American Revolution, March 24, 2019.

302   *"Do you think you could have found":* Ibid.

302   *"Before he uttered a word":* Ibid.

303   *"taken an oath":* Rod Andrew Jr., *The Life and Times of General Andrew Pickens* (Chapel Hill: University of North Carolina Press, 2017), 79.

303   *"plundered his plantation":* Ibid., 88.

303   *"a screen and early warning":* Ibid., 100.

304   *"state troops":* Lawrence E. Babits, *A Devil of a Whipping: The Battle of Cowpens* (Chapel Hill: University of North Carolina Press, 1998), 28.

304   *"calling on Morgan for ammunition":* Quoted in Andrew, 102.

304   *"Boys, get up, Benny's coming":* Quoted in Buchanan, *Guilford Courthouse,* 318.

304   *"The profession of arms":* Buchanan, *Guilford Courthouse,* 316.

305   *"Just hold up your heads":* Quoted in Albert Louis Zambone, *Daniel Morgan* (Yardley, PA: Westholme, 2018), 231.

306   *"12 killed and 60 wounded":* Babits, 151.

## CHAPTER 19: "Across the River, Just in Time"

PAGE

308   *"tents, excess clothing":* Buchanan, *Guilford Courthouse,* 340.

308   *"than those who were raised on it":* William A. Graham, *General Joseph Graham and his Papers on North Carolina Revolutionary History* (Raleigh, NC: Edwards & Broughton, 1904), 290.

309 *"Fatigued—hungry—alone":* Elizabeth F. Ellet, *The Women of the American Revolution* (New York: Baker & Scribner, 1849), Vol. 1, 298.

309 *"Take these":* Ibid., Vol. 1, 299.

309 *"For someone who wants to know":* David Purtell, "Future Remains Unclear for Site of Former Mill," *Salisbury Post*, March 15, 2015.

310 *"ciatick pain in my hip":* Morgan to Greene, January 24, 1781, quoted in Andrew Waters, *To the End of the World* (Yardley, PA: Westholme, 2020), 120.

311 *"You have the flower of the army":* Greene to Otho Williams, February 13, 1781, quoted in Lawrence E. Babits and Joshua B. Howard, *Long, Obstinate and Bloody: The Battle of Guilford Courthouse* (Chapel Hill: University of North Carolina Press, 2009), 34.

311 *"dejected and demoralized":* Babits and Howard, 34.

312 *"It was necessary to convince":* Greene to Jefferson, March 10, 1781, *FO*.

313 *"their night position":* Henry Lee, *Memoirs*, 257.

313 *"returning to their homes":* Ibid.

313 *"It has knocked up Toryism":* Pickens to Greene, February 26, 1781, quoted in Andrew, 121.

313 *"dreadful carnage":* Greene to Jefferson, February 28, 1781, *FO*.

313 *"It has had a very happy effect":* Ibid.

315 *"The North Carolina militiamen were justifiably nervous":* Babits and Howard, 100.

315 *"resting on a rail fence":* Roger Lamb, *An Original and Authentic Journal of Occurrences During the Late American War* (Dublin: Wilkinson & Courtney, 1809), 361.

315 *"a general pause":* Ibid.

315 *"fire two volleys and then retire":* Quoted in John Maass, *The Battle of Guilford Courthouse* (Charleston, SC: The History Press, 2020), 140.

316 *"rode directly into the Guards' formation":* Ibid., 166.

316 *"The wild horsemen attacked":* Ibid.

316 *"pushed back toward the woods":* Ibid., 167.

317 *"did what he had to do":* Buchanan, *Guilford Courthouse,* 379.

317 *"the incident as it has come to be described":* Babits and Howard, 162.

317 *"more than a quarter mile away":* Ibid.

317 *"either a rumor that Lee had heard":* Ibid.

317 *"losing all our hopes":* Morgan to Greene, February 20, 1781, quoted in Maass, 135.

317 *"certain":* Greene to Washington, March 18, 1781, *FO/EAD*.

317 *"But they left the most advantageous position":* Ibid.

318 *"I never did, and I hope never shall again":* Charles O'Hara to the Duke of Grafton, April 20, 1781, quoted in Babits and Howard, 172.

318 *"remained on the very ground":* Ibid.

318 *"totally defeated the rebel army":* Quoted in Maass, 177.

318 *"I shall take every measure":* Greene to Washington, March 29, 1781, *FO/EAD*.

319 *"food, clothing, quarters, pay":* Boatner, 760.

319 *"Officers who tried to intervene":* Lengel, 326.

319   ***"instantly execute a few"***: Washington to Robert Howe, January 22, 1781, *FO/EAD*.

319   ***"the most important assignment"***: Massey, 172.

320   ***"a tumultuous assemblage"***: Thomas Paine to James Hutchinson, March 11, 1781, quoted in Hawke, 115.

320   ***"Negroe, the property of a rebel"***: Quoted in John U. Rees, *'They Were Good Soldiers'* (Warwick, UK: Helion, 2019), 19.

320   ***"full Security to follow"***: Ibid.

320   ***"took advantage of wartime disruption"***: Gary B. Nash, "Thomas Peters: Millwright and Deliverer," in David G. Sweet and Gary B. Nash, eds., *Struggle and Survival in Colonial America* (Berkeley: University of California Press, 1981), 74.

321   ***"by joining the British"***: Ibid., 76.

321   ***"to stage the first large-scale rebellion"***: Ibid.

321   ***"discontent"***: Washington to Henry Laurens, March 20, 1779, *FO*.

321   ***"arming blacks on a large scale would spur an exodus"***: Lengel, 316.

321   ***"I saw no man, officer nor private"***: Quoted in Rees, 116.

322   ***"caught carrying messages"***: Cassandra Pybus, *Epic Journeys of Freedom* (Boston: Beacon Press, 2006), 21.

322   ***"because nobody recorded"***: Nash, "Thomas Peters," 72.

322   ***"a leading member"***: Ibid., 73.

323   ***"Don't be surprisd if my movements"***: Greene to James Emmet, April 3, 1781, quoted in Dennis M. Conrad, "General Nathanael Greene: An Appraisal," in Massey and Piecuch, 23.

324   ***"I give it decisively as my opinion"***: Washington to John Laurens, April 9, 1781, *FO/EAD*.

324   ***"our present force"***: Ibid.

324   ***"we are at the end of our tether"***: Ibid.

324   ***"now or never"***: Ibid.

324   ***"Here I am, getting rid of my wounded"***: Cornwallis to William Phillips, April 10, 1781, quoted in Willcox, 382.

324   ***"Now my dear friend, what is our plan?"***: Quoted in ibid., 382–83.

## CHAPTER 20:  The Midnight Ride of Jack Jouett

PAGE

328   ***"our great, faithful, and beloved friend and ally"***: Quoted in Unger, 90.

329   ***"I had left as a rebel and fugitive"***: Quoted in ibid., 94.

329   ***"horrors inflicted"***: Laura Auricchio, *The Marquis* (New York: Alfred A. Knopf, 2014), 82.

330   ***"retreat with honor"***: Quoted in Nathaniel Philbrick, *In the Hurricane's Eye* (New York: Viking, 2018), 72.

331   ***"always carried a pair of small pistols"***: Ewald, 295.

332   ***"I shall now proceed to dislodge La Fayette"***: Cornwallis to Clinton, in Tarleton, 353.

332 *"Okay, so this is the number one selling":* John Maass, speaking at the American Revolution Institute of the Society of the Cincinnati, January 28, 2016.

333 *"If you mean to be a historical figure":* Virginius Dabney, "Jack Jouett's Ride," *American Heritage,* Vol. 13, No. 1 (December 1961).

334 *"potent mint juleps":* Ibid.

334 *"by a troop of Light-horse":* "Deposition of Christopher Hudson Respecting Tarleton's Raid in June 1781, 26 July 1805," *FO.*

335 *"held overnight in a nearby coal shed":* John Maass, *The Road to Yorktown* (Charleston, SC: The History Press, 2015), 90.

335 *"destroyed all my growing crops":* Jefferson to William Gordon, July 16, 1788, *FO.*

336 *"We make it seem we are pursuing him":* Lafayette to the Chevalier de La Luzerne, June 16, 1781, in Idzerda, Vol. 4, 186.

336 *"the appearance of a retreat":* Ibid.

337 *"described their commander pretty well":* Michael Schellhammer, "The Nicknaming of General 'Mad' Anthony Wayne," *Journal of the American Revolution,* May 3, 2013.

339 *"This campaign is a good school for me":* Lafayette to the Vicomte de Noailles, July 9, 1781, in Idzerda, Vol. 4, 241.

339 *"grand scale":* Newport Mansions (https://www.newportmansions.org).

339 *"the grandest of Newport's summer 'cottages'":* Ibid.

339 *"promotions, distinctions and rewards":* Gilbert Chinard, in preface to Jean Edmond Weelen, *Rochambeau: Father and Son* (New York: Henry Holt, 1936), viii.

339 *"no inclination for the frivolous":* Ibid.

339 *"written with military brevity":* Ibid., vii.

339 *"severely suppressed his emotions":* Ibid.

340 *"he did not wish to suffer another debacle":* Robert Selig, *March to Victory* (Washington, DC: U.S. Army Center of Military History, 2007), 10.

340 *"disintegrate and cease to exist":* Orders quoted in Charles Lee Lewis, *Admiral de Grasse and American Independence* (Annapolis, MD: United States Naval Institute, 1945), 129.

340 *"Fixed with Count de Rochambeau":* Washington diary entry, May 22, 1781, *FO.*

340 *"commence an operation"... "it was thought":* Ibid.

340 *"extend our views to the Southward":* Ibid.

341 *"an act of redemption":* Selig, *March,* 10.

341 *"humiliating defeat":* Ibid.

341 *"massive reinforcements":* Ibid., 22.

341 *"the assistance of a powerful fleet":* Ibid.

342 *"at the moment the armistice":* Ferling, *Miracle,* 473.

342 *"the Genl is exceedingly anxious":* Quoted in Selig, *March,* 22.

# CHAPTER 21:  A Battle You Could Hear But Couldn't See

PAGE

344 *"The Day That Would Shake the World":* Robert Selig, *The Franco-American Encampment in the Town of Greenburgh* (Greenburgh, NY: Town of Greenburgh, 2020), 108.

344 *"several hours":* Robert Selig, March 18, 2021, online talk titled "Tuesday, 14 August, 1781. The Day That Shook the World," Washington-Rochambeau Revolutionary Route Association (https://w3r-us.org/scholars-resources/).

344 *"obliged":* Washington diary entry, August 14, 1781, *FO.*

345 *"told him that matters were too far advanced":* Comte de Lauberdière, *The Road to Yorktown*, translated and edited by Norman Desmarais (El Dorado Hills, CA: Savas Beatie, 2021), 122.

345 *"This sounds as if Rochambeau":* Selig, online talk titled "Tuesday, 14 August, 1781."

345 *"nominally the commander in chief":* Ibid.

345 *"was also, militarily, the weakest link":* Ibid.

345 *"and they all knew it":* Ibid.

345 *"It is almost certain":* Jonathan R. Dull, *The Miracle of American Independence* (Lincoln, NE: Potomac Books, 2015), 128–29.

346 *"major blows should be landed":* Quoted in Ferreiro, 209.

347 *"where we think you may be able":* Quoted in Robert Selig, "En Avant to Victory," in Edward G. Lengel, ed., *The 10 Key Campaigns of the American Revolution* (Washington, DC: Regnery History, 2020), 202.

347 *"indispensable":* Philbrick, *Hurricane's Eye*, 133.

348 *"Should a fleet Come in":* Lafayette to Washington, August 6, 1781, *FO/EAD.*

348 *"willing":* Cornwallis to Clinton, June 30, 1781, quoted in Benjamin Franklin Stevens, ed., *The Campaign in Virginia, 1781,* Vol. 2 (London: 1888), 37.

350 *"essentially serving as chief executive":* Charles Rappleye, *Robert Morris: Financier of the American Revolution* (New York: Simon & Schuster Paperbacks, 2011), 91.

350 *"is generally compared":* Ibid., 226.

350 *"primary administrator":* Ibid.

350 *"would be responsible":* Ibid., 227.

351 *"all his energy and available funds":* Ibid., 257.

351 *"I have already advised your Excellency":* Robert Morris to Washington, August 28, 1781, *FO/EAD.*

351 *"I am distressed beyond expression":* Washington to Lafayette, September 2, 1781, *FO/EAD.*

351 *"the present Time is as interesting & anxious":* Washington to Greene, September 4, 1781, *FO/EAD.*

351 *"I wish it to come":* Washington to Morris, September 6, 1781, *FO/EAD.*

352 *"short Bobs":* Rappleye, 259.

352 *"the only man in the city":* Ibid., 261.

352 *"a tall man acting as if"*: Barbara W. Tuchman, *The First Salute* (New York: Alfred A. Knopf, 1988), 260.

352 *"His features, his physiognomy"*: Count William de Deux-Ponts, *My Campaigns in America*, translated by Samuel Abbott Green (Boston: J. K. Wiggin and Wm. Parsons Lunt, 1868), 126.

352 *"A child, whose every wish"*: Ibid.

353 *"a lone rider"*: Rappleye, 261.

353 *"This was the first that could be called money"*: Martin, *Ordinary Courage*, 141.

354 *"It would have been a less painful circumstance"*: George Washington to Lund Washington, April 30, 1781, *FO/EAD*.

355 *"In our time"*: John Buchanan, *The Road to Charleston* (Charlottesville: University of Virginia Press, 2019), 108.

356 *"steadily and without faltering"*: Quoted in ibid., 225.

357 *"the country's premier installation"*: Joint Expeditionary Base Little Creek–Fort Story (https://www.cnic.navy.mil/regions/cnrma/installations/jeb_little_creek_fort_story.html).

357 *"The Pearl by the Bay and the Emerald on the Ocean"*: Ibid.

359 *"scouts, messengers, and mounted cavalry"*: James L. Nelson, *George Washington's Great Gamble* (New York: McGraw-Hill, 2010), 271.

360 *"Since the ships that sailed out of the bay the fastest"*: Philbrick, *Hurricane's Eye*, 184.

360 *"a most glorious opening"*: Samuel Hood to George Jackson, September 16, 1781, in French Ensor Chadwick, ed., *The Graves Papers* (New York: The Naval History Society, 1916), 87.

361 *"resembling a chevron of geese"*: Nelson, *Great Gamble*, 281.

## CHAPTER 22: "Little Short of a Standing Miracle"

PAGE

365 *"There is every reason to hope"*: Clinton to Cornwallis, September 24, 1781, quoted in Wickwire and Wickwire, 369.

365 *"Great time would have been gained"*: Tarleton, *History*, 385.

366 *"felt a great impulse"*: Callahan, 184.

366 *"who no doubt wished"*: Ibid.

367 *"ineffective due to illness"*: Jerome A. Greene, *The Guns of Independence* (El Dorado Hills, CA: Savas Beatie, 2013), 138.

367 *"driving off livestock, and stripping the fields"*: Pybus, 48.

367 *"Nothing but a treaty of alliance"*: Lafayette to Washington, July 20, 1781, *FO/EAD*.

367 *"During the siege we saw in the woods"*: Martin, *Ordinary Courage*, 153.

367 *"British guns ceased to respond"*: Jerome Greene, 196.

368 *"holes and Pits"*: Quoted in Jerome Greene, 203.

368 *"a kind of grotto"*: Yorktown journal of St. George Tucker, quoted in George F. Scheer and Hugh F. Rankin, *Rebels & Redcoats* (New York: Da Capo Press, 1987), 485.

368    *"nothing but a direct move"*: Cornwallis to Clinton, October 11, 1781, quoted in Stevens, 176.

368    *"had in his hands the one British naval force"*: Willcox, 435.

370    *"If Washington expected relief"*: Ron Chernow, *Alexander Hamilton* (New York: Penguin Press, 2004), 154.

370    *"battlefield honor . . . would be a useful credential"*: Ibid., 150.

370    *"sent a marathon letter"*: Ibid.

371    *"Rush on boys"*: Martin, *Ordinary Courage*, 149, 150.

371    *"Two nights ago, my Eliza"*: Alexander Hamilton to Elizabeth Hamilton, October 16, 1781, *FO*.

371    *"less than one quarter of a mile"*: Quoted in Jerome Greene, 240.

371    *"I had not less than six or eight"*: Quoted in ibid., 244.

371    *"Many historians assume"*: Van Buskirk, 267.

372    *"I cannot recommend"*: Cornwallis to Clinton, October 15, 1781, in Chadwick, ed., *The Graves Papers*, 140.

373    *"to a place to be appointed"*: Quoted in Jerome Greene, 352.

373    *"allowed Washington to retreat gracefully"*: Jerome Greene, 288.

373    *"Americans seized on the 'Upside Down' version"*: Thomas Fleming, *Beat the Last Drum* (New York: St. Martin's Press, 1963), 357.

374    *"without ever"*: Selig, *March*, 46.

374    *"Oh God! it is all over!"* Quoted in Henry P. Johnston, *The Yorktown Campaign and the Surrender of Cornwallis* (New York: Harper & Brothers, 1881), 180.

374    *"The Curtain of seperation will soon be drawn"*: Washington's Farewell Address to the Army, November 2, 1783, *FO/EAD*.

375    *"indulge himself"*: Ibid.

375    *"disadvantageous circumstances"*: Ibid.

375    *"singular interpositions of Providence"*: Ibid.

375    *"the unparalleled perseverence"*: Ibid.

375    *"little short of a standing Miracle"*: Ibid.

375    *"that was not on the spot"*: Ibid.

## EPILOGUE: "Let's Take a Ride"

PAGE

376    *"would receive one slave"*: Massey, 207.

376    *"Poor Laurens is fallen"*: Greene to Otho Holland Williams, September 17, 1782, quoted in Massey, 228.

377    *"I wonder why Quebec"*: Quoted in "Who Gets the General's Body?" *Life* magazine, September 3, 1951.

377    *"Live free, or die"*: Quoted in Stark, 313.

378    *"was as brutal as any in the war"*: Mark Edward Lender and James Kirby Martin, "Target New London: Benedict Arnold's Raid, Just War, and 'Homegrown Terror' Reconsidered," *Journal of Military History*, Vol. 83, No. 1 (January 2019), 92.

378   *"as an effort to spare American blood":* McBurney, 2.

378   *"courted financial disaster":* Alan Taylor, *Liberty Men and Great Proprietors* (Chapel Hill: University of North Carolina Press, 1990), 41.

379   *"Greene, Sumter, and Morgan may have injured him":* John Knight, *War at Saber Point* (Yardley, PA: Westholme, 2020), 225.

379   *"Congress passed the nation's first bankruptcy law":* Rappleye, 512.

380   *"as soon as possible":* Quoted in Richard B. Morris, *The Peacemakers* (New York: Harper & Row, 1965), 376.

380   *"managed to get a clause inserted":* Ibid., 381.

380   *"dishonorable":* Quoted in Pybus, 67.

380   *"We have been beating the bush":* Greene to Knox, September 29, 1781, quoted in Waters, 204.

380   *"Will you be a Planter?":* Joseph Reed to Greene, March 14, 1783, quoted in Gregory D. Massey, "Independence and Slavery: The Transformation of Nathanael Greene, 1781–1786," in Massey and Piecuch, eds., 250.

381   *"The word 'apotheosis' in the title":* Architect of the Capitol (https://www.aoc.gov/explore-capitol-campus/art/apotheosis-washington).

# Selected Bibliography

Allison, David K., and Larrie D. Ferreiro, eds. *The American Revolution: A World War.* Washington, DC: Smithsonian Books, 2018.

Anderson, M. T. *The Astonishing Life of Octavian Nothing, Traitor to the Nation*, Vol. 1, *The Pox Party.* Cambridge, MA: Candlewick Press, 2006.

———. *The Astonishing Life of Octavian Nothing, Traitor to the Nation*, Vol. 2, *The Kingdom on the Waves.* Cambridge, MA: Candlewick Press, 2008.

Andrew, Rod Jr. *The Life and Times of General Andrew Pickens.* Chapel Hill: University of North Carolina Press, 2017.

Atkinson, Rick. *The British Are Coming.* New York: Henry Holt, 2019.

Auricchio, Laura. *The Marquis.* New York: Alfred A. Knopf, 2014.

Babits, Lawrence E. *A Devil of a Whipping: The Battle of Cowpens.* Chapel Hill: University of North Carolina Press, 1998.

Babits, Lawrence E., and Joshua B. Howard. *Long, Obstinate and Bloody: The Battle of Guilford Courthouse.* Chapel Hill: University of North Carolina Press, 2009.

Ball, Edward. *Slaves in the Family.* New York: Farrar, Straus and Giroux, 1998.

Bass, Robert D. *Gamecock.* Orangeburg, SC: Sandlapper, 2000.

———. *The Green Dragoon.* Orangeburg, SC: Sandlapper, 1973.

Bell, J. L. *Boston 1775.* https://boston1775.blogspot.com/.

———. *Longfellow House-Washington's Headquarters National Historic Site Historic Resource Study.* Washington, DC: National Park Service, U.S. Department of the Interior, 2012.

———. *The Road to Concord.* Yardley, PA: Westholme, 2016.

Billias, George Athan. *General John Glover and His Marblehead Mariners.* New York: Holt, Rinehart and Winston, 1960.

Billias, George Athan, ed. *George Washington's Generals and Opponents.* New York: Da Capo Press, 1994.

Boatner, Mark Mayo III. *Encyclopedia of the American Revolution.* Bicentennial edition. New York: David McKay Company, 1974.

Borick, Carl P. *A Gallant Defense.* Columbia: University of South Carolina Press, 2012.

Brown, Christopher Leslie, and Philip D. Morgan, eds. *Arming Slaves.* New Haven, CT: Yale University Press, 2006.

Brumwell, Steven. *Turncoat*. New Haven, CT: Yale University Press, 2018.

Buchanan, John. *The Road to Charleston*. Charlottesville: University of Virginia Press, 2019.

———. *The Road to Guilford Courthouse*. New York: John Wiley & Sons, 1997.

Callahan, North. *Henry Knox: George Washington's General*. New York: Rinehart & Company, 1958.

Carey, Charles W. Jr. "Lord Dunmore's Ethiopian Regiment." Master's thesis, Virginia Polytechnic Institute and State University, 1995.

Carpenter, Stanley D. M. *Southern Gambit*. Norman, OK: University of Oklahoma Press. 2019.

Cecere, Michael. *The Invasion of Virginia 1781*. Yardley, PA: Westholme, 2017.

Chadwick, French Ensor, ed. *The Graves Papers*. New York: The Naval History Society, 1916.

Chernow, Ron. *Alexander Hamilton*. New York: Penguin Press, 2004.

———. *Washington: A Life*. New York: Penguin Press, 2010.

Clark, George P. "The Role of the Haitian Volunteers at Savannah in 1779: An Attempt at an Objective View." *Phylon*, Vol. 41, No. 4 (Winter 1980).

Clark, Stephen. *Following Their Footsteps*. Scarborough, ME: Clark Books, 2003.

Clary, David A. *Adopted Son*. New York: Bantam, 2007.

Cohn, Amy L., ed. *From Sea to Shining Sea*. New York: Scholastic, 1993.

Dameron, J. David. *King's Mountain*. Boston: Da Capo Press, 2003.

Desjardin, Thomas A. *Through a Howling Wilderness*. New York: St. Martin's Griffin, 2006.

Deux-Ponts, Count William de. *My Campaigns in America*, translated by Samuel Abbott Green. Boston: J. K. Wiggin and Wm. Parsons Lunt, 1868.

Di Spigna, Christian. *Founding Martyr*. New York: Broadway Books, 2019.

Draper, Lyman C. *King's Mountain and Its Heroes*. Cincinnati: Peter G. Thomson, 1881.

Dull, Jonathan R. *The Miracle of American Independence*. Lincoln, NE: Potomac Books, 2015.

Dunkerly, Robert M., and Irene B. Boland. *Eutaw Springs*. Columbia: University of South Carolina Press, 2017.

Dwyer, William M. *The Day Is Ours*. New Brunswick, NJ: Rutgers University Press, 1998.

Edgar, Walter. *Partisans and Redcoats*. New York: Perennial, 2003.

Ellis, Joseph J. *American Creation*. New York: Alfred A. Knopf, 2007.

———. *His Excellency*. New York: Vintage Books, 2005.

Ewald, Johann. *Diary of the American War*, translated and edited by Joseph P. Tustin. New Haven, CT: Yale University Press, 1979.

Fenn, Elizabeth A. *Pox Americana*. New York: Hill and Wang, 2001.

Ferling, John. *Almost a Miracle*. New York: Oxford University Press, 2007.

———. *Winning Independence*. New York: Bloomsbury, 2021.

Ferreiro, Larrie D. *Brothers at Arms*. New York: Alfred A. Knopf, 2016.

Fischer, David Hackett. *Paul Revere's Ride*. New York: Oxford University Press, 1994.

———. *Washington's Crossing*. New York: Oxford University Press, 2004.

Fleming, Thomas. *Beat the Last Drum*. New York: St. Martin's Press, 1963.

———. *Washington's Secret War*. New York: HarperCollins, 2005.

Forman, Samuel A. *Dr. Joseph Warren*. Gretna, LA: Pelican, 2012.

Frey, Sylvia R. *Water from the Rock*. Princeton, NJ: Princeton University Press, 1991.

Fuss, Norman. "Billy Flora at the Battle of Great Bridge." *Journal of the American Revolution*, October 14, 2014.

Golway, Terry. *Washington's General*. New York: Henry Holt, 2006.

Graham, James. *The Life of General Daniel Morgan*. New York: Derby & Jackson, 1856.

Greene, Jerome A. *The Guns of Independence*. El Dorado Hills, CA: Savas Beatie, 2013.

Griswold, William A., and Donald W. Linebaugh, eds. *The Saratoga Campaign*. Hanover, NH: University Press of New England, 2016.

Gross, Robert A. *The Minutemen and Their World*. New York: Hill and Wang, 1976.

Gruber, Ira D. *The Howe Brothers and the American Revolution*. Chapel Hill: University of North Carolina Press, 1972.

Hamilton, Philip. *The Revolutionary War Letters of Lucy and Henry Knox*. Baltimore: Johns Hopkins University Press, 2017.

Harris, Michael C. *Brandywine*. El Dorado Hills, CA: Savas Beatie, 2014.

———. *Germantown*. El Dorado Hills, CA: Savas Beatie, 2020.

Hawke, David Freeman. *Paine*. New York: W. W. Norton, 1974.

Henriques, Peter R. *First and Always*. Charlottesville: University of Virginia Press, 2020.

———. *Realistic Visionary*. Charlottesville: University of Virginia Press, 2006.

Higginbotham, Don. *Daniel Morgan: Revolutionary Rifleman*. Chapel Hill: University of North Carolina Press, 1961.

Hume, Ivor Noel. *1775: Another Part of the Field*. New York: Alfred A. Knopf, 2006.

Idzerda, Stanley J., ed. *Lafayette in the Age of the American Revolution: Selected Letters and Papers 1776–1790*. Vols. 1 and 4. Ithaca, NY: Cornell University Press, 1977.

Johnston, Henry P. *The Yorktown Campaign and the Surrender of Cornwallis*. New York: Harper & Brothers, 1881.

Kachun, Mitch. *First Martyr of Liberty*. New York: Oxford University Press, 2017.

Keegan, John. *The Face of Battle*. New York: Penguin Books, 1978.

Kelsay, Isabel Thompson. *Joseph Brant*. Syracuse, NY: Syracuse University Press, 1984.

Kennedy, Benjamin, ed. and trans. *Muskets, Cannon Balls & Bombs: Nine Narratives of the Siege of Savannah in 1779*. Savannah, GA: Beehive Press, 1974.

Ketchum, Richard M. *The Battle for Bunker Hill*. Garden City, NY: Doubleday, 1962.

———. *Saratoga*. New York: Henry Holt, 1999.

———. *Victory at Yorktown*. New York: Henry Holt, 2004.

———. *The Winter Soldiers*. New York: Henry Holt, 1999.

Kidder, William L. *Ten Crucial Days*. Lawrence Township, NJ: Knox Press, 2018.

Knight, John. *War at Saber Point*. Yardley, PA: Westholme, 2020.

Lancaster, Bruce, and J. H. Plumb. *The American Heritage Book of the Revolution*. New York: Dell, 1963.

Lauberdière, Comte de. *The Road to Yorktown*, translated and edited by Norman Desmarais. El Dorado Hills, CA: Savas Beatie, 2021.

Lee, Henry. *Memoirs of the War in the Southern Department of the United States*, 3rd edition. New York: University Publishing, 1870.

Lefkowitz, Arthur S. *The Long Retreat*. New Brunswick, NJ: Rutgers University Press, 1999.

Lender, Mark Edward. *Cabal!* Yardley, PA: Westholme, 2019.

Lender, Mark Edward, and Gary Wheeler Stone. *Fatal Sunday*. Norman: University of Oklahoma Press, 2016.

Lender, Mark Edward, and James Kirby Martin. "Target New London: Benedict Arnold's Raid, Just War, and 'Homegrown Terror' Reconsidered." *Journal of Military History*, Vol. 83, No. 1 (January 2019).

———. "A Traitor's Epiphany." *Virginia Magazine of History and Biography*, Vol. 125, No. 4 (2017).

Lengel, Edward G. *General George Washington: A Military Life*. New York: Random House, 2005.

Lengel, Edward G., ed. *The 10 Key Campaigns of the American Revolution*. Washington, DC: Regnery History, 2020.

Lepore, Jill. "How Longfellow Woke the Dead." *American Scholar*, March 2, 2011.

Lewis, Charles Lee. *Admiral de Grasse and American Independence*. Annapolis, MD: United States Naval Institute, 1945.

Lockhart, Paul. *The Drillmaster of Valley Forge*. New York: HarperCollins, 2008.

Luzader, John F. *Saratoga*. New York: Savas Beatie, 2008.

Lynch, Wayne. "Arnold in Command at Bemis Heights?" *Journal of the American Revolution*, November 14, 2013.

Maass, John. *The Battle of Guilford Courthouse*. Charleston, SC: The History Press, 2020.

———. *The Road to Yorktown*. Charleston, SC: The History Press, 2015.

Martin, David G. *A Molly Pitcher Sourcebook*. Hightstown, NJ: Longstreet House, 2003.

Martin, James Kirby. *Benedict Arnold: Revolutionary Hero*. New York: New York University Press, 1997.

Martin, James Kirby, and Mark Edward Lender. *"A Respectable Army,"* 3rd edition. New York: Wiley-Blackwell, 2015.

Martin, James Kirby, and David L. Preston, eds. *Theaters of the American Revolution*. Yardley, PA: Westholme, 2017.

Martin, Joseph Plumb. *Ordinary Courage: The Revolutionary War Adventures of Joseph Plumb Martin*, 4th edition, edited by James Kirby Martin. Chichester, UK: Wiley-Blackwell, 2013.

Massey, Gregory D. *John Laurens and the American Revolution*. Columbia: University of South Carolina Press, 2015.

Massey, Gregory D., and Jim Piecuch, eds. *General Nathanael Greene and the American Revolution in the South*. Columbia: University of South Carolina Press, 2012.

Mayer, Holly. *Belonging to the Army*. Columbia: University of South Carolina Press, 1996.

McBurney, Christian. *George Washington's Nemesis*. El Dorado Hills, CA: Savas Beatie, 2020.

———. *Kidnapping the Enemy*. Yardley, PA: Westholme, 2014.

———. *The Rhode Island Campaign*. Yardley, PA: Westholme, 2011.

McCullough, David. *1776*. New York: Simon & Schuster, 2005.

McDonald, Robert M. S., ed. *Sons of the Father*. Charlottesville: University of Virginia Press, 2013.

Morris, Richard B. *The Peacemakers*. New York: Harper & Row, 1965.

Murdock, Harold. *The Nineteenth of April 1775*. Boston: Houghton Mifflin, 1925.

Nash, Gary B. *The Unknown American Revolution*. New York: Penguin Books, 2006.

Neimeyer, Charles Patrick. *America Goes to War*. New York: New York University Press, 1996.

Nelson, James L. *Benedict Arnold's Navy*. Camden, ME: McGraw-Hill, 2006.

———. *George Washington's Great Gamble*. New York: McGraw-Hill, 2010.

Nelson, Paul David. "Guy Carleton Versus Benedict Arnold: The Campaign of 1776 in Canada and on Lake Champlain." *New York History*, Vol. 57, No. 3 (July 1976).

Neville, Gabriel. "The Tragedy of Henry Laurens." *Journal of the American Revolution*, August 1, 2019.

Oller, John. *The Swamp Fox*. Boston: Da Capo Press, 2016.

O'Shaughnessy, Andrew Jackson. *The Men Who Lost America*. New Haven, CT: Yale University Press, 2013.

Pancake, John S. *This Destructive War*. Tuscaloosa: University of Alabama Press, 1985.

Parker, John C. Jr. *Parker's Guide to the Revolutionary War in South Carolina*. West Conshohocken, PA: Infinity Publishing, 2013.

Philbrick, Nathaniel. *Bunker Hill*. New York: Penguin Books, 2014.

———. *In the Hurricane's Eye*. New York: Viking, 2018.

———. *Valiant Ambition*. New York: Viking, 2016.

Piecuch, Jim. *The Battle of Camden: A Documentary History*. Charleston, SC: The History Press, 2006.

———. *The Blood Be Upon Your Head*. Lugoff, SC: Southern Campaigns of the American Revolution Press, 2010.

———. *Three Peoples, One King*. Columbia: University of South Carolina Press, 2013.

Preston, David L. *Braddock's Defeat*. New York: Oxford University Press, 2015.

Puls, Mark. *Henry Knox*. New York: Palgrave Macmillan, 2008.

Pybus, Cassandra. *Epic Journeys of Freedom*. Boston: Beacon Press, 2006.

Quarles, Benjamin. *The Negro in the American Revolution*. Chapel Hill: University of North Carolina Press, 1996.

Quintal, George Jr. *Patriots of Color*. Boston: Boston National Historical Park, 2004.

Rakove, Jack. *Revolutionaries*. New York: Houghton Mifflin Harcourt, 2010.

Raphael, Ray. *The First American Revolution*. New York: The New Press, 2002.

Raphael, Ray, and Marie Raphael. *The Spirit of '74*. New York: The New Press, 2015.

Rappleye, Charles. *Robert Morris: Financier of the American Revolution*. New York: Simon & Schuster Paperbacks, 2011.

Rees, John U. *'They Were Good Soldiers.'* Warwick, UK: Helion, 2019.

Roberts, Kenneth. *Arundel*. Camden, ME: Down East Books, 1995.

———. *Rabble in Arms*. Camden, ME: Down East Books, 1996.

Roberts, Kenneth, ed. *March to Quebec: Journals of the Members of Arnold's Expedition*. Garden City, NY: Doubleday, 1953.

Saberton, Ian. *The American Revolutionary War in the South*. Tolworth, UK: Grosvenor House, 2018.

Sabin, Douglas P. *April 19, 1775: A Historiographical Study.* Concord, MA: Minute Man National Historical Park, 1987.

Schecter, Barnet. *The Battle for New York.* New York: Walker, 2002.

Scheer, George F., and Hugh F. Rankin. *Rebels & Redcoats.* New York: Da Capo Press, 1987.

Scoggins, Michael C. *The Day It Rained Militia.* Charleston, SC: The History Press, 2005.

Selig, Robert A. *The Franco-American Encampment in the Town of Greenburgh.* Greenburgh, NY: Town of Greenburgh, 2020.

———. *March to Victory.* Washington, DC: U.S. Army Center of Military History, 2007.

———. "Tuesday, 14 August, 1781: The Day That Shook the World." Online presentation, March 18, 2021. The Washington-Rochambeau Revolutionary Route Association, https://w3r-us.org/scholars-resources/.

Shepherd, Joshua. "A Melancholy Accident: The Disastrous Explosion at Charleston." *Journal of the American Revolution*, August 5, 2015.

Shy, John. *A People Numerous and Armed.* Ann Arbor: University of Michigan Press, 1990.

Spring, Matthew H. *With Zeal and with Bayonets Only.* Norman: University of Oklahoma Press, 2008.

Stark, Caleb. *Memoirs and Official Correspondence of Gen. John Stark.* Concord, NH: Edison C. Eastman, 1877.

Stevens, Benjamin Franklin, ed. *The Campaign in Virginia, 1781*, Vol. 2. London: 1888.

Sweet, David G., and Gary B. Nash, eds. *Struggle and Survival in Colonial America.* Berkeley: University of California Press, 1981.

Tarleton, Banastre. *A History of the Campaigns of 1780 and 1781, in the Southern Provinces of North America.* Dublin: Colles, Exshaw, et al., 1787.

Tuchman, Barbara W. *The First Salute.* New York: Alfred A. Knopf, 1988.

Unger, Harlow Giles. *Lafayette.* Hoboken, NJ: John Wiley & Sons, 2002.

Van Buskirk, Judith L. *Standing in Their Own Light.* Norman: University of Oklahoma Press, 2017.

Van Doren, Carl. *Secret History of the American Revolution.* New York: Viking Press, 1968.

Venter, Bruce M. *The Battle of Hubbardton.* Charleston, SC: The History Press, 2015.

Vowell, Sarah. *Lafayette in the Somewhat United States.* New York: Riverhead Books, 2015.

Ward, Christopher. *The War of the Revolution*, Vols. 1 and 2. New York: Macmillan, 1952.

Waters, Andrew. *The Quaker and the Gamecock.* Philadelphia: Casemate, 2019.

———. *To the End of the World.* Yardley, PA: Westholme, 2020.

Weelen, Jean Edmond. *Rochambeau: Father and Son.* New York: Henry Holt, 1936.

Wickwire, Franklin, and Mary Wickwire. *Cornwallis: The American Adventure.* Boston: Houghton Mifflin, 1970.

Wiencek, Henry. *An Imperfect God.* New York: Farrar, Straus and Giroux, 2003.

Wilkinson, James. *Memoirs of My Own Times*, Vol. 1. Philadelphia: Abraham Small, 1816.

Willcox, William B. *Portrait of a General*. New York: Alfred A. Knopf, 1964.

Wilson, David. *The Southern Strategy*. Columbia: University of South Carolina Press, 2008.

Zambone, Albert Louis. *Daniel Morgan: A Revolutionary Life*. Yardley, PA: Westholme, 2018.

# Illustration Credits

Thayendanegea (Joseph Brant). *Copy after Ezra Ames / National Portrait Gallery, Smithsonian Institution*

John Burgoyne. *Sir Joshua Reynolds, c. 1776 (photograph) / Library of Congress, Prints & Photographs Division*

Horatio Gates. *Charles Willson Peale, 1782 / Courtesy of Independence National Historical Park*

Boot Monument, Saratoga National Historical Park. / *Park Service photograph*

Battle of Brandywine. *Watercolor by William Augustus West / Reproduced by Permission of Durham University Library and Collections*

The Marquis de Lafayette. / *Charles Willson Peale mezzotint, after his 1781 painting / Philadelphia Museum of Art*

## SECOND INSERT:

Monmouth confrontation. *Booth's History of New York / New York Public Library*

Molly Pitcher mural. *Photograph by Bob Thompson*

Patriot Militia, an African-American soldier (w/c & gouache on paper), by Don Troiani. / *Private Collection © Don Troiani. All Rights Reserved 2022 / Bridgeman Images*

John Laurens. *Charles Willson Peale, 1780 / National Portrait Gallery, Smithsonian Institution*

Henry Laurens. *Engraving by John B. Neagle after Charles Willson Peale / National Portrait Gallery, Smithsonian Institution*

Nathanael Greene. *Oil on wood by John Trumbull / Yale University Art Gallery*

The Morning After the Attack on Sullivan's Island, June 29, 1776. *Watercolor by Henry Gray / Courtesy of the Gibbes Museum of Art / Carolina Art Association*

John André self-portrait. / *Yale University Art Gallery*

Sir Henry Clinton. *Engraving by Francesco Bartolozzi after John Smart / New York Public Library*

Banastre Tarleton. *Sir Joshua Reynolds, 1782 / © The National Gallery, London*

Lord Cornwallis. *Print by Francesco Bartolozzi after Hugh Douglas Hamilton, 1781 / Yale Center for British Art, Paul Mellon Collection*

Frontiersmen on marker at Kings Mountain. / *Photograph by Bob Thompson*

Waxhaws memorial, Buford, South Carolina. / *Photograph by Bob Thompson*

The Battle of Cowpens. *Detail from Charles McBarron painting / OH3 Photography for the National Park Service*

Thomas Sumter. *Engraving after Charles Willson Peale / New York Public Library*

Guilford Courthouse map. / *Library of Congress, Geography & Map Division*

Robert Morris. *Charles Willson Peale, c. 1782 / Courtesy of Independence National Historical Park*

The Comte de Rochambeau. *Oil on canvas by Joseph Désiré Court / National Portrait Gallery, Smithsonian Institution*

Admiral de Grasse. *Engraving after a 1782 portrait / New York Public Library*

Battle of the Virginia Capes. / *Courtesy of the U.S. Navy Art Collection, Washington, D.C. / U.S. Naval History and Heritage Command photograph*

Yorktown commemorative stamp. / *U.S. Postal Service, 1931*

Yorktown surrender. *Oil on canvas, John Trumbull / Yale University Art Gallery*

# Index